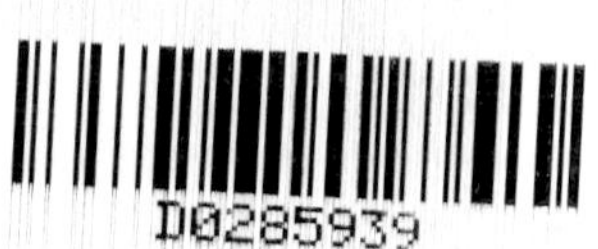

A History of Catholic Moral Theology in the Twentieth Century

A History of Catholic Moral Theology in the Twentieth Century

From Confessing Sins to Liberating Consciences

JAMES F. KEENAN, SJ

Published by the Continuum International Publishing Group
The Tower Building, 11 York Road, London SE1 7NX
80 Maiden Lane, Suite 704, New York NY 10038

www.continuumbooks.com

First published 2010
Reprinted 2010

British Library Cataloguing-in-Publication Data
A catalogue record for this book is available from the British Library.

ISBN 978-0-8264-2928-5 (hardback)
ISBN 978-0-8264-2929-2 (paperback)

Designed and typeset by Kenneth Burnley, Wirral, Cheshire
Printed and bound in the United States of America

CONTENTS

To Bobby

PREFACE

For the past fifteen years I have been teaching a doctoral seminar on the intellectual history of twentieth-century Catholic moral theology. One evening in New York, Frank Oveis, my friend and editor at Continuum, suggested I write a book-length manuscript on the subject. Two years later, I began to take up his suggestion.

When I taught the course I was mindful of introducing my students not only to the works that shaped the century but more importantly the persons. I hope in these pages that you will be able to see the intelligence, dedication, and vision of very specific theologians from around the globe.

As comprehensive as this work is, I restricted my investigation to fundamental moral theology, which concerns conscience, sin, love, virtue, authority, etc. I had to omit, therefore, all the areas of applied ethics: social, sexual, medical, and corporate ethics. Whereas today we believe that fundamental moral theology needs to be applied and applied ethics needs fundamentals, in the last century these subjects were kept separate.

As we study history, we want to know where history eventually arrives. We want to experience the journey of the story, but we also want to know the destination. With this in mind, at the end of each chapter on the revisionists, I present a contemporary work that captures the contribution of the chapter's main theme. In this way we can move through the last century with insight into our own time and place.

There are many people I want to thank: my colleagues and students at Fordham University and Weston Jesuit School of Theology; Michael Duffy and Julia Dowd at the Joan and Ralph Lane Center for Catholic Studies and Social Thought at the University of San Francisco; Ann Patrick from whom I appropriated the title of her wonderful book, *Liberating Conscience*; Jack Mahoney, Albert Jonsen, Renzo Pegoraro, Tom O'Meara, John O'Malley, Linda Hogan, and Antonio Autiero for their wisdom and advice; my Jesuit brothers at Boston College, in particular my community at Robert's House; my students and colleagues in the Boston College Theology Department, especially the ethicists, Lisa Cahill, Stephen Pope, Ken Himes, Dave Hollenbach, and John Paris; my friends who supported me especially through these last eight months of health challenges: Lúcás, Frank, Maura, Enrico, Tom, Toni, Gloria, Gary, Monica, Nick, Stan, Hoa, Bert, Mark, Tone, Diddy, Roy, Peter, Don, and Bethany. Finally, to my family whose histories of love and life have shaped my own, and especially my brother Bobby (1954-80) who was my companion as I grew up, with abiding love.

1
Background

In the beginning of the twentieth century, moral theology expressed itself in a textbook form, known as the 'moral manuals'. For a variety of reasons, from the 1920s onward, moral theologians began a sustained critique of these manuals. On the one hand they discredited the authority, sources, and content of the manuals. On the other hand, they began to propose alternatives to these manuals.

This innovation occurred by incorporating an historical-critical method into a much clearer theological context animated by biblical insights. These attempts were later stymied, however, when moral theologians fell into a contentious debate with the hierarchy over *Humanae Vitae*. In its aftermath most moral theologians and most bishops found themselves operating out of two very different and distinctive methodologies that responded to very different presuppositions.

After the promulgation of *Veritatis Splendor* (1993), moral theologians began trying to bridge the divide between themselves and bishops, and by the end of the century we see a more reconciling agenda. At the same time, moral theologians examined their own local contexts with greater attentiveness and later sought to dialogue cross-culturally with fellow moralists.

In brief, these developments, from the manuals through revisionist innovation and subsequent division to finally more reconciling agendas fixed on the local and the global concerns of theological ethics, mark the history of moral theology in the twentieth century.

Before beginning that history, let us look at the three periods of moral theology preceding the twentieth century: the writing of *Summas* from the twelfth to the fifteenth centuries; the use of casuistry in the sixteenth century; and the establishment of the moral manuals of the seventeenth through the nineteenth centuries. Let me also explain what I mean by moral theology.

Summa Confessorum and the *Summa Theologiae*

From the twelfth to the fifteenth centuries, moral theology operated on two tracks. First there was the instruction of the pastoral practice of absolving sins and giving penances. This track actually started much earlier, around the sixth century, with the penitential manuals, first used in Ireland and eventually appearing throughout Europe. They were called 'penitential' manuals because they assigned fixed penances for sinful acts organized according to the seven deadly sins.

Many of these manuals were handbooks written by abbots (and abbesses) who assigned the same penances for the same sins under the same circumstances. In this way these confessors were considered just judges as they assigned proportionate penances to their community members. These manuals were fairly brief, inasmuch as they dealt with sins committed for the most part by those few Christians who confessed: mostly monks, nuns, clerics, bishops, and occasionally devout nobility.

In 1215, Innocent III imposed on the Church universal the 'Easter Duty', that is, the obligation to receive Communion at least once a year during Easter. To fulfill this obligation, Christians had to be in the 'state of grace', and therefore each one had to confess their sins annually so as to fulfill their duty. For the first time the whole Church was involved in a sacrament that previously was practiced only by the ordained or vowed religious.

Henry Lea, the great Protestant Church historian, called Innocent's edict the most significant piece of legislation in the history of the Church. Not only did the laity now have to know how to confess their sins, the clergy had to learn how to hear them. Moreover, since the sins of monks and nuns tended to focus on their vows and religious practices and were generally less complex than those of people with families and businesses, the penitential manuals became very inadequate for this much larger and more diverse group of sinners. In the thirteenth century, the much more extensive *Summa Confessorum* were published. These texts did not simply aim at assigning universally fixed penances; they also guided confessors to learn how to discover the source of sin in the individual penitent. Here, confessors became trained not simply as just judges but also as physicians of souls.[1]

At the same time, for an elite group of religious and clerics there developed a highly intellectual track of theology, known as scholasticism. These theologians (Peter Abelard, Peter Lombard, Albert the Great, Thomas Aquinas, Bonaventure, Duns Scotus, and William of Ockham, to name a few) taught at the universities recently established (think here of Oxford, Bologna, Padua, Paris). Eventually, they gathered their teachings together in tomes known as the *Summa Theologiae*.

In sum, from the twelfth to the end of the fifteenth centuries, there were two very different tracks of moral theology: the practical and very specific *Summa Confessorum* and the highly academic *Summa Theologiae*. The genius of the later moral manuals is that they merged these tracks together: the foundational first half of the manuals was developed out of the academic *Summae* and the specific material for determining what belonged to sin and what did not, came, in the second half, from the confessional *summae*.

Casuistry

In the sixteenth century, Europe was bent on enormous expansionism. Westward, explorers from Portugal, Spain, France, Holland, Italy, and England began their conquest of the Americas. At the same time, they engaged in extensive trade negotiations with the East. With such new frontiers, the moral questions of the sixteenth century were altogether new.

For instance, the Church had held that usury was always sinful. Consider maritime insurance, that is, insurance for shipping vessels. In 1237, Pope Gregory IX ruled that paying collateral fees for shipping was a form of usury, and therefore sinful. In the sixteenth century, Europeans needed to insure their cargoes returning from the conquest of the Americas or from trade with the Middle East and Asia. They wondered: did the decretal apply to maritime insurance, or was such insurance morally licit?

In 1530, a group of Spanish merchants living in Flanders asked the University of Paris to address certain commercial practices. One question concerned maritime insurance, and the famous nominalist professor, John Mair, responded that just as the captain of a ship licitly insures that a ship moves from point A to point B, so too does a maritime insurance agent licitly insure that the worth or value of the cargo moves from point A to point B. This method, high casuistry as it was later called, was fairly universal, engaged by academics as well as confessors.[2]

The method of high casuistry is very different from low casuistry. Low casuistry is simple deductive logic, the application of a principle to a case. High casuistry does not begin its argument with principles precisely because the existing ones were inadequate. Instead, the casuistry of the sixteenth century started with a case that served as the principle once did, as the morally objective standard. In the case above, the captain of a ship was the accepted standard. Then another case, for instance, the maritime insurance agent, is measured against this. An analogical comparison between the standard and the new case ensued: was the work of the insurance agent morally analogous to the upright work of piloting a ship? The morality of the answer depended on two authorities: the internal authority of the argument itself (Is it cogent? Does the argument make sense?) and the external authority of the casuist who had to be a recognized moral theologian. This twofold authority became constitutive of the method of moral argument from the sixteenth through the twentieth centuries.

For roughly 100 years, moralists reinvestigated every question using this inductive, analogical reasoning: every form of moneyed activity, questions of lying, property, dueling, governance, war, international law, temporal authority, and even the killing of tyrants. Every type of case was reconsidered, from abortion to end of life.[3] And the casuists enjoyed these explorations; as Mair asked, 'Has not Amerigo Vespucci discovered lands unknown to Ptolemy, Pliny and other geographers up to the present? Why cannot the same happen in other spheres?'[4]

The moral manuals

By the seventeenth century, Europeans were exhausted with the high casuistry of the previous 100 years. Moral theologians, instead of entertaining arguments for new cases, began assembling the cases into summary statements: these became known as the *Summa Casuum Conscientiae*, the summary of the cases of consciences. These *Summa* became the material for the seminaries that Trent mandated (1545–63). They later developed into sophisticated textbooks, the 'moral manuals', which began appearing at the end of the eighteenth century.[5]

By stringing together the summaries of the sixteenth-century cases, moralists began to recognize certain patterns among the cases and articulated new methodological principles: double effect, co-operation, toleration, lesser evil. These became the textbook principles of the moral manuals, which lasted through to the twentieth century.[6]

Textbook readers applied these methodological principles deductively to new cases. Moreover, they gave the reader the impression that moral theology was unchanging; whereas the casuists of the sixteenth century saw each new case as an occasion for further investigations, in the later centuries, cases were simple conundrums to be dispatched by these varied principles. As a result the principles seemed to be ahistorical, even eternal, and certainly always a part of the method of moral theology. Still, any time a methodological principle was applied to a new case, the understanding of the principle and its applicability developed and in time this led (unwillingly?) to the realization that in moral theology, inevitably, nothing remains the same.[7]

Moral theology?

A few theologians argue that contemporary moral theology is so distant from the agenda of moral manualism that the title 'moral theology' is no longer valid as a description. Basically they contend that moral theology started as a specific theological field of inquiry taught in seminaries created by the Council of Trent. John A. Gallagher writes: '"Moral theology" is, I believe, no longer a helpful term with which to categorize the work of Curran, Schüller, McCormick, Fuchs, Häring or other revisionist theologians. Their theological positions and moral categories are simply too distinct from the prime analogue.'[8] For Gallagher, the prime analogue for 'moral theology' is the practical theological guidance that moral theologians gave to priests in their seminary formation, whether in the *Summa Casuum Conscientiae* or the later moral manuals.

I think Gallagher's claims are misplaced. Moral theology is an overarching concept. Those who wrote the *Summa Confessorum* were doing moral theology as much as those writing the *Summa Theologiae*. Similarly, the inductive logic of sixteenth-century casuistry is as much about moral theology as the deductive logic of the later moral manuals. Are these investigations noticeably different? Yes, of course, but our search for moral truth is categorically expressed differently in different periods of time and place. The twentieth century produced a very different alternative to the moral manuals, but the alternative is not contrary to the nature, that is, the *proprium* of moral theology.

Moral theology did not begin at Trent. It began when the Church gathered and asked how, as a people of God, they were going to live morally upright lives, as a response to their baptism in Christ. Moral theology, thus, can be found in the letters of Paul when he proscribes vices, discusses the eating of idol meat, argues against circumcising Gentiles, warns against ideological fractions in the community, and explains the stance that a Christian ought to have toward the state. Moral theology is equally evident when Augustine writes on marriage or the virtues, Ambrose gives us Christian duties, and Thomas Aquinas writes the *Pars Secunda* of the *Summa Theologiae*.

Like Gallagher, Norbert Rigali insists that using 'moral theology' to describe the work of theological investigation before Trent is 'anachronistic', that the locus of moral theology's inception is Trent, and, with Gallagher, concludes that moral theology has 'come to an end'.[9] But this is exaggeration. Moral theology is a constant: what Paul, Augustine, Ambrose, Thomas, Suárez, Slater, Davis, Tillmann, Häring, Ford, Cahill, and Farley are all doing is moral theology, whether they write a treatise, a summa, a revisionist thesis, or an essay in a theological journal. The nature of moral theology, however, is constantly shifting its method, its discourse partners, and its more immediate purposes; while its long-range purpose is to find for the Church the way to live the upright life of Christian discipleship, its short-range purpose might be to study the foundations of it as a science or to help confessors with penitents, abbots with their monks, or catechists with their catechumenate. Again, moral theology is the constant, it is the overarching concept about the Church's search for the moral response to Christ.

From the sixteenth to the twentieth centuries the morally upright stance was fairly minimal: avoid sin. Later, with twentieth-century revisionists, the stance was to become through charity a disciple of Christ. The divergence here is enormous, but in both instances the presumption is that theologians are seeking to articulate the morally upright life for the Church.

We will see, for instance, that in the 1930s to 1950s, German theologians were hesitant to speak of bioethics, while the English were enthralled with it. We will see some talking about the just-war tradition and others obsessed with girls' dresses, but in all these instances, though their method, concerns, and conclusions differ, their 'stuff' is always moral theology.

Even today we might refer to our work under the rubric of 'theological ethics'. It might seem to be a common umbrella under which we find multiple areas of investigation: social ethics, fundamental morals, bioethics, sexual ethics, church ethics, political ethics, etc. So, for instance, in July 2004 in Padua, Italy, when the first international cross-cultural conference was held for theologians in these different fields of inquiry, it was called 'Catholic Theological Ethics in the World Church'.[10] The term is applicable not because their inquiry is so distant from the prime Tridentine analogue, as if it were true that moral theology was minted as such at Trent, but because the nature of theological investigations is, while diverse, also overlapping. What were once separate areas, say bioethics and social ethics, can no longer remain as such: we are no longer able to do a bioethics that overlooks the social ethical questions regarding access to health care. Similarly we cannot do a sexual ethics that does not look to questions of justice as well. But saying that we are interested in theological ethics is no more a departure from the broader field of moral theology than those who worked on the penitentials, *Summae*, or casuistry. Theologians of the thirteenth century championed two extremely different *Summas*, while those of the sixteenth fought for casuistry, those from the seventeenth to the twentieth defended manualism, those from the mid-twentieth to twenty-first centuries turned to revisionism, and those in the twenty-first century highlight theological ethics. No period is less a manifestation of moral theology than another, because the most practical of the theological sciences must constantly adapt to and adopt from its context and presuppositions.

Three important contemporary texts on the history of moral theology each view that history through a continuous lens under the rubric of moral theology: the earliest, in 1972, by Giuseppe Angelini and Ambrogio Valsecchi, was a work on the historical design of moral theology;[11] John Mahoney's towering *The Making of Moral Theology: A Study of the Roman Catholic Tradition* began its investigations with Augustine and the pentientials;[12] and Renzo Gerardi's magisterial history of moral theology starts with the scriptures.[13] They are clear indications that moral theology is the constant umbrella term, but inevitably it proposes historically appropriate theological methods.

One other work specifically highlighted the diverse method, structure and immediate purpose of moral theology. In *The Origins of Moral Theology in the United States*, Charles Curran examines three moral theologians (Aloysius Sabetti, Thomas Bouquillon, and John Hogan) who taught and wrote in the United States at the dawn of the twentieth century in very different contexts for very different audiences. In each instance their work is moral theology.[14]

What Gallagher and Rigali overlook is that the nature of moral theology is to respond to the practical challenges of each period in history. To respond to these challenges, moral theologians must not only address the specific problems that arise, they must also investigate whether their method of responding and the operative theological presuppositions are adequate to the task. What we find in the twentieth century, then, is the enormously complex move from defining moral theology as the fixed science of human action to becoming a guide for the personal and communal development of the conscientious disciples of Christ. That move is the central focus of this work.

Notes

1 John Mahoney, 'The Influence of Auricular Confession', *The Making of Moral Theology* (Oxford: Clarendon Press, 1987) 1–36.

2 James Keenan, 'The Casuistry of John Major, Nominalist Professor of Paris (1506–1531)', *Annual of Society of Christian Ethics*, (1993) 205–22; Louis Vereecke, 'L'assurance maritime chez les théologiens des XVe et XVIe siècles', *Studia Moralia*, 8 (1970) 347–85.

3 Albert Jonsen and Stephen Toulmin, *The Abuse of Casuistry* (Berkeley: University of California Press, 1988); James Keenan and Thomas Shannon, eds, *The Context of Casuistry* (Washington, DC: Georgetown University Press, 1995).

4 From Major's *Commentary of the Fourth Book of the Sentences*, quoted in John Durkan, 'John Major: After 400 Years', *The Innes Review*, I (1950) 131–57, 135.

5 James Keenan, 'Was William Perkins' *Whole Treatise of Cases of Consciences* Casuistry?: Hermeneutics and British Practical Divinity' in Harald E. Braun and Edward Vallance, eds, *Contexts of Conscience in Early Modern Europe: 1500–1700* (New York: Palgrave, 2004) 17–31; 'The Birth of Jesuit Casuistry: Summa casuum conscientiae, sive de instructione sacerdotum, libri septem by Francesco de Toledo (1532–1596)' in Thomas McCoog, ed., *The Mercurian Project: 'Forming Jesuit Culture, 1573–1580'* (Rome: Institutum Historicum Societatis Iesu, 2004) 461–82.

6 Albert Jonsen explains the three phases to high casuistry. First, a morphological dissection of the circumstances and maxims in conflict in a case; then a taxonomy where casuists line up the cases to search for congruency among them; finally, there is the kinetic that develops emerging insights and articulates them into rules. Albert Jonsen, 'The Confessor as Experienced Physician: Casuistry and Clinical Ethics' in Paul F. Camenisch, ed., *Religious Methods and Resources in Bioethics* (Netherlands: Kluwer Academics, 1993).

7 John T. Noonan, Jr, 'Development in Moral Doctrine', *Context*, 188–204; Thomas Kopfensteiner, 'Science, Metaphor and Moral Casuistry', *Context*, 207–20.

8 John Gallagher, *Time Past, Time Future: An Historical Study of Catholic Moral Theology* (New York: Paulist Press, 1990) 270.

9 Norbert Rigali, 'From "Moral Theology" to the "Theology of the Christian Life": An Overview', *Origins* 34/6 (24 June 2004) 85–91.

10 James Keenan, ed., *Catholic Theological Ethics in the World Church: The Plenary Papers from the First Cross-cultural Conference on Catholic Theological Ethics* (New York: Continuum, 2007).

11 Giuseppe Angelini and Ambrogio Valsecchi, *Disegno storico della teologia morale* (Bologna: Dehoniane, 1972).

12 John Mahoney, *The Making of Moral Theology: A Study of the Roman Catholic Tradition* (New York: Oxford University, 1987).

13 Renzo Gerardi, *Storia della morale: Interpretazioni teologiche del'esperienza Cristiana* (Bologna: Edizioni Dehoniane, 2003).
14 Charles Curran, *The Origins of Moral Theology in the United States* (Washington, DC: Georgetown University Press, 1997).

2

The Moral Manualists

The moral manuals existed well into the first 60 years of the twentieth century. To appreciate their development, we examine three English texts spanning those years: the first edition (1906) of Jesuit Father Thomas Slater's *A Manual of Moral Theology for English-speaking Countries*;[1] the fourth edition (1943) of Jesuit Father Henry Davis's *Moral and Pastoral Theology in Four Volumes* (originally published in 1934);[2] and the eighth English edition (1951, a translation of the German thirteenth edition of 1949) of Capuchin Father Heribert Jone's *Moral Theology* (originally published in 1929).[3] These specific editions allow us to consider the very first English moral manual; the most important English edition during the Second World War; and the most international manual to appear from Germany. Quite apart from these specific editions, no other moral manuals had more influence on English-speaking clergy and the Church throughout the world than these three.

As a matter of fact, I know of no other manual than Jone's, translated into English. The German diocesan priest Joseph Mausbach (1861–1931) wrote a three-volume moral manual published in sequence from 1914 to 1918 which went through ten editions, the last edited by Gustav Ermecke in 1954. Mausbach sought to provide a dogmatic foundation for moral theology. One of his other works was translated into English, though it was not a moral manual but rather an apologia for Catholic moral theology.[4] Similarly, the French Sulpician, Adolphe Tanquerey (1854–1932), who taught in Paris and Baltimore and whose 2,000-page, three-volume moral manual went through more than a dozen editions, was never translated into English, but his brief synopsis of dogmatic theology was.[5]

Moral manuals were developed out of the community of clerics to which one belonged. For instance, the Jesuit moralists included: Jean-Pierre Gury (1801–66); Antonio Ballerini (1805–11); Augustin Lehmkuhl (1834–1918); Gennaro Bucceroni (1841–1918); Edouard Génicot (1856–1900); and Hieronymus Noldin (1838–1922). Gury's manual was the Jesuits' first after their restoration (1814) from their suppression (1773). Gury espoused the moral theology of the Redemptorist Alphonsus Liguori (1696–1787), and quickly Gury's manual became, as Charles Curran writes, 'the most influential manual of moral theology in the nineteenth century'.[6] With Gury's death in 1866, Ballerini edited Gury's seventeenth edition, and inasmuch as Ballerini had a distinctive read on conscience and morality, his edition of Gury prompted a lively, sustained, and critical debate between the Jesuits and the Redemptorists on conscience and the law.[7] With Ballerini's death in 1881, Jesuits in different countries made the Gury–Ballerini manual their own by adapting it to their own contexts. As Renzo Gerardi notes, 'At the beginning of the twentieth century, it was the most diffuse manual of moral theology in the theological schools.'[8]

In the United States, a Jesuit from Naples, Aloysius Sabetti (1839–98) began teaching Jesuits moral theology at Woodstock College, Maryland, in 1873, where he remained until his death 25 years later. In 1884, he edited his Gury–Ballerini edition and called it *Compendium theologiae moralis.*[9] Curran, who has written extensively on Sabetti, describes the title page as first written by Gury, updated by Ballerini, and 'shortened and accommodated for seminarians of this region by Aloysius Sabetti'.[10] Sabetti's manual went through thirteen editions in his lifetime and his successors edited another 21 editions, the final being published in 1939. Curran notes, 'Sabetti's manual was the most influential and long-lasting of the nineteenth-century moral manuals written in the United States. In addition to its use by the Jesuits, ten of thirty-two seminaries training diocesan priests in the mid-1930s still used Sabetti's textbook.'[11]

In the nineteenth and early twentieth centuries, the history of the moral formation of Dominicans, Redemptorists, Franciscans and diocesan priests followed similar tracks of development. The Redemptorists began with the phenomenal Alphonsus Liguori[12] and later with Jozef Aertnys (1829–1915). Dominicans followed Dominikus Prümmer (1866–1931) and then Benoit Merkelbach (1871–1942).

Thomas Slater (1855–1928)

Thomas Slater studied canon law and ecclesiology at Rome's Gregorian University and won a reputation for precision and clarity, evident in his first work, *De justitia et de jure* (1898). His lengthy *Principia theologiae moralis* (1902), clearly foundational to his later works, was a publishing failure, but his subsequent *Manual of Moral Theology* (1906) was for twenty years the most consulted manual in English, going through five editions, the last appearing in 1931. The *Manual* was later accompanied by his two-volume work, *Cases of Conscience for English-speaking Countries* (1911) and another large compendium, *Questions of Morality* (1915). By 1911, unable to see well, he retired from teaching and assisted at a parish in Liverpool as a confessor for his last seventeen years, writing occasional essays.[13]

Like other contemporary moral theologians at the beginning of the twentieth century, Slater was an innovator. After two centuries of moral manuals being published in Latin, twentieth-century manuals appeared for the first time in the vernacular. Slater's *A Manual of Moral Theology* is the first manual in the English language, and in the preface he acknowledged that he followed the initiative of authors in German, Spanish, French, and Italian.

The vernacular made the text more accessible to a greater audience. While he reminded the reader that the role of the moral theologian was to assist the priest in the confessional, Slater contended that persons other than priests could benefit from their texts and explicitly named Anglicans as prospective readers.[14]

Later writers emphasized similar hopes. Jone acknowledged that his work was for the pastor, but wrote that he 'will be happy to know his book is of benefit to the educated laity, interested in religious matters, whom it may help in solving such questions of conscience as occur in their daily lives'.[15] Davis reminded his readers that 'all men are casuists in the innumerable affairs of everyday life' and commended his readers, both priests and others, to understand this.[16]

Still, the primary audience for these moral manuals was the priest, who, as the *Catholic Catechism of the Council of Trent* reminds us, sits in 'the tribunal of the confessional'.[17] John Mahoney underlines this connection between the moral theologian and the confessor: 'There is no doubt that the single most influential factor in the development of the practice and of the discipline of moral theology is to be found in the growth and the spread of "confession" in the Church.'[18]

In the preface, Slater noted that the manuals 'are necessary for the Catholic priest to enable him to administer the sacrament of penance and to fulfill his duties'.[19] This duty restricted him from writing on other matters, and so he pled that the manuals 'should not be censured for not being what they were never intended to be'. Then, in remarkably stark terms, he described the manuals of moral theology as books of moral pathology:

> They are the product of centuries of labor bestowed by able and holy men on the practical problems of Christian ethics. Here however, we must ask the reader to bear in mind that the manuals of moral theology are technical works intended to help the confessor and the parish priest in the discharge of their duties. They are as technical as the text-books of the lawyer and the doctor. They are not intended for edification, nor do they hold up a high ideal of Christian perfection for the imitation of the faithful. They deal with what is of obligation under the pain of sin, they are books of moral pathology.[20]

Slater acknowledged that if readers were looking to learn how to become better disciples, they should look elsewhere: to the manuals of ascetical, devotional, or mystical theology, where they would find the 'high ideal of Christian perfection'. 'Moral theology', he added, 'proposes to itself the humbler but still necessary task of defining what is right and wrong in all the practical relations of the Christian life. This all, but most especially priests, should know.'

Slater concluded the stunning preface, bisecting the natural law's fundamental principle, 'Do good and avoid evil.' 'The first step on the right road to conduct is to avoid evil.' By referencing the doing of the good, that is, Christian perfection to ascetical manuals, Slater held that the natural law has only a singular task: to guide us to avoid evil.[21]

These parameters were explicitly abandoned by Vatican II. In the *Decree on Priestly Formation*, the issue of Christian perfection was reinserted into the ambit of moral theology. We read: 'Special care must be given to the perfecting of moral theology. Its scientific exposition, nourished more on the teaching of the Bible, should shed light on the loftiness of the calling of the faithful in Christ and the obligation that is theirs of bearing fruit in charity for the life of the world.'[22]

Yet before Vatican II, Slater's insistence that moral theology was only about avoiding evil was hardly unique. Davis wrote: 'It is precisely about the law that Moral Theology is concerned. It is not a mirror of perfection, showing man the way of perfection.'[23] The manuals of moral theology were not designed to help one become a disciple, but rather to help keep a penitent from becoming lost for ever. A decade after Davis, Edwin Healy underlined this important task: 'The method of outlining clearly the sinfulness of the various actions dealt with has as its aim the rectifying of false consciences, the clarifying of doubts, and the dispelling of scruples.'[24]

Slater's *Manual* was classical in form and divided into two parts. The first was 200 pages long and made up of five 'books': human acts, conscience, law, sin, and the theological virtues. The second part consisted in four books: the ten commandments, contracts, the commandments of the Church, and the specific duties of clergy, religious, and 'certain laymen' (physicians and those with different roles in the courts). These 460 pages focused on fairly institutional issues. Alone, the commandments covered 270 pages, with 112 dedicated to the combined seventh and tenth commandments and another 90 to the book of contracts.[25] While 30 pages each were dedicated to the first and fourth commandments, a mere twenty were dedicated to the fifth, and ten each to the second and third. Only sixteen pages were dedicated to the combined sixth and ninth commandments, with one topic, consummated sins against nature (masturbation, sodomy, and bestiality), appearing in Latin, presumably so as not to lead a less educated reader into sin.[26]

At the outset of his first part, in the treatment of human acts, Slater defined the task of moral theology: 'To frame rules for human conduct according to the teaching of the Catholic Church, to decide what actions are good and what bad according to the principles of Christian faith.'[27]

What did Slater mean by the teaching of the Catholic Church? Slater's teachings differed significantly from what we will see in successive generations. Slater cited St Paul, Thomas Aquinas, Alphonsus Liguori, Francisco Suárez, Januarius Bucceroni, and Viktor Frins. By 'the teaching of the Catholic Church', he clearly meant what theologians who wrote on morality had been handing on for centuries: that is, the moral tradition. Later, as the century progressed, moral theologians relied more and more on ever-emerging 'teachings' from Rome. Unlike his successors, however, Slater means something different from magisterial teaching, inasmuch as that teaching was, until the 1930s, but a small part of the tradition's exposition of moral theology.

In the second book, on conscience, he wrote that 'conscience signifies a dictate of the practical reason deciding that a particular action is right or wrong'.[28] He then invoked 'certainty', a key concept for the manualists, derived from Thomas's *Summa* II.II. 70.2. 'In order to act lawfully and rightly, I must have at least moral certainty of the imperfect kind that the proposed action is honest and right.'[29]

Since perfect certainty about a moral judgment was often elusive, the required degree of moral confidence was imperfect certainty: are we at least adequately convinced that our action is right or not? The assumption that we are adequately sure of the rightness of our action does not guarantee that our action will be morally right. Slater added that if my conscience was in error, that does not negate the goodness that I intentionally willed.[30]

Still, if one lacked imperfect certitude, then one experienced practical doubt; acting out of such a conscience was not lawful. Therefore the conscientious but doubtful Catholic must search for imperfect certainty and, therefore, needs to consult an expert, the parish priest.

In the consultation both the doubtful lay person and the priest had an array of options. The differences pertained to the quality of argument needed for imperfect certainty when recognized authors proposed differing opinions: must a priest choose a weightier and stricter interpretation of the law even when another opinion is evidently valid though less weighty and less restrictive in its interpretation? In 1577 this question was answered by the Dominican Bartolomeo de Medina who argued that because the latter argument had cogency and was held by a recognized theologian, there was no need to follow the former.[31] This approach was called 'probabilism' and gave to the lay person and the priest the freedom in conscience to accept any opinion so long as it was well argued and from an authoritative source, that is, that it had both internal and external certitude.

Later conservative moral theologians advanced the contrary position, arguing that their interpretation was in support of the weightier and stricter, that is, the more probable or 'probabilior' opinion. To mediate this difference, the Redemptorists later proposed 'equiprobabilism', which contended that a more lenient opinion ought to have as weighty an argument as the more strict interpretation.

Slater embraced the probabilist opinion which he defined as: 'When there is only question of committing sin or not, it is lawful to follow a solidly probable opinion, even though the opposite may be more probable.'[32] He defended probabilism in three pages and concluded with an argument for its adequacy. Here he dismissed the premise that the solution founded on the stronger (more probable) argument was in fact more true.

> The greater the probability of the other view does not make it certain, nor is the more supposed greater probability a sure guarantee that the more probable view is the more true. It very frequently happens that an opinion which is considered more probable at one time is thought less probable or altogether improbable at another. Moreover, degrees of probability are very difficult to determine. What seems more probable to one theologian seems less to another, or even to the same at a different time. And even if it be granted that one opinion is certainly and absolutely more probable, the opposite may for all that remain solidly probable.[33]

Slater's position on probabilism was a typically Jesuit one, different from the equiprobabilism of Redemptorists or the probabiliorism of most Dominicans (the Dominican Medina founded probabilism, though his successors opted for the more limited rule of interpretation, probabiliorism). Not all Jesuits were probabilists, nor were all probabilists Jesuits. The three manualists we are examining – Slater, Davis and Jone, a Capuchin priest – were all probabilists.

Inasmuch as he was endorsing a hermeneutics which held that any credible manualist with a credible argument was a legitimate moral choice, Slater gave greater validity to the writings of almost all manualists and freed clergy to choose to advise the laity from the full range of manualists' opinions. Probabiliorists, on the other hand, contended that the clergy's options were more restrictive: generally speaking, only the more rigid interpretation was valid unless a weightier argument could be made for a more lenient interpretation. Probabiliorists were therefore more suspicious of the degree of freedom that probabilists were extending both to fellow manualists and to the clergy who were adopting these differing opinions.[34]

Still, despite a manualist's general hermeneutics of interpretation, there was a gentlemen's agreement among them not to discredit one another's position. A manualist basically proposed his own position, occasionally arguing that it represented 'a common opinion', but rarely did he declare another opinion as illicit, and if one ever did, he rarely identified the proponent. Though non-manualists like Blaise Pascal mocked or derided one school, in his case, the Jesuit probabilists, the entire hermeneutical 'debate' among manualists was shaped by an active, respectful tolerance: each school enjoyed a recognized legitimacy.[35] If ever a complaint was registered, it was often against those whose strictness unnecessarily burdened the laity.

After defending the probable conscience, Slater turned sympathetically to the scrupulous conscience and advised the confessor to find the cause of scruples, to prescribe a remedy, and then to tell the penitent, 'who through scruples thinks he commits sin in every action, to act boldly and fearlessly, that he may do whatever is not obviously forbidden, and that it is impossible for one who wishes to serve God to commit sin, especially grave sin, without being well aware of it'.[36]

In the second part, Slater turned to the 'matter' of morality. Throughout, Slater made his case and cited authorities for his positions, using a wide variety of experts. If a matter was 'settled', that is, if he could call it a law, he invoked a pontiff's teaching, a national law, or some other form of legislation; otherwise, if it was not yet settled, he invoked another moralist or offered his own opinion.

He divided the fourth commandment into seven chapters; each framed some issue of authority and subservience: duties of children to parents; parents to children; guardians to children; between parents; masters and servants; masters and scholars; and rulers and subjects. In the first chapter, he briefly discussed the piety and obedience children owe their parents, stating that the obligation of obedience ceases with the child's emancipation in England at 21 years of age. To this he appended a note regarding the different state laws in the United States on the emancipation of a minor.

He began the second chapter with love, piety, and emotional and material support, and then specifically mentioned the obligation to breast-feed: a mother 'is bound at least under venial sin to nourish it with her own milk, unless some good reason excuse her'.[37] He quickly turned to education:

> The Church condemns all non-Catholic schools, whether they be heretical and schismatical, or secularist, and she declares that as a general rule no Catholic parent can send his young children to such schools for educational purposes without exposing their faith and morals to serious risk, and therefore committing a grave sin.[38]

He added that only a bishop, and not a priest, could deny the sacraments to parents who act in this regard. Here he cited the Third Plenary Council of Baltimore (9 November–7 December 1884), and then argued that if a bishop (as happened in St Louis) expressly prohibited all parents in his diocese from sending their children to a non-Catholic school, then no priest may absolve such parents if they continue to send their children.[39]

Later, he turned to university education, noted that the Holy See allowed English Catholics to attend Oxford and Cambridge, but granted no analogous permission in the United States, since the Third Plenary Council was not at all in favor of such a policy. Still, exceptions were granted by the Council if two conditions could be met: that there was grave cause and that 'suitable means are to be employed in order that danger to faith and morals be rendered remote'. If a student did not observe these means, he should not be absolved; if his parents condoned his conduct, they should not be absolved either.[40] Clearly, no other topic was as extensively parsed by Slater as this one, simply because on this matter the Holy See and the specific Episcopal offices made their decisions law.

In the third chapter, he turned to matters of custody; for these, national policies from England and the United States were invoked. The fourth chapter, only two pages, concerned duties between husband and wife and, with the exception of Ephesians 5.22–24, Slater cited no authorities. A wife is to be subject and obedient to, but not a slave or servant of, her husband; if she shows great contempt for him and neglects his commands, she sins grievously. Likewise, he is bound by justice and piety to support her and sins grievously if he treats her with harshness or neglect. Slater concluded: 'The wife would not be guilty of sin if she took from her husband without his knowledge what was necessary for decent support of family.'[41]

Leo XIII's *Rerum Novarum* (15 May 1891) was invoked five times in the fifth chapter, and in most instances, at length, stipulating the duties of employers to employees on just working conditions, respectful treatment and fair wages.[42] Citing Romans 13.1–2 and then Leo XIII's *Diuturnum* (29 June 1881), Slater concluded the fourth commandment, reflecting on the connection between a local authority and divine right:

> It has been the constant teaching of the Catholic Church that all public and legitimate authority is of divine right, in the sense that God is the Author of man's nature by which he is a social animal, formed to live in society, which necessarily implies a distinction between rulers and ruled. The rulers may, indeed, be designated in various ways, their power may be more or less absolute; this power may be in the hands of one or of many, but it is derived from God.[43]

On the fifth commandment, Slater treated six issues: suicide, capital punishment, justifiable homicide, killing the innocent, war, and dueling. Throughout, he appealed to applications of the principle of double effect.[44] In the first chapter, he established that since 'God is the Author of life and death, He has reserved the ownership of human life to Himself', 'we have not the free disposal of our lives'. Thus suicide, which has one's death as 'the direct and immediate object of the will', was prohibited,[45] but that did not mean that one could not do something that could cause one's own death. He applied the principle of double effect to the case of the captain of a ship who, fearing in wartime that his ship will be seized and become a danger to his own country, destroys the ship, knowing that he and his crew will lose their lives. The captain 'does not intend the destruction of human life; the immediate effect of his action is to prevent the ship from falling into the enemy's hands. The public advantage counterbalances the loss.'[46]

With his usual economy, he differentiated in one single paragraph suicide from forgoing extraordinary means to preserve one's life. He gave two instances of such means: a painful and costly operation and one that required travel. Regarding the latter, he considered the case of one who would die if he were to spend the winter in England; Slater judged he 'is not bound to expatriate himself and go and live in a milder climate'.[47]

He justified capital punishment with arguments from Romans 13.4 and 'natural reason'. He began the chapter on justifiable homicide stating simply, 'In defense of my own life from unjust attack I may use whatever violence is necessary and even to the length of killing the aggressor.' He then added that no one should use greater force than necessary, nor act out of vengeance or anticipation of attack. Under these limitations, one may use such violence to defend limbs, property (as long as it is of considerable amount), and chastity. He noted that some theologians once held that one could commit justifiable homicide over an insult, but noted that Popes Alexander VII and Innocent XI condemned these positions.[48]

On killing the innocent, he noted that not even the good of the State makes it right to take an innocent life, though he invoked the principle of double effect to demonstrate the liceity of civilian deaths in an attack on a 'beleaguered town'. He declared the direct procuring of abortion as an intrinsic evil, but noted that a pregnant woman may appropriate life-saving means even if that means were indirectly to cause the fetus's death. Finally, he argued against the direct killing of a fetus to save the mother's life, 'even if otherwise both child and mother were certain to die'. His position is historically interesting inasmuch as it had been held until the end of the nineteenth century that a woman could defend herself against a fetus which threatened her life.[49] His argument is worth reading, in part because of its disturbing reversal in depicting the mother as the unjust assailant.

> Some theologians used to think that such operations were lawful if the mother's life could not otherwise be saved, because the child might be considered a material unjust assailant of its mother's life, and so be lawfully killed . . . However, in no sense can it be allowed that the child is an unjust assailant of a mother's life; it is where nature placed it, through no fault of its own, and it has a right to be there and to be born. If either is an unjust assailant of the other's life, it is the mother, who voluntarily undertook the obligations of motherhood . . . This doctrine is now theologically certain after the repeated declarations of the Holy See that no operation which tends directly to the destruction of the life of the fetus is lawful.[50]

He appended no references to other moralists holding similar positions.

While in three pages he invoked several popes and the Council of Trent to demonstrate the unequivocal wrongness of dueling, in four pages he upheld the certain teaching of Catholic theology on just war.

Finally, the sixth and ninth commandments were treated in four chapters: the nature of impurity, consummated sins of impurity, consummated sins against nature, non-consummated acts of impurity. He began the first chapter: 'The means devised by God for the preservation and increase of the human race is the union of the sexes, which has as its primary object, the procreation of children.' He upheld the teaching that there was no light moral matter concerning sins of impurity: 'All sins of impurity of whatever kind or species are of themselves mortal.'[51] He invoked 1 Corinthians 6.9–10, Galatians 5.19, and Matthew 5.28.

Under the consummated sins of impurity he treated in six paragraphs the following sins: fornication, adultery, incest, criminal assault, rape, and sacrilege, the last five violating other virtues as well. On the consummated sins against nature, he treated in Latin, masturbation, sodomy, and bestiality. Clearly the parsing of the first sin evidenced widespread pastoral anxiety.[52] Sadly, in the final chapter he treated touching, kissing, and embracing as sins.

Henry Davis (1866–1952)

Davis entered the Jesuits at seventeen in 1883. He spent 40 years training both clergy and laity (at least physicians) on morality. His four-volume work, *Moral and Pastoral Theology*, underwent eight editions and revisions. In 1952 he authored a one-volume summary of his manual. In addition to occasional essays, he also worked in the history of moral theology, editing Suárez's *De Legibus* (1944) and St Gregory's *Pastoral Care* (1950).[53]

While he wrote in the preface of the first edition that, as in Slater's manual, the 'chief aim of this work is to present the common teaching of modern Catholic authors on Moral Theology', still, there was a remarkable shift in the self-understanding of the moral theologian. Beyond a doubt, the publication of the *Code of Canon Law* in 1917 made moral theologians more aware that they were not the only ones offering norms for moral conduct. The influence of the code is unmistakable. Davis began the preface of the first edition writing, 'Several Manuals in English on Moral Theology have been published within recent years. *The Manual of Moral Theology* of Fr. T. Slater, S.J., held an honored place for many years, but its author was unable to incorporate in the later editions of his works, as much as of the codified Canon law as he would have wished.' After commenting on the limits of other works, he wrote: 'Since a knowledge of Canon law is essential to the student of Moral Theology, and since frequent reference must be made to the canons that bear on the Sacraments' a work such as his was needed.[54]

As the twentieth century unfolded, the Vatican, from its different dicasteries, began instructing on moral matters with greater frequency and specificity. These instructions changed moral theology from being a guild of arbiters of the moral tradition to becoming more and more interpreters of contemporary magisterial utterances. This shift cannot be underestimated in the shaping of twentieth-century moral theology.

An indication of the shift is clear in Davis's preface to the fourth edition:

> Some emendations and additions have been made in the fourth edition of this work, which are necessary in view of both recent Instructions issued by the Sacred Roman Congregations, and replies given by the Pontifical Commission for the Interpretation of the canons of the Code of Canon Law. The Author has embodied in this edition all necessary material published in the *Acta Apostolicae Sedis* up to December 1941 inclusive.[55]

The two 'recent' instructions included in the fourth edition were the problem of a social tolerance of prostitution and the issue of female dress. On the latter instruction, first issued on 12 January 1930, Davis presented a two-page 'faithful translation' of the twelve main points. A look at these is instructive in terms of appreciating the direct influence of the Sacred Congregation on ordinary life.

The first point stated that 'parish priests most of all and preachers, should, on occasion, address words of severe admonition to women that they should employ dress that bespeaks modesty and serves as an ornament and a safeguard of their virtue'. The second and fourth points called on parents and school mistresses respectively to foster modesty and chastity in the children. The third point told parents to 'deter their daughters from public gymnastic exercises'. The fifth through eighth points instructed school mistresses, women of religious institutes, and pious associations of women to aim at checking abuses in modest dress and to ban those who violate such codes. Remarkably, the ninth resorts to excommunication and as such should be quoted in full.

> Girls and women who dress unbecomingly are to be refused Holy Communion, and not allowed to be sponsors in Baptism or Confirmation, and should occasion demand, they shall be forbidden admittance into the Church.

The tenth urged that feast days of the Blessed Virgin be used as occasions to preach on modesty. The eleventh instructed diocesan councils every year to develop strategies 'for the more efficacious promotion of female modesty', and the twelfth required bishops and other local ordinaries 'to give an account of these matters every third year to the Sacred Congregation'.[56] In 1943, while England was in the midst of the Second World War, this is the only transcription of a Vatican instruction that appeared at length in the fourth edition of Davis's work.

The concern about the education of children in Slater developed into a fixation on the dress of girls and young women by Davis's time. Vatican directives coupled with punitive sanctions were published more and more often. The instruction on female dress was but an indicator of these teachings.

As we look at Davis's first two volumes, we see how his work was much more expansive than Slater's. For instance, before treating human acts, Davis's first treatise is on 'Moral Theology: Its Meaning'. The treatise on law covers 85 pages. Though sin has a mere 50 pages, the theological virtues occupy more than 100 pages.

The second volume is dedicated to the Decalogue. The proportionality among the commandments is somewhat similar to Slater's. The seventh and tenth commandments are more than 150 pages. The second, third, and eighth commandments are each under 20 pages. The fifth commandment is 60 pages, with much material, as we shall see, on bioethical issues.

In the very beginning of this volume he defined moral theology as:

> That branch of Theology which states and explains the laws of human conduct in reference to man's supernatural destiny, the vision and fruition of God. As a science, it investigates the morality of human acts, that is, the moral good and the moral evil in conduct in relation to man's ultimate end. It is a practical science because it has to regulate action.[57]

Later he clarified its relationship with canon law:

> Canon law is the body of church law which regulates man's conduct as a member of the visible society of the Church, that is, it imposes a certain discipline on man in his external relations within society. Human acts must conform to the laws of the church, since it is, for man, a divinely appointed teacher and ruler. But it is only in this external relationship, in the *forum externum* that Canon law imposes specific lines of conduct, whereas Moral Theology considers the obligation in conscience, termed the *forum internum*, that arises whensoever the Church, through its canons, imposes such definite rules of conduct.[58]

By this point in the twentieth century, the practical teachings of moral theology and canon law have become different sides of the same coin.

He defined conscience as 'an act of practical reason'.[59] He noted that 'if conscience were never interfered with by passion or ignorance there would be only one kind of conscience, namely the true conscience'.[60] An innocent assertion, we would be hard pressed to find such a one in anyone's writings today.

The simplicity of his assumptions allowed him to describe a variety of ways in which one lacks a true conscience. He gave a startlingly long list of categorically problematic consciences (the false, doubting, perplexed, scrupulous, and laxed conscience), allowing us to see just how easily and frequently the average Catholic avers from the true conscience.[61]

To make a right decision, 'cool reason' was needed, and though it was never mentioned, we cannot but wonder how 'detached' (a very Jesuit virtue) the Catholic conscience should be, especially from the passions, and, we might add, human relationships. Indeed, at one point he discussed 'the pure intention':

> A pure intention is to be highly commended and with prudence aimed at. It consists in the exclusion of all that is opposed to the love of God for His own sake, such as vanity, sloth, sensual ease, selfishness. The highest and purest intention excludes every element of self-interest. Thus S. Francis Xavier excluded in his hymn of love, the motive of seeking his own celestial happiness, and loved God with a love that had no admixture of self-interest.[62]

Davis turned to law: 'Conscience discerns obligations but does not create them. Obligations arise from law, which determines a certain standard of action, according to which we must act.'[63] Davis invoked the distinctions of law from Thomas's *Summa Theologiae*, discussing first the eternal law, and then the natural law, assuming Thomas's definition that 'the Natural Law is nothing else than the rational creature's participation in the Eternal law'.[64] He later adds, 'Practically Natural law means for us that which is in accord with right reason.'[65]

The a-historicity of the natural law was vigorously defended by Davis. He entertained questions about the law as invariable and universal, and turned to the secondary precepts which 'are said to be dispensed, but this is a less accurate way of speaking. No real natural precepts are dispensed. Thus as polygamy, slavery and divorce have been permitted by the author of nature, they cannot be conceived as being against any natural precept that effects the essence of nature.'[66]

He treated *epikeia*, which 'is an interpretation of law in a particular case against the letter of the law, but in accordance with the spirit of it, as reasonably supposed to exist in the mind of the legislator'.[67] In an interesting development, he allowed *epikeia* to be practiced by anyone, though prudently and reasonably. *Epikeia* has its limits:

> There are legalists who never see beyond the words of the law; anarchists repudiate all law. The equitable man will steer a middle course, for laws are made, more especially by the Wisest of all Lawgivers, God Himself, not to restrict liberty, but to enable us to use it aright . . . Natural law and divine law do not admit of the use of *epikeia*, since the Divine Author of such law has foreseen every contingency.[68]

On sin, he noted that for a mortal sin to occur, there must be 'serious matter, full advertence to the gravity of this matter, and full consent to the act of sinning'.[69] Discussing full advertence, Davis referred to other authors and argued that these authors have caused confusion by failing to be clear and by departing from the tradition:

> A lamentable confusion has been created by writers who speak of virtual advertence as sufficient to constitute mortal sin. In any true sense such a

> term is unintelligible, for when a person sins, he must actually know he sins . . . Such confusion of thought is the result of not clearly defining terms, and also – which is almost worse – of departing from commonly-received meaning of terms.[70]

Davis wanted not only to be clear and orthodox, he also wanted to remind his own peers of their obligation to avoid confusion for those who labored in the pulpit and the confessional and not to impose burdens heavier than the tradition espoused. Clarity unraveled confusion; confusion led to chaos; chaos led to unnecessary burdens.

Behind so much of this material was a certain vision of good order in which each understood her or his role. Not surprisingly, when he turned to the capital vices, the first was pride, 'the inordinate desire to excel'.[71] Humble workers, not ambitious visionaries, conveyed the nature of the true, early-twentieth-century Catholic.

Davis's treatment of charity mostly concerned co-operation in the wrong-doing of another. The lucidity of his expression prompted these passages to be quoted with some frequency. Not only were the rules clear, so were the examples. Davis presented a variety of cases: a servant bearing letters concerning illicit assignations; a priest giving Communion to an unworthy recipient; nurses assisting in operations in hospitals; judges presiding over divorces; husbands practicing withdrawal; the sale of furniture to 'heretical places of worship'; etc.[72] The painstaking clarity of Davis paid off when matters were murky or grey. He tended to illuminate exactly where the traditional lines had been drawn so as to let priests and laity comfortably negotiate what appeared to be ambivalent issues by following his probable, clear opinion.

The second volume of the fourth edition was published in 1945, two years after the first volume. There Davis presented the treatise on the Decalogue, where we see how Vatican teaching immediately affected Catholic life. But we also find Davis's own descent into the particular with considerable vigor. For instance, among the sins against the first commandment were those contrary to religion by excess. Davis parsed twelve of them: magic, divination, casting of lots, automatic writing, invocation of the devil, etc.[73] On contracts that were adjudicated under the seventh commandment, Davis discussed twenty different ones: from a promise, gift, or a last will and testament, to leases, insurance, employment, stake-holding, and lotteries.[74] On the fourth commandment, we find the same concern regarding the education of children as we saw in Slater; however, Davis has no fewer than eight appendices from Pope Pius XI (on the education of children, sex education, co-education, and even naturalism).[75]

In light of the Second World War, I propose we examine Davis on the fifth commandment. The commandment was divided into ten sections: three on foundational issues (the precept, preservation of life, and murder and suicide) and seven practical applications (dueling, war, capital punishment, indirect killing, mutilation and sterilization, abortion, and ectopic embryos). He concluded the chapter with three appendices: some medical views on ectopic pregnancies; some medico-moral problems; and contagious diseases. The second appendix treated 22 different problems, from fibroid cysts, cancer of the cervix, eclampsia, to premature delivery, caesarean deliveries, and sterilization, to organ transplants, euthanasia, and embalming.[76]

The framework for arbitrating most of these issues rested with the fundamental assumption about the boundaries between the rights of God and the limited freedom of the human in light of God's rights: 'By Natural law, man enjoys the use not the dominion of his life. He neither gave it nor may he take it away. God only is the author of life. He must preserve it by the use of ordinary means; he is not bound to employ extraordinarily expensive methods.'[77]

Thus, on suicide Davis held: 'It is never permitted to kill oneself intentionally, without either explicit divine inspiration to do so, or – probably – the sanction of the State in the case of a just death penalty.'[78] Among practical issues related to suicide, he treated hunger strikes. Noting that much had been written on both sides (but not offering any citations), Davis argued that if an imprisonment was just, a hunger strike would never be just; but if the imprisonment was unjust then a hunger strike could be held to win one's release 'if there is a good chance of being freed from prison before death ensues'. If the strike were held simply to shame the prison authorities, then the probable death would be too great an evil to legitimate the strike. Interestingly, he did not raise the question whether a group of prisoners can strike for the purpose of winning the eventual release of all. Could all intend to fast until death, if they believed that eventually they would win and some would then be released before their deaths?

Other instances of suicide dealt with 'indirect' death. He discussed the legitimacy of the following cases: the messenger pursued by an enemy who preferred drowning to surrender; the officer who exposed himself to enemy fire so as to induce his men to the courage of a full charge; and the soldier who jumped from an overloaded ship so as to lighten the load. Remarkably, he also argued that a virgin may (but is not required to) leap to her death to preserve her virginity. He used the principle of double effect to say that by leaping, her death 'is not directly wished but only permitted'. Finally, he concluded with another case, arguing that acts of 'bodily mortification may shorten life, but they are lawful if prudently used. Divine inspiration may suggest serious penances that shorten life by a great deal.'[79]

On dueling he cited six papal condemnations.

The section on war covered a mere four pages. After presenting the traditional standards for just war, he remarked that when the grounds for war are 'not certainly just, it is more generally taught that war may not be undertaken'. Though, like Slater, he argued that one could not act from a doubtful conscience, still soldiers 'may usually presume their country is in the right; in doubt, they are bound to obey'. Were we to ask whether Davis is inconsistent, he would argue, I believe, that the soldiers acted not from doubt but in confidence of their obligation to obey the State.

He dedicated only two sentences to unjust war and soldiering: 'If the war is manifestly unjust, a soldier may not lawfully inflict any damage on the enemy, though he may, of course, defend his life. Soldiers who freely join up after a war has begun, must satisfy themselves that the war is just.'[80]

Though upholding non-combatant immunity, he noted that air raids on fortified towns and munition facilities 'are permissible, but reasonable care must be taken, if possible, though usually this is impossible, to spare the lives and property of non-combatants. Indiscriminate air raids on non-combatants to sap the morale of a people, and on places of no military significance are wrong.' Still, he raised the very real case of a ship, either a passenger or hospital vessel, without munitions, which could possibly become later an instrument for aggression. Though the action is 'deplorable, we think the sinking may be justified, for what is attacked is the ship, the deaths of those on board are incidental and not wished, and the loss of a few lives is nothing in comparison with the defeat of a nation'. He concluded: 'When a nation's existence is at stake, the principles of humanity – as they are called – must be regretfully sacrificed to the very existence of a people, but never the principles of justice.'[81]

Davis, like his predecessors, thought of the killing of humans precisely and singularly in terms of God's Lordship over life and not of the intrinsic worth of human life itself. He thought simply of what God forbade and permitted; inasmuch as God forbade direct killing of the innocent, the ambit for indirectly killing human beings was significantly permissive. Like others, he gave a pass to collateral damage. (In his encyclical of 1981, *Evangelium Vitae*, Pope John Paul II both upheld God's Lordship and asserted that human life is itself sanctified. For John Paul, taking human life unjustly violated both the will of God and the integrity of the human being made in God's image.)

Davis addressed the insidiousness of reprisals, but then, in a lapse that reflected some of the horror of the war, he wrote: 'Soldiers, however, in the heat of battle, or in desperate situations, cannot be expected to see the application of true principles through the medium of war. The State that acts on the principles of justice and forbearance from evil in victory and defeat, will preserve the honour of its people and save its soul.'[82] At one point, however, we have to press Davis and ask, is there any point at which the actions of soldiers are attributable to themselves?

On capital punishment, he declared, 'God has given to the State the right over life and death . . . This moral power of the State has been universally acknowledged by the Christian tradition.'[83]

Under the topic of indirect killing, he argued that self-defense against an actual or imminent threat is legitimate even if the death of the assailant is necessary. He added, 'The harm anticipated must be very grave, such as loss of life, mutilation, loss of chastity, loss of temporal goods of great value, absolutely or even relatively.'

On sterilization he raised the case of eugenically sterilizing 'defectives and criminals'. While he noted that three Catholic writers defended the practice, he argued against it not on principles of human dignity or autonomy, but by noting that 'it is a direct and intentional invasion of a natural right, which is not forfeited by mere defectiveness'. He accompanied his argument with eleven citations from other manualists holding the same position. As always, the hermeneutics of God-given natural rights provided the context for applying principles to specific cases.

The legalism of Davis provided a way of discerning right from wrong. The system of laws was rooted in a metaphysical world, distinct from the ambiguities and apparent contradictions of everyday ordinary life. It accommodated historical claims into the context of a universal law that never changes. Thus, as new cases emerged, the manualist astutely applied the law, but the law remained intact. In moments of catastrophic upheaval, the manualist's ability to apply these principles was almost as stabilizing and comforting as the principles themselves. But inevitably the so-called imperfect yet probable certitude that was offered was based on these universal and unchanging principles.

Though there were developments in manualists' teachings, there was not the admission of new principles, for example the intrinsic dignity of human life, nor was there the possibility of considering once-accepted norms as no longer valid. Thus Davis, an opponent of slavery, still acknowledged that it existed as a natural, though no longer accessible, right; when John Paul II declared slavery an intrinsic evil, he directly contradicted it as a natural principle. No twentieth-century manualist would have done that.[84]

Davis concluded the second volume with two treatises. The first concerned 'certain precepts of the church', that is, eleven sections on fasting and abstinence. The final treatise concerns church law on books, particularly their censorship and prohibition. This 'development' was nowhere in evidence in Slater.[85]

Heribert Jone (1885–1967)

Heribert Jone was born on 30 January 1885 in Schelklingen, Germany, and died 82 years later on Christmas Day in Stuehlingen, Germany. He entered the Capuchins at nineteen and was ordained in Cologne at 25. For six years, 1913–19, he was a missionary in the Caroline Islands in the Pacific. He returned to Europe for doctoral studies in canon law at Rome's Gregorian University which he completed in 1922. He subsequently taught in Münster, Germany, from 1924 to 1949. He wrote a *Commentary for the Code of Canon Law* in 1917 and first published his *Katholische Moraltheologie* in 1929. This classic went through eighteen editions in the original German and was eventually translated into eight other languages. Though his work was rather juridical, narrow, and at times obsessively precise, in his ordinary life he was known as a very amiable and compassionate teacher who had an irrepressible inclination for telling jokes.[86]

If Davis was clear and thorough, Jone was quick and convenient. In the original edition, in 1929, Jone wrote that his text is for busy priests and 'aims to provide them with quick and convenient answers to moral questions'. He added that he made special effort to work the new Code into the text.[87]

For the thirteenth edition, in 1949, he noted that he had 'always endeavored to incorporate the decisions of the Holy See in each new edition', but 'the number of these improvements has mounted considerably in the course of years and consequently many parts of this newest edition differ very much from the corresponding parts of the first edition'.

Then in an evident (but the only) reference to the war and Europe's reconstruction, he remarked on 'the necessity of this present revision' due to the fact 'that no new edition has appeared for several years because of European conditions'.[88]

The translator, Urban Adelman, also noted how much new material there was. As an indication of how legalistic exactitude became the mark of Catholic teaching, he cited three tables in the American edition: Catholic hospital codes; State regulations concerning marriage (this is a chart of the then 48 States' regulations regarding minimum age to marry with or without parental consent, whether common law marriages were recognized, whether miscegenation was prohibited, and whether medical certificates were required); and the time of midnight.[89] This last table reckoned to show how many minutes 'our clocks are ahead of or behind true local time'. This assisted in matters regarding private celebration of the Mass, recitation of the divine office, receiving Holy Communion, and observing the laws of fasting and abstinence. More than 100 cities were measured. As he noted, midnight in Albany is 12.05 a.m.[90]

Jone put five parts (human acts, the law, conscience, sin, and virtue) under the first 'book', 'First Principles'. For the most part, Jone was, like the others, a defender of probabilism. He warned confessors that they may exhort penitents to become better, but they ought not to urge their own more restrictive opinions if a less burdensome and probable judgment existed: 'In practice, the confessor should endeavor to freely choose the more perfect thing himself and should likewise advise his penitents to do the better thing. Let him not forget, however, that he has no right to impose his own opinion on his penitents as long as the contrary view is solidly probable.'[91]

The one section that shows considerable development over the Jesuits was in the first chapter on human acts where Jone provided a section called 'The Imputability of Human Acts'. While the effects of a directly voluntary action were always imputed to an agent, the effects of an indirectly voluntary action could also be imputed to an agent. Jone depended on Thomas Aquinas who asked in the *Summa Theologiae* (II.II. 19.6) whether the actions of an erroneous conscience could be attributed to an agent. Thomas had asked the question (II.II. 19.5) whether we could ever disobey our consciences without sinning, and responded, 'Never.' In article 19.6 Thomas asked, if we obey our consciences but its judgment is erroneous, are we responsible for the now-known-to-be-wrong action? Thomas responds that if the agent *could have learned by more proper investigation or reflection* what would have been the actually right action, then the agent indirectly willed the wrong action and was therefore responsible for the action as such. Jone wrote that a wrong action which is committed by an agent who does not intend it as such is imputable to the agent if he or she had the competency to know that these effects would result from her or his action, if some effect could have been foreseen in any way, and if it was in the power of the agent to omit the action. Jone effectively elaborated on Thomas's conditions of imputablility.

On the obstacles to the human act, Jone developed the topic far more than we have seen. In Slater, the obstacles were simply ignorance, concupiscence, fear, and violence,[92] and Davis added habitual obstacles as in vices that have not yet been checked.[93] Jone provided a host of nervous conditions that diminished the agent's moral responsibility: neurasthenia, hysteria, compulsive disorders, melancholia, hypochondria, inferiority, etc.[94] We saw in Davis a tendency to find the conscience of the agent more ignorant, confused, and incompetent than in Slater; in Jone we find the penitent more prone to psychological disorders. In both cases, while compassion for the sinner was probably what motivated them, still the newer writers found more occasions to view the ordinary penitent as less capable, less responsible, and less mature. Clearly the average lay person is, in the eyes of the moralists and confessors, progressively less able to discern and execute morally right conduct.

When Jone turned to the commandments, we find again that a tendency in Davis is fully realized here. The 'precepts' of the three theological virtues (faith, hope, and charity), along with the specific duties, obligations, and necessities of the virtues, are now incorporated under the commandments (prior to the Decalogue itself).[95] The language is thoroughly legalistic. In this much more juridical exposition, charity as union with God, self, and neighbor gets replaced by the duty of fraternal charity to the obligation of almsgiving; noticeably absent was any recognition of the virtues as providing a second self that inclined the agent easily and happily to deeper union with God, self, and neighbor.

The meticulousness of Jone appeared throughout the commandments. For instance, under the third commandment he explained that:

> Servile works are forbidden even though done gratis, as a form of recreation, or for some pious purposes. About two and a half or three hours of such work, according to its arduousness, is a grievous sin. Thus, operating a modern washing machine, which consists in putting the clothes in the machine, pressing a button, removing and hanging clothes, would be only a venial sin.[96]

He later acknowledged that indispensable housework is legitimate Sunday work.[97]

He provided innumerable excuses for missing Mass, including

> persons who cannot endure the air of the church (e.g., certain neurotic persons and sometimes pregnant women in the first or last months of pregnancy) . . . women and children who would incur the grave displeasure of their husbands or parents by attending mass . . . those who have reason to think that by staying at home they can hinder sin; or who would suffer injury to their good name or possessions by going to Church.[98]

For the fourth commandment, regarding the education of children, Jone stated the simple facts: attendance in Catholic schools was obligatory; canon 374 forbade attendance in non-Catholic schools; only the local Ordinary could rule on exceptions.

For the fifth, aside from material on ectopic pregnancies and premature deliveries and the lists of lawful and unlawful hospital procedures,[99] Jone had little time for the bioethical issues that we saw in Davis. His section on war is even pithier and astonishing. Without any reference to the just-war tradition, Jone described the morality of war simply with these words:

> Both offensive and defensive war is lawful for a just cause which must be serious enough to justify the great evils associated with war. The *lawfulness* of war is evident from the fact that one is allowed to defend himself against an unjust aggressor or to prosecute his rights with force if there is no higher authority that will protect them. It is always presupposed that there is no other means to obtain justice, e.g., by arbitration, etc.[100]

On participation in warfare, he had the same position as Davis: a soldier may fight in a doubtful war; no one may take part in an evidently unjust war. He added, 'In modern times, it is almost always impossible for the private citizen to solve doubts concerning the justice of war.'[101] On methods of warfare, he wrote: 'In waging war anything necessary or useful for the attainment of the end is lawful provided it is not forbidden by either divine or international law.' He then briefly referred to non-combatants, but for the most part seemed more interested in the seizure of property:

> It is lawful to exact things necessary for war such as the rulers of a country themselves might demand in the interest of good government. With permission of the commander private soldiers may appropriate such things if necessary. If they have taken anything against the will of their officers they are bound to restitution, that is, if authorities have not consented in order to respect private property.[102]

He concluded this section with a brief discussion on atomic warfare. He upheld the possible use of the atomic or hydrogen bomb, which did not in itself violate any principle *per se*, by offering three insights: today's concept of 'total war' greatly restricts the concept of the non-combatant; the modern conscription of industry and manpower made all persons members of the war effort; and it is difficult to harness the defensive action of a people threatened by a godless tyranny. Clearly thinking of the emergent Cold War, Jone contended that while atomic weapons must be greatly restricted, they could be justifiable.[103]

Jone was expansive with the sixth commandment. He wrote at length about direct and indirect voluntary pollution, in particular the issue of seeking 'relief from itching in the sex organs'. He covered a variety of expressions of sodomy and gave his most sustained attention to external sins of modesty, wherein he listed at least 70 problematic situations, among which we find:

> It is venially sinful to glance at the indecent parts of another of the same sex or to look at them out of curiosity.
>
> It is venially sinful out of curiosity to observe animals mating if no sexual pleasure is caused.
>
> Touching animals indecently is generally not gravely sinful, unless it is done with an evil intention or for a long time or until the animal suffers pollution.[104]

These comments are followed by internal sins against chastity (again matters of 'pollution') and finally he concludes on sexual perversions.[105]

Like all the other manualists, Jone wrote more on the seventh and tenth commandments.[106] Like Davis, he wrote about the property rights of children and married women,[107] and covered topics like ownership, contracts, restitution, and reparations.

He concluded his book on the commandments by looking at the precepts of the Church (fasting, abstinence, and annual confession), the censorship and prohibition of books, and then something not present in Slater or Davis, ecclesiastical penalties in general and individual censures (excommunication, interdicts, and suspension). These sanctions are a full 22 paragraphs, eleven times the length of the chapter on war.[108] Clearly, the more directive and juridical the Church became, the more punitive it did as well.

Conclusion

Manualist theology at the beginning of the twentieth century shaped the clergy's own disposition toward the pastoral care of Catholics on moral matters. Manualists operated out of a very legalistic world in which the principles themselves were safeguarded by their very interpreters. These principles were indelibly linked to a vision of moral truth that was fairly certain, universal, ahistorical, and remote.

The manualist himself exuded a competency to interpret these principles. He was well read both in his own colleagues' works and in canon law. He understood experientially the priesthood and its ministry. He accepted the moral laws that hovered over his discipline and tried compassionately and instructively to hand on his own practical wisdom to those around him. He endorsed the schema that the priest and the lay person could choose the opinion of whoever they wanted, as long as it was someone from their guild, and did not contradict a defined teaching. He also knew that priests and people were busy, so he did not want to waste their time with long arguments; terseness was the style.

As the century unfolded, however, five developments occurred within the manualist tradition. First, the Vatican defined more and more. To the extent that it did, to that extent, the moralist became the translator of the teaching and no longer a scholar offering an informed opinion. By the eve of Vatican II, in fact, the manualist became primarily dependent on Vatican dictates. Second, the agenda of moral theology was altered by these teachings. While the Vatican teachings regarding war and killing were few, their attentiveness to the necessity of Catholic education, to prohibitions of theological books, and to matters dealing with the appearance of women, highlighted that their interests were more set on controlling life within the Church. As time went on, Catholic manualists are more and more concerned not with facing the challenges of the world but rather with conforming to the rigors of the Church. Third, with greater research into human psychology, the manualists' perception of the lay Roman Catholic as a wounded and uncertain penitent became more and more evident. As the century progressed, manualists considered the laity as growing in greater and greater incompetency. Though the manualist was always known as a physician of souls, now he became the psychiatric care-giver of the inculpable sinner. Fourth, he became more and more opposed to innovation. In particular, he chided those who looked for moral theology to be more integrated into both dogmatic or fundamental theology and ascetical or devotional theology. In fact, as other church leaders tried to persuade the manualist in this more holistic direction, the more the manualist receded from moral theology into canon law. Fifth, the metaphysical principles that the manualists followed were unable to address the real critical issues of the day. One only has to see that girls' dresses and sperm received more attention than atomic weapons to appreciate how distant the manualists were from the world as it emerged out of the rubble of the Second World War and faced the possibility of nuclear war.[109]

Notes

1 Thomas Slater, *A Manual of Moral Theology for English-speaking Countries* (London: Benziger Brothers, 1906).

2 Henry Davis, *Moral and Pastoral Theology in Four Volumes*, 4th edn (New York: Sheed and Ward, 1943).

3 Heribert Jone, *Moral Theology*, 8th edn, trans. Urban Adelman (Westminster: Newman Press, 1951).

4 Joseph Mausbach, *The Catholic Moral Teaching and Its Antagonists Viewed in the Light of Principle and of Contemporaneous History*, trans. Anna Buchanan (New York: J. F. Wagner, 1914) from *Die katholische Moral und ihre Gegner, grundsätzliche und zeitgeschichtliche Betrachtungen* (Cologne: Bachem, 1913).

5 Adolphe Tanquerey, *A Manual of Dogmatic Theology*, trans. John J. Byrnes (New York: Desclée Co., 1959) from *Brevior synopsis theologiæ dogmaticae* (Paris: Desclée, 1911).

6 Charles Curran, *Catholic Moral Theology in the United States: A History* (Washington, DC: Georgetown University Press, 2008) 7. Gerardi makes the same assessment in *Storia della Morale*, 415.

7 Raphael Gallagher, 'The Moral Method of St Alphonsus in the Light of the "Vindiciae" Controversy', *Spicilegium Historicum Congregatinis SS.mi Redemptoris* 45 (1997) 331–49. See Gerardi, 413–15.

8 Gerardi, 414.

9 Aloysius Sabetti, *Compendium theologiae moralis*, 7th edn (New York: Pustet, 1892).

10 Curran, 17.

11 Ibid., 21.

12 See Gerardi, 399–404.

13 Thomas Slater, *De justitia et de jure* (London: Burns and Oates, 1898); *Principia theologiae moralis* (London: Burns and Oates, 1902); *Cases of Conscience for English-speaking Countries* (New York: Benziger, 1911–12); *Questions of Morality* (New York: Benziger, 1915); *A Short History of Moral Theology* (New York: Benziger, 1909); *Religion and Human Interests* (New York: Benzinger, 1918); *The Morals of Today* (New York: Benziger, 1920); *The Foundation of True Morality* (New York: Benziger, 1920); *Christ and Evolution* (London: Burns, Oates & Washbourne Ltd, 1923); *Points of Church Law, Mysticism, and Morality* (New York: P. J. Kennedy, 1924); *Back to Theology* (New York: Benziger, 1925).

14 'The writer is not without hope of its doing good even among non-Catholics. Among these, the moral theology of the Catholic Church is little understood and constantly misrepresented and maligned. Of course, it does not merit the bad reputation which Protestant and Jansenist slander has fastened on it.' Slater, *A Manual of Moral Theology*, 5.

15 Jone, v. With the exception of the prefaces and translator's note, when citing or referring to Jone's work, the numbers refer to the paragraphs and not actual pages.

16 Davis, I. 3.

17 http://www.catholicapologetics.info/thechurch/catechism/trentc.htm.

18 Mahoney, *The Making of Moral Theology*, 1.

19 Slater, 6.

20 Ibid., 5–6.

21 Ibid., 6.

22 *Optatam Totius*, 16. http://www.vatican.va/archive/hist_councils/ii_vatican_council/documents/vat-ii_decree_19651028_optatam-totius_en.html, .

23 Davis, I. 4.

24 Edwin Healy, *Moral Guidance* (Chicago: Loyola University Press, 1942) 1.

25 Contrary to many impressions, the seventh commandment always commanded more attention from casuists; see James Keenan, 'The Birth of Jesuit Casuistry'.

26 See Mark Jordan, *The Invention of Sodomy in Christian Theology* (Chicago: University of Chicago Press, 1997).

27 Slater, 18.
28 Ibid., 53.
29 Ibid., 60.
30 Ibid., 60–1. Slater's position confirms the long-standing affirmation that an act made in good but erroneous conscience remains good. See James Keenan, 'Can a Wrong Action Be Good? The Development of Theological Opinion on Erroneous Conscience', *Église et Théologie* 24 (1993) 205–19; Brian Johnstone, 'Erroneous Conscience in *Veritatis Splendor* and the Theological Tradition', Joseph Selling and Jan Jans, eds, *The Splendor of Accuracy* (Grand Rapids, Michigan: Eerdmans, 1994) 114–35; Werner Wolbert, 'Problems Concerning Erroneous Conscience', *Studia Theologica* 50 (1996) 162–75; Josef Fuchs, 'Was heisst "Irriges Gewissen"', *Fur eine menschliche Moral* (Freiburg: Herder, 1997) 54–64, Gerald Gleeson, 'Conscience and Conversion', *Australian EJournal of Theology* 1.1 (August 2003), http://dlibrary.acu.edu.au/research/theology/ejournal/aet_1/GGleeson.htm.
31 Mahoney, 136.
32 Slater, 70.
33 Ibid., 72.
34 On probabilism, see Albert Jonsen and Stephen Toulmin, *The Abuse of Casuistry* (Berkeley: University of California Press, 1988); Mahoney, *The Making of Moral Theology*; Louis Vereecke, *De Guillaume d'Ockham à Saint Alphonse de Liguori: études d'histoire de la théologie morale moderne, 1300–1787* (Rome: Alfonsianum University Press, 1986).
35 Blaise Pascal, *Provincial Letters* (London: Wipf and Stock Publishers, 1997).
36 Slater, 79.
37 Ibid., 274.
38 Ibid., 275–6.
39 Ibid., 276–7.
40 Ibid., 277–81, at 279.
41 Ibid., 288.
42 Ibid., 289–95.
43 Ibid., 297–8.
44 See Lucius Iwejuru Ugorji, *The Principle of Double Effect: A Critical Appraisal of its Traditional Understanding and Its Modern Reinterpretation* (Frankfurt Am Main: Peter Lang, 1985).
45 Slater, 302.
46 Ibid., 303.
47 Ibid., 304.
48 Ibid., 308–9.
49 John Connery, *Abortion: The Development of the Roman Catholic Perspective* (Chicago: Loyola University Press, 1977); John T. Noonan, Jr, 'An Almost Absolute Value in History', Noonan, *The Morality of Abortion: Legal and Historical Perspectives* (Cambridge, MA: Harvard University Press, 1970).
50 Slater, 314–15.
51 Patrick Boyle, *Parvitas Materiae in Sexto in Contemporary Catholic Thought* (Lanham: University Press of America, 1987); James Brundage, *Law, Sex and Christian Society in Medieval Europe* (Chicago: University of Chicago Press, 1987).
52 Slater, 330–4. See also Giovanni Cappelli, *Autoerotismo: Un problema morale nei primi secoli cristiani?* (Bologna: Edizioni Dehoniano, 1986). Hubertus Lutterbach, 'Die Sexualtabus in den Bussbüchern', *Saeculum* 46 (1995) 216–48.

53 Henry Davis, *Moral and Pastoral Theology: A Summary* (New York: Sheed and Ward, 1952). His other works include: *Birth Control: The Fallacies of Dr M. Stopes* (New York: Benziger Brothers, 1928); *Eugenics: Aims and Methods* (London: Burns, Oates & Washbourne Ltd, 1930); *State Sterilization of the Unfit* (London: Burns, Oates & Washbourne, 1931); *Selections from Three Works of Francisco Suárez, S.J.: De legibus, ac Deo legislatore, 1612; Defensio fidei catholicae, et apostolicae adversus anglicanae sectae errores, 1613; De triplici virtute theologica, fide, spe, et charitate, 1621* (Oxford: Clarendon Press, 1944). He translated Pope Gregory I, *Pastoral Care* (Westminster, Md: Newman Press, 1950).
54 Davis, vii.
55 Ibid., ix.
56 Ibid., I. 355–6.
57 Ibid., 1.
58 Ibid., 2.
59 Ibid., I. 65.
60 Ibid., I. 65.
61 Ibid., I. 67–78, Bartholomew Kiely.
62 Ibid., 52. Still on ordered love of self out of charity see I.312–14.
63 Ibid., I. 117.
64 Ibid., I. 125.
65 Ibid., I. 127.
66 Ibid., I. 128.
67 Ibid., I. 187.
68 Ibid., I. 188–9.
69 Ibid., I. 213.
70 Ibid., I. 216.
71 Ibid., I. 236.
72 Ibid., I. 341–52.
73 Ibid., II. 11–30.
74 Ibid., II. 365–408.
75 Ibid., II. 90–139.
76 Ibid., II. 183–99.
77 Ibid., II. 141.
78 Ibid., II. 142
79 Ibid., 145–6.
80 Ibid., II. 149.
81 Ibid., II. 149–50.
82 Ibid., II. 150.
83 Ibid., II, 151, he cites Exodus 22.18; Romans 13.14).
84 John T. Noonan, Jr, *The Church that Can and Cannot Change* (Notre Dame: University of Notre Dame Press, 2005).
85 The two treatises are found in Davis, II. 427–40 and 441–60.
86 Interview with Dr Antonio Autiero, 19 June 2007, Münster.
87 Jone, v.
88 Ibid., vi.
89 Ibid., vii.
90 Ibid., 357.
91 Ibid., 97.
92 Slater, 30–40.
93 Davis, I, 16–33.

94 Jone, 29–37.
95 Ibid., 117–54.
96 Ibid., 192.
97 Ibid., 194.
98 Ibid., 198.
99 Ibid., 212–13 respectively.
100 Ibid., 218.
101 Ibid., 218.
102 Ibid., 219.
103 Ibid., 219.
104 Ibid., 234–40.
105 Ibid., 241–4.
106 Ibid., 245–367.
107 Davis, II. 273–80; Jone, 253.
108 Jone, 420–42.
109 The civilian toll was around 47 million, including about 20 million due to war-related famine and disease. The military toll was about 25 million, including about 5 million prisoners of war.

3

Initiating Reform: Odon Lottin

Introduction

In 1972, in the first sustained history of moral theology, Giuseppe Angelini and Ambrogio Valsecchi described the twentieth century as undergoing a renewal in fundamental moral theology unlike anything seen since the thirteenth century, and yet they were, at that time, hardly able to anticipate its outcome.[1]

The most significant influence in this renewal was the shift in the nineteenth century from the action to the person as the norm for morality. In the moral manuals the point of departure for moral analysis was the action itself: the major task of the priest then was to help the lay Catholic avoid wrong actions, and if they were not avoided, then to absolve the agent of the effects of these wrong actions.

In the nineteenth century the point of departure for philosophers was the person: herein was the famous turn to the subject.[2] This shift was welcomed in Protestant circles long before it was in Catholic circles. Its influence in Catholic circles emerged predominantly through the biblical scholarship of Protestants who introduced the historical critical method for our understanding of the scriptures. Other fields of inquiry, particularly psychology, sociology, and cultural anthropology, began considering the human being no longer as a philosophical object of analysis but as an historical acting subject.

As Joseph Möller explained, the turn to the subject arose precisely in the search for objective truth.[3] Objective truth without consideration of the agent was neither truthful nor objective. But just as philosophers and theologians were trying to understand the relationship between the moral subject and objective truth, they also took a particular interest in history.[4] Some of the events of the twentieth century were enormously disturbing: did we learn from history; were we shaped by it; did we govern it? These were the questions to be understood.

At the same time, society itself was on the move: urbanization followed the dawn of the Industrial Revolution which in turn ignited rapid demographic shifts, and these subsequently shaped our understanding of not only the family unit itself but also our duties and relationships toward that unit.

In this light, moral theologians in the beginning of the twentieth century attempted to meet these challenges, but did so in the context of a continuous debate among themselves.

In Germany, from 1900 to 1930 a lively discussion arose about the sources of Christian ethics. In particular, a question arose about authority, and German professors, enjoying a certain autonomy from Rome, began to question hierarchical authority. Simultaneously, Protestant philosophers and theologians began, in the name of and in defense of the Christian conscience, a sustained critique of the positivism of the Catholic hierarchy's many regulations. In time, this critique crystallized in targeting the casuistry of the neo-scholastic manualists.

These Protestants were not against casuistry *per se*, so much as they were opposed to how casuistry was being done. In 1927, for instance, the Anglican Kenneth Kirk offered probably the most significant defense and reform of casuistry in his *Conscience and Its Problems: An Introduction to Casuistry*.[5] Inevitably the Protestant critics believed that the integrity of the Christian moral judgment should not be compromised by moral norms imposed from without: the moral life was to heed the conscience, not another's dictates.

Catholic moral theologians responded to this critique in three different ways: acceptance, rejection, and an attempt to incorporate the Protestant critique into the traditional manuals (this was, for instance, the nature of Joseph Mausbach's apologia). This last group saw in Thomas's treatises on the virtues a way of turning to the subject; they sought to integrate these treatises into their manuals while at the same time prescribing norms for the subject, but Angelini and Valsecchi note that in the end their manuals were not notably different from the other manualists'.[6]

In this light, if there was to be renewal, it would be in part by repudiating the neo-scholastic manuals and by seeking a specifically positive identity for Catholic moral theology. There were three major steps to this end, each with its own trailblazer: recovering history (Odon Lottin), recovering the Bible (Fritz Tillmann), and recovering the primacy of charity (Gilleman). To them we now turn.

Odon Lottin (1880–1965)

Thirty years ago, the great historian of theological ethics, Louis Vereecke, commenting on the growing number of studies dedicated to the history of moral theology, wrote: 'It is no longer necessary to demonstrate the possibility of a history of moral theology.'[7] This 'young discipline', as he called it, has been developing exponentially over the past 50 years, above all because of the work of Dom Odon Lottin.

Lottin's contributions shaped and animated the shifts that we see over the twentieth century. His writings demonstrated that the history of ideas is complex, that some notions go forward while others are arrested, and that progress can never be fully adequately preconceived because the discourse of ideas is subject to a variety of historical variables, intentional and accidental.[8]

Lottin rendered moral theologians historically sensitive to the development of ideas not simply within schools of thought, but also within the writings of individual theologians. His claim, for instance, that Thomas Aquinas later in his life changed his position on the way in which reason 'moves' the will, challenged the belief that Aquinas's works could be studied and cited without any attention to dates of publication. This belief might seem preposterous today, but 60 years ago it was easily assumed. Inasmuch as many neo-scholastic manualists insisted on universal claims, Lottin's historical claim that Thomas developed his own thoughts challenged the unchanging notion of objective truth held by some of his contemporaries.

After studies in the minor and major seminary of Liège, Joseph Lottin was sent to the Belgian seminary at Louvain, studying under Joseph Mercier, Maurice de Wulf, Désiré Nys, and Simon Deploige. From them he learned the historical-critical method. He also studied with Alfred Cauchie and Paulin Ladeuze, founders of the *Revue d'Histoire ecclésiastique*. He was ordained a priest in 1904 and finished his licentiate in 1907. In 1910 he was appointed to Louvain and began visiting the relatively new (founded in 1899) Benedictine Abbey du Mont César, which community he entered in 1914. In pronouncing his vows that year, he was given the name Odon.

In 1920 he wrote on worship and the virtue of religion.[9] In 1929 he founded the influential *Recherches de Théologie ancienne et médiévale* (*RTam*) and the *Bulletin de Théologie ancienne et médiévale* (*BTam*). In the 1930s he published two small historical texts, one on Godfrey of Fontaines, the other on the natural law according to Thomas Aquinas and his predecessors.[10] From 1942 to 1960 he wrote his four-volume study (roughly 3,000 pages): *Psychologie et morale aux XIIe et XIIIe siècles*. Here he revolutionized our understanding of scholasticism in general, and Thomas Aquinas in particular.[11]

Though the first three volumes of *Psychologie et morale* were published in the 1940s, three other works were published in the same decade. He wrote on the sources of the moral tradition[12] and then on religious life in general and the Benedictine charisms specifically.[13] Then he published his first moral theological synthesis, the two-volume work, *Principes de Morale*. The first volume is subtitled, *Exposé Systématique*. Its index *looks* like the moral manuals: the moral act, the law, imputability, the conscience, and the virtues, but there are no ten commandments, nor are there any specific utterances about specific moral practices. In fact the entire work is an attempt to convey not what the neo-scholastics held, but what the twelfth- and thirteenth-century scholastics did. Rather than being a text for hearing confessions, the first volume of *Principes* was actually a theological foundation for anyone interested in the formation of conscience. The second volume is subtitled: *Compléments de Doctrine et*

D'Histoire. Here he gave the historical debates and resolutions on 28 topics, such as synderesis, erroneous conscience, the connection of the virtues, the gifts of the Holy Spirit, etc. It served as a companion to the first volume, historically engaging the development of foundational scholastic moral arguments but then commenting on their doctrinal significance. Here, Lottin was reintegrating moral theology into what was then called dogmatic theology, but today is known as systematic theology.[14]

In 1954 he published his revolutionary *Morale Fondamentale*. In the preface, he noted that several recent attempts to renew moral theology had been made. He cited as examples, Joseph Mausbach, Arthur Vermeersch, and Benoît Merkelbach. He then added that a more praiseworthy effort had been launched by those looking toward an Aristotelian ethic coupled with an appreciation of the specificity of Christian ethics, particularly its supernatural end. He noted that these studies relied on recent patristic and biblical scholarship, looking to better understand revelation and the tradition, and added that his project was inspired by Thomas Aquinas who illuminated rather than harnessed innovative studies.[15] On the first page of the text proper, he insists that moral theology ought not to be divided according to the Decalogue, but rather according to the moral and theological virtues, and that moral method ought to be inductive, not deductive.[16]

In 1957 he published another work on religious life,[17] and then *Au Coeur de la Morale Chrétienne*. In the latter's preface, he noted that *Morale Fondamentale* was not published as a manual for students but rather as an exposé of the questions being discussed by moral theologians. Because of its success, he had been asked to write a foundational text for young theologians as well as educated, interested laity.

To appreciate his contribution to moral theology, let us look at him as an historian of theological ethics, then as a critic of the post-scholastic period that extended from the fifteenth- and sixteenth-century casuists to the subsequent moral manualists, and finally as the first true revisionist, who by discerning the actual historical roots of theological ethics was able to renew the field as a truly theological enterprise.

Lottin the historian

Lottin's historical-critical method was developed from a set of assumptions very different from those of the manualists who were his contemporaries in moral theology. He wanted to investigate how medieval theologians developed their arguments. Truth was not, for him, a series of always held, ahistorical, universal utterances. He did not believe he would find one position held by all, always. He presumed, instead, that the scholastics did not all share the same understandings of free will, conscience, law, and norms, etc. On the contrary, they debated and contradicted one another and sometimes even themselves. Though the concerns were similar, their quests for moral understanding and truth led them to differing positions. The tradition, then, was not monolithic; it was a series of debates and engagements that historically developed. He wanted to know that history.

Disputed questions included: Could a pagan be virtuous? Did Socrates or Plato truly have virtue? The early scholastics, from Peter Abelard and Peter Lombard to Albert the Great, held that true virtue could be found only in the Christian. Though there were four acquired cardinal virtues (justice, temperance, fortitude, and prudence), the received position (from Augustine) was that without the infused virtue of charity, no acquired virtue was true virtue. Inasmuch as the gift of charity could only be found in those who had received the gift of faith, only those with faith in Christ could have true virtue. The pagans would not have been surprised to learn that the Christian scholastics did not think they had the theological virtues of faith, hope or charity; still, they would probably have been puzzled that the scholastics denied that they had justice, temperance, fortitude or prudence, as well. In short, according to the early scholastics, the pagans were completely without virtue.

Lottin notes that from the beginning of Thomas's writings, that is, from his *Commentary on the Sentences of Peter Lombard*, Thomas recognized that the action of a pagan, if it conformed to right reason, was good.[18] For Lottin, as for Thomas, questions regarding the acquired virtues were about matters of character development conforming to right reason. These virtues were different from the infused virtues which made us supernaturally perfect. The pagan may not know the perfection of charity, but the pagan could know and acquire the virtues of prudence and justice.

Thomas's departure from Augustine and the other scholastics eventually prompted a new stream of thought on virtue. The premise of the development of such thought meant that our own understandings of moral concepts, judgment, and truth are themselves tentative. Though we saw that the manualists, particularly the probabilists, appreciated the elusiveness of absolute moral certitude, they avoided considering the ramifications of the historicity of both their own judgments as well as the metaphysics behind their judgments. They were not inclined to consider that what we might hold today with moral certitude might not be what we would hold tomorrow, if we were to learn something new or to discover something as erroneous.

Lottin's strong interest in the history of ideas and the assumptions that led to those investigations prompted him to set out and establish a chronology of the works of the high scholastics.[19] From this, Lottin's extensive investigations in *Psychologie et morale* would show that Thomas, among others, was constantly developing his thoughts and that earlier positions might well not be the same as later ones. He believed what others thought was unthinkable: that Thomas would have significantly changed his own positions. To admonish those who could not think this way, he remarked that Thomas Aquinas was not a Melchizedek without mother or father, but a man.[20]

Lottin discovered a significant change in Thomas's later thought concerning the reason and the will. Thomas had long asserted that the will had the freedom to accept or reject whatever objects the reason proffered it for consideration. Without that assertion, we would all be slaves to our reason: each of us could only consider whatever our reason proposed, and none of us could try to think otherwise. Still, Thomas made two other assertions that significantly compromised the freedom of the will. These assertions were: the will does not move itself as the reason does, but that the will is moved by the reason, and that the reason moves the will the way an end does.

Here then is the problem: if the reason were to present the will with anything, how could the will refuse the offer? If the will does not move itself but is only moved by reason, how could the will move the reason to think further or otherwise? While Thomas asserted the will's freedom, he offered no grounds for the assertion. If the reason moves the will, how can the will tell the reason to reconsider its offer?

Lottin found that, in later writings, Thomas differentiated between *that* the will wills and *what* the will wills. First, he argued that in presenting objects, the reason acts as the formal cause (no longer did he make reference to the final cause). He attributed the final cause of the will to God, who placed in us the desire for union with our perfect end, God. He then argued that the will moves itself (as efficient cause) other than by the reason (formal cause). Thus, the will can move the reason to consider other objects again and again and again.[21] Second, for the specific act of what the will wills, Thomas held that the will can only will among whatever objects reason offers, but it cannot will something that reason has not offered it; that would be, in a word, unthinkable.[22]

When Lottin reported his findings, he was either rebuffed or ignored. Rosemary Lauer dismissed the claim, arguing that Thomas had no implicit contradictions earlier and that the later writings are only a refinement.[23] Lottin responded.[24] Later, in 1950, the American Jesuit moral philosopher George Klubertanz claimed that Lottin's discovery provided an epistemologically more integrated view of human activity.[25] In another article, in 1961, Klubertanz castigated moral philosophers and theologians for not appropriating this dynamic structure, noting in a survey of a long list of writings that no major contemporary philosopher or theologian appropriated the discovery, except Bernard Lonergan, who used it for his *Grace and Freedom*.[26] Later, Klubertanz developed Lottin's findings into his own virtue philosophy, going from the integrated relationship between the will and the reason to the involvement of human agents in their own actions which occasion their growth in virtue.[27]

In 1971, Klaus Riesenhuber dedicated a major work to Lottin's findings, *Die Transzendenz der Freiheit zum Guten: der Wille in der Anthropologie und Metaphysik des Thomas von Aquin*.[28] Riesenhuber's study showed that the basic thrust of contemporary theological ethics toward the call to Christian discipleship through self-determination, or, as it later became known, as an autonomous ethics in a theological context, was well founded in Thomas's significant changes on the reason and the will.[29] Riesenhuber later presented his findings to an American audience of Catholic philosophers in 1973.[30]

While the debate continued about whether Lottin correctly identified a significant shift in Thomas's later writing on the will,[31] his influence on Riesenhuber prompted other German investigations into the historical context of Thomas's thought. Wolfgang Kluxen's philosophical investigations[32] were coupled with moral theological ones by Karl-Wilhelm Merks and the Congolese moral theologian teaching in Switzerland, Benezet Bujo.[33] These tried to bridge the historical work of the thirteenth century to today's claims about autonomous ethics in a theological context.

Lottin's work was also an incentive for important historical research by Dominicans. James Weisheipl paved the way with his study of Thomas's life and works.[34] After Weisheipl's death, Jean-Pierre Torrell wrote his account of the life and work of Thomas.[35] Leonard Boyle examined the thirteenth-century Dominican deliberations at Angnani that led to Thomas's decision to write the *Summa Theologiae*.[36] Boyle described the deeply pastoral agenda of the *Summa* written for the training of young Italian Dominicans who were not assigned to become university professors but simply to be theologically well-trained pastors. Boyle's work validated Lottin's own insistence that moral theology needed to locate its practical teachings first as the fruit of its systematic foundations and then within the context of dogmatic theology. Later, Torrell gave further insights into the *Summa*'s historical background and purpose, as well as its legacy.[37] Simon Tugwell then analyzed the influence of Dominican spirituality on Aquinas's theology.[38] Finally, Brian Davies presented a comprehensive study of Thomas's work.[39] Now more than an Aristotelian work, the *Summa* is seen as a very Dominican theological synthesis of the thirteenth century.

Lottin the critic

Lottin was a sharp critic of the moral manuals. In *Morale Fondamentale*, he differentiated his work from all manualists, even those seeking some innovation. There he criticized the wretched past of moral theology, blaming the priest confessor as the principal cause for his disinterest in moral theology. According to Lottin, the priest confessor was not interested in anything except that which directly affected his being a confessor.

He attacked recent developments wherein canon law had taken over moral theology, forcing it to focus exclusively on external acts, when in fact, historically speaking, moral theology had been primarily interested in the internal life. Overtaken by canon law, moral theology lost its moorings in dogmatic theology and in the biblical and patristic sources of theology. Moreover, by its insistence on avoiding wrong external acts, not only had it lost its purpose, that is, to pursue the Christian vocation, but it lost its deep connection to ascetical and mystical theology.[40]

He then criticized the centrality of the Decalogue in the manualist method.

He argued that the manualists used the Decalogue because it focused on what we should avoid. This was not an adequate vehicle for the greatness of the Christian moral life, and though he admitted that the Decalogue did have some prescriptions along with prohibitions, it had a rather incomplete set of responsibilities to God and neighbor, and none at all to self.[41]

Finally, he critiqued the probabilists. Calling their command of the field of moral theology 'profoundly regrettable', he noted that the probabilists never instructed the laity to be virtuous; all they did was offer a variety of actions as permitted. They never proposed the virtuous actions that a true Christian should practice.[42]

Later, in *Au Coeur de la Morale Chrétienne*, he commented on the 'poor manuals *ad usum confessariorum*' wherein not a trace of biblical inspiration can be found. Interestingly, he returned to the question of why the moral manuals were so singularly interested in sin, and this time blamed the very numerous mediocre Christians who asked their confessors to give them minimalist expectations for the moral life. If we were to turn to the great theologians of the Middle Ages, however, we would find their living dependence on the scriptures, the tradition, and classic philosophy. Finally, he noted that after Thomas Aquinas, moral theology fell into a terrible decline: 'It separated itself from its living sources, Scripture and dogmatics; it amputated its limbs of ascetical and mystical theology; it introduced a number of canonical questions which sought no solution in biblical texts; and it became much more interested in sin than in virtue.'[43] Clearly, Lottin wanted to kick the dust of the manuals from his shoes as he covered new terrain.

Revisionist builder

As opposed to the limited work of the manualists, Lottin looked historically for the actual roots of moral theology so as to let moral theology flourish in its own proper theological setting. As Lottin noted, after the scholastics the moralists forgot the virtuous ends, both natural and supernatural, of the moral life. Instead fixated on sin, the authors of casuistry and the later confessional and then moral manuals progressively uprooted moral theology from its dogmatic sources and eventually transplanted morals into the field of canon law. There the manualists taught a highly canonical and normative morals that instructed the priest in naming what the Christian was to avoid, but offered no moral guidance on what should be pursued both internally and externally.

To get moral theology to its proper home, Lottin argued that morality was deeply dependent upon dogmatics. 'Dogmatics, in a word, presents us God's part in the work of our salvation, morals organizes our part.'[44] Dogmatics and historical theology are Lottin's theological companions, as was evident not only in the second volume of *Principes Morale*, but in all his writings.[45]

Lottin saw the end of morality as the right realization of the person and the community in and according to God's salvific plan. Far from writing a moral pathology, Lottin believed that morality conveyed humanity's greatness: 'The true grandeur of being human resides in morality, because one's moral life is one's own self manifesto, the fruit of one's own personality.'[46] Elsewhere he wrote that morality does not come from beyond the person, but rather is immanent and immanently changes and leads the person to become more of a Christian.[47] For this reason the entirety of Lottin's *Morale Fondamentale* aimed at the formation of the Christian conscience. What all ministers should look to do is to help the members of the Church to lead conscientious lives.[48] This is why Thomas wrote the *Summa*; this is why Lottin found in history the validation of his own project.

His striking break with the manualists is most evident in the hermeneutical context in which he establishes the conscience as foundational to the moral life. No longer do we find the manualists' pathology of conscience: doubtful, laxed, scrupulous, uncertain, erroneous, etc. Here we find instead the 'formation' of conscience, some 45 pages. Here, too, we find his instruction on the resolution of doubt, not by advising the laity to consult the parish priest or to look up what a probabilist permits, but rather by helping them to form their consciences. Toward this end, he dedicated the remaining 130 pages of his book to the virtuous life and prudential judgment.[49] The Christian conscience is formed by the virtues, and these are acquired, developed, and maintained by learning what prudence means.[50]

By turning to prudence, Lottin liberated the Christian conscience from its singular docility to the confessor priest. He instructed church members to become mature, self-governing Christians, and insisted that Christians have a lifelong task, a progressive one, as he called it,[51] toward the ideals of both the natural and supernatural virtues. By turning to prudence, Lottin urged his readers to find within themselves, their community, their faith, the Church's tradition and the scriptures, the mode and the practical wisdom for determining themselves into growing as better Christians.[52]

The turn to prudence did not just involve the agent; it engaged the entire notion of moral objectivity. Is the objectively right determined by particular ethicists who give their judgments on what is sinful and what is permitted or is it in the conscientious Christian's prudential determination of the particular judgment?

This will be the question that later leads Josef Fuchs to rethink his entire moral theology and to lead other moralists into the revisionist school. That school in many ways was started by this Benedictine monk studying the history of the moral theology of the scholastics. The more Lottin looked into these texts, the more he found the turn to the person, to virtues, and to prudence.

But we should also acknowledge that Lottin's emphasis on the personal right realization through the virtues was not a move away from community. While the moral manuals simply prohibited certain forms of activity and never guided us into becoming better neighbors (though they did aim to keep us from becoming worse ones), Lottin argued from Thomas that our personal good was derived from the common good.[53]

After Lottin: The 'uses' of history

After Lottin, Louis Vereecke dominated the last 30 years of the twentieth century in the historical study of moral theology. For the most part, he restricted his research to modern history, from the years 1300 to 1787, concentrating especially on the writings of moral theologians from William of Ockham to Alphonsus Liguori.[54] Vereecke's studies focused on diverse topics such as the relationship between law and morals in Jean Gerson, dominical observance and medical ethics in Antoninus of Florence, the economic ethics in Peter of Palu and John Mair, and sexual and marital ethics throughout the modern period. Vereecke highlighted an attentiveness to local claims, the influence of circumstances on moral reasoning, the significance of historical context, and the inevitable development of moral doctrine. Vereecke insisted that these issues belong to the *proprium* or the nature of moral theology. Most importantly, the formation of the human conscience stood as Vereecke's primary concern as he investigated how modern theologians discerned the demands of the word of God in the context of human responsibility.[55]

Like Lottin, the historian of moral theology often uncovered the tools that liberated Christians to form and follow their consciences. In order to appreciate Lottin's own legacy, let us consider several ways in which history has, since Lottin, affected the field of moral theology: validating innovation, insisting on the progress of moral truth, and retrieving abandoned or endangered ideas. By bringing history into moral theology, Lottin initiated perhaps the most significant shift in twentieth-century moral theology.

At the beginning of his magisterial *The Law of Christ*, Bernhard Häring presented a brief 'historical survey of moral theology'. These pages served as a guarantee that his work was well within the tradition. Continuity with the moral tradition validated many Roman Catholic moral claims.

Häring's decision to present a brief history was ingenious, precisely because he used it to establish his own innovative claims as traditional exactly as he broke with the theology of the historical period immediately before his, that is, the manualism of the seventeenth through the twentieth centuries. Engaging history, Häring claimed that inasmuch as his theology squared with several key periods in the Catholic tradition, he was more traditional than his more immediate predecessors.[56] Häring's break with the neo-scholastics was not only about the matter and form of the manualists, but also about their use of history. The manualists presupposed that their teachings were universally true by virtue of their historical unchangeableness. In a way, they distorted and even attempted to destroy history's claims by insisting that nothing changes over the centuries. The words 'as we have always taught' became over time a rhetorical insurance for the validity of their teachings.[57]

Moreover, inasmuch as, inevitably, every manualist depended on Thomas Aquinas as the well-spring of moral teaching, each attributed to Thomas a variety of principles and concepts that were only formulated after Thomas lived. Though the principle of double effect was first articulated in the seventeenth century, manualists routinely referred to it as being in the *Summa Theologiae*.[58] Worse is the attribution to Thomas of positions inimical to his thought. For instance, the concept 'intrinsic evil' was first expressed by the fourteenth-century Dominican Durandus of St Pourcain, the most significant opponent to the legacy of Thomas Aquinas; yet still manualists referred to Thomas's use of the concept, though he never had the concept and never would have used it.[59]

Over the past twenty years, three kinds of works have significantly undermined the validity of the presupposition regarding the unchangeableness of the moral tradition: critical reviews of particular moral teachings; studies of how manualists 'developed' moral teachings; and theological arguments that illustrated that moral theology must progress if it is to be faithful to its call to recognize and realize moral truth. Investigations into claims of historically continuous moral teachings have often been proven false. For instance, Giovanni Cappelli studied the claim that church teaching on masturbation was unchanged, but found no comment on masturbation until the fifth century when, as monastic communities were developing, the sexual lives of monks came under scrutiny by two theologians, John Cassian (365–433) and Caesarius of Arles (470–543). They commented on the 'vices' of the 'solitary' life, particularly masturbation, sexual fantasies and even nocturnal emissions, and wrote extensively about the monks' need to subdue any influence of sexuality at all. Their concerns were not with the act of masturbation, but with the monks who vowed chastity. The monks' promise made masturbation an illicit act; the act itself was not considered sinful.[60] In fact, as Cappelli, Louis Crompton, and James Brundage each observe, prior to Cassian, masturbation was not considered a sexual offense for anyone.[61]

Other studies made similar claims. Mark Jordan examined seven medieval texts on homosexuality and concluded that, far from being consistent, any attempt to make a connection among the texts proved impossible. Jordan called the tradition's teaching 'incoherent'.[62] Bernard Hoose studied an array of church teachings on matters of life and death, sexuality, and even crime and punishment, and found that claims to continuous teaching were simply not true.[63] Another study betrays its very agenda by its long title: *Rome Has Spoken: A Guide to Forgotten Papal Statements and How They Have Changed through the Centuries*.[64] Behind these works were not simply claims of inconsistency, contradiction, and even incoherence, but more importantly the insight that continuity with the tradition is not itself the truth guarantor of any particular teaching.[65]

Studies of the manualists proved that, despite claims to the contrary, manualists were co-operators in the necessary historical development of the moral tradition. Here, John T. Noonan, Jr, has set the standard for historical research in his studies of abortion, contraception, and usury.[66] He understands that history cannot leave a teaching or principle untouched: every application of a principle to a situation affects our understanding of the principle itself. Inevitably these historical applications lead to developments in these principles and eventually in moral doctrines.[67]

Noonan has offered a new text looking at areas where the Church not only changed, but shamefully did not. In particular, Noonan studies the Church's long-standing hesitancy to repudiate its teachings on the legitimacy of slavery, and argues that inevitably love and faith moves us to change so as to arrive at moral truth.[68]

In recent years moral theologians have been influenced by Noonan's research. Charles Curran studied the logic of a particular manualist, Aloysius Sabetti, to see the varied ways in which the manualist 'applied' a principle to a case.[69] Thomas Kopfensteiner, using the deductive casuistry of the manualists, illustrated the significance that the science of hermeneutics brings to historical development.[70] His selection of the manualists is important: unlike the high casuists who used their casuistry precisely to develop new moral teachings by entertaining a variety of previously unconsidered circumstances, the manualists resisted assiduously the influence of circumstances and were convinced that moral truth standards were found in the unchangeable. Despite their convictions and resistance, their teachings developed over time. Raphael Gallagher took up the claims of Noonan and Kopfensteiner and examined how the manualists engaged the principle of totality in their teachings on transplants, and demonstrated how and why the moral tradition necessarily developed in the field of medical ethics.[71]

Behind these claims of discontinuity and development, moral theologians have been asserting a third claim: not only does history necessitate development, but moral theology must also occasion such a development. This was Häring's claim against the manualists: their resistance to development was a betrayal of moral theology's mission, which is the pursuit of moral truth. Josef Fuchs agreed and wrote that the Christian has received a new competency through Christ to overcome evil with good, and therefore is called continually to improve the human world through innovation.[72] Likewise, Klaus Demmer argued that the moral task of reversing bias and decline in human history shares analogously in the death and resurrection of Christ.[73] Finally, Marciano Vidal studied recent papal statements to find an implicit endorsement of the necessity of moral development or what Vidal called 'progress'.[74]

These historical investigations have served as correctives and repudiate the manualists' general claims regarding the unchangeability of moral truth. Other studies have turned to history to reclaim specific foundational insights that have fallen prey to unexamined, harmful presuppositions. Here, research has focused on casuistry, conscience, natural rights, and natural law.

Albert Jonsen and Stephen Toulmin, through their study *The Abuse of Casuistry*, restored the credibility of casuistry by heeding the admonition of the Anglican casuist, Kenneth Kirk: 'The abuse of casuistry is properly directed, not against all casuistry, but only against its abuse.'[75] Jonsen and Toulmin argued that, contrary to earlier held assumptions, casuistry is an inductive method that grounds its truth standards in the experienced, well-solved, historical cases rather than in abstract principles with pretensions of universal claims.[76]

Their ground-breaking work generated other foundational contributions that have made the study of casuistry remarkably rich. Edmund Leites provided a timely collection of essays from various academic disciplines that address the way casuistry mediates the tension between conscience and law as found in a variety of both religious and civil cultures.[77] Thomas Shannon and I edited a collection of essays on the differing historical contexts of casuistry. John O'Malley's study of the Society of Jesus provided the foundations for further studies on Jesuit casuistry, while Antonio Poppi investigated the moral theology of the early Franciscans and specifically their work on casuistry.[78]

Others have investigated casuistry with greater specificity. James Pollock studied the casuistry of Francois Genet.[79] Richard Miller investigated the casuistry of Jeremy Taylor.[80] G. Scott Davis wrote on Francisco de Vitoria, Domingo de Soto, and Juan Gines de Sepulveda,[81] and I studied John Mair (also known as John Major), Robert Persons, William Perkins, and Francesco de Toledo.[82] Julia Fleming examines both historical and contemporary casuistry on such practices as lying, deception, gambling, and detraction.[83] More recently, her study on Juan Caramuel, often considered the prince of the laxists, prompted a renewed appreciation for casuistry.[84] Eric Genilo has done a compelling study of the two casuistries that John Ford developed.[85] Toon van Houdt presented the economic casuistry of major sixteenth- and seventeenth-century thinkers.[86] Each of these works was designed to restore casuistry as a credibly critical and contemporary form of moral reasoning.

Paul Valadier has taken on a number of historically unexamined presuppositions that are dangerous to the primacy of the conscience. First, he admits that the postmodern world provides no moral tradition and leaves in doubt whether conscience can be properly formed to make its own moral judgments. But he asks whether communitarians such as Michael Oakeshott and Alasdair MacIntyre are correct when they suggest that the pretext of the liberty of conscience undermines moral traditions. Furthermore, he critiques their proposals that we ought to withdraw to moral communities in order to reconstruct those long-neglected traditions and to enforce their values despite any claims of conscience. Valadier contends, instead, that throughout history, the consciences of various communities' leaders have given shape and content to whatever traditions their communities developed. The consciences of individuals are themselves the sources of the teachings of local traditions.

Second, with regard to the claims that modern moral disagreement reveals an underlying but avoidable moral chaos, Valadier argues that moral traditions, like consciences, have not been and should not be free of internal disparities and inconsistencies. To bring home his point, he takes aim at a French icon, Blaise Pascal, whom, he notes, French intellectuals have notoriously failed to critique. Valadier argues that Pascal deceived many into assuming that moral truth is not like the practical world, but rather universal, simple, and perpetually consistent regardless of circumstances. At length, and with particular dexterity, Valadier also bares the naive epistemological assumptions and dangerous theological beliefs that prompted Pascal's enormously popular attack on Jesuit casuistry.[87]

Brian Tierney, through his investigation of medieval church law, provided a vigorous defense of natural rights, arguing that while the Stoics and Cicero defined *ius naturale* as the universal, objective natural law recognizable by all, twelfth-century canonists described it as a force, faculty or power inherent in individual human persons. These early canonists developed the first expressions of natural rights from an anthropological vision of the person as rational, self-aware, and morally responsible. In fact, contrary to the claims of Michel Villey, Leo Strauss, Alasdair MacIntyre, and others, Tierney proved that 'medieval society was saturated with a concern for rights'.[88]

Finally, Jean Porter demonstrated convincingly that from the twelfth century, the scholastics' idea of the natural law is embedded in the world of theology.[89] In particular, the schoolmen routinely turned to revelation in the pursuit of natural law so as to justify their appeals to the natural law and to derive much of the concrete moral content of the natural law. In turn they employed the natural law as a framework for interpreting scripture as a moral document.

Porter helps us to understand that the scholastics were not at all harnessed by the need to compartmentalize sources of moral insight. While they differentiated between the conventional and the natural, they saw no incompatibility between moral data emanating from rational insight or the natural or supernatural order. Nor did they consider any difference between the rational and the pre-rational as more than a difference of degree. Rather, they recognized an affinity among rational reflection, the natural world, and the light of scripture. They did not exclude other sources of moral insight, for example from other religious and civil traditions; nor did they view their own findings as applicable exclusively to Christians. Finally, they would not have understood contemporary tendencies to bracket natural law theories from virtue ethics inasmuch as they understood the virtues as the right realization of natural inclinations.

Underlying all of these investigations are remarkably similar claims. First, they are about fundamental moral concepts and offer enormous foundational relevance for moral theology, on conscience, casuistry, natural law, and natural rights. Second, these concepts deal with methodological issues needed to ascertain moral truth: conscience is the source, casuistry is the method, human rights and the common good are the stuff, and natural law is the context for moral reasoning. Third, each investigation asserts the theological relevance that these concepts enjoy; the historical research helps us to appreciate why and how faith and ethics are engaged so intimately. Fourth, these investigations for the most part are not about practices but about ideas. Fifth, similarly, inasmuch as these are the investigations of ideas, not surprisingly we find academicians investigating academicians. Tierney looks at eleventh-century canonists, Porter at twelfth-century scholastics, Toulmin and Jonsen at sixteenth-century university casuists, and Valadier at the Enlightenment.

Thus, moral theologians have yet to take advantage of the works of social history in grasping whether historical ideas were ever accepted by the public or whether they were even congruent with contemporary practices, a distinction that historians raised years ago while reflecting on the use of the confessional.[90] We are only beginning to appreciate this possible 'disconnect' between published ideas and public practices. Yet the disconnect is quite possible, as Bryan Massingale has illustrated when he laments that precisely during the civil rights movement, American Catholic moralists evidenced no interests whatsoever in US race relations.[91] The academy and the public do not always share the same concerns, nor certainly the same discourse.

Still, we are only at the dawn of understanding how moral theology has functioned over the centuries and how much research needs to be done about specific practices. These investigations help us think more clearly not only about the past but also about the richness these concepts offer modern needs. By correcting earlier presuppositions, these authors effectively liberate the concepts from restricting interpretations that made them problematic for present-day research.

Who would have thought, following the demise of manualism, that we would be embracing casuistry and natural law so quickly? The turn to history made that possible, for we are embracing these foundational issues not as the manualists and canonists did, but rather as the theologians before them did.

A contemporary work: John Mahoney, *The Making of Moral Theology: A Study of the Roman Catholic Tradition*

After Lottin, two very different scholars presented historical investigations of portions of the Roman Catholic moral tradition. Noonan studied the development of moral teaching on very specific topics: abortion, contraception, divorce, usury, etc. Louis Vereecke wrote about moral theologians from the fourteenth to the eighteenth centuries by looking at their cases, particular interests, philosophical influences, etc. But, like Lottin, neither ever presented a comprehensive study of the influences that shaped the entire moral tradition, nor did they therefore set about evaluating those influences. Mahoney's *The Making of Moral Theology: A Study of the Roman Catholic Tradition*, did just that.

In 1972, Angelini and Valsecchi wrote their history of moral theology. Later, in 1985, Servais Pinckaers published his study of the sources of moral theology.[92] These salutary efforts, however, never approached the breadth, depth, and scope of Mahoney's accomplishment: an investigation into the central historical themes that formed moral theology. Here is a 'cumulative treatment of the subject which at the same time conveys its historical progression, development and fortunes'.[93] As Oliver O'Donovan astutely observed: 'We must not miss the importance of his turn to history as a mode of pursuing moral theology. In teaching us that our contemporary disagreements need to be understood in the light of the past that has pursued them, he directed the community of theological moralists along a path that they badly need to explore.'[94]

In eight chapters, Mahoney named and examined six major forces that constituted the moral tradition: auricular confession, the legacy of Augustine, the distinction between nature and supernature, magisterial authority, subjectivity, and the language of law. He then turned to a contemporary read of the convergence of those influences by explicating the writing of *Humanae Vitae* and concluding with a glimpse of his own hope for the future. Through these chapters he provided a kaleidoscopic view of moral theology, by offering a series of filters to understand the primary concerns of ethics.

Mahoney's focus on auricular confession irrevocably affected our understanding of the development of moral theology.[95] Since the thirteenth century, when confession became the great preoccupation of Roman Catholic priests and laity, moral theology became primarily a sin-based ethics warning Catholics about wrongdoing and offering little by way of positive counsel for the pursuit of a rightly ordered life. Mahoney counterbalanced 'this commitment to spiritual pathology' with his own critical call to pursue a more positively oriented moral theology, one that witnesses to the conscience, recognizes diversity, liberates the oppressed, recovers mystery, and promotes the love of neighbor and community.[96]

Mahoney resisted the urge to consider moral theology as solely expressed in the manualist tradition. In this way, Mahoney decided to see Catholic morality as Lottin and the other great revisionists did; that is, as something richer and more formidable than the moral manuals themselves.

Mahoney had, I think, another reason for going beyond manualism: a sustained interest in promoting the relevance of the Holy Spirit for moral theology. After his dissertation on the Holy Spirit in the writings of Thomas Aquinas, Mahoney published a collection of essays on the Spirit, fruits of the dissertation, as well as the development of other ideas.[97] The essays were published in 1981, the very year Mahoney gave the Martin D'Arcy lectures, which were the first instance of what would later become *The Making of Moral Theology*. Similarly, in the last pages of *The Making of Moral Theology*, Mahoney turns to the idea of *koinonia* or 'the fellowship of the Holy Spirit' (2 Corinthians 13.14).[98] Mahoney recognized that no historical period did more to eliminate the presence of the Spirit than manualism, a point evident in the texts quoted from Slater, Davis and Jone in the previous chapter. In order to allow for the influence of the Spirit, Mahoney had to acknowledge that moral theology was more than manualism.

Mahoney rejected any reductionistic attempts on moral theology and clearly allied himself with those who called to expand the shaping of moral theology to be more scriptural (Tillmann), more spiritual (Gilleman), and more theological (Häring and Fuchs). Still, unlike Lottin, Noonan and Vereecke, Mahoney was much less interested in historical investigation for the sake of retrieval than for the sake of deconstruction. Lottin and Gilleman looked back to history to retrieve elements long lost by the manualists. Mahoney wanted effectively to find out what was holding it back.

The reviewers noted that Mahoney wrote not about the tradition's riches, but rather the restraining elements. Philip Endean rightly noted that Mahoney takes 'us back to free us from what can so easily be an unreflective bondage to our past and our traditions'.[99] Oliver O'Donovan agreed and located Mahoney's book as belonging to the 'genre of theological self-mystification – the most elegant and entertaining example of its kind. He has given his indictment with lucidity and irony . . . It is, in fact, a book all about the bad influences which "conspired" to form Moral Theology.'[100] Some reviewers asked whether there might have been a more positive engagement with the shaping of moral theology. David Brown, for instance, commented that 'what one misses from this liberal Catholic is any sympathetic engagement with the past'.[101] But Peter Byrne suggested that Mahoney is not offering the 'harsh exposé of an external sceptic, but the gentle, if persistent, reflection of one who is engaged in examining the basis of his own thinking'. He concluded: 'The resulting effect is to remind us of the limitations and eccentricities of Catholic moral theology that surround its great contribution to the development of the Western moral tradition.'[102]

As we conclude this chapter, we note five recent books that capture the breadth of contemporary interest in the evolution of the moral tradition. In his *Storia della Morale: Interpretazioni teologiche dell'esperienza cristiana. Periodi e correnti, autori e opera*, Renzo Gerardi introduces us to an encyclopedic categorizing of all the major figures who affected the Christian moral life over the past twenty centuries, including not only ethicists (predominantly) and theologians, but also inspired figures like Hildegard, Teresa of Avila, John of the Cross.[103] In *Catholic Moral Theology in the United States: A History*, Charles Curran provides the first study of the Catholic moral theology within a nation's historical development.[104] Finally, in Karl-Heinz Kleber we receive the lessons of history.[105]

Two new scholars study specific issues. In *The Concept of Sexual Pleasure in the Catholic Moral Tradition*, India's Shaji George Kochuthara argues that the trajectory of theological development of teachings on sexual pleasure eventually recognized its intrinsic value. While patristic theologians developed a Christian apologetics on the body, importing from philosophy a more negative perspective than found in the scriptures, later theologians, notably Thomas Aquinas, Martin LeMaistre, John Mair, Thomas Sanchez, and Alphonsus Liguori, provided enough theological innovation that when the Church wanted to explore more fully and openly the question of sexual pleasure as a good, the theological resources were there.[106]

From Germany, Alexander Flierl presents a fascinating book on the history of moral teaching on everyday lying.[107] According to Flierl, from the early life of the Church there has always been two schools of thought: one describing the lie as an absolutely wrong action, the other referring to scriptural cases[108] and validating as morally legitimate certain exceptions. With Augustine, Aquinas, and Kant contending that lying is always wrong, Flierl argues that their counterparts, John Chrysostom, Bonaventure, and Samuel Puffendorf, disagreed.[109] Even today, Flierl argues, ethicists are found on both sides of the divide: Germain Grisez's unconditional repudiation of every lie contrasts with Eberhard Schockenhoff's differentiation between a simple falsehood and a lie.[110] In both works, the themes of validating innovation, retrieving abandoned teachings, and promoting the idea of moral progress are much in evidence.

Reclaiming their history, moral theologians followed the lead of Odon Lottin and discovered that the *proprium* of moral theology was more humane and truthful than the neo-scholastic manualists suggested. By looking backwards, moral theologians found a new way of looking ahead. Inevitably, through historical investigations of major authors and their texts, moral theologians would re-discover the scriptures.

Notes

1 Angelini and Valsecchi, 164.

2 Michael Himes, 'The Human Person in Contemporary Theology: From Human Nature to Authentic Subjectivity', Ronald Hamel and Kenneth R. Himes, eds, *Introduction to Christian Ethics: A Reader* (New York: Paulist Press, 1989) 49–62.

3 Joseph Möller, 'Truth', *Sacramentum Mundi* (London, Burns and Oates, 1970) V. 308–13.

4 Adolph Darlap and Jörg Splett, 'History and Historicity', *Sacramentum Mundi*, III, 31–9.

5 Kenneth Kirk, *Conscience and Its Problems: An Introduction to Casuistry* (London: Longmans, Green, and Co., 1927).

6 Angelini and Valsecchi, 168.

7 Louis Vereecke, 'Histoire et morale', *Studia Moralia* 12 (1974) 81–95, at 81.

8 Odon Lottin, *Psychologie et morale aux XIIe et XIIIe siécles* (Gembloux, Belgium: J. Duculot) Volume I, 1942; II, 1948; III, 1949; IV, 1960 (hereafter, *Psychologie et morale*).

9 Odon Lottin, *L'Ame du Culte: La Vertu de Religion* (Louvain: Abbaye du Mont César, 1920).

10 Lottin, *Le Droit Naturel Chez Thomas D'Aquin* (Bruges: Ch. Beyaert, 1931); *Le Quodlibet XV et Trois Questions Ordinaires de Godefroid de Fontaines* (Louvain: Institut Supérieur de Philosophie, 1937).

11 The biographical and bibliographical material is well presented in Mary Jo Iozzio, *Self-Determination and the Moral Act: A Study of the Contributions of Odon Lottin, O.S.B.* (Leuven: Peeters, 1995) 1–9. Throughout this chapter I am indebted to Iozzio's work.

12 Lottin, *Aux Sources de Notre Grandeur Morale* (Louvain: Abbaye du Mont César, 1946).

13 Lottin, *Considérations sur L'État Religeux et la Vie Bénédictine* (Louvain: Abbaye du Mont César, 1946).
14 Odon Lottin, *Principes de Morale* (Louvain: Abbaye du Mont César, 1946) (hereafter *PM*).
15 *'On l'a dit cent fois, saint Thomas d'Aquin est pour l'esprit un phare, non une borne.'* Odon Lottin, *Morale Fondamentale* (Belgium: Tournai, 1954) vi (hereafter *MF*).
16 On inductive logic, *MF*, 38ff.
17 Lottin, *Le plus haut Service* (Brussels: La Pensee Catholique, 1957).
18 *MF*, 273–5.
19 Ibid., 190ff.
20 Iozzio, 7.
21 *MF*, 50–1.
22 *PM*, I. 262. Lottin repeatedly returned to this shift in Thomas's writing, see 'La date de la Question dispute "*De malo*" de saint Thomas d'Aquin', *Revue d'Histoire ecclésiastique* 24 (1928) 373–88; *MF*, 50–1.
23 Rosemary Lauer, 'St Thomas's Theory of Intellectual Causality in Election', *New Scholasticism* 28 (1954) 299–319; Joseph Lebacqz, *Libre arbiter et jugement* (Bruges: Desclée de Brouwer, 1960).
24 Lottin, 'La Preuve de la liberté chez saint Thomas d'Aquin', *RTam* 23 (1956) 323–30. Similarly he responded to Thomas Deman and Servais Pinckaers, 'Psychologie de l'acte humain', *RTam* 29 (1962) 250–67.
25 George Klubertanz, 'The Unity of Human Activity', *The Modern Schoolman* 27 (1950) 75–103.
26 Klubertanz, 'The Root of Freedom in St Thomas's Later Works', *Gregorianum* 42 (1961) 701–24. Bernard Lonergan, *Grace and Freedom* (New York: Herder and Herder, 1971) 93–7.
27 George Klubertanz, *Habitus and Virtues* (New York: Appleton-Century-Crofts, 1965).
28 Klaus Riesenhuber, *Die Transzendenz der Freiheit zum Guten: der Wille in der Anthropologie und Metaphysik des Thomas von Aquin* (Munich: Berchmanskolleg, 1971).
29 The work of Lottin, Klubertanz, and Riesenhuber eventually became the heart of my own dissertation on Thomas. Later, I published my study as *Goodness and Rightness in Thomas Aquinas's Summa Theologiae* (Washington, DC: Georgetown University Press, 1992).
30 Riesenhuber, 'The Bases and Meaning of Freedom in Thomas Aquinas', *American Catholic Philosophical Quarterly* 48 (1974) 99–111.
31 See for instance Daniel Westberg's criticisms of Lottin, Riesenhuber and me, as well as Iozzio's own observations. Daniel Westberg, *Right Practical Reason* (Oxford: Oxford University Press, 1995); Iozzio, 128–77.
32 Wolfgang Kluxen, ed., *Thomas von Aquin im Philosophischen Gesprach* (Munich: Alber, 1975); *Philosophische Ethik bei Thomas von Aquin*, 2nd edn (Hamburg: Meiner, 1980).
33 Karl Wilhelm Merks, *Theologische Grundlegung der Sittlichen Autonomie* (Düsseldorf: Patmos, 1978); Benezet Bujo, *Moralautonomie und Normenfindung bei Thomas von Aquin* (Paderborn: Schoningh, 1979).
34 James A. Weisheipl, *Friar Thomas D'Aquino*, 2nd edn (Washington: Catholic University of America, 1983).
35 Jean-Pierre Torrell, *Saint Thomas Aquinas* (Washington, DC: Catholic University of America Press, 1996).

36 Leonard Boyle, *The Setting of the Summa Theologiae of Saint Thomas* (Toronto: Pontifical Institute of Mediaeval Studies, 1982).
37 Jean-Pierre Torrell, *Aquinas's Summa: Background, Structure, & Reception* (Washington, DC: Catholic University of America Press, 2005).
38 Simon Tugwell, ed., *Albert and Thomas: Selected Writings* (New York: Paulist, 1988).
39 Brian Davies, *The Thought of Thomas Aquinas* (New York: Oxford University, 1993); Davies, ed., *Aquinas's Summa Theologiae: Critical Essays* (Lanham, MD: Rowman & Littlefield Publishers, 2006).
40 *MF*, 23–5. He entitles this section, 'Causes de l'inferiorité actuelle de la théologie morale.'
41 Ibid., 14. See the criticisms by Enrico Chiavacci on the Decalogue, where he argues against its presumed primacy of place in the Hebrew Bible. Chiavacci, *Teologia Morale Fondamentale* (Assisi: Cittadella Editrice, 2007) 43–8.
42 Ibid., 331.
43 Lottin, *Au Coeur de la Morale Chrétienne* (Tournai: Declees, 1957) 6.
44 Lottin, 'Le dogmatique, en un mot, nous présente la parte de Dieu dans l'oeuvre de notre sanctification, la morale organiste la parte de l'homme.' *MF*, 13. See Iozzio 42–4. Jacques Leclerq writes simply, 'La morale séparée du dogme cesse d'être chrétienne.' *L'enseignement de la morale chrétienne* (Paris: Editions du Vitrail, 1950) 21. The Redemptorist, Francis J. O'Connell, writes in 1958: 'The earlier theologians usually treated both dogmatic and moral theology as two aspects of the one science of theology. Since the seventeenth century there has been a tendency to discuss them separately so that the impression given is that they are two distinct sciences. This is incorrect, for theology, whether speculative or practical, is one science in as far as its formal object or motive is the same, divine revelation, as analyzed and applied by human reason.' Francis J. O'Connell, *Outlines of Moral Theology* (Harrison, New York: Roman Catholic Books, 1958) 4.
45 Iozzio notes (163–5) the profound influence that Pope Leo XIII's *Aeterni Patris* (4 August 1879) had on Lottin in urging theology to an historical rediscovery of its own authentic roots. See Gerard McCool, *From Unity to Pluralism: The Internal Evolution of Thomism* (New York: Fordham University Press, 1992).
46 Lottin, 'La vraie grandeur de l'homme résides dans sa moralità, parce que cette moralità est son oeuvre à lui, le fruit de sa personnalité.' *Aux Sources* 20, quoted in Iozzio 51.
47 'La morale n'est pas chose impose du dehors: ses fondaments sont immanents à la nature meme de l'homme.' *MF*, 116–17; see Iozzio 71.
48 *MF*, 297–339 ff.
49 Ibid., 341–470.
50 Ibid., 363–9, 379–81, 448–52.
51 Ibid., 54ff.
52 Later, Daniel Mark Nelson, *Priority of Prudence* (University Park, PA: Penn State Press, 1992) argued in a similar way.
53 *MF*, 189–201.
54 Louis Vereecke, *De Guillaume d'Ockham a Saint Alphonse de Liguori* (Rome: Collegium S. Alfonsi de Urbe, 1986); *Conscience morale et loi humaine selon Gabriel Vasquez S.J.* (Paris: Desclee, 1957). On Liguori, see Marciano Vidal, *Frente al rigorismo moral, benignidad pastoral, Alfonso de Liguori (1696–1787)* (Madrid: PS, 1986); Frederick Jones, *Alphonsus de Liguori: The Saint of Bourbon Naples, 1696–1787* (Westminster, Md: Christian Classics, 1992).

55 Réal Tremblay and Dennis Billy, eds, *Historia: Memoria Futuri* (Rome: Editiones Academicae Alphonsianae, 1991). On Redemptorist writings on the history of the conscience, see Marian Nalepa and Terence Kennedy, eds, *La Coscienza morale oggi* (Rome: Editiones Academicae Alphonsianae, 1987) 109–280.

56 Bernhard Häring, *The Law of Christ*, 3 vols, trans. Edwin Kaiser (Westminster: Newman, 1961) 1–33.

57 See Charles Curran, ed., *Readings in Moral Theology No. 13: Change in Official Catholic Moral Teachings* (Mahwah: Paulist Press, 2003).

58 While Joseph Mangan argued that Thomas Aquinas first articulated the principle of double effect, Josef Ghoos proved otherwise. Ghoos showed that the moral solutions from the thirteenth to the sixteenth centuries were of isolated concrete cases. In the sixteenth century, Bartolomeo de Medina (1528–80) and Gabriel Vasquez (1551–1604) began to name the common factors among relevant cases. Later, John of St Thomas (1589–1644) articulated the factors and named the four conditions of the principle for the first time. Joseph Mangan, 'An Historical Analysis of the Principle of Double Effect', *TSs* 10 (1949) 41–61; Josef Ghoos, 'L'Acte à double effet: Étude de théologie positive', *Ephemerides theologicae lovanienses* 27 (1951) 30–52. See James F. Keenan, 'The Function of the Principle of Double Effect?' *TS* 54 (1993) 294–315. Lottin agrees with Ghoos in *MF*, 268.

59 See John Dedek, 'Moral Absolutes in the Predecessors of St Thomas', *TS* 38 (1977) 654–80; 'Intrinsically Evil Acts: An Historical Study of the Mind of St Thomas', *The Thomist* 43 (1979) 385–413; 'Intrinsically Evil Acts: The Emergence of a Doctrine', *Recherches de theologie ancienne et medievale* 50 (1983) 191–226. The reader should not miss that Dedek's last study appeared in the journal Lottin founded.

60 Giovanni Cappelli, *Autoerotismo: Un problema morale nei primi secoli cristiani?* (Bologna: Edizioni Dehoniano, 1986).

61 James Brundage, *Law, Sex and Christian Society in Medieval Europe* (Chicago: University of Chicago Press, 1987); Louis Crompton, *Homosexuality and Civilization* (Cambridge: Harvard University Press, 2003).

62 Mark Jordan, *The Invention of Sodomy in Christian Theology* (Chicago: University of Chicago Press, 1997).

63 Bernard Hoose, *Received Wisdom?: Reviewing the Role of Tradition in Christian Ethics* (London: Geoffrey Chapman, 1994).

64 Maureen Fiedler and Linda Rabben, eds, *Rome Has Spoken: A Guide to Forgotten Papal Statements and How They Have Changed through the Centuries* (New York: Crossroad, 1998).

65 Karl-Wilhelm Merks, 'De irenenzang van de tradites: Pleidooi voor een universele ethiek', *Bijdragen* 58 (1997) 122–43; Brian Johnstone, 'Can Tradition be a Source of Moral Truth? A Reply to Karl-Wilhelm Merks', *Studia Moralia* 37 (1999) 431–51.

66 Noonan, *The Scholastic Analysis of Usury* (Cambridge: Harvard University, 1957); *Contraception: A History of Its Treatment by the Catholic Theologians and Canonists* (Cambridge: Harvard University, 1965); ed., *The Morality of Abortion*.

67 John T. Noonan, Jr, 'Development in Moral Doctrine', in *The Context of Casuistry*, ed. James Keenan and Thomas Shannon (Washington, DC: Georgetown University Press, 1995) 188–204.

68 Noonan, *A Church that Can and Cannot Change*.

69 Charles Curran, 'The Manual and Casuistry of Aloysius Sabetti', *The Context of Casuistry*, 161–80.

70 Thomas Kopfensteiner, 'Science, Metaphor and Moral Casuistry'.

71 Raphael Gallagher, 'Catholic Medical Ethics: A Tradition Which Progresses', James F. Keenan, ed., *Catholic Ethicists on HIV/AIDS Prevention* (New York: Continuum, 2000) 271–81 (hereafter *CEHP*).

72 Josef Fuchs, 'Innovative Morality', *Moral Demands and Personal Obligations* (Washington, DC: Georgetown University Press, 1993) 114–19.

73 Klaus Demmer, 'Die autonome Moral: Eine Anfrage an die Denkform', Adrian Holderegger, ed., *Fundamente der theologischen Ethik: Bilanz und Neuansatze* (Freiburg: Herder, 1996) 261–76.

74 Marciano Vidal, 'Progress in the Moral Tradition', *CEHP*, 257–70.

75 Kenneth E. Kirk, *Conscience and Its Problems* (London: Longmans, 1927) 125.

76 Jonsen and Toulmin, *The Abuse of Casuistry*.

77 Edmund Leites, ed., *Conscience and Casuistry in Early Modern Europe* (New York: Cambridge University, 1988).

78 John O'Malley, *The First Jesuits* (Cambridge: Harvard University Press, 2007); Antonio Poppi, *Studi sull etica della prima scuola Francescana* (Padua: Centro Studi Antoniani, 1996).

79 James Pollock, *Francois Genet: The Man and His Methodology* (Rome: Gregorian University, 1984).

80 Richard Miller, 'Moral Sources, Ordinary Life, and Truth-telling in Jeremy Taylor's Casuistry', in *The Context of Casuistry* 131–58; *Casuistry and Modern Ethics: A Poetics of Practical Reasoning* (Chicago: University of Chicago, 1996).

81 G. Scott Davis, 'Conscience and Conquest: Francisco de Vitoria on Justice in the New World', *Modern Theology* 13 (1997) 475–500; 'Humanist Ethics and Political Justice: Soto, Sepulveda, and the "Affair of the Indies",' *Annual of the Society of Christian Ethics* (1999) 193–212. See also his *Warcraft and the Fragility of Virtue* (Moscow, Idaho: University of Idaho, 1992).

82 Keenan, 'The Casuistry of John Major, Nominalist Professor of Paris (1506–1531)', *Annual of Society of Christian Ethics* (1993) 205–22; 'William Perkins (1558–1602) and the Birth of British Casuistry', *The Context of Casuistry*, 105–30; 'How Casuistic is Early British Puritan Casuistry? Or, What Are the Roots of Early British Puritan Practical Divinity?', John O'Malley, ed., *The Jesuits: Cultures, Sciences, and the Arts, 1540–1773* (Toronto: Toronto University Press, 1999) 627–40; 'Unexpected Consequences: A Jesuit and Puritan Book, Robert Persons' *Christian Directory* and Its Relevance for Jesuit Spirituality Today', *Studies in the Spirituality of the Jesuits* 33/2 March 2001, 1–26; 'Was William Perkins' *Whole Treatise of Cases of Consciences* Casuistry?'; 'The Birth of Jesuit Casuistry: *Summa casuum conscientiae, sive de instructione sacerdotum, libri septem* by Francesco de Toledo (1532–1596)'. See also my essays on the contemporary application of casuistry: 'Making a Case for Casuistry: AIDS and its Ethical Challenges', Jon Wetlesen, ed., *Hva er Kasuistikk?: Om moralsk laering og refleksjon i tilknytning til forbilder og eksempler* (Oslo: Oslo University Press, 1998) 163–86; 'Fallstudien, Rhetorik und die amerikanische Debatte über die ärztliche Suizidbeihilfe' ('Cases, Rhetoric, and the American Debate about Physician Assisted Suicide') Adrian Holderegger, ed., *Das medizinisch assistierte Sterben: Zur Sterbenhilfe aus medizinischer, ethischer, juristischer und theologischer Sicht* (Freiburg: Herder, 1999) 157–74; 'Applying the Seventeenth Century Casuistry of Accommodation to HIV Prevention', *TS* 60 (1999) 492–512.

83 Julia Fleming, 'By Coincidence or Design? Cassian's Disagreement with Augustine Concerning the Ethics of Falsehood', *Augustinian Studies* 29 (1998) 19–34;

'Deception by Means of Incomplete Truth', *Josephinum Journal of Theology* 6 (1999) 21–30; 'The Ethics of Lying in Contemporary Moral Theology: Strategies for Stimulating the Discussion', *Louvain Studies* 24 (1999) 57–71; 'Reputation Reconsidered: The Contemporary Relevance of Casuist/Manualist Legacies Concerning Detraction', *Studia Moralia* 39 (2001) 159–74.

84 Julia Fleming, *Defending Probabilism: The Moral Theology of Juan Caramuel* (Washington: Georgetown University Press, 2006).

85 Eric Genilo, *John Cuthbert Ford: Moral Theologian at the End of the Manualist Era* (Washington, DC: Georgetown University Press, 2007).

86 Toon van Houdt, 'Money, Time, and Labour: Leonardus Lessius and the Ethics of Lending and Interest Taking', *Ethical Perspectives* 2 (1995) 18–22; 'Tradition and Renewal in Late Scholastic Economic Thought: The Case of Leonardus Lessius (1554–1623)', *Journal of Medieval and Early Modern Studies* 28 (1998) 51–75; with Martin Stone 'Probabilism and its Methods: Leonardus Lessius and his Contribution to the Development of Jesuit Casuistry', *Ephemerides Theologicae Lovanienses*, 75 (1999) 359–94.

87 Paul Valadier, *Eloge de la conscience* (Paris: Seuil, 1994).

88 Brian Tierney, *The Idea of Natural Rights: Studies on Natural Rights, Natural Law, and Church Law* (Atlanta: Scholars Press, 1997) 54.

89 Jean Porter, *Natural and Divine Law: Reclaiming the Tradition for Christian Ethics* (Grand Rapids: Eerdmans, 1999); *Nature As Reason: A Thomistic Theory of the Natural Law* (Grand Rapids: Eerdmans, 2004).

90 John Bossy, 'The Social History of Confession in the Age of the Reformation', *Transactions of the Royal Historical Society* 25 (1975) 21–38.

91 Bryan Massingale, 'The African American Experience and US Roman Catholic Ethics: "Strangers and Aliens No Longer"?' Jamie Phelps, ed., *Black and Catholic: The Challenge and Gift of Black Folk: Contributions of African American Experience and World View to Catholic Theology* (Milwaukee: Marquette University, 1997) 79–101.

92 Servais Pinckaers, *Les sources de la morale chrétienne: sa méthode, son contenu, son histoire* (Paris: Editions du Cerf, 1985); *The Sources of Christian Ethics*, trans. Sr Mary Thomas Noble (Washington: Catholic University of America, 1995).

93 John Mahoney, *The Making of Moral Theology: A Study of Roman Catholic Tradition* (New York: Oxford University, 1987) viii.

94 Oliver O'Donovan, 'The Making of Moral Theology', *Journal of Theological Studies* 39 (1988) 348–50, at 350.

95 On this history, see James Dallen, *The Reconciling Community* (New York: Pueblo, 1986); Thomas Tentler, *Sin and Confession on the Eve of the Reformation* (Princeton: Princeton University, 1977); Bernhard Poschmann, *Penance and the Anointing of the Sick*, trans. Francis Courtney (New York: Herder and Herder, 1964).

96 Mahoney, *The Making of Moral Theology*, 29; Keenan, 'John Mahoney's *The Making of Moral Theology*', *Oxford Handbook of Theological Ethics*, Gilbert Meilaender and William Werpehowski, eds (Oxford: Oxford University Press, 2005) 503–19.

97 Mahoney, *Seeking the Spirit: Essays in Moral and Pastoral Theology* (London: Sheed and Ward, 1981).

98 Mahoney, *The Making of Moral Theology*, 343.

99 Philip Endean, 'The Making of Moral Theology', *The Month* 18 (1988) 683–5, 683.

100 O'Donovan, 349.

101 David Brown, 'The Making of Moral Theology', *Scottish Journal of Theology* 42 (1989) 130–1, at 130.

102 Peter Byrne, 'The Making of Moral Theology', *Religious Studies* 24 (1988) 543–4, at 543.

103 Renzo Gerardi, *Storia della Morale: Interpretazioni teologiche dell'esperienza cristiana. Periodi e correnti, autori e opera* (Bologna: Edizioni Dehoniane, 2003).

104 Curran, *Catholic Moral Theology in the United States: A History.*

105 Karl-Heinz Kleber, *Historia Docet: Zur Geschichte der Moraltheologie*, Studien der Moraltheologie 15 (Münster: Lit Verlag, 2005).

106 Shaji George Kochuthara, *The Concept of Sexual Pleasure in the Catholic Moral Tradition* (Rome: Gregorian University Press, 2007).

107 Alexander Flierl, *Die (Un-)Moralder Alltagslüge?! Wahrheit und Lüge im Alltagsethos aus Sicht der katholischen Moraltheologie*, Studien der Moraltheologie 32 (Münster: Lit Verlag, 2005).

108 See Genesis 27; 29.23; 31.35; 34.14–25; 38.13–26; Exodus 1.17–20.

109 Flierl, at 231. He compares the six authors from pages 78–231.

110 Ibid., 203–20, 232.

4

Retrieving Scripture and Charity: Fritz Tillmann and Gérard Gilleman

Though the word 'retrieval' is much overused, it appropriately applies to the legacy of Dom Odon Lottin: he retrieved the historical context of the development of moral theology and, in doing so, discovered the need for moral theology to be reunited with dogmatic, biblical, and ascetical theology. At the same time, in his own moral theology he gave us a thick, positive, developmental, anthropological vision of the moral person in the key of virtue.

Still, while he critiqued and broke away from the deeply negative direction that the moral manuals pursued in connection with their legal and canonical bonds, he did not do a moral theology that was rooted in scripture, developed from dogmatic theology, or embedded in spiritual theology. Instead he summoned his readers to begin imagining anew how moral theology could again be rooted in fundamental, biblical, and ascetical theology. Who would effectively lead moral theologians to do their investigations and research in relation to these other forms of theological reflection?

In the next chapter we will look at the crowning theological synthesis which Bernhard Häring achieved in writing *The Law of Christ*. Here, let us consider the two earlier trailblazers who revised the agenda of moral theology: one who wrote a moral handbook in the key of scripture; the other who wrote a moral theology that emerged from a dynamic spirituality.

As parallel as their work and interests were, as persons they were completely different. The one working in scripture, Fritz Tillmann, was originally an accomplished biblical scholar and a German diocesan priest forced by a Vatican congregation out of his field of work. The other, Gérard Gilleman, was a Belgian Jesuit doctoral student whose dissertation when published became arguably the most important single work in moral theology in the twentieth century. The student, however, did not publish the dissertation; his academic adviser did, because the newly minted scholar was sent to India to teach in a seminary, never to write again and never, effectively, to be heard of again outside of India. He died at 92 in Calcutta on 24 May 2002.

Fritz Tillmann (1874–1953)

On 10 May 2003, on the occasion of the 100th anniversary of the Pontifical Biblical Commission, the then-Cardinal Joseph Ratzinger reflected on two names that appeared in 'the decree of the Consistorial Congregation of 29 June 1912, *De quibusdam commentariis non admittendis*'. One of them was: 'Fritz Tillmann, the editor of a commentary on the New Testament labelled as unacceptable'. The commentary included an essay by Friedrich Wilhelm Maier, 'a friend of Tillmann, at the time a qualified lecturer in Strasbourg. The decree of the Consistorial Congregation established that these comments *expungenda omnino esse ab institutione clericorum*. The Commentary . . . had to be banned and withdrawn from sale since, with regard to the Synoptic question, Maier sustained the so-called two-source theory, accepted today by almost everyone.'

Not only was the author Maier held accountable, but the editor, Tillmann, was as well. The Cardinal added: 'This also brought Tillmann's and Maier's scientific career to an end. Both, however, were given the option of changing theological disciplines.'

According to the Cardinal, Maier did not take the offer and became, instead, a prison chaplain. Tillmann did decide to change fields and, in the Cardinal's words, 'became a top German moral theologian. Together with Theodor Steinbüchel and Theodor Müncker, he edited a manual of *avant-garde* moral theology, which addressed this important discipline in a new way and presented it according to the basic idea of the imitation of Christ.'[1]

Until 1912, Tillmann had been a successful and influential biblical theologian. The English titles of his German works evidence the research that he did: *The Son of Man: Jesus's Self-understanding of his Messianic Nature* (1905); *The Future Coming of Christ according to the Pauline Epistles* (1909); and *The Self-understanding of the Son of God: The Foundation of the Synoptic Gospels* (1911).[2]

In 1919, he wrote his first moral theological work: *Personality and Community in the Preaching of Jesus*.[3] In 1934, he collaborated with Theodor Steinbüchel and Theodor Müncker on a three-volume work, which he edited, entitled *Die katholische sittenlehre* (*Catholic Moral Teaching*). Steinbüchel wrote the first volume on philosophical foundations; Müncker authored the second, on the epistemological and psychological foundations; and Tillmann wrote the third, *Die Idee der Nachfolge Christi*, on the idea of the disciple of Christ.[4]

Tillman's volume was a tremendous success. Seventy years after its publication, Karl-Heinz Kleber writes that in the search to express what the foundational principle of moral theology ought to be, Tillmann came forward and named it: the disciple of Christ. Others followed Tillmann's lead. Kleber names: Gustav Ermecke, Johannes Stelzenberger, Bernhard Häring, Gérard Gillemann, and René Carpentier.[5] No less than Odon Lottin remarked, 'One could not recommend too highly a reading of Fritz Tillmann's *Die Idee der Nachfolge Christi* (1934).'[6]

In 1937 he published a more accessible text for lay people, *Der Meister Ruft*

(*The Master Calls*). This work had an even greater impact on theological discourse. M. J. Congar remarked that the new work presented a handbook of lay morality, not as a list of sins, but as virtues dominated by the idea of the following of Christ and guided by scripture.[7]

Still Tillmann had his detractors. Andreas Hartman asked whether such a moral theology could address all the issues faced by contemporary Christians.[8] Otto Schilling suggested that his approach provided less clear guidelines than the manualists did.[9] Later, when the English translation appeared, Felix Cardegna gave it a brief notice in *Theological Studies*, commenting that the work was hardly a complete treatment of moral theology.[10]

Nevertheless, D. Thalhammer astutely observed two significant achievements. First, Tillmann managed to distill all his previous work, especially *Die Idee der Nachfolge Christi*, into an integrated and accessible expression for interested lay readers. More importantly, he demonstrated that it was possible to create a sound, moral theology based directly on Christian revelation.[11]

More recently, Johannes Reiter confirmed Thalhammer's observations and added that Tillmann's Christological accent in moral theology influenced a series of subsequent German authors such as Johannes Steinberger and Bernhard Häring.[12]

Demonstrating in 1937 a biblically based moral theology was, in my estimation, nothing short of miraculous. We need only to read Lottin's laments about the lack of biblical theology in moral theology to stop for a minute and ask, where did Lottin incorporate it? Indeed, the fair reader will find more scripture quoted in Slater or Jone than in Lottin. Admittedly, Slater and Jone used biblical texts to substantiate their particular claims, and clearly, in this sense they hardly had a biblical theology but rather a form of proof-texting. But Lottin and his admirers, while assuredly familiar with historical scholastic texts and while advocating a biblically based and informed moral theology, did not know how to incorporate what they knew was missing. Interestingly, Lottin knew that the virtues would be the best way to bridge biblical theology with moral theology, but as both a great historian and moral theologian he simply could not have had yet another competency.

Catholic moral theology could not make the much-needed and extraordinarily urgent turn to the Bible if it did not have within its guild a superb scripture scholar. One can hardly imagine a moral theologian credibly developing a biblically based moral theology. Tillmann's exile from the land of exegesis and his finding safety and sanctuary in the field of moral theology became itself the fundamental occasion for realizing one of the most significant developments in twentieth-century Roman Catholic moral theology.

The English translation of the 1937 *The Master Calls* is divided into five parts: principles, love of God, love of self, love of neighbor, and social relations. The first four parts are roughly 80 pages each, the final is 35 pages long. Without a doubt, a work based on the threefold command of love was radically new.

'Principles' begins with 'The Fundamental Idea of the Following of Christ', accompanied by the words of Luke 9.23, 'And he said to all, "If anyone wishes to come after me, let him deny himself and take up his cross daily, and follow Me."' The passage is key: the call of discipleship is addressed not to a few, but to all 'whom faith would lead to become His disciples'.[13] Tillmann's selection of biblical texts underlining the universality of Jesus's summons offered to the whole Church a way of imagining and anticipating a theologically educated laity bent on ministry and service.

Highlighting the immensity and grandeur of the call, Tillmann wrote: 'The goal of the following of Christ is none other than the attainment of the status of a child of God.' Here, Tillmann offered three requisites: 'realization of the very highest degree of religious demands and conduct'; 'a willingness to undergo any sacrifices for the sake of the great task enjoined'; and an 'absolute conformity to the will of God'.[14] These conditions were not matters of privacy or isolation. 'Christ's over-all teaching concerning the new man, his duties, and his position with regard to God and His kingdom, excludes all isolation, whether in general or in particular, and points out directions and duties which tend toward the community.'[15] The pursuit of Christ has never been in separation from love of neighbor or for the needs of the world; Christ is the soul of a community.

After stating that baptism supplies the essential foundation of discipleship,[16] Tillmann discussed our rebirth and new creation, quoting extensively from St Paul and St John. Enunciating that the first power of the new life is the gift of the Holy Spirit, while the second is union with Christ, he concluded noting that 'the Johannine concept of the communion of the disciple with his Lord becomes identified with the Pauline concept of Christ's life in the baptized person'. Citing Romans 8.19–23, he added that our hope is to be 'made free to share in the magnificent liberty of the children of God'.[17]

From discipleship and baptism, he turned to the will of God. Reflecting on John 4.34, 'My food is to do the will of him who sent me, to accomplish his work', Tillman argued that the will of God is the foundation of the moral life, 'the disciple's daily bread. It is his life in general and in particular; it is his calling and his labors; it is everything.'[18]

How, then, could we respond to God's will to become disciples? Tillmann followed the lead of Lottin and suggested the virtues as the primary place to begin our life as disciples. He pointed to the preaching of Jesus who saw in our 'interior disposition' the beginning of every moral act, whether good or bad.[19] Tillmann commented extensively on Matthew 5.21–29 and added that conscience goes hand in hand with the interior life: 'The Lord taught that all moral action and all moral bonds must have an interior basis, and that any contradiction between inner conviction and external conduct is nothing but hateful hypocrisy.'[20]

Tillmann reflected on the beginning of our journey: to accept the call of discipleship is to make a decision that must be 'absolute and irrevocable'.[21]

Tillmann cited Luke 9.59–61, 14.28–33 and added, 'No man can escape this decision; the call to God's kingdom does not admit excuses.'[22]

The journey of following in the footsteps of Christ is a call to pursue perfection, a call that Paul reiterates time and again (1 Corinthians 2.6; Philippians 3.15; Colossians 4.12). Tillmann describes Christian perfection as 'the religious and moral fullness attainable by the individual Christian here on earth'.[23] He concluded that the attainment of perfection is 'the task and goal of every Christian'.[24]

The language of perfection was usually, though not exclusively, for those in religious life; they lived the state of perfection, their houses of formation were schools of perfection. Still, exceptions were often noted. Thomas Aquinas, for instance, argued that religious life was a school of perfection, but added that not everybody in the school was perfect, and conversely, not everybody who lived the perfect life was in a school of perfection.[25] Tillmann, by turning to Paul, broke down the differentiations among laity, clergy and religious, identifying Christian baptism as the universal call to perfection.

Even though the teachings of Jesus and Paul were universal in their call, the tradition (for a host of reasons) reserved service for a few rather than for all. Those few were called to be disciples and therefore called to pursue perfection. Desiderius Erasmus thought otherwise and wrote his argument in the *Enchiridion Militis Christiani* (*The Handbook of the Christian Soldier*) in 1504. This work is the prototype for all later attempts to develop a distinctively lay (non-monk) spirituality that could accommodate the call of all Christians. Erasmus described the *Enchiridion* and explained that the 'good life is everybody's business, and Christ wished the way to be accessible to all men, not beset with impenetrable labyrinths of argument but open to sincere faith, to love unfeigned, and their companion, the hope that is not put to shame'.[26]

With Tillmann, Erasmus's claim implicitly reappeared in the twentieth century, and from Tillmann's time onward the call to perfection and discipleship for all Christians became eventually a traditional claim. This is affirmed yet again recently by the Irish moral theologian Enda McDonagh who observed, 'One of the gains of moral theology presently has been the realization that the call to perfection applies to all Christians.'[27]

By using the language of perfection, then, Tillmann stayed within the discourse of virtue, since virtue perfects the human.[28] With the virtues he also built a much-needed bridge to ascetical theology, wherein we find the schools of perfection. Here he focused more on the character traits and inner dispositions, rather than on specific external actions as the moral manuals had. After Tillmann, those who work in biblical ethics frequently turn to the virtues as the most appropriate mode of conveying such an ethics.

For Tillmann, the road to perfection required the virtues of humility and self-denial. Humility was not known in the Roman world; it was the fruit of Jesus's new teaching. This virtue teaches us three lessons: 'the pure and absolute truth regarding man's relation to God'; 'the unvarnished truth about ourselves'; and the abandonment of every form of degradation. In short, humility is active self-knowledge and expresses itself in gratitude.[29]

After humility comes exercises of self-denial, which is asceticism. These exercises must conform to each person's own personality and must be exercised within reasonable limits. Moreover, only those who have self-esteem can express self-denial: self-denial is not a 'forcible suppression . . . leading to stupefaction and death'. The gospel does not consider our passions as obstacles but rather as aids to further development. 'The flame must not be snuffed out, but must be purified and regulated, so that it may illumine and warm, not blind and consume.'[30]

Tillmann concluded the part on perfection by reflecting on sin, a contradiction of God's will and a denial of the honor due to God. In light of his holistic claims, Tillmann added that the gravity of a sin 'depends on the significance of the act in the religious and moral life'.[31]

In the second part, the love of God, Tillmann turned to piety. All true piety is 'directed toward the honor of God'.[32] Piety is not a conceptual activity but rather a deeply relational one, that includes three experiences of a fundamental and decisive nature: our absolute dependence on God, our sin and guilt, and the mercy and grace of God.[33]

The beginning of piety is found in being a creature: it is enkindled by Jesus Christ; reverence and love are the soul of piety. Thus we are to imitate Christ in his piety.[34] Therein, we also experience the three fruits of piety: the ability to stand in the presence of God; to have trust in God; and to have an absolute obedience to God.[35]

Piety leads, in turn, to the three theological virtues. Tillmann discussed the essence of faith, starting with Hebrews 11.1, that is, that 'faith is the substance of things to be hoped for, the evidence of things not seen'. Faith differs from knowledge, because faith is 'an assent resting on liberty'.[36] From here, Tillmann reflected on living faith, doubts and difficulties of faith, and sins against faith, which are primarily indifference (Revelation 3.15) and frivolity (1 John 4.1).

He initiated the chapter on hope with a reflection on 1 Thessalonians 4.13 and saw hope as bound up with our striving.[37] Since hope is embedded in Christ's redemptive work, 'Divine hope begets the precious fruit of Christian joy.'[38] The sins of hope are found in two ways, by excess or defect regarding desire and confidence. One sins against hope by being too attached to the goods of this world or by such a desire for the next world that it obfuscates the responsibilities in this one. Its sins are despair and presumption. Despair is 'a renunciation of help from God and His grace'. He differentiated the sin of despair which is expressed in one's freedom, from the despair of a pathological nature, where an 'individual becomes a victim of feelings of fear and self-accusation which have no spiritual basis'. Moreover, those who sin from despair ought to be differentiated from those 'of refined spiritual sensibilities' who experience deep disappointments and failures in the moral and religious life. He counseled these to try to discover the source of their failures, but not to undertake anything beyond their powers. He defined presumption as 'the frivolous expectation that God will grant eternal beatitude without any merit on the part of the individual'. It begins with 'a devil-may-care attitude'.[39]

Finally he called charity 'the distinctive mark of Christ's religion'.[40] Here, Tillmann reflected on the bond of perfection in Galatians 5.6, Romans 13.8, 10, Ephesians 3.16–19, and Colossians 3.12–14. He defined charity as an internal and active union with God.[41] Its sin is hatred of God, the greatest of all sins.[42]

The remaining chapters in part two are on the virtue of religion, prayer, the sacrifice of the Mass, oaths and vows, and sins against religion. While the object of the three theological virtues is God, embraced in God's 'own plenitude as supreme being', the object of the virtue of religion 'comprises all those actions which give recognition to the supremacy of God and express the subjection of the creature'.[43] Religion is an acquired virtue directed to God, best expressed in our need to worship as a visible expression of our interior disposition toward God.[44]

Following the Augustinian and Thomistic triple order of charity, that is, the love of God, self, and neighbor, Tillmann turned in the third part to self-love using Ephesians 5.29, 'No one has ever hated his own flesh; on the contrary, he nourishes it and cherishes it.' Nonetheless, Tillmann was suspicious of a natural self-love and contrasted a Christian self-love with one that rejects Christianity: 'Christian love of self signifies respect for the regenerated and reborn man, respect that rests on esteem and veneration for that which is holy.'[45] He distinguished the ways in which Paul referred the body to either the flesh (our damnation) or the spirit (our redemption). Through it all, however, the body remains with the soul in the human possibility for meeting God. 'It is correct, but insufficient to say that we care for the body to make it the fit instrument of the soul. The body is more than that; it is the companion of the soul. Only when a body is united with a soul does a man exist, and it remains the companion of the soul for all eternity.'[46]

In an astonishing move, Tillmann descended here into great specificity, entertaining questions of health and hygiene: cleanliness (an expression of self-esteem); proper nutrition, temperance and moderation; the problem of drunkenness and drug use; the right choice of clothing (mean between extremes); importance of the home, rest, recreation, and the rules governing them; bathing and swimming; art; gymnastics; abstinence (necessary for the alcoholic, but otherwise moderation should be the norm since Paul refused to consider wine as forbidden, Romans 14.14; Colossians 2.16),[47] vegetarianism, and nudism ('The emancipation from the Christian faith and from Christian morals has no where shown itself more patently than in the devotees of this nudism').[48]

Afterwards, his section on suicide is remarkably sensitive. On the one hand he considered those who argue in favor of suicide: those 'who assert that in the whole world man has no right he can more call his own more than that over his person and his life. It must be admitted that when there is no belief in a Supreme Being it is difficult to prove the immorality of suicide.' On the other hand, he acknowledged the fact that 'as a general rule, information regarding the causes of suicide is extremely meager and unreliable'. Reporting on an investigation of 124 cases of attempted suicide, he noted that in only one case was the person mentally healthy; in the majority of instances, the person was not in a permanent mental condition, but was 'burdened with a psychological predisposition'.[49]

After death, he discussed sexuality. After commenting on its purpose, that is, to procreate, and then on 'the sexual impulses and the sexual life' as 'something good and holy',[50] he turned to the fundamental equality of the sexes. Interestingly, on these two pages Tillmann invoked more scriptural texts (28 citations) than almost any other two pages in the entire book. Arguing that 'from the very beginning Christian teaching considered the two sexes equal', he cited and commented on Genesis, Proverbs, and the Gospels. Reflecting on a variety of encounters of Jesus with the Samaritan women, the sisters of Lazarus, and even the adulteress, he wrote that Jesus 'respected women. Frequently and with evident affection, He describes in His parables the daily life of the woman with its labors, sorrows and joys.' Tillmann concluded that 'therefore the equality of woman and man in their vocation is fundamental', quoting Galatians 3.26–28.[51]

The equality of the sexes still yielded differences. He wrote that the 'natural calling of woman is marriage and motherhood'.[52] He added that 'there is a certain subordination of woman to man. All things considered, woman stands more in need of protection and care than does man.'[53] He described how the Industrial Revolution led to a breakdown of classic structures, which in turn led to feminism, which threatened 'the characteristic function of the peculiar qualities of the woman'. Remarkably, while his pro-equality pages were inundated with scriptural references, these pages were remarkably light on scripture, with only two citations, Ephesians 5.25 and 1 Corinthians 11.3. Still, he concluded by noting that it 'certainly would be erroneous to speak of a physical, intellectual or even moral inferiority as far as woman is concerned'.[54]

Tillmann then addressed chastity, modesty, and virginity, and the latter's excellence over the married state. Celibacy is 'nothing else than virginity placed at the service of God and of the Church'.[55] Under the sins against chastity, he described how during puberty young people begin the practice of masturbation. 'Little by little it begins to dominate thoughts and imaginations, slowly wears down the will to resist, gradually makes the individual lose interest and joy in serious work, by and by robs him of confidence in himself, of hope in the possibility of bettering his condition and estranges him from the practices of religion.'[56] The passage highlights the obsessive estimation that manualists and others had of masturbation.

His description of homosexuality follows: 'The conscious centering of the sexual impulse on a partner of the same sex, generally several years younger . . .

Quite often it is the result of an abnormality; certainly this constitutes a great misfortune for the individual, but not a crime.' Tillmann concluded with two insights. First, one cannot argue that a psycho-physical predisposition gives validity to homosexual activity. Second, the pastor should treat every homosexual as an individual and give attention to their concrete situations.[57]

His most innovative writing pertained to the respect for intellectual and moral life. Throughout, Tillmann has been appreciative of the fact that the virtues emerge in each person differently. Thus, the right realization of ourselves as intellectual and moral agents similarly differs for every individual.[58] Still, the unique development of the person is not isolated from the needs and goods of the community.

In this section, we find a profound respect for general culture: it 'lifts man above himself and lets him participate in the cultural heritage; if this is not absorbed superficially and as a dead thing, but elaborated and a vital part of man, then it 'cultivates' him. Consequently it is not the amount of knowledge that a man possesses that gives him culture; indeed it is possible to be learned and yet very uncultured.'

Tillmann understood that culture depends on our understanding; the two are deeply interconnected: no education, no culture; no culture, no education. To the concept of culture necessarily belongs the idea of elaborating knowledge, of taking possession of it intellectually, and of assimilating it so that it becomes a personal patrimony.[59]

Later he added, 'If an individual does not share in the cultural heritage of the community, he tears the vital bond that he should have with it and becomes incapable of contributing to its intellectual life.' Yet, Tillmann was always driven by realism, for neither education nor culture should be exaggerated: knowledge 'may quite readily accompany boorishness and moral degradation'.[60]

The obligation to participate through one's vocation in the life of the general culture means that 'no useless and idle members may be tolerated in it'. The responsibility to realize one's vocation arises from the needs of the community and from the diversity and specialty of individual inclinations and abilities. As the link between the personal and the social, vocation 'represents the goal of personal effort and the personal achievement which society imposes on a man . . . only through it can the individual enter into the national and social collectivity. Only thus does labor acquire its full meaning.'[61]

Again and again, Tillmann returned to these considerations, balancing and integrating the personal with the social. 'Behind everything that happens is God's all embracing plan, which takes into consideration mankind as a whole as well as the individual person in particular.'[62]

Moreover, Tillmann noted how constitutive leisure was for culture, especially as expressed in family and civic life. Every person needs 'enough leisure to share in his family's life and to participate in a reasonable manner in the educational and cultural heritage of his community . . . Where working conditions disrupt family life and degrade man to the level of beast, they are not only immoral, but necessarily shatter the very foundations of society.'[63]

As he turned to work, he again acknowledged the context of the social. Work is 'a moral performance of a free man for the welfare of the community. Work has significance far beyond its mere utility; it has a moral character in relation to the collectivity. Work makes social life possible.'[64] He added that only a highly developed culture can provide 'the background for a true appreciation of the dignity of labor and its religious and moral value. Primitive peoples have always regarded work as a burden and have put it on the shoulders of women and slaves . . . Only in revealed religion does work attain to a higher meaning and its proper dignity.'

Tillmann offered three ways in which work has religious and moral significance. First, work forms part of man's lot: 'he is born to labor as the bird is born to fly (Job 5.7). Hence, work is life, and only that human life can be called worthwhile which is filled with toil and work.' Second, through work, we realize ourselves as images of God. Tillmann referred here to John 5.17, 'My Father works even until now, and I work.' Third, 'work is a form of expiation and penance for fallen man, and at the same time a means of salvation and purification'.[65]

In the fourth part, the love of neighbor, Tillmann reflected on the love of enemy which gave to neighbor love an absolute universality: 'With one stroke Christ demolished the limitations of the Old Testament, which restricted love to the members of the same tribe or the same nation.'[66] By incorporating love of enemies as constitutive of neighbor love, Tillmann found the newness of the command to love the neighbor.

Because of its unique and challenging nature, Tillmann offered strategies for realizing the love of enemy. In conflicts he encouraged the disciple to make 'the first step and employ every means to facilitate a re-establishment of peace' and urged 'an indefatigable patience which never despairs, but confidently looks forward to the moment of reconciliation'.[67] He then offered the commandment's minimum requirements:

> To try to discover good in the enemy.
> To desire uprightly whatever may truly benefit the enemy.
> To be ever ready to forgive him sincerely and to be reconciled to him.
> To show this benevolent disposition at least through the common forms of courtesy and charity which are owed to all.[68]

Considering the disciple's responsibilities for neighbor, Tillmann started with the duty to provide a good example, citing John 13.15.[69] He then turned to fraternal correction, the sin of scandal, and co-operation in the sin of others. Later he treated justice, rights, and property, and invoked the papal social encyclicals, commenting on the limits and social function of property as well as the Church's differing stances toward capitalism and socialism.[70]

The last part, a brief section on social relations, was a reflection on two issues: Christian marriage and family, and Church and State.

Tillmann's breakthrough is inestimable. First, as a scripture scholar he derived from the scriptures an appropriate identity for the Christian agent, the disciple. His proposal of this identity has had a lasting influence on moral theology. Second, he developed his argument into a vigorous academic text, *Die Idee der Nachfolge Christi*, which allowed him to engage his colleagues on the intellectual foundations of his proposal. Third, he made this idea accessible and concrete by *The Master Calls*. He also made the text extraordinarily comprehensive, never departing from the double insight that the text had to be fundamentally (and exclusively) based on scripture (there are no other types of citations) and the text had to give an anthropological shape to the vocation of discipleship.

Fourth, wisely he turned to the virtues, most appropriately because, as any reader of the New Testament will note, virtue is the language of Paul and the Evangelists. Virtue is the language of the Hebrew Bible as well. Thus, entering into moral theology, he did not abandon scriptural language, but found in virtue the worthy bridge between scripture and moral theology. Fifth, coupled with this, the architectonic structure of the work, two parts bookending the threefold love command, placed charity at the very heart of his ethics. Revelation conveys the singular primacy of charity.[71]

Sixth, he never dismissed the basic pastoral call that the moral theologian had. Certainly, the manualists' reader was the priest confessor, but Tillmann's work, while easily accessible to the laity, was especially attentive as, in the areas on suicide and homosexuality, to the pastoral challenges of the contemporary priest, counselor, confessor, and preacher. Finally, as a member of the guild of moral theologians, Tillmann gave his colleagues a text that became a paradigm for others.

Gérard Gilleman (1910–2002)

Before turning to Gilleman's specific contributions, we need now to recognize that the innovators claimed that moral truth was not realized as much in solitary external actions as in overarching internal personal dispositions. Integral to this claim was the belief that moral truth was not found primarily in negative principles – about what actions were to be avoided – but rather in the person who pursued the good. The locus of moral truth began to change: at the beginning of the century, moral truth was found in the long-held norms and, analogously, in their application by moral theologians. By the century's end, moral truth was found in the lives of active Christians, living as embodied disciples of Christ.

This more positive, interior, and integrated direction for finding moral truth was of extraordinary moment, and Gilleman's own contribution helps to highlight the nature of this innovation. Gilleman examined the most internal and gracious of all virtues, charity, by studying the *Summa Theologiae* of Aquinas in light of the work of the Jesuit moral theologian Émile Mersch (1890–1940).

In three successive works, Mersch examined the mystical body of Christ: first through historical investigations, then in its relevance for morality, and finally in its own theological significance.[72] Gilleman found in Mersch compelling grounds for identifying the Christian with the filial self-understanding of Jesus, the Son of God. In that self-understanding, Gilleman found that charity establishes our union with God.

Moral theology's necessary congruence with ascetical theology became apparent. The reunion of the former, identified by the manualists as the avoidance of evil, with the latter's interest in the personal pursuit of the good, reintegrated the first principle of the natural law – to do good and avoid evil – under one discipline. This was a remarkable departure from Thomas Slater's or Heribert Jone's manual. Gilleman wrote: 'The task of Christian morality and of asceticism which is intimately linked to it, is to render the intention and exercise of charity in us always more and more explicit.'[73]

The turn to human interiority led to an understanding of moral truth as needing to be realized in the human being. By 1960, then, moral truth was no longer propositional, but rather ontological. An illustration of this change is found in *Sacramentum Mundi*'s entry on 'Truthfulness'.

> Truth is defined primarily as ontological, the basic intelligibility of things, with God as the First Truth. Further, God is held to be knowable but incomprehensible, while man is understood as a being created in order to know and love God, who finds therefore his true self in being blessed by God and giving himself to God. The main task of an ethics of truth is then to remain as absolutely open as possible for the truth in whatever guise man encounters it, and to unconditionally follow out the known truth in action. The ethics of truth will mainly take the form of an ethics of the disposition, insisting on the formal attitude. Hence an ethics of truth cannot do without reflection on one's personal consciousness and its implications.[74]

Establishing the measure of moral truth in the right realization of the human person called by charity to be a member of the community of the disciples of Christ becomes the foundational shift in moral theology in the twentieth century.

In 1947, the Belgian Jesuit Gérard Gilleman defended his dissertation at the Institut Catholique in Paris under the guidance of the French Jesuit, René Carpentier. His topic was the role of charity in moral theology.[75] Shortly after submitting his dissertation, he was assigned to teach dogmatic theology at St Mary's Theological College in Kurseong, India. He left his mentor the task of publishing a French edition of the revised dissertation.

In the editor's note, Carpentier modestly wrote that, due to an appointment, Gilleman was 'unable to do himself the considerable work of revision, completion and even recomposition that he judged necessary for the publication of his work'. Carpentier added, 'I performed this work of revision in full agreement with him – agreement made easy by friendship and a profound kinship of thought.'[76]

Carpentier published Gilleman's work in 1952. After a second edition appeared in 1954, Carpentier found two Canadian Jesuits, one French-speaking (André Vachon) and the other English-speaking (William F. Ryan), to become the translators for the English edition.

It is hard to over-estimate the influence of Gilleman's work. In their two-volume work, *Contemporary Moral Theology*, American Jesuits John Ford and Gerald Kelly presented in four pages Gilleman's 'widely acclaimed work'.[77] Later they remarked that, though Gilleman was more interested in shaping the form rather than the content of moral theology, still his influence was overwhelming. They wrote:

> At present we seem to be in a period of transition in the development of the moral theology course. The valuable elements contained in modern approaches to the subject are being sifted out from what is not worthwhile for practice, and from what is dangerous in tendency, or even false. It remains to be seen, for instance, to what extent the primacy of charity, as magnificently conceived by Gilleman and systematized by him, can be incorporated into the ordinary seminary course of moral theology. It is actually being attempted in more than one seminary.[78]

Gilleman's argument was very persuasive. Later, others would follow his lead.[79] One instance of his influence is the recent encyclical by Pope Benedict XVI, *Deus Caritas Est.*[80] Though the Pope does not cite Gilleman, clearly his influence is quite evident.[81]

Until recently there was the assumption that Gilleman derived most of his ideas from his mentor, René Carpentier, who was long an advocate of an integrated moral/spiritual theology. In 1950, for instance, Carpentier had argued that the real task of moral theology was the pursuit of growing in charity.[82] But Vincent LeClercq has argued from the dissertation and the two French editions, that fundamental claims in *The Primacy of Charity* are original in and rightly attributed to Gilleman.[83]

In his introduction, Gilleman, like Lottin and Tillmann before him, criticized the moral manuals: 'Law rather than love is their dominant theme. Where there should be a spiritual impulse, we find a fixed body of doctrine. Even inspiration and liberty are precisely codified.'[84] Like Lottin, he argued that moral theology had lost its moorings in dogmatic theology. Gilleman commented that this first occurred in the fifteenth century when morals became an autonomous discipline, citing specifically St Antoninus of Florence whose *Summa theologiae moralis* (1419) began without any rootedness in dogmatic theology. The result was 'a moral theology far too negative and concerned chiefly with minimal obligations; virtues were passed over in favor of commandments and law . . . . Their theological content was so scanty that they scarcely merited the name *Theologiae morales*.'[85]

He observed, too, that contemporary innovations by moralists have tried to reconnect moral theology to dogmatics, but now a second task has emerged: to rediscover 'the dominant theme of charity, the soul of Christian tradition'. He noted, 'love, the inner soul of moral theology, has not yet come into its own in our manuals, if we except the works of F. Tillmann and a few others like the remarkable book by B. Häring (*Das Gesetz Christi*, 1954).'[86]

In attempting to recover charity, he aimed for a moral theology that is primarily about the interior life. From that interior life, each Christian can discover what each shares with the other, that is, the life of charity in them. This interior life, then, is not for the private life but for the whole of humanity, particularly in its sociality. Here, then, we engage what the modern person seeks: an objective for the longing for interior fulfillment. Gilleman articulated this vision:

> By introducing charity as the pivot of its formulation, moral theology will not only come into closer contact with Christ but will also meet the best aspirations of the modern conscience. For among all other values love is most able to bring together the living subject and the moral object. By its insatiable demands it liberates all the generous impulses of the individual without minimalizing precise duties; without diminishing the importance of his own person, it drives a man into the society of other men.[87]

Gilleman emphasized the newness of the gift of charity: 'It was the very structure of this morality that was new, for it contained the germ of an ontology of man and of his actions of which philosophers could never dream.' He concluded his central introductory observation: 'The core of the "good news" was this: God is charity; and we no longer are merely his creatures or participations, but we are really his sons invited *in Filio* to communion with the Father. With this the whole world was renewed; man could no longer live as before.'[88]

In learning that God is love and that we are in Jesus Christ, God's own children, we assumed an identity that would be 'terribly exacting'.[89] 'In its very structure, the Christian life is a beloved cross, a cross carried in the wake of love.'[90] We are to adopt the divine habits of charity 'with all their drastic demands' and we learn these habits by being a 'disciple of Christ', 'according to the very significant title of F. Tillmann's work'.[91]

In concluding the introduction, Gilleman stated quite clearly the purpose of his study: 'To apply to the formulation of each and every question of moral theology the universal principle of St. Thomas: *Caritas forma omnium virtutum*.'[92]

The work is divided into three parts: a brief 'historical' section on the relevant texts of Thomas; a methodological section that develops a charity-centered theology; and a practical part that highlights how ethics functions in ordinary life.

The historical part is a review of Thomas's *Summa Theologiae* to demonstrate that charity is not one virtue among others but rather the form or the first mover of all graced human activity. Only charity allows us to be in union with God, ourselves and our neighbor. In union with God, we can act out charity and perform acts of justice, temperance, and fortitude.

Gilleman showed that any moral action can be based on some previous intention: I act generously so as to deepen a friendship. Another acts courageously in the pursuit of justice. For an act of charity, however, there can be no previous intention. If I act out of the love of God, I cannot claim that I do so for another intention, because then I would no longer be acting out of charity.[93] He concluded this, arguing that, for Thomas, 'charity is, in a very real sense, the soul of the moral life; it is everywhere present in our activity'.[94] He added.

> If charity-love is everywhere present in the moral life, it is its very absence that is sin. Sin, considered as a human act, owes its whole ontological reality to love of the ultimate end, but by choosing a particular good which contradicts this love, it renounces grace and infused charity and so does not lead to the ultimate end. Hence a moral theology which takes sin as its starting point does not feel any need of relating its object to charity love.[95]

The methodological part aimed to re-construct a charity-centered moral theology, through three stages of a syllogism. First, our moral actions mediate our spiritual tendency. Second, that tendency is charity. Therefore, every virtuous act mediates charity. Gilleman achieved the syllogism by reflecting on the human as body and soul, and on the human action as material and spiritual; that is, the action itself and its motivating source.[96] The spiritual within us is what he called our 'tendency'.

Gilleman's term 'tendency' is not unlike Thomas's 'inclination'. The latter term suggests that within the human is the desire for flourishing, that is, full realization. At once the term suggests what is and what is not yet. By focusing on the inclination or tendency, we reflect then on our present condition as opposed to our ultimate destiny. There is a certain humility regarding the nature of the end to which we are inclined. Assuredly the end is union with God, neighbor, and self, for that is what charity attains. But that charity-tendency keeps seeking that union; it desires its full realization, a realization not yet experienced. Through the concept of tendency, then, we capture a sense of the dynamic tension between what we seek and what we will actually have realized lastingly in the kingdom. 'Our own intellect can only understand its knowledge of real being because it is dynamic, that is, because it lives on our fundamental tendency of love.'[97]

In the ordering of love, Gilleman claimed that the love of God precedes the love of self because in charity we are closer to God than even to ourselves.

'There is no way of escaping the fact that the ontological cohesion of any being is possible only through actual participation in Being. Our love for God is a more intimate constituent of ourselves than love for our own selves!'[98]

Moreover we ought not to separate love of God from God. 'Jesus Christ came to reveal something entirely new concerning love in God. Not only does God have love, but He is *agapè* (1 John 4.8), which Thomas interprets in saying "*Ipsa essentia divina caritas est*" (II.II.23.2.ad1).'[99] Inasmuch as this love of God is within us, we are divinized: 'Charity commands the powers now that they are divinized . . . For the Christian in the state of grace, all good voluntary action is necessarily elicited by a divinized will, that is to say, by charity-love.'[100]

Through sustained reflective exercises, we develop within us the acquired virtues which further realize other dimensions of our selves. But our pursuit of these virtues – justice, temperance, fortitude, and prudence – is prompted and directed by the charity-love tendency within us. The virtues, then, express the exigencies of charity in the various fields of our activity and they are specifically named after the immediate virtues that elicit them. But effectively they are means for expressing that tendency within us.[101] 'An ideal Christian should consist in making each day an uninterrupted series of acts of charity.'[102]

In concluding the second part, Gilleman wrote beautifully and forcefully about the moral life:

> Christian moral life, with its multitude of humble as well as significant acts, is a creation springing from the gushing sources of charity. In the heart of the commonplace realities scattered along the course of our days, it is possible to perceive God's activity passing through us. Our moral life, the result of liberty creating our spiritual person, appears at last in its naked reality: it is a work of love springing at once from God's heart and from ours.[103]

In the final part, Gilleman referred to Fritz Tillmann on discipleship, René Carpentier on charity, and Josef Fuchs on love as the foundation of the moral life.[104] From them, he developed the practical qualities for a loving disciple of Christ: generous communion with others, Christ-centeredness, devotion toward others, filial sanctity, and a mortified life nourished by the sacraments. Then, he concluded that a charity-driven moral theology changes our understanding of the law, which now exists at the service of love.

Remembering that Gilleman defended his dissertation in 1947, that his revised dissertation was not published until 1952, and that the second edition of 1954 became the basis for the 1959 English translation, we can see that these events became themselves occasions for initiating again and again the argument for the original premise of a deeply affective, spiritual foundation for moral theology founded on charity.[105] Moreover, throughout the 1950s others followed the Gilleman initiative, most notably his mentor Carpentier, but also others, from Fuchs to Ford and Kelly.

Gilleman's initiative was the logical extension to the Tillmann project. In the love command, Tillmann gave a deep directionality to the material agenda of Catholic moral theology; in the idea or concept of discipleship, he gave Christians a moral identity, and in the use of the scriptures, he gave us a 'new' text. What Tillmann's project needed was an empowering ascetical theology to animate the disciple. Gilleman answered that need by advocating for a charity-inspired spiritual tendency.

A contemporary work: William C. Spohn's *Go and Do Likewise: Jesus and Ethics*

In 1983, William Spohn wrote *What Are they Saying about Scripture and Ethics?* There, he marked the specificity with which moral theologians read the scriptures.

> When theologians turn to the Scripture for moral guidance they are not acting like moral philosophers. They turn to a history rather than a theory of ethics, to a canonical text whose credential is inspiration by God and not merely logical consistency. Christians turn to Scripture to discover more than the right thing to do; they want to act in a way that responds to the God of their lives.[106]

With great ecumenical interests, the book quickly became a reference text for providing a typology of the various models of approaching scripture so as to understand its moral instruction. Therein Spohn offered six models which he described as 'a sign not of scholarly chaos but of the irreducible richness of the Scripture itself'.[107]

The first model was the command of God, seen as a personal and clear call, best expressed in the twentieth century by the courageous and brilliant Lutheran pastor and resister, Dietrich Bonhoeffer.[108] The second, 'Scripture as a reminder', is so called because Fuchs used it in his first major work on natural law: the natural law gives us moral norms, but the scripture reminds us of their urgency.[109] Later, one of Fuchs' best-known students, Bruno Schüller, insisted that scripture provided no moral instruction but rather moral exhortation.[110] The third model is the call to liberation. Here he turned to the pioneering work of Gustavo Gutiérrez to describe the call to act for the oppressed because God is on their side.[111] Spohn also saw in early feminist writings, particularly by Letty M. Russell[112] and Phyllis Trible,[113] a similar hermeneutics in their approach to scripture. In the fourth approach, we find scripture read so as to understand how God is acting in our situation today. Spohn cited the responsibility ethics of H. Richard Niebuhr who saw in the immediacy of our history God's action in the world.[114] The fifth model is the call to discipleship. Rather than citing Tillmann, Spohn referred to the writings of three contemporary Protestants, Stanley Hauerwas, Sally McFague, and John Howard Yoder, who call us to reflect on the narrative theology of scripture so as to understand what God calls us to in Jesus Christ.[115] The final model is Spohn's own, 'Scripture as basis for responding love', which he described as giving us 'the motive and the norm for loving others in the witness of God's love in Scripture that has been confirmed in the agent's experience'.[116] Spohn's small book served as an incentive for a great deal of work on scripture and ethics.[117]

Sixteen years later, Spohn published a sustained argument for this model. In *Go and Do Likewise*,[118] Spohn insisted that virtue ethics was 'the most appropriate avenue' for an approach to scripture.[119] As we will see later, virtue ethics becomes a significant alternative to principle-based ethics; the former offers a more personal and communal-based ethics. The evolution of virtue ethics ought to come as no surprise; we saw already in the hermeneutics of Lottin and Tillmann that the development of an entire ethical system based on virtue would inevitably have to emerge.

Taking its lead from Aristotle who argued that moral action derives from moral persons, this system, today called 'virtue ethics', seeks to develop first in the person and the community the proper character traits or suitable virtues to promote right moral action and the right moral goals or ends of the good life. As Spohn wrote, 'Virtues are means to the good life and components of it.'[120]

In this system, then, moral rules and norms for action derive from the virtues being developed in the person and the community. Rules for action are integral to the system, but the point of departure always concerns the needed virtuous qualities for people and their communities.[121]

Spohn offered three reasons for the appropriateness of virtue ethics for biblical theology:

> (a) It fits the narrative form of the New Testament and can explain how the particular story of Jesus shapes the moral character of individuals and communities. (b) It attends to the deeper levels of moral existence which the teaching of Jesus addressed: the heart, the personal center of convictions, emotions, and commitments. (c) It fits the dominant mode of moral discourse in the New Testament, namely, paradigms that establish certain patterns of disposition and action that guide action.[122]

This third reason includes the role exemplary figures play in defining particular virtues. Spohn noted that while virtues as skills need examples to show what virtues mean practically, they take on different expressions in different cultural contexts.[123]

Virtue ethics considers identity, and our identity needs a story, a temporal framework which 'synthesizes our diverse moments of experience into a coherent whole'.[124] Personal identity 'comes through a process of identification with [this] larger narrative framework – a story – and with a community that tries to live out this story'.[125] Our choices and actions help form our tendencies and dispositions (which in turn help inform and direct our subsequent choices and actions) and hence play a central role in the moral formation of our character.[126]

In his book, Spohn successfully accomplished four significant goals. First, in order to engage the scriptural texts, he suggested analogy as an appropriate vehicle for discussing the virtues and practices embedded in the scriptural narratives and translating them into contemporary contexts. Second, virtues provided the conceptual bridge to go from one historico-cultural context to another. Third, the virtuous spiritual practices of contemporary communities of faith are the means for dynamically growing as a community of disciples. Fourth, reconciliation, solidarity, and compassion are the key virtuous dispositions both for receiving the texts and for developing the moral perception to understand them.

Ten years after his work, Roman Catholic moral theology, which long considered scripture as no more than a reminder of the moral life, now finds through the medium of virtue ethics the resources for living an animated life of love and justice based on revelation. The work of Tillmann and Gilleman lives on.[127]

Notes

1 Pope Benedict VI, *Relationship between Magisterium and Exegetes*, 10 May 2003, http://www.vatican.va/roman_curia/congregations/cfaith/pcb_documents/rc_con_cfaith_doc_20030510_ratzinger-comm-bible_en.html. I am grateful to Lúcás Chan Yiu Sing whose research on Tillmann led me to this essay as well as to the reviews of Tillmann's books.

2 Fritz Tillmann, *Der Menschensohn: Jesu Selbstzeugnis für seine messianische Würde* (1905); *Die Wiederkunft Christ: nach den Paulinischen Briefen* (1909); *Das Selbstbewusstsein des Gottessohnes: auf Grund der synoptischen Evangelien* (1911).

3 Tillmann, *Personlichkeit und Gemeinschaft in der Predigt Jesu* (Schwann, 1919).

4 Theodor Steinbüchel, *Die philosophische Grundlegung*; Theodor Müncker, *Die psychologische Grundlegung*; Fritz Tillmann, *Die Idee der Nachfolge Christi*; in Fritz Tillmann, ed., *Die katholische sittenlehre* (Dusseldorf: Patmos, 1934).

5 'Als Formalprinzip, bzw. Wie man richtiger sagen sollte Moralgrundprinzip, stellte Fritz Tillman die "Nachfolge Christi" heraus. Andere folgten diesem Beispiel.' Karl-Heinz Kleber, *Historia Docet*, 89.

6 Lottin, *MF*, 15.

7 M.-J. Congar, 'Der Meister Ruft' in 'Bulletin de Théologie', in *Revue des Sciences Philosophiques et Théologiques* 27 (1938) 641.

8 Andreas Hartmann, *Stimmen der Zeit* 134 (1938) 204–5.

9 Otto Schilling, *Theologische Quartalschrift* 119 (1938) 250–1.

10 Felix Cardegna, 'The Master Calls', *TS* 22 (1961) 716.

11 D. Thalhammer, 'Der Meister Ruft', *Zeitschrift für Katholische Theologie* 62 (1938) 451.

12 Johannes Reiter, 'Die Katholische Moraltheologie Zwischen den Beiden Vatikanischen Konzils', Hubert Wolf, ed., *Die Katholischtheologische Disziplinen in Deutschland 1870–1962. Ihre Geschichte, ihre Zeitbezug* (Paderborn: Schöningh, 1999) 231–42.

13 Fritz Tillmann, *The Master Calls: A Handbook of Morals for the Layman*, trans. Gregory J. Roettger, (Baltimore: Helicon Press, 1960) 3.

14 Ibid., 4–7.
15 Ibid., 9–10.
16 Ibid., 15.
17 Ibid., 23.
18 Ibid., 30.
19 Ibid., 36.
20 Ibid., 38.
21 Ibid., 41.
22 Ibid., 42.
23 Ibid., 46, 47.
24 Ibid., 47.
25 Thomas Aquinas, *Summa Theologiae* II.II. 184. 4. See additionally his comments throughout questions 184 and 186.
26 Desiderius Erasmus, 'Letter to Paul Voltz', ed. John O'Malley, *Enchiridion Militis Christiani*, *Collected Works of Erasmus: Spiritualia* (Toronto: University of Toronto Press, 1988) LVI, 9.
27 Enda McDonagh, *Doing the Truth: The Quest for Moral Theology* (Notre Dame: University of Notre Dame Press, 1979) 15.
28 See Joseph Kotva, 'A Kind of Perfectionism', *The Christian Case for Virtue Ethics* (Washington, DC: Georgetown University Press, 1997) 37–8.
29 Tillmann, *The Master Calls*, 57.
30 Ibid., 63.
31 Ibid., 77.
32 Ibid., 86.
33 Ibid., 87.
34 Ibid., 93.
35 Ibid., 94–5.
36 Ibid., 100–1.
37 Ibid., 113.
38 Ibid., 116.
39 Ibid., 122–4.
40 Ibid., 125.
41 Ibid., 140.
42 Ibid., 141.
43 Ibid., 142.
44 Ibid., 143.
45 Ibid., 184.
46 Ibid., 190–1.
47 Ibid., 201.
48 Ibid., 202.
49 Ibid., 205.
50 Ibid., 208.
51 Ibid., 209–10.
52 Ibid., 210.
53 Ibid., 211,
54 Ibid., 212.
55 Ibid., 216–17.
56 Ibid., 221.
57 Ibid., 221.
58 Ibid., 222.

59 Ibid., 223.
60 Ibid., 224.
61 Ibid., 225.
62 Ibid., 226.
63 Ibid., 228–9.
64 Ibid., 229–30.
65 Ibid., 231.
66 Ibid., 255.
67 Ibid., 268.
68 Ibid., 268–9.
69 Ibid., 274.
70 Ibid., 204–308.
71 See, for instance, Ceslaus Spicq, *Charity and Liberty in the New Testament* (New York: Alba Press, 1965); *Agape in The New Testament* (St Louis: Herder, 1963).
72 Émile Mersch, *Le Corps mystique du Christ: Études de théologie historique* (Brussels: Desclée de Brouwer, 1936); *Morale et corps mystique* (Paris: Desclées de Brouwer, 1937); *La Theologie du corps mystique*, 2 vols (Paris: Desclées de Brouwer, 1944).
73 Gérard Gilleman, *The Primacy of Charity in Moral Theology* (Westminister, MD: Newman Press, 1959) 82 (Hereafter *Primacy*).
74 Waldemar Molinski, 'Truthfulness', Karl Rahner et al., eds, *Sacramentum Mundi: An Encyclopedia of Theology* (New York: Herder & Herder, 1970) 313–18, at 313.
75 Gérard Gilleman, *Le role de la charité en théogie morale: essai méthodologique* (Paris: Institut Catholique de Paris, 1947).
76 Gilleman, *Primacy*, v.
77 John Ford and Gerald Kelly, *Contemporary Moral Theology* (Westminster: Newman Press, 1964) I. 76–9, at 76.
78 Ibid., 101.
79 Renzo Caseri, *Il principio della carità in Teologia morale. Dal contributo di G. Gilleman a una via riproposta* (Milano: Glossa, 1995).
80 Benedict XVI, *Deus Caritas Est*, 25 December 2005 http://209.85.215.104/search?q=cache:5LYqbqvjd_AJ:www.vatican.va/holy_father/benedict_xvi/encyclicals/documents/hf_ben-xvi_enc_20051225_deus-caritas-est_en.html+Deus+Caritas&hl=en&ct=clnk&cd=1&gl=us.
81 The Editors at *America* made the connection in 'A More Excellent Way', *America* 194.5 (13 February 2006).
82 René Carpentier, 'Le Sens du Bien Commun', *Nouvelle Revue Théologique* 67 (1945) 32–55; 'Conscience', *Dictionnaire de Spiritualité, Ascétique et Mystique* (Paris: Beauchesne, 1950) 13, col. 1547–75. See later works, 'Vers une morale de la charité', *Gregorianum*, 34.1 (1953) 32–55; *Life in the City of God: An Introduction to the Religious Life* (New York: Benziger, 1959); 'Evangelical Counsels', Karl Rahner, ed., *Encyclopedia of Theology: A Concise Sacramentum Mundi* (New York: Continuum, 1975) 467–70.
83 Vincent Leclercq, '*Le Primat de la Charité* de Gilleman et la *Conscience* de Carpentier: Le Renouveau Théologal de la Vie Morale', *Studia Moralia* 44 (2006) 353–75.
84 Gilleman, *Primacy*, xxviii–xxix.
85 Ibid., xxx.
86 Ibid., xxxi.
87 Ibid., xxxiv.
88 Ibid., xxii.
89 Ibid., xxiii.

90 Ibid., xxvi.
91 Ibid., xxvi.
92 Ibid., xxxvi.
93 Ibid., 34.
94 Ibid., 49.
95 Ibid., 50.
96 Ibid., 84–5.
97 Ibid., 135.
98 Ibid., 132.
99 Ibid., 135.
100 Ibid., 156.
101 Cf. Ibid., 180ff.
102 Ibid., 186.
103 Ibid., 188.
104 At Ibid., 205, see Josef Fuchs, 'Die Liebe als Aufbauprinzip der Moraltheologie', *Scholastik* 29 (1954) 79–87.
105 See my 'Catholic Moral Theology, Ignatian Spirituality, and Virtue Ethics: Strange Bedfellows', *Supplement to the Way: Spirituality and Ethics* 88 (1997) 36–45. Conversely, Jean Porter proposed a spirituality that follows from moral theology, 'Virtue Ethics and Its Significance for Spirituality', 26–35.
106 William C. Spohn, *What Are They Saying about Scripture and Ethics?* (Mahwah: Paulist Press, 1984) 1.
107 Ibid., 3
108 Dietrich Bonhoeffer, *The Cost of Discipleship* (New York: Macmillan, 1963).
109 Josef Fuchs, *Natural Law: A Theological Investigation* (New York: Sheed and Ward, 1965).
110 Bruno Schüller, 'The Debate on the Specific Character of a Christian Ethics: Some Remarks', Charles E. Curran and Richard A. McCormick, eds, *Readings in Moral Theology No. 2: The Distinctiveness of Christian Ethics* (New York: Paulist Press, 1980) 207–33.
111 Gustavo Gutiérrez, *A Theology of Liberation* (Maryknoll, NY: Orbis Press, 1973).
112 Letty M. Russell, *Human Liberation in Feminist Perspective: A Theology* (Philadelphia: Westminster Press, 1974).
113 Phyllis Trible, *God and the Rhetoric of Sexuality* (Philadelphia: Fortress Press, 1978).
114 H. Richard Niebuhr, *The Responsible Self* (New York: Harper and Row, 1963).
115 Stanley Hauerwas, *A Community of Character* (Notre Dame: University of Notre Dame Press, 1981); Sally McFague, *Speaking in Parables* (Philadelphia: Fortress Press, 1975); John Howard Yoder, *The Politics of Jesus* (Grand Rapids: Eerdmans, 1972).
116 Spohn, *What Are They Saying*, 106.
117 For the most salient essays from the 1970s see Charles Curran and Richard McCormick, eds, *Readings in Moral Theology No. 4: The Use of Scripture in Moral Theology* (New York: Paulist Press, 1984). For more recent contributions, see James Bretzke, 'Scripture and Ethics', *A Morally Complex World: Engaging Contemporary Moral Theology* (Collegeville: Liturgical Press, 2004) 79–108; Ibid., 'Scripture and Ethics: Core, Context, and Coherence', James Keating, ed., *Moral Theology: New Directions and Fundamental Issues* (Mahwah: Paulist Press, 2004) 88–107; Lisa Sowle Cahill, 'The Bible and Christian Moral Practices', Lisa Cahill and James Childress, eds, *Christian Ethics: Problems and Prospects*, (Cleveland, OH: The Pilgrim Press, 1996) 3–17; Thomas Deidun, 'The Bible and Christian Ethics',

Bernard Hoose, ed., *Christian Ethics: An Introduction* (London: Cassell, 1998) 3–46; Daniel J. Harrington and James F. Keenan, *Jesus and Virtue Ethics: Building Bridges between Biblical Studies and Moral Theology* (New York: Sheed and Ward, 2002); Ibid., *Paul and Virtue Ethics* (New York: Rowman and Littlefield, forthcoming); Richard Hays, *The Moral Vision of the New Testament* (San Francisco: Harper-Collins, 1996); Kenneth Himes, 'Scripture and Ethics: A Review Essay', *Biblical Theology Bulletin* 15, No. 2 (1985) 65–73; Frank Matera, *New Testament Ethics: The Legacies of Jesus and Paul* (Louisville, KY: Westminster John Knox, 1996); Paulinus Ikechukwu Odozor, 'Scripture and Ethics', *Moral Theology in an Age of Renewal: A Study of the Catholic Tradition Since Vatican II* (Notre Dame: University of Notre Dame Press, 2003) 135–64; Jeffrey Siker, *Scripture and Ethics: Twentieth-Century Portraits* (New York: Oxford University Press, 1997); Allen Verhey, *The Great Reversal: Ethics and the New Testament* (Grand Rapids, MI: Eerdmans, 1984); Ibid., *Remembering Jesus: Christian Community, Scripture, and the Moral Life* (Grand Rapids, MI: Eerdmans, 2002).

118 William C. Spohn, *Go and Do Likewise: Jesus and Ethics* (New York: Continuum, 1999).

119 Just before his untimely death, Spohn reiterated his claim: 'The most adequate ethical approach to Scripture is that of character and virtue ethics. While the ethics of principles and the ethics of consequences are also represented in the texts, they are subordinate to the ethics of character.' Spohn, 'Scripture', Gilbert Meilaender and William Werpehowski, eds, *Oxford Handbook of Theological Ethics* (Oxford: Oxford University Press, 2005) 93–111. This is also the argument in Harrington and Keenan's *Jesus and Virtue Ethics*.

120 Spohn, *Go And Do Likewise*, 42.

121 On the relationship between virtues and norms, Keenan, 'Virtues, Principles and a Consistent Ethics of Life', Thomas Nairn, ed., *The Consistent Ethic of Life: Assessing its Reception and Relevance* (Maryknoll: Orbis, 2008) 48–60. Also, Daniel Daly, *From Nature to Second Nature: The Relationship of Natural Law, Acquired Virtue, and Moral Precepts in Thomas Aquinas's Summa Theologiae,* PhD dissertation, Boston College, 25 March 2008.

122 Spohn, *Go And Do Likewise*, 28.

123 Ibid., 32–3.

124 Ibid., 174.

125 Spohn, *What are They Saying about Scripture and Ethics?*, 81–2.

126 Spohn, *Go and Do Likewise*, 29.

127 Some other essays by Spohn include: 'The Reasoning Heart: An American Approach to Christian Discernment', *TS* 44.1 (1983) 30–52; 'The Use of Scripture in Moral Theology', *TS* 47.1 (1985) 88–102; 'Virtue and American Culture', *TS* 48.1 (1986) 123–35; 'The Moral Dimensions of AIDS', *TS* 48.1 (1988) 89–109; 'Parable and Narrative in Christian Ethics', *TS* 51.1 (1990) 100–14; 'Passions and Principles', *TS* 52.1 (1991) 69–87; 'The Recovery of Virtue Ethics', *TS* 53.1 (1992) 60–75; 'The Magisterium and Morality.' *TS* 54.1 (1993) 95–111; 'Jesus and Christian Ethics.' *TS* 54.1 (1995) 92–107; 'Spirituality and Ethics: Exploring the Connections.' *TS* 58.1 (1997) 109–23; with William R. O'Neill, 'Rights of Passage: The Ethics of Immigration and Refugee Policy', *TS* 59.1 (1998) 84–106; 'Conscience and Moral Development.' *TS* 61.1 (2000) 122–38.

5

Synthesis: Bernhard Häring

In the 1950s, Catholic moral theologians split over theological methods: they either stayed with the manualists and taught moral theology as an aid for the priest confessor or they followed the lead of the revisionists and began looking for a moral theology that was more positive, more theological and more attuned to human experience. In an essay reflecting on the development of moral theology during that period, the Jesuit Richard McCormick (1929–2006) characterized the former as 'all too often one sidedly confession-oriented, magisterium-dominated, canon law-related, sin-centered and seminary-controlled'.[1] He added that its theological anthropology looked like: 'the agent as solitary decision-maker'.[2]

The reformers focused on the life of the baptized Christian living in community. They addressed more fundamental theological issues: our self-understanding in light of the event of Jesus Christ (Mersch); the role of charity in sustaining our deep tendency toward the moral life (Gilleman); the role of historical development in the life of the Church and of the individual person (Lottin); and the call to discipleship (Tillmann).

Bernhard Häring summed up the interests of the reformers: 'Moral theology, as I understand it, is not concerned first with decision making and discrete acts. Its basic task and purpose is to gain the right vision, to assess the main perspectives, and to present those truths and values which should bear upon decisions to be taken before God.'[3]

From fundamental morals to new norms through new values

The moral theologians' turn to foundations in moral theology did not mean abandoning the responsibility to offer guidance in the concrete situations. Rather than simply giving their pithy judgments as the manualists had done, however, they began to do what Häring proposed. They developed from the new theological foundations the 'truths and values' that would provide the

Church with a more visionary way of acting morally. To achieve this, they would need to avoid the extremes of abstract theological investigations and the obsessive particularity of manualist norms.

When, for instance, the bishops of the papal birth control commission assigned Josef Fuchs the task to write the so-called 'majority report', which would contend that in conscience married couples could practice birth control for the sake of responsible parenthood, they were not looking for him to offer an exposé on the fundamental option or a treatise on intentionality. But they were also not asking for a simple norm as the manualists would have offered: 'Yes, married couples may use birth control responsibly.' Rather, the bishops were looking for a contemporary fundamental stance on the relationship between marriage and child-bearing and the roles that the Christian conscience and church teaching have in moral decision-making. In short, they wanted actual guidance in how those decisions were to be made.[4]

When the United States Conference of Catholic Bishops asked Bryan Hehir to write what would become *The Challenge of Peace: God's Promise and Our Response*, they expected his explanation of the theological foundations of peace, the Christian issues of protecting human life, and whether and when the resort to war was morally feasible.[5] In these and many other instances, people were looking to moral theologians to articulate those 'truths and values' which would offer specific guidance for action.

The metaphysical foundations of the moral manuals undermined our ability to witness to the way moral truths and their norms are developed, shaped and received. In rediscovering our history, in shaping a vision of Jesus Christ, and in having through charity the ability to hear and respond to his call, we are able to understand better the journey that lies before us. We recognize, then, the call to articulate new norms that might assist us as guideposts along the way.

Before entering into the unique synthesis accomplished by Häring, then, we might want to get ahead of our historical investigation for a moment to illustrate how hierarchy and theologians eventually offered new foundational premises or expanded older ones and promoted new truths, new values, new virtues, new self-understanding, and even new norms (or at least new applications of norms). All of this emerged as part of the effects of the creative development of moral theology that happened *after* Häring's *The Law of Christ*, that is, over the last 50 years.

By doing this exercise, those impatient with foundational language might be able to appreciate that eventually the revisionists got us not only to a better theological foundation and a more humane and social methodology, they also helped us to answer more adequately practical challenges. This action is only right, since the end of all being and the end of all moral processes are the same: to act.

Many new values have emerged since Häring's landmark work; we will consider four of them: sanctity of life, consistent life ethics, the preferential option for the poor, and solidarity.

It is difficult to think of another phrase more commonly associated with contemporary Catholic moral teaching than 'sanctity of life'. Surprisingly, the term itself is rather new: no Catholic dictionary or encyclopedia before 1978 had an entry on it. For instance, in the fifteen-volume *New Catholic Encyclopedia of 1967*, the term has no entry. (It later appeared as a modest afterthought in an unsigned entry in the later supplement.)[6] There is no entry in the new theological dictionaries from the United States, England, or Germany.[7] There was only a passing reference in an Italian counterpart.[8]

'Sanctity of life' has its roots in modern Christian writings, most commonly in the assertion of God's dominion over human life. In 1908, the Jesuit moralist Thomas Slater discussed suicide and declared, 'The reason why suicide is unlawful is because we have not the free disposal of our own lives. God is the author of life and death, and He has reserved the ownership of human life to Himself.'[9] The prohibition against killing was founded on the belief that we do not own our lives, God does. Therefore, we are not free to dispose of them.

Later, Pope Pius XI declared in *Casti Connubii*, 'The life of each is equally sacred and no one has the power, not even public authority, to destroy it.'[10] In this context, our life was an object, a sacred object because it belonged to God.[11]

The modern expression 'sanctity of life' first appeared as the sacredness of human life in the encyclical *Mater et Magistra*,[12] though there it still functioned as a euphemism for God's dominion.[13] In *Humanae Vitae*, life is sacred because its owner, God, willed it so; like other objects that God owned and sanctified – the marriage bond and the Temple, for example – life cannot be violated. [14] The sacredness rests not in anything intrinsic to the marriage bond, the Temple, or human life; it rests on the claim of God, who made and owns the sacral quality of the marital bond, Temple, and human life.

Pope John Paul II significantly developed the term by recognizing the sanctity of life as intrinsic to the human person. In 1987, in his apostolic exhortation, *Christifideles Laici*, the Pope spoke at length about the inviolable right to life, saying, 'The inviolability of the person, which is a reflection of the absolute inviolability of God, finds its primary and fundamental expression in the inviolability of human life.'[15] Nowhere did he refer to God's dominion or prerogatives. Rather, the argument was simply that we are in God's image; as God's person is inviolable, so is God's image.

In the same year, in the Congregation for the Doctrine of the Faith's declaration on reproduction, *Donum Vitae*, we find the two trends in the tradition wedded: 'From the moment of conception, the life of every human being is to be respected in an absolute way because man is the only creature on earth that God has "wished for himself" and the spiritual soul of each man is "immediately created by God"; his whole image bears the image of the Creator.' The document continues: 'Human life is sacred because from its beginning it involves the "creative action of God" and it remains for ever in a special relationship with the Creator, who is its sole end. God alone is Lord of life from its beginning until its end: no one can, under any circumstance, claim for himself the right directly to destroy an innocent human being.'[16]

This latter section is repeated later in paragraph 53 of *Evangelium Vitae* and became the single text in the *Catechism of the Catholic Church* (paragraph 2258) to interpret the fifth commandment. In it we see key elements: that human life is singular; that we are created in God's image; that we are uniquely created by God for a special relationship with God, which is, in turn, our destiny; and that, as source and end of human life, God is Lord of life.[17] While not at all abandoning the 'God's ownership or dominion' argument, the Pope gave it newer meaning by highlighting the intrinsic uniqueness of the human subject in God's image.[18]

The human is not to be killed, therefore, because of the intrinsic sanctity of life. Human life is not simply an object that God owns: human life is a subject bearing the inviolable image of God. In John Paul II's personalist writings, we see within human life an indelible mark of its sacredness.

The reader might be puzzled that the late pontiff is included in the revisionist work of developing new values. It might be helpful to think of him as a good deal like Joseph Mausbach, offering a whole new foundation for thinking about moral issues but integrating classicist longstanding norms into his teaching. The Pope could develop those norms, but what differentiates him from the revisionists is not that development, which after all reflects historicist instincts. Rather, while the revisionists presented a variety of values to guide the consciences of others in making their moral judgments, the Pope promulgated a number of norms that required submissive adherence from everyone's conscience.

Still, because of this new expanded teaching on life issues, the Pope revisited the teaching on capital punishment which the Church permitted for centuries. In light of the Pope's teaching in *Evangelium Vitae*, the *Catechism* was edited and now teaches that only in the rarest instance is the death penalty morally valid and that those cases in which the execution of the offender is an absolute necessity 'are very rare, if not practically non-existent' (2267).[19] The normative teaching on capital punishment is now evolving toward its abolition because of the intrinsic nature of the sanctity of life.[20]

The moral relevance of 'sanctity of life' was made more morally compelling by another new fundamental concept. On 6 December 1983, in his Gannon Lecture at Fordham University, Cardinal Joseph Bernardin launched an argument for a consistent life ethics. While sanctity of life would help us to appreciate the dignity of the human being as being intrinsically in the image of God, the Bernardin concept would prompt us to consider and apply the sanctity of life argument to every stage and every area of life. It would certainly compound the urgency of changing the teaching on capital punishment, but it would also bring sanctity of life to other ethical issues that were not previously considered under that rubric, like health care, education, and employment.

From 1983 to 1996, the Cardinal gave 35 lectures and speeches on the topic.[21] We are only now beginning to understand the impact of those discourses.[22]

The 'preferential option for the poor' was articulated by Gustavo Gutiérrez.[23] While there was no such concept before the 1960s, today it is a constitutive part of the moral theological tradition of the Roman Catholic community and has normative claims on us. It affects not only the way the Church as an institution prophetically advocates on behalf of the poor, but it also allows us to propose to governments and NGOs the need to consider the just allocation of resources, through corrective policies which empower the poor. Moreover, many religious and lay movements see in this option the possibility of a new direction to incorporate those who have long been ignored on the margins, especially with regard to the access of labor, education, and health care. Finally, it imposes on the Church normative guidelines for its ethical practices with its own employees.

The concept has universal claims in the Church. Even when liberation theology came under the critique of the Congregation for the Doctrine of the Faith in 1984, Cardinal Joseph Ratzinger was careful not to undermine the claims of the option of the poor: 'This warning should in no way be interpreted as a disavowal of all those who want to respond generously and with an authentic evangelical spirit to the "preferential option for the poor."'[24] Since then, the claim 'preferential option for the poor' is no longer a local, Latin American moral claim; today it can be found in every Catholic social ethical discourse on every continent and in every level of our hierarchy.[25]

Finally, John Paul II again developed another concept, solidarity, taking it from a variety of other, more secular movements, but making it a keystone in his own understanding of the Catholic social tradition. Just as Bernardin's consistent ethics of life fortified the claims of John Paul's sanctity of life, similarly John Paul's solidarity gave the preferential option for the poor greater claim. In a variety of major encyclicals, but especially *Laborem Exercens* (*On Human Work*, 1981), *Sollicitudo Rei Socialis* (*On Social Concern*, 1987), and *Centesimus Annus* (*On the Hundreth Anniversary of Rerum Novarum*, 1981), Pope John Paul II developed the virtue of solidarity into a host of insights into concrete right moral conduct in such a way that the language is foundational to Catholic social tradition.[26]

These newly minted but foundational concepts generated more contemporary understandings about what Jesus Christ expects of us. They empowered us to revisit a variety of agendas so as to stipulate the ways we should live and act. Interest in fundamental issues did not mean that moral theology would be more remote from practical concerns than the manualists were; on the contrary, by reinvestigating the fundamental concerns, moral theologians would discover a new freedom to understand the demands of being a disciple under the new law of Christ.

For the reformers, then, there was a deep connection between their fundamental concerns and the world in which they lived, and that link was founded on experience. As we saw in Chapter 2, contemporary experience barely appeared in the manuals. In fact, it can be claimed that it is precisely experience that differentiates the reformers from the moral manualists. McCormick, for instance, noted: 'There is a residue of truth in the general assertion that for some decades Catholic moral theology proceeded as if its responsibility was to form and shape experience, but hardly ever to be shaped by it.'[27] For the revisionists, experience had an evident claim. Again McCormick stated: 'One of the richest and most indispensable sources of moral knowledge is human experience and reflection. To be ignorant of it or to neglect it is to doom moral theology to irrelevance and triviality.'[28] On this emphasis on experience we turn to Bernhard Häring whose writings exude experience.

Bernhard Häring (1912–98) and *The Law of Christ*

In 1954, Bernhard Häring published in German the 1,600-page magisterial manual, three-volume, *Das Gesetz Christi* (in English: *The Law of Christ: Moral Theology for Priests and Laity*).[29] Of his 104 published books, this is certainly his landmark contribution.[30]

The opening words of the Foreword were decisive: 'The principle, the norm, the center, and the goal of Christian Moral Theology is Christ.'[31] Each word was central: Christ is the principle, the foundation, the source, the wellspring of moral theology; Christ is the norm, indeed a positive norm, a norm about being, a norm about persons as disciples; Christ, not the human, is the center; and Christ is the goal, for charity is union with God for ever.

The first volume was on general moral theology. The second volume is composed of two 'books': our fellowship with God and with humanity. The third volume concerns our ascent to the all-embracing majesty of God's love and is the most practical of the three.

Throughout these volumes, Häring worked with three premises. First, he established the perfect ideal of life in Christ and with Christ, and therein insisted on the ideal of radical conformity with Christ through the exercise of Christian virtue. Second, he acknowledged the limits of the law beyond which lies the dread realm of death and loss of life. Law may be described as an expression or manifestation of the reality of creation and redemption: it is the reverse side of the loving divine bounty. For our own welfare, the law may be compared to an off-limits warning of the abyss of death. Third, with its sound basis in law, moral theology reaches to the summit of perfection.

The Law of Christ has just celebrated its fiftieth anniversary. In his superb lead essay in a collection celebrating the anniversary, the Irish Redemptorist Raphael Gallagher makes clear that ethics derives from the Church reflecting theologically on the Gospels.[32] As Gallagher, Eberhard Schockenhoff and Josef Römelt each show, Häring's point of departure was always theology, and from there he sought through ethics to engage culture and its sciences, with an appreciation for an interdisciplinary approach to understanding the human situation.[33] This theological foundation prompts Norbert Rigali, in noting the lasting influence of Bernhard Häring, to declare that the subject of moral theology's present incarnation is 'unmistakably Christian: life in Christ. There can be no question that the new discipline is theology.'[34]

Gallagher names four experiences that shaped Häring's landmark work: having studied the moral manuals; having lived through the war; having been formed in the Redemptorist tradition; and, having learned from his reforming predecessors.[35]

Reflecting on his superior's request to study moral theology, Häring reported that 'I told my superior that this was my very last choice because I found the teaching of moral theology an absolutely crushing bore.'[36] In subsequently pursuing his studies, Häring found that the experience was profoundly, personally unhelpful. He realized that if he found little benefit in its study, so would the laity. He began to see that the moral theology that he needed had to be designed for others as well.

> In 1936 when I came to study moral theology under the guidance of a professor who was a canon lawyer, he used the manual of Aertnys-Damen; we students found ourselves in crisis and even disgusted. For my personal-in-depth development I found other ethical writers of great value. Thus I created a deviation between the official morality for the preparation of the office of confessor and the personal work for a morality to live and to announce.[37]

Häring's attempts to design a new moral theology had to be orientated towards a notion of moral truth that could be realized from the depths of persons. This project led him to an interior conviction to continue the reform of theology even if it meant censure and silencing. In a way, his life was mirrored by the very premises with which he worked: he knew the truth, not through utterances, but through profound life experiences.

Unlike Davis and Jone, Häring's experience of the war shaped the breadth and depth of his project: the war empowered him to stand and witness to truth in the face of a criminal regime: 'During the Second World War I stood before a military court four times. Twice it was a case of life and death. At that time I felt honored because I was accused by the enemies of God. The accusations then were to a large extent true, because I was not submissive to that regime.'[38]

His wartime experiences convinced him that in crises people realize their true selves and reason from the depths of their commitments. He witnessed to how many uneducated Christians recognized the truth, were convicted by it, and stood firm with it. Häring found truth not primarily in what persons said but in how they acted and lived. The war experiences irretrievably disposed him to the agenda of developing a moral theology that aimed for the bravery, solidarity, and truthfulness of those committed Christians he met in the war.[39]

While he encountered heroes and heroines, he also witnessed to 'the most absurd obedience by Christians toward a criminal regime. And that too radically affected my thinking and acting as a moral theologian. After the war, I returned to moral theology with the firm decision to teach it so that the core concept would not be obedience but responsibility, the courage to be responsible.'[40] He realized therein the need to develop not a conforming, obediential moral theology, but rather one that summoned Christians to a responsive and responsible life of discipleship.

A third experience was his life in the Redemptorist order; from reading the writings of Alphonsus to preaching parish missions, Häring developed an intimate understanding of the end of moral instruction and the need for that instruction to care for the whole person. Alphonsus's work prompted him to develop an integrated moral theology, that is, one that was theologically demanding, pastorally sensitive, and spiritually sustaining.[41]

The influence of the Redemptorist tradition on Häring cannot be overstated. Before Häring, the severity of the manualists' teachings was often complemented by the local pastor's ministerial sensitivity that effectively (especially in the confessional) suspended the former's judgments. Lay Catholics learned to find consolation in the confessional because the law as it was applied there was far more understanding and receptive to their experience than the manuals were. Often this resulted in two teachings on the same matter: the public, exceptionless universal instruction by the manualists, and the private, compassionate judgment of the local confessor. We will see more on this later, but Häring realized that if the confessor could appreciate the experience of the lay person, then the moral teacher had to as well.

The Redemptorists, especially in the person of Häring, would bring a much more integrated moral theology into the life of the Church. Not only would he integrate the moral and the pastoral, but following both the revisionists and the legacy of Alphonsus, he would weave moral theology into the pattern of dogmatic theology.

Finally, Gallagher insists that studying at Tübingen gave Häring an experience of the reformers. Häring relied on Lottin, Tillmann, Mersch, and Gilleman, but appropriated the insights of three other theologians as well. The first was Johannes Stelzenberger (1898–1972) who, after being released in 1949 from a Russian prisoner of war camp, held the chair in moral theology at Tübingen from 1950 to 1965. Instead of focusing on discipleship or the self-understanding of Jesus, he looked to the kingdom of God.[42] Like Lottin, Stelzenberger only discussed this theological approach and never provided a moral theological application as Tillmann did with *The Master Calls*.[43]

The second figure was Gustav Ermecke (1907–87) who taught moral theology and social doctrine at Paderborn from 1950 and at Bochum from 1965. Ermecke believed that the best way of reforming moral theology was to develop a strong theological basis for fundamental moral theology as a complement to the practical casuistic manuals. Ermecke believed, then, in the necessity of the manuals, though for their new foundations he contended that being made in the image of Christ required us to develop a Christ-centered foundational moral theology. But, unlike Stelzenberger and Tillmann, he argued against a single unifying category for moral theology (like the kingdom or discipleship) and that moral theology ought to aim to be comprehensive.[44]

Finally, Häring also depended on his professor and doctoral dissertation director from Tübingen, Theodor Steinbüchel, who celebrated the work of Fritz Tillmann.[45] Steinbüchel provided Häring with a way of appreciating both graced human freedom and the call to decision-making as key elements for realizing the call to pursue moral truth.[46]

Häring's work represents a certain coming together of almost 40 years of a variety of attempts to resituate moral theology as a theological enterprise, deeply connected to dogmatic (Lottin, Mersch, Stelzenberger, Ermecke), biblical (Tillmann and Steinbüchel), and ascetical (Gilleman) theology. Moreover, it also represents a decisive break with the manuals. Early nineteenth-century attempts sought a new theological foundation for moral theology but still turned to the manualistic logic in order to write about the practical order. Later, Ermecke and others suggested a more intentional coupling of the Decalogue's application in the manuals with an *imitatio Christi* as the foundational theology. Other moral theologians realized that the practical order could not be adequately addressed in the twentieth century by following, in any way, the manualist logic. Among these reformers who abandoned the manual tradition, only Tillmann provided concrete norms for action. Now, it would belong to Häring to do a 'synthesis' of fundamental moral theology, rooted in dogma, scripture, and spirituality, and at the same time able to generate new modes of constructing normative guidance for right moral conduct.

In the first of the three volumes, Häring presented his foundations of moral theology in six parts. The first surveyed the history of moral theology and provided the basic concepts for doing moral theology: responsibility, fellowship, and an *imitatio Christi*. In the second part he developed a theological anthropology based on the call to follow Christ: the human is a whole being, body and soul; dependent on community which itself bears human values; and located in history, a history marked by sin but called through discipleship to restoration. For that restoration he proposed worship as the primary vehicle for reform. This foundation, in turn, let him comment extensively on the 'true basis of morality', human freedom. Realization of that freedom depends on our knowledge of God, the development of our consciences, and the realization through action of our call to responsibility. The third part, the moral duty of the disciple of Christ, turned to the quintessential concerns of traditional moral theology: norms and law; the moral object in itself and in situation; the moral motive; and the problem of indifferent actions. Part four focused on sin, with special attention to the biblical roots of teachings on sin and then a consideration of the capital sins. Part five turned to conversion, with extensive comments on contrition, confession, satisfaction, and atonement. The final part focused on life after conversion in pursuit of the perfection of the virtues, which included the four cardinal virtues (prudence, justice, fortitude, temperance) and humility (a very Redemptorist virtue).

Of its innumerable contributions, we attend to five central themes: an entirely positive orientation; an emphasis on history and tradition; human freedom as the basis of Christian morality; the formation of the conscience; and the relevance of worship for the moral life.

The first paragraph of the first chapter of the first volume captured (much as Tillmann did) the positive call to moral theology. It was riveting:

> The moral theology of Jesus is contained in its totality in the glad tidings of salvation. The tremendous *Good News* is not actually a new law, but the Sovereign Majesty of God intervening in the person of Christ and the grace and love of God manifesting itself in Him. In consequence all the precepts of the moral law, even the most sacred, are given a new and glorious orientation in divine grace and a new focus, the Person of the God-man. There is nothing novel in the call to repentance for all sin. What is new is the glad tidings announcing that *now* the time for the great conversion from sin and the return to God is at hand.[47]

Häring summoned the reader: the moment of *Kairos* is now. Christ, the glad tidings, beckons us. 'We understand moral theology as the doctrine of the imitation of Christ, as life in, with, and through Christ . . . the point of departure in Catholic moral theology is Christ, who bestows on man a participation in his life and calls on him to follow the Master.'[48]

Fifty years after Slater's manual, we find little emphasis on moral pathology. While the manuals deliberated on scrupulous, erroneous, doubtful, and perplexed consciences, Häring instructed on the formation of an upright conscience that needed to be obeyed. While the manualists invoked motive to attend to the matter of culpability, he reflected on motive's relationship to the love of God, hope, and the love of neighbor. And while he spent 40 pages on sin, he dedicated 100 pages to conversion and another 80 to the perfecting virtues.

Still, there was no license in this positive agenda: probability was endorsed but with critical warnings; indifferent actions were ruled out in that everything we do is marked by goodness or badness; and the truly free Christian was called to be humble.

As we saw in Chapter 3, at the beginning of *The Law of Christ*, Häring provided a slim 33-page 'historical survey of moral theology'. These pages served as a sort of guarantee that Häring's presentation would be within the tradition. His decision to invoke the authority of history finds precedent in the writings of several innovators, who acknowledged their discontinuity with the manualists, while still claiming to be 'traditional'. However, rather than turn to general historical claims, these moral theologians turned either to the scriptures or to Thomas Aquinas. Häring's roots were more pervasive, running extensively through the tradition which he called 'a stream of life and truth under the guidance of the Holy Spirit, who introduces each generation in its dynamic historical context into the one great truth revealed by Jesus Christ'.[49]

True to his Redemptorist vocation, Häring upheld and interpreted the tradition and, while critical of its past, he could not but contribute to it. For this reason we see in innumerable Redemptorists a strong tendency toward retrieving the tradition. The pre-eminent historian of moral theology, Louis Vereecke, served as an evident reminder of this charism,[50] but long-time editor of *Studia Moralia*, Raphael Gallagher, has continually called us to reflect on the tradition, whether editing the selected writings of Alphonsus Liguori, comparing the Redemptorist and Jesuit interpretative traditions on Thomas Aquinas, or reflecting on the development in medical ethics papers.[51] From Ireland's Sean O'Riordan[52] to Spain's Marciano Vidal, their writings witness to the tradition. Not surprisingly, when Karl-Wilhelm Merks raised fundamental questions about whether the tradition ought always to be a source for moral judgment, another Redemptorist, the Australian Brian Johnstone, came to its defense.[53]

Still, the central theme of Häring is not history but freedom, because our history is written in Christ and Christ calls us to freedom. 'We recognize the true nature of our freedom when we perceive values and experience the challenge of the morally good.' 'In essence, freedom is the power to do good. The power to do evil is not of its essence.'[54]

Noticeably different from his predecessors, Häring privileges human freedom as foundational to moral goodness. For Häring, freedom is the possibility of responding to God's call to do God's will. But that freedom is itself a gift. As God calls, God provides. Sin is the refusal to accept the gift and the call; it is therefore the defeat of freedom and the entrance into slavery.

There are many reasons for Häring's turn to freedom: the Facist and Nazi movements that imprisoned millions across the European continent; the subsequent developments in the philosophy of existentialism; the incredibly obsessive control of the manualists and the ever-encroaching Vatican dictates; the Soviet expansionism into Eastern Europe; and the growing appreciation in ordinary European culture of human freedom.[55] Moreover, theologians, particularly his doctoral director, Theodor Steinbüchel, had been writing on freedom.[56]

Raphael Gallagher offers another reason for the turn to freedom: revelation. Häring has 2,031 scriptural citations in *The Law of Christ*, and 659 come from Paul, 'the apostle of Christian freedom'.[57] These glad tidings are precisely that which makes us free. We have law as a pedagogue, teaching us how to proceed and revealing to us, forensically, our sins. But the gospel, the law of Christ, makes us free to follow him. The Galatian message of Paul rings true in the life experiences of Häring, particularly those during the war; by his own testimony, Häring was free to stand and witness. Personal freedom is the foundation for doing good and for doing moral theology.

From freedom we move to conscience as a spiritual disposition and as a moral and religious phenomenon. In short, conscience is the voice of God which we must obey in freedom. We need to form our consciences and, generally speaking, ought to observe the claims of the law.

In Volume 2, Häring divided his concerns into two parts, life in fellowship with God and with neighbor, with most matter attending the first fellowship. In that first part, he focused on the theological virtues, humility and religion. Like Lottin and Tillmann, Häring found moral formation in the virtues.[58] His responsibility ethics was therefore primarily virtue based.

The virtue of religion and its practice of worship is unmistakably innovative. Through religion, Kathleen A. Cahalan sees Häring's integration of moral and sacramental theology. His understanding of virtue as not only interior and personal but communal and public, prompted him to explore the ramifications of a virtue that moves an entire community of believers to respond collectively to the God who calls us: 'Our entire activity in the world must have a religious formation, for all our acts must be ordered to the loving majesty of God. This means that all our moral tasks are at the same time religious tasks.'[59]

Later Häring deliberated on the two primary manifestations of neighbor love: care for the other's bodily well-being and salvation. In the sins against neighbor love, he commented simply on scandal and co-operation.

In the third volume, Häring's aim to be comprehensive led him to work out, in part, the relationship between virtue and law. Here he reflected on the concrete responsibilities of the moral person. In the first part of the third volume, Häring simply repeated his section on the cardinal virtues and humility. He then examined the realization of Christian love in community, by considering the family and the attendant duties to parents and children; the State and its duties and powers as well as the obligations and rights of citizens; and the Church and her pastoral ministry of love. He turned to matters of health, first reflecting on forms of killing, then to the concept and responsibilities surrounding health. In turning to sex, he wrote about it in the context of life with Christ, and while he spends some 30 pages on sins against chastity, for the most part he constructed a positive, moral–sacramental theology of marriage and virginity. Still, we find here hundreds of different topics, from 'false approaches to the mastery of passion' and 'intercourse of the sexually impotent and sterile' to 'the love prelude' and 'the so-called "safe period"'. In this section there is great wisdom, both pastoral and moral, and sensitivity in his willingness to enter into a variety of specifics that must have been a source of considerable anxiety for many devout Catholics. Yet, we cannot but wonder as to how much social control the clergy's teachings had over the sexual lives of its lay members that such a plethora of concerns is examined.

The second longest section in this volume is the use of earthly goods, which considers the acquisition of property, contracts (thirteen species, from promises and rentals to annuities), theft and fraud, reparations for injustices, and the basis for a just economic order. He concluded his work on truthfulness, honor, and beauty, which he applied to matters of film, radio, television, and the mass media.

Upon concluding *The Law of Christ*, the reader cannot but sense a comprehensive view of the moral life, rooted in the theological tradition, with an enormous amount of awareness of the best advice in pastoral, moral, and sacramental theology.[60] Besides being integrative of all the areas of practical theology (with the extraordinary exception of little reference to canon law), it is also incredibly rich in its bibliographical reporting. Every part of the three volumes is marked by an extensive listing of the theological works upon which Häring built his argument. When one finishes these three lengthy volumes, one wonders not only at how much he has written, but how much he has read. As Rigali and others noted, with Häring's *Law of Christ*, moral theology came of age as a theological discipline.[61]

Vatican II

With *The Law of Christ*, moral theologians had a solid foundation for their revisionists' claims. There was no longer a need to go back over the claims of Lottin, Tillmann, Mersch or the others. There was no need to make anew a case for revisionism: now it was contemporary moral theology. The claims of previous writers were validated now by the realization of a new manual of moral theology. As such, it was foundational for moral theologians as they faced the 1960s, and most especially Vatican II and the papal commission on birth control.

Aside from the much-anticipated work of the papal commission (see the next chapter), two conciliar documents especially merit our attention. First, when the document on priestly formation, *Optatam Totius*, defined seminary education, it offered a simple, two-sentence statement on moral theology. This comment not only validated the revisionists' work, but admonished the seminaries to incorporate the scriptures in their study of moral theology and to embrace more clearly the virtue of charity and the role of discipleship. Since its promulgation, the paragraph has become a kind of a terse manifesto of the revisionists' agenda. It reads:

> Special care must be given to the perfecting of moral theology. Its scientific exposition, nourished more on the teaching of the Bible, should shed light on the loftiness of the calling of the faithful in Christ and the obligation that is theirs of bearing fruit in charity for the life of the world.[62]

One example of its pivotal role in moral theology is a 50-page article written in 1966 by Josef Fuchs on the moral theology according to Vatican II. The very first words of the essay are those from *Optatam Totius*.[63]

Second, at the Council, Häring served on pre-conciliar and conciliar commissions and was the secretary of the editorial committee that drafted the *Pastoral Constitution on the Church in the Modern World, Gaudium et Spes.*[64] Charles Curran notes that Häring was referred to as 'the quasi-father of Gaudium et Spes'.[65]

Among his contributions, three are particularly noteworthy. First, the anthropological vision was based on the human as a social being. Moral issues were not treated as primarily individual, but rather communal and even global. Moreover, even though sin is pervasive in the document, still the vision is fundamentally positive as the Church stands with the world in joy and hope. A new moral theological foundation was emerging that hardly looked like Jone's, but it did look like Häring's.

The French theological ethicist Philippe Bordeyne argues in his work on the moral theology of *Gaudium et Spes* that here the Church conveyed a deep sympathy for the human condition, especially in all its anxieties, and stood in confident solidarity with the world. The entire experience of ambivalence that so affected the world in its tumultuous changes of the 1960s was positively entertained and engaged.[66] Finally, in looking at contemporary moral challenges, the Church encouraged an interdisciplinary approach in understanding and promoting a globalized vision of modernity.[67]

Out of this framework the Council shaped its teaching on conscience, evidently indebted to Häring's extensive description of conscience in *The Law of Christ.* His work anticipated, inspired, and formed some of the most important words from the Council, the now famous definition of conscience, which deserves to be quoted in its entirety.

> In the depths of his conscience, man detects a law which he does not impose upon himself, but which holds him to obedience. Always summoning him to love good and avoid evil, the voice of conscience when necessary speaks to his heart: do this, shun that. For man has in his heart a law written by God; to obey it is the very dignity of man; according to it he will be judged. Conscience is the most secret core and sanctuary of a man. There he is alone with God, Whose voice echoes in his depths. In a wonderful manner conscience reveals that law which is fulfilled by love of God and neighbor. In fidelity to conscience, Christians are joined with the rest of men in the search for truth, and for the genuine solution to the numerous problems which arise in the life of individuals from social relationships. Hence the more right conscience holds sway, the more persons and groups turn aside from blind choice and strive to be guided by the objective norms of morality. Conscience frequently errs from invincible ignorance without losing its dignity. The same cannot be said for a man who cares but little for truth and goodness, or for a conscience which by degrees grows practically sightless as a result of habitual sin.[68]

The teaching on conscience is, I think, the emblematic expression of the hopeful expectations that were raised by Häring and affirmed by Vatican II. Universally, conscience becomes the point of departure for revisionists, as witnessed by the plethora of books and essays on the topic. For instance, the German Josef Fuchs, the Australian Terence Kennedy, and later the American Charles Curran, all publish collected essays on the topic.[69] Full-length books are written by Eric D'Arcy from Australia, Linda Hogan from Ireland, Kevin Kelly from England, Anne Patrick from the United States, Herbert Schlögel from Germany, Osamu Takeuchi from Japan, and Paul Valadier from France.[70] Conscience becomes the locus for developing the moral judgment, which, as we will see later, becomes the standard of moral objectivity.

Finally, Häring's theology of marriage also emerges from the constitution: marriage is a 'communion of love' (47), an 'intimate partnership' (48); it is no longer seen as a contract, but as a covenant (48). Rather than asserting procreation as the singular end of marriage, the council fathers argued: 'Marriage to be sure is not instituted solely for procreation' (50).[71] Such positive, non-legalistic, but deeply affirming language was a new phenomenon for Vatican teaching on marriage.

England's Kevin Kelly is probably the theological ethicist who has written more extensively on marriage than any colleague, particularly on the relationship between experience and the teaching tradition. He saw in *Gaudium et Spes* a watershed moment in the Church's teaching. He writes:

> In the Pastoral Constitution, *Gaudium et spes*, nn. 47–52, the Council Fathers clearly accepted a personalist approach to marriage as helping us to appreciate much more positively the gift of human sexuality and its important role within the marriage relationship. They moved away from a predominantly functional view that regarded procreation as the primary purpose of marriage. Instead they used the language of 'relationship' (covenant) to speak of marriage. The bishops were prepared to recognize that the sexual expression of a couple's love reflects and communicates God's own love for us. They even went so far as to warn couples that sexual abstinence could threaten their faithfulness to each other and thus pose a danger to the stable home life needed by their children. All of this was light years away from St. Augustine's insistence that sexual acts were sinful because they disturbed the calmness of mind demanded by rational self-control and needed to be 'excused' by the reasonable purpose of procreation. In contrast, Vatican II's personalist approach spoke of children as the 'fruit' of married love, not its purpose.[72]

Still, the hopes of developing church teaching even further hit an enormous impasse precisely in the final stages of the document's preparation. Then, after a week of tumultuous debate over birth control,[73] the Council concluded with these words: 'the sons of the Church may not undertake methods of birth control which are found blameworthy by the teaching authority of the Church in its unfolding of the divine law' (51). For all the joy and hope that the Council offered to married couples, when it came to the issue of responsible parenthood, the Council fathers were not ready to substantiate their theology of marriage with the teaching of conscience which they had just articulated. Instead, they reiterated the teaching of *Casti Connubii*. The divides between theology and norm, and between conscience and teaching, became all too apparent, and, in a word, foreboding.

In a recent collection of essays from Leuven University, *Vatican II and its Legacy*,[74] Joseph Selling sees in *Gaudium et Spes* the foundational outline for fundamental moral theology.[75] Georges De Schrijver comments on how the document has been received and reformulated at the Latin American Episcopal Conferences of Medellín, Puebla, and Santo Domingo.[76] And Mary Elsbernd studies how *Gaudium et Spes* is 'reinterpreted' in *Veritatis Splendor*. Though we will examine *Veritatis Splendor* at the end of the next chapter, we may appreciate the 'development' between Vatican II and Pope John Paul II's encyclical, by considering three points that she makes to demonstrate how the magisterium itself 'reconstructs' the tradition.

> First the theological anthropology of *Gaudium et Spes* has been recast into a dualistic and individualistic concept in *Veritatis Splendor*. Second, *Veritatis Splendor* has recontextualized *Gaudium et Spes* quotations on change, conscience, dialogue with modern culture, human autonomy, and social institutions by placing them into paragraphs stressing law and precepts. Third, relying on a selective wording of *Gaudium et Spes*, *Veritatis Splendor* has reworked the role of the moral theologian into a disseminator of magisterial teaching.[77]

She concludes: 'While claiming a continuity with *Gaudium et Spes*, *Veritatis Splendor* in fact peers backward through *Gaudium et Spes* to a moral theology of late eighteenth and early nineteenth centuries which did rely on a legal framework, an individualistic anthropology and the origins of moral theology in the sacramental practice of confession.'[78]

In order to appreciate how these changes did develop, we need to see in the next chapter the emergence of neo-manualism which occurred simultaneous to the work of Häring. Before we do, we need to linger a little longer with the legacy of Häring as we consider the comprehensive work of two of his most famous disciples, Charles Curran and Marciano Vidal.

Two contemporary works: Charles Curran's *The Catholic Moral Tradition Today: A Synthesis*; Marciano Vidal's *Nueva Moral Fundamental: El hogar teológico de la Ética*

Two contemporary works capture the legacy of Häring in their common interests in reviewing the tradition so as to propose a more relational–responsible understanding of discipleship. They are the syntheses of the senior moralist in the United States, Charles Curran, and the senior moralist in the Spanish language, Marciano Vidal.

Charles Curran (1934–), a diocesan priest from Rochester, New York, studied in Rome from 1959 to 1961, where he completed two doctorates. Earlier, he read Häring's *The Law of Christ* and remarked that, of everyone with whom he studied in Rome, Häring had 'the most significant influence on my thought'. He writes: 'My reading of Häring and my intellectual curiosity were pushing me to explore moral theology beyond the classroom manuals . . . Häring presented a life-centered moral theology based on the covenant – the good news of God's gracious gift of love and life and our response to it.'[79]

In 1960, while working on his dissertation at the Gregorian University (on the prevention of conception after rape), he was invited by the Redemptorist Domenico Capone to enroll in the Alphonsianum's newly established doctoral program. After much arm-twisting, under Capone's tutelage Curran wrote his second dissertation on 'Invincible Ignorance of the Natural Law according to St Alphonsus'. Defending both dissertations in 1961 (he was the Alphonsianum's first student to be awarded the doctorate), Curran learned that by studying the tradition, he would discover (as Lottin always taught) its deep complexity.

In 1963, the eminent moral theologian at Leuven University, Louis Janssens, authored an essay endorsing the birth control pill,[80] which generated a variety of essays from American moralists.[81] In time, like many others, Curran began to see contraception as a morally valid choice for responsible parents. In 1968, while teaching at the Catholic University of America, he edited a collection of essays by diverse theologians considering the claim of moral absolutes.[82] In that same year he published *A New Look at Christian Morality*[83] and drafted a petition against the encyclical *Humanae Vitae*, which more than 600 scholars signed.[84]

During the 1970s, Curran became an American powerhouse in moral theology, publishing a number of books on fundamental moral theology[85] and specific contemporary moral issues.[86] At the same time he developed an argument for the relevance of dissent to moral teaching and later wrote a sustained defense of it.[87]

In 1979, the Congregation for the Doctrine of the Faith (CDF) began an investigation of his writings and in 1986 declared that he was no longer a Professor of Catholic Theology: he was removed from teaching at the Catholic University of America. The issues against him were twofold: the matter and defense of his public dissent, and his specific stances on contraception, masturbation, homosexuality, premarital intercourse, and the indissolubility of marriage[88]

As CDF investigated Curran, he remained a prolific author and lecturer. In 1980, he published a landmark essay, an overview of fundamental moral, along with a proposed agenda for the next decade. Within that agenda, Curran called for greater attention to stance, that is, the fundamental perspective out of which we read all of reality. He argued that the stance should include the five Christian mysteries: creation, incarnation, sin, redemption, and resurrection destiny. Curran's strong theological foundations were unlike any other American writing at the time.

Like revisionists before him, he also contended that we needed a more evident Christian anthropology, but also, in the aftermath of the upheaval of the 1960s, a more sustained reflection on norms and concrete decision-making.[89] Finally, in surveying contemporary ethical models of moral reasoning, he found them lacking and proposed instead a relational–responsibility model. The model is evidently indebted to Häring's own responsibility ethics, but it makes more explicit the claims to relationality.[90]

In 1999, Curran laid out his own synthesis of the Catholic moral theological tradition. Like his Redemptorist professors, Curran's context was the tradition. Unlike reformed Protestant theologies, Curran argued, the Catholic tradition affirms mediation, that is, that the divine expresses itself not immediately to the person, but through the world and the Church. While Catholicism sees the sacraments as the quintessential mediations of God's work, it also accepts the Church's own theological tradition as the mediation of God's word and God's will. Above all, the Church itself is the mediator of God's life and love since it is the 'way God has entered into his saving love with us'.[91]

In this light, he argues in his first chapter for an ecclesial context for moral theology.[92] He notes how few moral theologians attend to this context: 'Catholic moral theology in the past has paid little or no explicit attention to the church and its influence on the discipline.' The only exceptions to this claim are the historical investigations of Vereecke and Angelini's *Disegno Storico*.[93]

The second, third, and fourth chapters on stance, ethical models, and the person, respectively, are a working out of his 1980 essay. In the fifth chapter, he contextualizes the virtues into his relational–responsibility model and discusses how they mediate our relationship with God, others, the world, ourselves, and power. In the sixth chapter, he turns to moral principles by distinguishing his claims from those of the hierarchical magisterium; he turns to his relational–responsibility model and looks for a more personalist and historical understanding of principles. He then launches a critique against the concept of absolutes in the form of intrinsically evil actions.

His last two chapters are on conscience and church teaching. For the former, he looks for a more holistic understanding of conscience, one that does not reduce it to questions of culpability or the syllogistic application of principles to situations, but insists on 'the law of growth' that guides our self-understanding in the formation of conscience. He attributes the law to Alphonsus and Häring. In the last chapter he sees the teaching Church as the whole Church, and while critiquing the exercise of the contemporary hierarchical magisterium, provides a defense of dissent as constitutive for the right development of moral teaching.

A recent *festschrift* highlights Curran's specific contributions to the particular renewal of moral theology. Three of the many worthy essays merit attention for appreciating Curran's contributions. Margaret Farley's recognition of the inadequacy of any particular point of view prompts her to propose the grace of self-doubt so as to train moral teachers to be aware of the need to look beyond their own perspectives.[94] That need has always been at the source of Curran's frequent call to dialogue.

In light of Curran's emphasis on dialogue, James Gustafson calls Curran the 'Ecumenical Moral Theologian Par Excellence' and names six criteria for an ethicist to be an ecumenical one: to master one's own tradition; to have sufficient knowledge of another tradition's teachings as they pertain to the issues within one's own; to establish an agenda within one's own tradition for a critical dialogue with other traditions; to apply that agenda to other traditions; to employ the comparative method; and to propose 'a somewhat systematic, comprehensive, and defended interpretation of Christian ethics that attends to materials from more than one tradition'.[95] The grasp of one's own tradition, something that Häring and Curran have both mastered, becomes the possibility for appreciating and dialoguing with another.

Raphael Gallagher specifically compares Curran's contributions with European interests and notes that the Europeans could learn from Curran about a 'soteriological Christology, the understanding of the developmental nature of history, and the validity of a plurality of methods in moral theology'. From the Europeans Curran could 'pay greater attention to hermeneutics, have a more philosophically rounded anthropology, and give more attention to the analytic aspects of questions rather than the synthetic aspects'.[96]

Curran remains the senior figure in American Catholic ethics. After his removal from Catholic university, he eventually was appointed in 1991 to the Elizabeth Scurlock Chair in Human Values at Southern Methodist University in Dallas.[97] During this time, in addition to *The Synthesis*, he has written several other books, on the history of Catholic social teaching, on the history of moral theology in the United States, and on the moral theology of Pope John Paul II.[98] With these books we see the 'traditionalism' of Curran's moral theology, but we also see his longstanding commitment to educating the laity in the tradition, much as his mentor had done 50 years earlier.

Marciano Vidal (1937–), a member of the Redemptorist order, did his dissertation at the Alphonsianum in 1967. He quickly became a prolific author and lecturer, writing on topics ranging from fundamental morals, marriage, family, euthanasia, and civil society.[99] He has directed over 25 dissertations and 125 licenses.[100] It is impossible to find anyone more influential in the Spanish language in theology.

Throughout his writings is an evident indebtedness to both Alphonsus and Häring.[101] Vidal found in Alphonsus a morally and pastorally sensitive figure who did not compromise moral truth, but who accompanied the Christian into a more mature life of Christian responsibility. Neither laxist nor rigorist,

Alphonsus brought a moderation which Vidal repeatedly argued was needed for the contemporary Church. In one of his central expositions of Redemptorist morals, Vidal argued for a morality from and for redemption. Here he developed both Alphonsus and Häring as defenders of the conscience, as mediators of the law and conscience, and as proponents of an emancipative solidarity through morality.[102]

In 1981 he authored the massive, four-volume, *Moral de Actitudes*, treating fundamental morals, bioethics, sexuality, and social ethics.[103] By 1997, the work enjoyed enormous reception and had gone through eight editions. In 1991 he published *Diccionario de Ética Teológica*[104] and in 1994 he did a critical commentary on Pope John Paul II's encyclical *Veritatis Splendor.*[105] In late 1997, these three works became the focus of an investigation of Vidal's writings by the Congregation for the Doctrine of the Faith. Like Curran's, the case received a great deal of attention both nationally and throughout the Church.[106]

In 2001 the Congregation issued its 'Notification' on the writings of Vidal.[107] It reported the following:

> The Christian ethic that results from this is 'an ethic influenced by faith', but the influence is weak, because it is juxtaposed in fact to a secularized rationality laid out completely on a horizontal plane. Therefore, *Moral de Actitudes* does not stress sufficiently the ascending vertical dimension of Christian moral life. And the great Christian themes, such as redemption, the Cross, grace, the theological virtues, prayer, the beatitudes, the resurrection, judgment, and eternal life, are hardly mentioned and exert almost no influence on his presentation of moral teachings.[108]

It then raised a series of questions about his positions on masturbation, birth control, homosexuality, and artificial fertilization, that is, matters relating to sexuality and reproduction, matters not unlike the topics in the Curran investigation. The 'Notification' concluded that none of the three works were to be used for theological formation and that Vidal had to revise his four-volume work.

Vidal recently commented on the investigation, noting the particular 'hardness' of the ordeal. Though the 'Notification' by the Congregation for the Doctrine of the Faith which Vidal signed did not in any way question 'the author, his intentionality, the totality of his publications or his ministry', still it declared that *Moral de Actitudes* was 'not to be used for theological formation', a particularly painful decision because the manual was born and used in the context of teaching theology students for several generations. Vidal's comments are instructive. He had remained silent about the investigation for these years for a variety of reasons: his own personal non-aggressive nature, his humility, and his spirituality. But he concluded his interview remembering how the theological tension of the 1950s bore fruit in Vatican II: 'My silence does not signify a distrust in either the judgment of history or of God.

I believe in the wisdom of the Gospel: "Nothing hidden will not be revealed".'[109]

Just before the 'Notification' appeared, Vidal published his mature work, the 999-page *Nueva Moral Fundamental: El Hogar Teológico de la Ética.*[110] Here Vidal provides a breathtaking treatment of the contemporary enterprise of moral theology. Dividing his work into three main parts, he presents morals within the design of God, the life of the Church, and the public arena. He concludes with a theological discourse on the constitution, epistemology, and method of moral theology.

This comprehensive, refreshingly theological, forward-looking work begins with the image of God as foundational to morals, emphasizing the particular relevance of the Trinity, and then exploring the significance of the Father as mystery, Son as the incarnate Word, and the Holy Spirit as impulse for the moral life. He divides the second part (a mere 420 pages!) into an historical overview of the various methodological periods of moral theology (scholasticism, casuistry, manualism, etc.) and a systematic analysis of how moral theology is mediated by the Church, inculturated in the world, and attentive to the future. He concludes with the public, civil, and rational claims that moral theology makes on us.

Among Vidal's many talents is his constructive use of the magisterium in order to demonstrate its significance and relevance.[111] But he also introduces us to some of the best of moral theology out of Europe and North and South America, with a special nod to Spanish moral theologians. Throughout the work we see the deep transcendence of the theological tradition located in the ordinariness of human life.[112]

A recent *festschrift* (at 1,028 pages it has the expansiveness that we have come to expect from Spanish moralists) celebrated his 'style',[113] which he calls 'a morality of pastoral care' ('*una moral de la benignidad pastoral*') and derives from Alphonsus Liguori.[114] The work is divided into six sections: a study of Vidal himself; the sources of Christian ethics; the foundations of Christian ethics; the person as the core of Christian ethics; society and its moral dimensions; and Christian ethics and interdisciplinary dialogue. Throughout, Vidal is seen as recognizing human suffering and tragedy as well as human hopes and joys. But he also sees his writing as a work of 'liberation' that bears personal costs.[115]

Like Häring, these two moral theologians have offered integrated views of moral theology, particularly in their numerous works for a theological formation of the Catholic Church. Like Häring, they believe in and are committed to the inevitable competency of the laity. As priests and as theologians, they take seriously the experience of the laity, not as grounds for a strict but forgiving morality, but as the foundation for a responsibility ethics for mature Christians.

In their writings, we find, as we did in Häring, a living confidence in the Church and in its ability to instruct. Despite any actions from the Congregation, they remain probably the most productive figures shaping moral theology, even now, more than 40 years after their studies at the Alphonsianum. Their works, like their lives, bear witness to the credibility of their projects. In that sense they follow their mentor pre-eminently.

Notes

1 Richard McCormick, 'Moral Theology 1940–1989: An Overview', *TS* 50 (1989) 3–24, at 3.

2 Ibid., 22.

3 Bernhard Häring, *Free and Faithful in Christ: Moral Theology for Clergy and Laity* (New York: Seabury Press, 1978) 6.

4 'Schema for a Document on Responsible Parenthood' appeared in English as the 'Responsible Parenthood, the Majority Report of the Papal Birth Control Commission', in Robert McClory, *Turning Point: The Inside Story of the Papal Birth Control Commission, and How Humanae Vitae Changed the Life of Patty Crowley and the Future of the Church* (New York: Crossroad Publishing, 1995) 171–87.

5 National Conference of Catholic Bishops, *The Challenge of Peace: God's Promise and Our Response: A Pastoral Letter on War and Peace, May 3, 1983* (Washington, DC: United States Catholic Conference, 1983).

6 *New Catholic Encyclopedia: Supplement, 1967–78* (New York City: McGraw-Hill, 1978) vol. 16, pp. 400–1.

7 Joseph Komonchak, ed., *New Dictionary of Theology* (Wilmington, DE: Michael Glazier, 1987); F. Cross, ed., *The Oxford Dictionary of the Christian Church* (Oxford: Oxford University Press, 1974); and K. Rahner and H. Vorgrimler, *Theological Dictionary* (New York City: Herder and Herder, 1965).

8 Bernhard Stoeckle, ed., *The Concise Dictionary of Christian Ethics* (New York City: Seabury, 1979); P. Palazzini, ed., *Dictionary of Moral Theology* (Westminster, MD: Newman Press, 1962).

9 Slater, *A Manual of Moral Theology* I, 302.

10 Pope Pius XI, *Encyclical Letter on Christian Marriage*, 31 December 1930: http://www.vatican.va/holy_father/pius_xi/encyclicals/documents/hf_p-xi_enc_31121930_casti-connubii_en.html.

11 Gerald Coleman sums up the tradition well: 'Human persons, then, have only a right to the use of human life, not to dominion over human life. What makes killing forbidden is that it usurps a divine prerogative and violates divine rights'. Gerald Coleman, 'Assisted Suicide: An Ethical Perspective', in Robert Baird and Stuart Rosenbaum, eds, *Euthanasia* (Buffalo, NY: Prometheus Books, 1989) 108.

12 'All must regard the life of man as sacred, since from its inception, it requires the action of God the Creator. Those who depart from this plan of God not only offend His divine majesty and dishonor themselves and the human race, but they also weaken the inner fibre of the commonwealth'. Pope John XXIII, *Mater et Magistra*, 1961, para. 194. The 'sanctity of life' phrase became key in *Humanae Vitae* (1968, para. 13). There Pope Paul VI used it to affirm the limited dominion that the human has over human life and human generativity.

13 Richard M. Gula writes: 'Closely related to the principles of sanctity and sovereignty is the divine law prohibiting killing as found in the fifth commandment'. *Euthanasia* (New York City: Paulist Press, 1994) 26.

14 See James Keenan, 'The Concept of Sanctity of Life and its Use in Contemporary Bioethical Discussion', Kurt Bayertz, ed., *Sanctity of Life and Human Dignity* (Dor-

drecht: Kluwer Academics, 1996) 1–18; Joseph Boyle, 'Sanctity of Life and Suicide: Tensions and Developments within Common Morality', Baruch Brody, ed., *Suicide and Euthanasia* (Kluwer Academics, Boston, 1989) 221–50.

15 John Paul II, *Christifideles Laici*, 30 December 1988, para. 38: http://www.vatican.va/holy_father/john_paul_ii/apost_exhortations/documents/hf_jp-ii_exh_30121988_christifideles-laici_en.html.

16 Congregation for the Doctrine of the Faith, *Donum Vitae*, 1987, Introduction, para. 5: www.nccbuscc.org/prolife/tdocs/donumvitae.htm.

17 See James Keenan, 'The Moral Argumentation of Evangelium Vitae', in Kevin Wildes, ed., *Choosing Life: A Dialogue on Evangelium Vitae* (Washington, DC: Georgetown University Press, 1997) 46–62; and 'History, Roots and Innovations: A Response to the Engaging Protestants', in Reinhard Hütter and Theodor Dieter, eds, *Ecumenical Ventures in Ethics: Protestants Engage Pope John Paul II's Moral Encyclicals* (Grand Rapids: Eerdmans, 1997) 262–88.

18 Pope John Paul II, *Evangelium Vitae*, 25 March 1995: http://www.vatican.va/holy_father/john_paul_ii/encyclicals/documents/hf_jp-ii_enc_25031995_evangelium-vitae_en.html.

19 *Catechism of the Catholic Church*: http://www.scborromeo.org/ccc.htm. The final words are again from John Paul II, *Evangelium Vitae*, para 56.

20 See John Langan, 'Situating the Teaching of John Paul II on Capital Punishment: Reflections on *Evangelium Vitae* 56', *Choosing Life*, 210–22; Helen Prejean, 'Response to John Langan's Essay', ibid., 231–5; Mark Latkovic, 'Capital Punishment, Church Teaching, and Morality: What is Pope John Paul II Saying to Catholics in *Evangelium Vitae?*', *Logos: A Journal of Catholic Thought and Culture* 5.2 (2002) 76–95; E. Christian Brugger, *Capital Punishment and Roman Catholic Moral Tradition* (Notre Dame: University of Notre Dame Press, 2003).

21 Joseph Bernardin, *Seamless Garment: Writings on the Consistent Ethic of Life*, in Thomas Nairn, ed. (Maryknoll: Orbis, 2008).

22 See James Walter, 'What Does Horizon Analysis Bring to the Consistent Ethic of Life?', *The Consistent Ethic of Life*, 1–15; Ron Hamel, 'The Consistent Ethic of Life: A Corrective Vision for Health Care', ibid., 16–33; and Patricia Beattie Jung, 'Constructing a Consistent Ethic of Life: Feminist Contributions to Its Foundation', ibid., 61–77.

23 Gustavo Gutiérrez, in *Theology of Liberation: History, Politics, and Salvation* (Maryknoll, New York: Orbis, 1973).

24 Congregation for the Doctrine of the Faith, *Instruction on Certain Aspects of the 'Theology of Liberation'*, 6 August 1984, introduction: http://www.vatican.va/roman_curia/congregations/cfaith/documents/rc_con_cfaith_doc_19840806_theology-liberation_en.html.

25 Gerald Twomey, *The 'Preferential Option for the Poor' in Catholic Social Thought from John XXIII to John Paul II* (Lewiston, New York: Edwin Mellen Press, 2005).

26 See Patricia A. Lamoureux, '*Laborem exercens*', in Kenneth R. Himes, *Modern Catholic Social Teaching: Commentaries and Interpretations* (Washington, DC: Georgetown University Press, 2005, heareafter *MCST*) 389–414; Charles E. Curran, Kenneth R. Himes and Thomas Shannon, '*Sollicitudo rei socialis*', *MCST*, 415–35; and Daniel Finn, '*Centesimus Annus*', *MCST*, 436–67.

27 McCormick, 'Moral Theology: 1940–1989', 20.

28 Ibid.

29 Häring, *Das Gesetz Christi* (Freiburg: Verlag Wewel, 1954); *The Law of Christ* (Paramus, New Jersey: The Newman Press, 1961).

30 See the Memoriam to Häring on the Alfonsianum website: http://www.alfonsiana.edu/In%20Memoriam/EN%20-%20IM%20Haring2.htm.

31 Häring, *The Law of Christ*, vii.

32 Raphael Gallagher, 'Das Gesetz Christi: Seine Bedeutung für die Erneuerung der Moratheologie', in Augustin Schmied and Josef Römelt, eds, *50 Jahre 'Das Gesetz Christi'* Studien der Moraltheologie 14 (Münster: LIT Verlag 2005) 11–42. Later translated, 'Bernhard Häring's The Law of Christ: Reassessing its Contribution to the Renewal of Moral Theology in its Era', *Studia Moralia* 44 (2006) 317–51.

33 Eberhard Schockenhoff, 'Pater Bernhard Häring als Wegbereiter einer konziliaren Moraltheologie', *50 Jahre 'Das Gesetz Christi'*, 43–68.

34 Norbert Rigali, 'On Theology of the Christian Life', *Moral Theology*, 3–23, at 19.

35 Also Giuseppe Quaranta, *La Cultura pieno Sviluppo dell'Umano: Il Concetto e la funzione della cultura nel pensiero di Bernhard Häring* (Rome: Alfonsianum Press, 2006).

36 Häring, *My Witness for the Church* (Mahwah: Paulist Press, 1992) 19.

37 Häring, *Teologia Morale Verso il Terzo Millennio*, class notes (Rome: Alfonsianum University, 1987), the last course Häring offered.

38 Häring, *My Witness*, 132.

39 Häring, *Embattled Witness: Memories of a Time of War* (New York: Seabury Press, 1976).

40 Ibid., 23–4.

41 Marciano Vidal, 'Bernhard Häring – Ein Theologe in der alfonsianischen Tradition', *50 Jahre 'Das Gesetz Christi'* 143–73.

42 Johannes Stelzenberger, *Lehrbuch der Moraltheologie: Die Sittlichkeitslehre der Köningsherrschaft Gottes* (Paderborn: Ferdinand Schöningh, 1953); Josef Rief, 'Johannes Stelzenberger zum Gedenken', *Theologischen Quartalschrift* 152 (1972) 380–7.

43 See Angelini and Valsecchi's comments, 174.

44 Gustav Ermecke, *Katholische Moraltheologie* (Münster: Aschendorff, 1953); Sein Und Leben in Christus: uber Die Seinsgrundlagen Der Katholischen Moraltheologie (Paderborn: Schöningh, 1985); on Mausbach and Ermecke see Vincent MacNamara, *Faith and Ethics: Recent Roman Catholicism* (Washington, DC: Georgetown University Press, 1985) 19–23.

45 Theodor Steinbüchel and Theodor Muncker, eds, *Aus Theologie und Philosophie: Festschrift fur Fritz Tillmann zu seinem 75. Geburtstag* (Patmos: Dusseldorf, 1950).

46 Theodor Steinbüchel, *Der Zweckgedanke in der Philosophie des Thomas von Aquino* (Münster: Aschendorff, 1912); *Existenzialismus und christliches Ethos* (Heidelberg: F. H. Kerle, 1948); *Religion und Moral* (Frankfurt: Knecht, 1950); *Zerfall des christlichen Ethos im XIX. Jahrhundert* (Frankfurt: Knecht, 1951).

47 Häring, *Law*, 3.

48 Ibid., 61.

49 Häring, 'The Role of the Catholic Moral Theologian', Charles Curran, ed., *Moral Theology: Challenges for the Future* (Mahwah: Paulist Press, 1990) 32–47, at 30.

50 In addition to his works already cited, see the festschrift, Réal Tremblay and Dennis Billy, eds, *Historia: Memoria Futuri: Mélanges Louis Vereecke* (Rome: Editiones Academiae Alphonsianae, 1991).

51 Raphael Gallagher, *Alphonsus de Liguori: Selected Writings* (Mahwah: Paulist Press, 1999); 'Interpreting Thomas Aquinas: Aspects of the Redemptorist and Jesuit Schools in the Twentieth Century', in Stephen Pope, ed., *The Ethics of Aquinas* (Washington, DC: Georgetown University Press, 2002) 374–84; 'Catholic Medical Ethics: A Tradition which Progresses', *CEHP*, 171–81.

52 See the collection of essays edited by Raphael Gallagher and Sean Cannon, *Sean*

O'Riordan: A Theologian of Development (Dublin: Columba Press, 1998).

53 Karl-Wilhelm Merks, 'De Strenenzang van de tradities: Pleidooi voor een universele ethick', *Bijdragen* 58 (1997) 122–43; Brian Johnstone, 'Can Tradition be a Source of Moral Truth? A Reply to Karl-Wilhelm Merks', *Studia Moralia* 37 (1999) 431–51. See also Johnstone, 'From Physicalism to Personalism', *Studia Moralia* 30 (1992) 71–96.

54 Häring, *Law of Christ*, 99.

55 See Stephen Schloesser on this period, 'Against Forgetting: Memory, History, Vatican II', *Theological Studies* 67 (2006) 275–314.

56 For instance, Theodor Steinbüchel, *Existenzialismus und christliches Ethos* (Heidelberg: F. H. Kerle, 1948); *Religion und Moral* (Frankfurt: Knecht, 1950).

57 Gallagher, 'Bernhard Häring's *The Law of Christ*', 336. Jeffrey Siker provides a very insightful study of Häring's use of scripture, in 'Bernhard Häring: The Freedom of Responsive Love', *Scripture and Ethics: Twentieth Century Portraits* (New York: Oxford University Press, 1977) 59–79.

58 Häring, *Timely and Untimely Virtues* (New York: St Paul Publications, 1986).

59 Bernhard Häring, *The Law of Christ II* (Westminster, Md: Newman Press, 1963) 124, as quoted in Kathleen A. Cahalan, *Formed in the Image of Christ: The Sacramental-Moral Theology of Bernard Häring, C.Ss.R.* (Collegeville: Liturgical Press, 2004), 161.

60 On the connection between moral and sacramental theology, see Eliseo Ruffini, 'Simbolismo, Sacramentalità e Stile di Vita Cristiano', in Tullo Goffi, ed., *Problemi e Prospettive di Teologia Morale* (Brescia: Queriniana, 1976) 289–314. Don Saliers has been at the forefront of developing the relationship between liturgy and ethics, see his 'Liturgy and Ethics: Some New Beginnings', in E. Byron Anderson and Bruce Morrill, eds, *Liturgy and the Moral Self: Humanity at Full Stretch Before God* (Collegeville: Liturgical Press, 1998) 15–37; Also Philippe Bordeyne and Bruce Morrill, *Sacraments: Revelation of the Humanity of God – Engaging the Fundamental Theology of Louis-Marie Chauvet* (Collegeville: Liturgical Press, 2008).

61 Marciano Vidal's *Nueva Moral Fundamental: El hogar teológico de la Ética* (Bilbao: Desclée de Brouwer, 2000).

62 *Optatam Totius*, 28 October 1965, para. 16: http://www.vatican.va/archive/hist_councils/ii_vatican_council/documents/vat-ii_decree_19651028_optatam-totius_en.html.

63 Josef Fuchs, 'Theologia moralis perficienda; votum Concilii Vaticani II', *Periodica de re morali, canonica, liturgica* 55 (1966) 499–548 (in English: 'Moral Theology According to Vatican II', *Human Values and Christian Morality*) (Dublin: Gill and Macmillan, 1970) 1–55; see also, Paulinus Ikechukwu Odozor, who begins his book with the passage as well: *Moral Theology in an Age of Renewal: A Study of the Catholic Tradition Since Vatican II* (Notre Dame: University of Notre Dame Press, 2003) 1; see also his discussion of the Council, 17–43.

64 Häring also assisted in other documents, among them the chapters on the laity and the call to holiness in *Lumen Gentium* and the oft-quoted paragraph 16 from *Optatam Totius*.

65 Charles Curran, 'Bernhard Häring: A Moral Theologian Whose Soul Matched His Scholarship', *National Catholic Reporter* 34 (17 July 1998) 11.

66 Philippe Bordeyne, *L'Homme et son angoisse: La Theologie Morale de 'Gaudium et Spes'* (Paris: Cerf, 2004).

67 Besides Bordeyne, Josef Römelt advanced Häring's project on interdisciplinary co-operation between ethics and the social sciences, see his '*Fides quarens Scientiam*,

Das Gespräch Bernhard Härings mit den Humanwissenschaften am Beispiel der Ethik der Familie und der Bioethik', *50 Jahre*, 93–114; Aniceto Molinaro, 'Scienze Umane, Filosofia, Etica', in Tullo Goffi and Giannino Piana, eds, *Vita Nuova in Cristo: Morale fondamentale e generale* (Brescia: Queriniana, 1983) 39–76.

68 *Gaudium et Spes*, 7 December 1965, para. 16: http://www.vatican.va/archive/hist_councils/ii_vatican_council/documents/vat-ii_cons_19651207_gaudium-et-spes_en.html. See Sabatino Maiorano, 'Coscienza e Verità Morale nel Vaticano II', *La Coscienza Morale Oggi* 29–271. See Terence Kennedy, 'L'idea di coscienza morale secondo S. Tommaso D'Aquino', 145–76; Karl Golser, 'La coscienza, concetto chiave di una pastorale della misericordia', ibid., 553–73.

69 Josef Fuchs, ed., *Das Gewissen* (Düsseldorf: Patmos Verlag, 1979); Charles E. Curran, ed., *Readings in Moral Theology No. 14: Conscience* (Mahwah: Paulist Press, 2004).

70 Eric D'Arcy, *Conscience and its Right to Freedom* (London: Sheed and Ward, 1961); Linda Hogan, *Confronting the Truth: Conscience in the Catholic Tradition* (Darton, Longman and Todd, and Paulist Press, 2001); Kevin Kelly, *Conscience: Dictator or Guide* (London: Geoffrey Chapman, 1967); Anne Patrick, *Liberating Conscience* (New York: Continuum, 1997); Herbert Schlögel, *Nicht Moralisch, Sondern Theologisch: Zum Gewissenverständnis von Gerhard Ebeling* (Mainz: Matthias-Grünewald Verlag, 1992); Osamu Takeuchi, *Conscience and Personality* (Chiba, Japan: Kyoyusha, 2003); Paul Valadier, *Éloge de la conscience.* Other essays by moral theologians include Richard Gula, 'Conscience', *Christian Ethics*, 110–22; William E. May, 'Conscience Formation and the Teaching of the Church', Ronald Hamel and Kenneth Himes, eds, *Introduction to Christian Ethics* (Mahwah: Paulist Press, 1989) 397–406. On pastoral connections with moral theology through conscience, see Dennis Billy and James Keating, *Conscience and Prayer: The Spirit of Catholic Moral Theology* (Collegeville: Liturgical Press, 2001); Sidney Callahan, *In Good Conscience* (New York: HarperCollins, 1991); Charles Shelton, *Morality of the Heart* (New York: Crossroad, 1990).

71 Todd A. Salzman and Michael G. Lawler, *The Sexual Person: Toward a Renewed Catholic Anthropology* (Washington, DC: Georgetown University Press, 2008) 41–7.

72 Kevin T. Kelly, 'Divorce and Remarriage', *A Call to Fidelity*, 97–112, at 98–9. See also his *Divorce and Second Marriage: Facing the Challenge* (Kansas City, MO: Sheed & Ward, 1997); 'Divorce and Remarriage' *Christian Ethics*, 248–65; 'Divorce' in Adrian Hastings et al., eds, *The Oxford Companion to Christian Thought* (Oxford: Oxford University Press, 2000) 172–3.

73 See John O'Malley, *What Happened at Vatican II?* (Cambridge: Harvard University Press, 2008) 284–9; Jan Grootaers and Jan Jans, *La regulation des naissances à Vatican II: Une semaine de crise* (Leuven: Peeters, 2002).

74 Mathijs Lamberigts and Leo Kenis, eds, *Vatican II and its Legacy* (Leuven: Leuven University Press, 2002, hereafter *Vatican II*); Enrico Chiavacci, 'La Riflessione Cristiana sul Sociale Nella *Gaudium et Spes*', *Teologia Morale Fondamentale*, 279–92.

75 Joseph A. Selling, '*Gaudium et Spes:* A Manifesto for Contemporary Moral Theology', *Vatican II*, 145–62.

76 Georges De Schrijver, '*Gaudium et Spes* on the Church's Dialogue with Contemporary Society and Culture: A Seedbed for the Divergent Options Adopted at Medellín, Puebla, and Santo Domingo', *Vatican II*, 289–327.

77 Mary Elsbernd, 'The Reinterpretation of *Gaudium et Spes* in *Veritatis Splendor*', *Vatican II*, 187–205, at 188; also published in *Horizons* 29 (2002) 225–39. See also

Herminio Rico, *John Paul II and the Legacy of Dignitatis Humanae* (Washington, DC: Georgetown University Press, 2002).

78 Elsbernd, 201.

79 Charles E. Curran, *Loyal Dissent: Memoir of a Catholic Theologian* (Washington, DC: Georgetown University Press, 2007) 14.

80 Louis Janssens, 'Morale conjugale et progestogènes', *Ephemerides Theolgicae Lovanieneses* (1963) 787–826.

81 Francis Swift, 'An Analysis of the American Theological Reaction to Janssens' Stand on The Pill', *Louvain Studies* 1 (1966) 19–54.

82 Curran, ed., *Absolutes in Moral Theology?* (Washington, DC: Corpus Books, 1968).

83 Curran, *A New Look at Christian Morality* (Notre Dame: Fides Press, 1968).

84 The text can be found in Gregory Baum, 'Introduction', in Ambrogio Valsecchi, *Controversy: The Birth Control Debate 1958–1968* (Washington, DC: Corpus Books, 1968) xi–xii.

85 Curran, *New Perspectives in Moral Theology* (Notre Dame: Fides Press, 1974); *Ongoing Revision: Studies in Moral Theology* (Notre Dame: Fides Press, 1975); *Themes in Fundamental Moral Theology* (Notre Dame: University of Notre Dame Press, 1977); *Transition and Tradition in Moral Theology* (Notre Dame: University of Notre Dame Press, 1979).

86 Curran, *Contemporary Problems in Moral Theology* (Notre Dame: Fides Press, 1970); *Medicine and Morals* (Washington, DC: Corpus Books, 1970); *Issues in Sexual and Medical Ethics* (Notre Dame: University of Notre Dame Press, 1978).

87 Curran, *Faithful Dissent* (Kansas City: Sheed and Ward, 1986). See Hans Küng and Jürgen Moltmann, eds, *The Right to Dissent* (New York: Seabury Press, 1982); Charles E. Curran and Richard A. McCormick, *Dissent in the Church* (Mahwah: Paulist Press, 1988).

88 Besides *Loyal Dissent*, on the matter of the investigation of Curran's writings see Richard McCormick, 'L'Affaire Curran', *The Critical Calling* (Washington, DC: Georgetown University Press, 1989) 111–30.

89 Curran, 'Method in Moral Theology: An Overview from an American Perspective', *Studia Moralia* 18 (1980) 107–28.

90 On Curran's method, see Keenan, 'The Moral Agent: Actions and Normative Decision Making', in James J. Walter, Timothy O'Connell and Thomas Shannon, eds, *A Call to Fidelity: On the Moral Theology of Charles E. Curran* (Washington: Georgetown University Press, 2002) 37–54 (hereafter *A Call to Fidelity*).

91 Curran, *The Catholic Moral Tradition Today: A Synthesis* (Georgetown University Press, 1999) 3.

92 See also Herbert Schlögel, 'Kirchenbilder in der Moraltheologie', *Stimmen der Zeit*, 210 (1992) 109–14; idem, 'In Medio Ecclesiae. Ekklesiologische Aspectke in der Moraltheologie', in Klaus Demmer and Karl-Heinz Ducke, eds, *Moraltheologie im Dienst der Kirche* (Leipzig: Benino, 1992) 57–67.

93 Curran, *The Catholic Moral Tradition Today*, 1.

94 Margaret Farley, 'Ethics, Ecclesiology, and the Grace of Self-Doubt', *A Call to Fidelity*, 55–77, at 69.

95 James Gustafson, 'Charles Curran: Ecumenical Moral Theologian Par Excellence', *A Call to Fidelity*, 211–34, at 214–15.

96 Raphael Gallagher, 'Curran's Fundamental Moral Theology in Comparison with European Catholic Approaches', *A Call to Fidelity*, 235–52, at 247.

97 See Curran's account, 'Life after Condemnation', *Loyal Dissent*, 161–86.

98 In recent years Curran published five other works with Georgetown University

Press: *The Origins of Moral Theology in the United States* (1997); *Catholic Social Teaching, 1891–Present: A Historical, Theological, and Ethical Analysis* (2002); *The Moral Theology of Pope John Paul II* (2005); *Loyal Dissent*; *Catholic Moral Theology in the United States: A History* (2008).

99 Marciano Vidal, *El nuevo rostro de la moral* (Madrid: Edic. Paulinas, 1976); *Modelos de una ética cristiana* (Madrid: Mañana, 1977); *Moral del matrimonio* (Madrid: Perpetuo Socorro, PS, D.L., 1980); *Ética civil y sociedad democrática* (Madrid: Desclée de Brouwer, 1984); *Familia y valores éticos* (Madrid: Promoción Popular Cristiana, 1986); *Crisis de la institución matrimonial: hechos, causas, orientación* (Madrid: Fundación Santa María, 1987); *Eutanasia: un reto a la conciencia* (Madrid: San Pablo, 1994); *Moral de opción fundamental y de actitudes* (Madrid: San Pablo, 1995).

100 http://www.iscm.edu/Curriculum%20Vidal.htm.

101 Vidal, *Frente al rigorismo moral, benignidad pastoral: Alfonso de Liguori* (1696–1787) (Madrid: Perpetuo Socorro, 1986); 'La "Praxis": Rasgo caracteristico de la moral alfonsiana y reto a la teologia moral actual', *Studia Moralia* 25.2 (1987) 299–326); 'S. Alfonsus de Liguori morallista: Significato storico e messagio attuale', *Historia: Memoria Futuri*, 275–301.

102 Vidal, 'Morale cristiana e cultura', in L. Alvarez-Verdes and Sebastian Majorano, eds, *Morale e redenzione* (Rome: Academia Alfonsiana, 1983) 95–127.

103 Vidal, *Moral de Actitudes: Moral Fundamental; Moral de la Persona y Bioetica Teologica; Moral del Amor y de la Sexualidad; Moral Social* (Madrid: Perpetuo Socorro, 1981).

104 Vidal, *Diccionario de Ética Teológica* (Madrid: Divino Verbo, 1991).

105 Vidal, *La propuesta moral de Juan Pablo II: comentario teológico-moral de la encíclica 'Veritatis splendor'* (Madrid: PPC, 1994).

106 http://www.ciberiglesia.net/discipulos/04/04actualidad_marciano_vidal.htm.

107 Cardinal Joseph Ratzinger, 'Notification regarding certain writings of Fr. Marciano Vidal, C.Ss.R.', (16 May 2001) 6–7: http://www.vatican.va/roman_curia/congregations/cfaith/documents/rc_con_cfaith_doc_20010515_vidal_en.html.

108 Ibid.

109 Benjamín Forcano and José Antonio Lobo, 'Intervista a M. Vidal', *Rivista di Teologia Morale* 137 (2003) 113–22.

110 Marciano Vidal, *Nueva Moral Fundamental: El Hogar Teológico de la Ética* (Biblioteca Manual Desclée, Bilbao: Desclée de Brouwer, 2000).

111 See his 'Progress in the Moral Tradition', *CEHP*, 257–70.

112 Vidal, 'Por qué he escrito una "Nueva" Teologia Morale', *Moralia* 23 (2000) 513–26.

113 John O'Malley developed this term, 'The Style of Vatican II', *America*, 188.6 (24 February 2003) 12–15.

114 M. Rubio, V. García and V. Gómez Mier, eds, *La ética cristiana hoy: horizontes de sentido, Homenaje a Marciano Vidal* (Madrid: Perpetuo Socorro, 2003) 44.

115 Patricia Lamoureux, 'The Criterion of Option for the Poor and Moral Discernment: The visions of Marciano Vidal García', *Louvain Studies*, 21 (1996) 261–87.

6

The Neo-Manualists

Developments in moral theology are prompted not only by moral theologians but also by those in dogmatic, or what is later known as systematic theology. Theologians like Yves Congar, Karl Rahner, and Edward Schillebeeckx provided a number of foundations for moral theology, on topics such as Christ, the Church, magisterial authority, and love. But in the English-speaking world, starting in the 1950s the Canadian Bernard Lonergan offered a host of insights into a new epistemology.[1] Foundational to his work was the turn to the subject.

In that turn Lonergan wanted to discuss not only how it affects our anthropology, but also our Christology.[2] In 1967, three articles were published that profoundly affected our understanding of moral truth: 'The Dehellenization of Dogma', 'The Transition from a Classicist World-View to Historical-Mindedness', and 'Theology in its New Context'.[3] Over the next 30 years these three essays would influence moral theology considerably.[4] Lonergan's distinction between the classicist and the historicist became foundational. These distinctions were not differences in kind, however, but in degree; no one is a pure classicist or historicist.

For classicists, the world is a finished product and truth has already been revealed, expressed, taught, and known. In order to be a truth it must be universal and unchanging. Clarity is key. Its logic is deductive: we apply the principle to the situation and we derive an answer from the syllogism.

The moral law is found, then, in that which is always true, never changes, and always applies. The truth-claims of a statement are demonstrated when we can claim possession of the same truth for centuries: consistency in historical transmission generates phrases like, 'As we have always taught . . .' Change in moral teaching is, then, problematic; it suggests that at one point a teaching was right and, in a later (or earlier) instance, wrong. Similarly, classicists resist contextualization. The truth cannot be compromised by local claims; if it is, it is dismissed as culturally relativistic. The universality and constancy of the truth-claim is central.

Four other assumptions must be understood. First, classicists identify God's characteristics with those of God's will and God's law. As God is, so is God's teaching. God is eternal, unchanging, universally the same. Similarly, God's willed teachings have the same qualities. Second, the Church is the guardian of that deposit of the truth; her leaders cannot change church teaching because they must not undermine God's will. Their role is to promote and proclaim again and again the constant teaching of the Church. Third, for this reason the credibility of the Church is known for its constancy; were the Church to change established teaching, it would jeopardize the grounds of confidence that the faithful have in her. Fourth, the reason why people do not adhere to the truth is not because they do not or cannot understand it, or that it is unreasonable. Rather, the innate weaknesses and wickedness of human beings hinder their ability to follow the law of God. Thus call for reform of the law is a charade. No one wants to reform the law but rather to abandon its claim on us.

A fine example of these presuppositions being operative in church teaching can be found in Pius XI's encyclical *Casti Connubii* (1930) which upheld a clear classicism in the teachings on marriage, and in particular, the practice of contraception. The Pope writes:

> Since, therefore, openly departing from the uninterrupted Christian tradition some recently have judged it possible solemnly to declare another doctrine regarding this question, the Catholic Church, to whom God has entrusted the defense of the integrity and purity of morals, standing erect in the midst of the moral ruin which surrounds her, in order that she may preserve the chastity of the nuptial union from being defiled by this foul stain, raises her voice in token of her divine ambassadorship and through Our mouth proclaims anew: any use whatsoever of matrimony exercised in such a way that the act is deliberately frustrated in its natural power to generate life is an offense against the law of God and of nature, and those who indulge in such are branded with the guilt of a grave sin.[5]

Elsewhere, the Pope demonstrably argued that the Church unhesitatingly maintained the continuity of these teachings, by turning to a similar position by his predecessor Leo XIII.

> It is a divinely appointed law that whatsoever things are constituted by God, the Author of nature, these we find the more useful and salutary, the more they remain in their natural state, unimpaired and unchanged; inasmuch as God, the Creator of all things, intimately knows what is suited to the constitution and the preservation of each, and by his will and mind has so ordained all this that each may duly achieve its purpose. But if the boldness and wickedness of men change and disturb this order of things, so providentially disposed, then, indeed, things so wonderfully

> ordained, will begin to be injurious, or will cease to be beneficial, either because, in the change, they have lost their power to benefit, or because God Himself is thus pleased to draw down chastisement on the pride and presumption of men.[6]

As popes in the twentieth century tended toward classicism, so did a few of their theologians. Ann Patrick disputes the classical paradigm of Roman Catholic moral theology; she notes its defense of intrinsic evil, its intolerance of circumstances and of particularity, its suspicion of the subject, and its promotion of moral objectivity as universal and unchangeable. These foundational concepts are a platform for an ecclesiology that assures its members that objective truth is found not in the particularity of a member's insight and experience, but in the constant teachings of the Church. In turn, it promotes a uniform identity for its members and at the same time inhibits the original competency of the individual conscience.[7]

Historical-minded theologians look at the world and at truth as constantly emerging. They argue that we are learning more, not only about the world, but about ourselves. As subjects we are affected by history: we become hopefully the people whom we are called to become. What the world and humanity will be is not yet known, but rests on the horizons of our expectations and the decisions we make and realize. The moral law then looks to determine what at this period corresponds to the vision we ought to be shaping. It admits that the final word on the truth is outstanding but emerging.

Contrary to their detractors, historicists do not argue that truth is constructed or manufactured; rather truth is 'discovered' in history by historical persons. Truth has its objectivity, but it is only gradually being grasped by us in our judgment over time, through experience, and with maturity.

Moreover, though historicists believe in the importance of the situation and of circumstances, they are not situational ethicists. That ethics developed by Joseph Fletcher argued that the moral agent has no mediating norms between the self and the concrete: only the law of love is to be radically expressed in the here and now. We have seen, however, from Lottin to Curran, that every revisionist believed in the need for mediating moral guidance through the stance and values that we need for right acting.[8]

Experience differentiates the two perspectives of classicism and historicism. The manualists did little to recognize and incorporate human experience, though the confessors themselves did. When it comes to moral teaching, classicists see experience as an attempt to diminish the truth-claims of an evident teaching. Historicists are anxious, however, about whether they adequately grasp and understand human experience.

Historicists are suspicious of deductive logic; in their estimation, real truth is found through analogy. They believe that truth is found by comparing one situation to another. They are modest about their judgments and assertions, and usually quite tentative about any truth-claim; they tend away from clarity and entertain circumstances as significantly and substantively relevant. The particularity of the situation is key.

Historicists, then, are much more inclined to context. As we saw in the previous chapter, they are more inclined to values and visions. Unlike the manualists, they accept change in teaching on usury, capital punishment, or contraception when that change illustrates a greater approximation to the law of love. Like Lottin, Vereecke, and Mahoney, they enjoy studying the history of church teaching, to see how the community of faith tries to understand from one generation to another the values and visions of moral truth.

In sum, the classical worldview depends on what is already known; historical-mindedness responds to the knower: our ability to recognize the truth as it emerges through the data of experience very much depends on our own moral nature. Following Aristotle, historicists acknowledge that we see reality as we are.

Furthermore, if we remember that these are differences not in kind but in degree, then we can appreciate that no period and no work is relentlessly attached to one perspective: while Plato was classically fixed on his ideas and forms, Heraclitus was very historical-minded. When we turn to the Bible, the texts seem fairly historicist, in part because each book unveils revelation and because humanity is slow to understand. Still, its basic truths are eternal.

Third, the governing notions of objectivity are, nonetheless, very different, not only about history and universality but also about the agent. For the classicist, the agent does not enter into the equation of moral truthfulness: the moral truth remains the same for all. If I want to know the truth, I should be as detached from the situation as possible. For the historicists, the agent is integrally involved in the morally objective judgment.

Finally, the Church's identity is deeply affected by its self-understanding as moral teacher. Inasmuch as it understands itself in the classicist mode, it will resist innovation as beyond its competency, where teachings have already been defined. These teachings sometimes limit the ambit of papal options. A fine example of this stance can be found in Pope John Paul II's teaching on women's ordination to the priesthood:

> Although the teaching that priestly ordination is to be reserved to men alone has been preserved by the constant and universal Tradition of the Church and firmly taught by the Magisterium in its more recent documents, at the present time in some places it is nonetheless considered still open to debate, or the Church's judgment that women are not to be admitted to ordination is considered to have a merely disciplinary force.
>
> Wherefore, in order that all doubt may be removed regarding a matter of great importance, a matter which pertains to the Church's divine constitution itself, in virtue of my ministry of confirming the brethren (cf. Lk 22.32) I declare that the Church has no authority whatsoever to confer priestly ordination on women and that this judgment is to be definitively held by all the Church's faithful.[9]

The distinction between classicism and historicism plays out in the Catholic Church throughout the second half of the twentieth century.

John Ford (1902–89) and Gerald Kelly (1902–64)

The revisionists, especially Lottin and Häring, were strong historicists and their opponents were usually classicists. One pair of theologians who staunchly opposed these innovations were John Ford and Gerald Kelly, American Jesuit casuists who wrote the 'Notes in Moral Theology' for *Theological Studies* from 1941 to 1954. They were ardent defenders of the classical nature of the moral law. For instance, in a 1958 lecture on natural law, Ford taught:

> Given a principle of natural law, firmly established, e.g. 'parricide is immoral', it is valid for all men, at all times, in all places, and if the proposition is stated with sufficient precision, in all circumstances. There are no exempt days, no exempt territory. There is no such thing as a moral holiday where natural law is concerned.[10]

Their classicism could work very positively. The distinction between ordinary and extraordinary means of life support could be firmly and universally taught and gave individual Catholics considerable latitude when facing end-of-life issues. A strong, absolute prohibition against direct killing gave a broad ambit to Catholics to consider withholding or withdrawing treatment when facing painful death. Similarly, in advocating against war-time atrocities, the clarity of the law and its historical consistency empowered them to take unwavering stances when others hesitated or looked the other way.

However, that same unchanging clarity could stand without apology or explanation against any form of contraception, even when there was clear evidence that the teaching on the question had previously changed and that assumptions about responsible parenthood were again radically changing.[11]

For all their classicism, there was certainly a fair amount of complexity about these two Jesuits. Kelly, for instance, can rightly be called the father of medical ethics, because of his teachings on ordinary and extraordinary means of life support. In 1950, for instance, he asked whether oxygen and intravenous feeding had to be used to preserve the life of a patient in a terminal coma and argued: 'I see no reason why even the most delicate professional standard should call for their use. In fact, it seems to me that, apart from very special circumstances, the artificial means not only need not but also should not be used, once the coma is reasonably diagnosed as terminal. Their use creates expense and nervous strain without conferring any real benefit.'[12]

Ford, a moral theologian at Weston School of Theology, became well known for an electrifying essay against obliteration bombing, right in the crucible of the Second World War, that is, in 1944.[13] Ford did what his European colleagues on either side of the war did not do: criticize and condemn the saturation bombing of cities. In this as in many matters, Ford was singular.

These were two very credible manualists looking to preserve manualism. In 1964, their two-volume *Contemporary Moral Theology* served as an example of the classicist's resistance to the historical-minded model.[14]

They were also zealous in looking to Rome for moral teaching. Though Davis and Jone expressed a certain respect for the frequent teachings coming from Rome, Ford and Kelly developed an actual theology about the theologian, not primarily as searching for the moral truth but as receiving it from Rome. Ford and Kelly were not at all like Slater, Davis or Jone. One reads a certain exasperation in the latter's attempts at keeping up with the Vatican declarations. In Ford and Kelly we find instead an ever-expanding welcome and, even, an encouragement for such papal exercises.

Ford and Kelly believed that the first place to look for a moral problem is to Rome: 'The principal approach to any theological treatise should be the teaching of the magisterium, especially of the Holy See itself, when such teaching is available.'[15] These were fundamental claims: for instance, in 1964 they commented on the difference between ethics and moral theology: 'Moral Theology studies man in the supernatural order, possessed of a spiritual destiny; it is a science based not only on reason – nor principally on reason – but especially on revelation and on the teaching of the church. Reason is the supreme argument in ethics; authority is the sovereign guide of the theologian.'[16]

Ford and Kelly were convinced that Rome was the only authentic interpreter of the laws of God. 'It is only through conformity with the teaching of the Church that the individual conscience can have security from error. The "autonomy of the individual conscience" cannot be reconciled with the plan of Christ and can produce only "poisonous fruit".'[17]

Since Rome set the agenda, they never accorded Rome more authority than Rome claimed. Prior to *Humanae Vitae*, each challenged other moral theologians who claimed that Rome prohibited more than Rome did. For instance, in 1959 a theologian argued that 'documents of the Holy See have convinced me that "rhythm" cannot be recommended as a Christian solution for overpopulation. In my opinion Rome has spoken and the case is settled.' Ford responded, 'Rome has not spoken.'[18]

When Rome had not yet defined or resolved a matter, moralists were free to offer their opinions. Ford offered his regularly. Of course, this was not Ford seizing illicit authority, but rather, again, Ford following the Roman agenda.

Eric Genilo notes, however, that Ford generally offered more than an opinion, and when he did, his argument was far more historicist than classicist, as for instance, speaking on selective conscientious objection.[19] His historicism was even more evident in his writings on alcoholism, which he argued was primarily a physical and not a moral disability. One commentator writes that on this topic Ford abandoned a legalistic sin-centered approach and instead offered one grounded in both 'a biblical, creation-centered perspective and in ascetical sources that spoke in a more modern idiom of virtue and attention to rightly-ordered and disordered relationships'.[20]

The only instance where Ford publicly overstepped the Roman agenda was when he was frustrated with the way *Humanae Vitae* was received and attributed to the teaching an infallible status. This status was not invoked by Pope Paul VI, nor by any of his successors or even the Congregation for the Doctrine of the Faith.[21]

With this exception aside, Ford and Kelly *always* let Rome take the lead: 'To fulfill his acknowledged duty of explaining the papal teaching, a theologian must in some measure interpret it; and all that can be reasonably demanded of him is that he follow sound theological norms of interpretation.'[22]

Today most contemporary moral theologians, following Häring, interpret magisterial utterances critically within the context of the entire tradition. Ford and Kelly did not employ any such critical reception; their hermeneutics of interpretation was completely dependent on whatever authority the magisterium claimed.

Ford and Kelly inverted the order of authority that the high casuists used. The former recognized the external authority of the papacy and of Roman dicasteries *before and, in fact, sometimes without* considering the internal authority of the argument. They used no critical reason *vis-à-vis* a magisterial utterance; that a claim was magisterial (external authority) was, for Ford and Kelly, itself the guarantor of its truthfulness. Thus, 'in interpreting them [papal pronouncements], [the moral theologian] should have read . . . especially for the papal intention as manifested in the historical context of the pronouncements'.

To look for moral truth, all the moral theologian had to do is listen to the propositional utterances from Rome and then explain them. 'Theologians have the same duty as the faithful in general to give the religious assent required by papal teaching . . . as a theologian he must study the papal pronouncements and incorporate them into his teaching and writing.'[23]

Their dependence on the agenda Rome sets was summarized in a stunning statement:

> An earnest student of papal pronouncements, Vincent A. Yzermans, estimated that during the first fifteen years of his pontificate Pius XII gave almost one thousand public addresses and radio messages. If we add to these the apostolic constitutions, the encyclicals and so forth, during the same period of fifteen years, and add furthermore all the papal statements during the subsequent years, we have well over a thousand papal documents . . . Merely from the point of view of volume, therefore, one can readily appreciate that it was not mere facetiousness that led a theologian to remark, that even if the Holy See were to remain silent for ten years, the theologians would have plenty to do in classifying and evaluating the theological significance of Pius XII's public statements.[24]

Ford and Kelly's approach was eventually critiqued by their peers. In a lengthy review of the second volume of their work, Daniel Callahan described the authors as 'loyal civil servants' and 'faithful party workers' and dismissed their work 'as years behind the (theological) revolution now in progress'.[25]

The hierarchy as neo-manualist teachers

As more moral theologians turned to the person to find moral truth, the hierarchy began to teach even more frequently using the methodology of the manualists. Like the manualists, popes and bishops believed that moral truth was found primarily in norms and principles. While moral theologians were searching for truth-to-be-realized in the lives of Christians, hierarchical leaders were still thinking of truth as propositional, since this is what they had learned from their manualist teachers in seminary days. Furthermore, popes and bishops began to consider themselves as competent in moral matters. At first they commented on social issues, speaking as social ethicists would, but by the papacy of Pius XII, popes and bishops were writing about birth control, abortion, pain relief, life support, ectopic pregnancies, and a host of other issues.

Likewise, they began to assert the claim that consistency was a constitutive guarantor of the truthfulness of their claims and began to preserve their own teachings as normative by citing them, updating them and commenting on them. Progressively, throughout the century, popes, bishops, and curial officials promulgated moral teachings in a variety of fields: fundamental, medical, sexual, and social ethics. Like the moral manuals that were commentaries on earlier important manualists' summaries, church documents became commentaries on predecessors' utterances. A central feature of any contemporary papal or episcopal document was and is the frequent citation of previous teaching moments by such authorities. The same self-generating and self-validating practices that the manualists used for three centuries became the tools of twentieth-century popes and bishops. The positivism that emerged from the manualists likewise emanated from these documents – David Kelly calls it an 'ecclesiastical positivism'.[26]

From the Council of Trent through the mid-twentieth century, papal, episcopal, and curial offices generally responded to any petitions regarding newly admitted circumstantial questions by directing petitioners to the judgments of 'approved' manualists. But with the repudiation of the manuals by moralists themselves, papal, episcopal, and curial offices began giving their own answers; and along the way, with the exception of certain social statements, most of these judgments were, not surprisingly, about actions to be avoided.

With time, other episcopal leaders looked less to their own moral theologians and with greater frequency turned to the very office that appointed them to their positions. By the end of the twentieth century, bishops saw the pope and his curial officials (and themselves) as competent to decide moral matters.

Not surprisingly, just as for three centuries moral truth had been identified in this context with the utterances of the manualists, so in the twentieth century, with this emerging moral magisterium, moral truth became identified with papal and episcopal utterances.[27]

These papal teachings enjoyed evident similarities with the manualists' work, but they departed from that tradition in four significant ways. First, manualists belonged to differing schools of interpretation. Often, Jesuits were different from Redemptorists and Dominicans, yet even within these orders there were differences among individual manualists. With a papal magisterium there were no alternative viewpoints, nor was there the constitutive structural tolerance that manualists observed. Second, following from this, probabilism allowed local pastors and their laity the freedom to choose from among the manualists, but pastors today have no such choice about these new papal, curial, and episcopal teachings, not only because the papal magisterium claims the highest authority for its argument, but also because inevitably papal, curial, and episcopal office has the actual power to compel assent, something that manualists never had. Third, popes and curial bishops are usually not trained in moral theology and their competency derives basically from the advisers they appoint. Finally, moral manualists were never guardians of the Church's identity, and therefore did not confuse the need for a community's historical identity with the need to determine their own moral claims as truthful.

In light of these differences, popes and bishops assumed a competency from their self-understanding as guarantors of the moral truth of the communities that they shepherded. Inevitably, the statements of popes, bishops, and curial officials reflected the judgment of someone who knew moral theology only to the extent that he allowed himself to be influenced by competent consultants. Much here depends on whether the bishop chooses an adviser with adequate training, who can understand and express professionally and fairly the viewpoints of his colleagues. The fact that many continue to follow a method based on the belief that moral truth is found in utterances about external actions, and often derive 'expert' advice from those considerably at odds with recent developments in moral theology, suggests that for all the good will in the world, a fair understanding of the claims of most contemporary moral theologians is nearly impossible.

Thus, the moral theologians' critical abandonment of the method of the manualists and the papal, episcopal, and curial decisions to replace the manualists, has had an extraordinary effect. The scientific research of moral theologians – that is, their continuous search for critical moral truth – goes on in the precincts of their own investigations: in their classrooms, their publications, and their conferences. But in an entirely different way, church teaching emerges more interested in order and uniformity than in critique and diversity, more interested in consistency and universality than in the contextual questions, more willing to suppress moral beliefs, differences, and exceptions for the sake of identity. The reason for this is that church officials are simply not convinced that the moral theologians' methods can provide the needed guidance and certainty for the laity that these officials believe ought to be offered.

Moral teaching, then, is presently taking place and developing on two different tracks. One pursues moral truth in the person of Christ and the realization of that truth in the very human lives of Christians; the other, in specific and (possibly) long-held propositional utterances. The gulf between these two tracks widens. For instance, those who advise magisterial authority participate less frequently in professional conferences of moral theologians, at which most moral theologians present their research for scientific critique. They are, instead, more at the disposition of those officials who rely on their judgments not only to write statements of instruction, but also to review, to estimate, and, if they deem it necessary, to censure the work of contemporary moral theologians.

Humanae Vitae

Before the Council, with the exception of a few revisionists, Ford and Kelly's belief in the frailty of reason and the surety of church teaching was fairly pervasive. For instance, the German Jesuit teaching at Rome's Gregorian University, Josef Fuchs (1912–2005) had published a work on the natural law in 1955 that garnered immediate attention and international praise. In his work, he wrote: 'We have an adequate knowledge of the meaning and order of sexuality, the essence and duties of married life, of temporal goods and their place in social and individual life.'[28] Thus the magisterium's 'duty within the actual order of salvation is to form the consciences of all men, primarily those in charge of public life'.[29]

Still, from 1957 moral theologians were publishing articles about birth control, and a variety of questions was being raised. Theologians allied with very different approaches to the question. Often the distinctions among theologians would seem minuscule to the lay reader, but in the long run these essays and the debates they generated were in many ways the prelude to the papal commission on birth control.[30]

During the first meetings of the papal commission which Pope John XXIII established, Häring and others were thought to be tending toward reform of the teaching on birth control. Purportedly, in an effort to counterbalance their attempts, Pope Paul VI appointed a number of more conservative archbishops, bishops and theologians to the commission, among them Fuchs. On the commission, Fuchs began listening to the testimony of married couples and eventually abandoned his conviction that moral truth was founded necessarily and primarily in long-held norms articulated by the magisterium.

In Fuchs' own life, we find that the shift of locating truth not in propositions but in persons was not a simple intellectual one. Moral theologians did not come to these convictions through simple meditations, but rather from seminal experiences. By listening to others, Fuchs slowly recognized that his original supposition was inadequate, and began to explore critically a key question posed by Karl Rahner: whether the method of directly applying a norm to a case is also adequate for determining moral truth. If that question were posed to Josef Fuchs in 1952, his answer would have been a resounding yes; by 1968, it was an equally decisive no.[31]

Beyond the singular issue of birth control, Fuchs reassessed his entire understanding of moral theology. He realized that the competency of a moral decision depended on the ability to consider adequately the various claims on an agent. From the testimonies of married couples, he saw that their understanding of the various claims on them was more comprehensive and more adequate than the general teachings of Rome. Fuchs acknowledged here that one found moral truth through the discernment of an informed conscience confronting reality.

Fuchs' intellectual conversion became an important impetus for others. Let me cite two significant examples of the impact Fuchs' conversion had on others. Recently Jack Mahoney, author of *The Making of Moral Theology*, recounted to me a meeting of Jesuit moral theologians in 1964. Each year these moralists gathered at Shrub Oak, the Jesuit philosophy school in New York State. They would discuss many and very diverse cases and would poll each for his opinion on the topic. At this meeting, there were 30 to 35 Jesuit moralists, including Richard McCormick, Gerald Kelly, Cal Poulin, John Connery and others (Ford was in Europe at the time). When they turned to the topic of birth control, they did not question the birth control teaching from *Casti Connubii*. Instead they took the case of whether a woman could use the birth control pill to regulate her menstrual cycle, a position that most moralists thought was morally debatable. One Jesuit priest after another gave his opinion, but the last person to speak was Richard McCormick. He said, 'I hear Joe Fuchs is reconsidering his understanding of the morality of birth control.' Mahoney reports that there was an audible 'collective intake of breath'. Then, one after another, the Jesuits said, 'Can we talk about church teaching on birth control?' Josef Fuchs' change gave his brother Jesuits the permission to examine a topic that previously was off-limits.[32]

Second, on the commission, Fuchs was appointed by his peers to become the principal draftsman of the report that represented the views of fifteen of the nineteen theologians.[33] This report recognized that married persons in conscience needed to determine whether the serious issue of birth control ought to be a means toward realizing themselves as responsible parents. In presenting the report, Fuchs explained that the locus for finding moral truth had shifted from utterances to persons: 'Many confuse objective morality with the prescriptions of the Church . . . We have to realize that reality is what it is. And we grow to understand it with our reason, aided by law. We have to educate people to assume responsibility and not just to follow the law.'[34]

Later the commission's governing group of cardinals and bishops asked Fuchs why he had changed his entire understanding of moral decision-making. He responded by narrating his own doubts arising in 1963: how he stopped teaching for a year (1965–66) at the Gregorian University because he could not take responsibility for teaching a doctrine he did not accept; and how in 1965 he ordered the university press not to reprint his work *De Castitate*.[35] In light of his answers, the episcopal committee voted first on whether contraception is an intrinsic evil (nine, no; three, yes; three, abstentions) and then formally approved Fuchs' majority report.[36]

At the same time, John Ford was on the same commission. He had nominated the once conservative Fuchs to be on the commission and was surprised that Fuchs had become the leading spokesman for those endorsing change. Ford took two measures. He became the author of the minority report, a response to the majority report. He also, as Genilo reports from Ford's own journals, became an occasional visitor of Pope Paul VI, reminding him repeatedly that as Pope he had the responsibility to uphold the teaching of his predecessors. This position was not unique to Ford; both the Italian Franciscan Ermenegildo Lio from the Holy Office and the Pope's own personal theologian, Carlo Colombo, gave similar counsel.[37] These three theologians instructed Pope Paul VI that as Pope he did not have moral authority to overturn *Casti Connubii*.[38]

Reporting on one (23 November 1965) of his several audiences with the Pope, Ford wrote: 'He [Paul VI] wanted to know whether at least onanism (was) o.k. I said no . . . [Paul VI] kept asking? But wouldn't it be right to do this or that medically with the pill . . . He pressed the medical uses of the pill . . . I spoke of his conscience that prevents him from repudiating C.C. [*Casti Connubii*].'[39]

In 1988 Ford spoke publicly on another audience with the Pope, during which they discussed the positions being proposed on the commission.

> I did have the impression that he did not talk about the proponents of these new positions as though they were 'Formati Doctores' speaking about the faith. But when I said to Pope Paul, 'Are you ready to say that *Casti Connubii* can be changed?' Paul came alive and spoke with vehemence: 'No!' he said. He reacted exactly as though I was calling him a traitor to his Catholic belief.[40]

Eventually Pope Paul VI rejected the majority report.

> The conclusions arrived at by the commission could not be considered by Us as definitive and absolutely certain, dispensing Us from the duty of examining personally this serious question. This was all the more necessary because, within the commission itself, there was not complete agreement concerning the moral norms to be proposed, and especially because certain approaches and criteria for a solution to this question had emerged which were at variance with the moral doctrine on marriage constantly taught by the magisterium of the Church.[41]

Two central teachings appear in the encyclical. First, the Pope taught that no one could, through withdrawal or any other practice of birth control, attempt to inhibit the procreative possibilities of sexual intercourse: 'Each and every marital act must of necessity retain its intrinsic relationship to the procreation of human life.' Second, he based the teaching on another: the divinely willed connection between the unitive and procreative ends of the marital act: 'This particular doctrine, often expounded by the magisterium of the Church, is based on the inseparable connection, established by God, which man on his own initiative may not break, between the unitive significance and the procreative significance which are both inherent to the marriage act.'[42]

Much could be said about *Humanae Vitae*. We could look at the entire document for other noteworthy claims; we could look at the ways it was received, or not; we could consider the 'development' in doctrine wherein we move from the primary, procreative end of marriage in *Casti Connubii* to the assertion of *Humanae Vitae*'s the dual end of the unitive and the procreative. This has been covered, however, by numerous authors.[43] For our purposes, we should simply say that, with *Humanae Vitae*, we see a rejection of the revisionists' innovative approach and the first significant papal endorsement of neo-manualism after Vatican II.

With its publication, an inevitable collision between the two approaches to moral theology arose. Previously, proponents from one track did not deny the others' right to teach, but with the encyclical, the Pope claimed that the consciences of all the faithful must adhere to the continuous teaching of an utterance defined as universally, and absolutely, morally true. Thus, just as Ford assumed that the experts on the commission who entertained the possibility of changing *Casti Connubii* were no longer 'approved theologians', so did others.

In 1983 Fuchs provided some commentary on this phenomenon:

> Since the Council of Trent, but especially in the last century, a strong juridical understanding of the magisterium as 'demanding assent' has become central; this was not so earlier. According to this understanding, the moral theologians' task should be understood primarily and extensively as the scholarly reflection and confirmation of already existing magisterial directives in moral questions. This is how it is expressed above all in Pius XII's encyclical *Humani Generis* (1950). Even today, this understanding is widespread although the Second Vatican Council began to shift the emphasis by its reference to the whole People of God as bearer of the Holy Spirit.[44]

Fuchs' concern was that the neo-manualism of the magisterium lacked the tolerance and diversity of even the manualists themselves, and inhibited the Christian conscience and, thereby, moral truth. He stipulated four particular dangers. First, there was the tendency to positivism that 'can hinder the research of moral theology as well as the living process of the establishment of moral truth. This process is never definitively finished.' The second danger was the encouragement of the belief that we encounter God's instructions, made known through positive revelation, in concrete moral directives. The majority report that elucidated values for guiding married couples was rejected; the encyclical insisted instead on unchanging and prohibitive norms. Third was a 'cramping or narrowing of moral–theological reflection'. Finally, 'the situation sketched here is apt to promote a permanent "moral immaturity" in the establishment of moral truth (in L. Kohlberg's sense), or the formation of "super-egos" in Freud's sense – as one may observe in lay people, priests, moral theologians, and bishops'.[45]

In the wake of *Humanae Vitae* arose the question to whom did moral theologians owe their primary allegiance in the pursuit of moral truth in the Church? The answer to that question was dependent on understanding who or what the Church is. Vatican II had defined the Church not primarily as hierarchy but rather as 'People of God' and 'Body of Christ'; according to Yves Congar this change was fundamental for understanding the nature of the Church.[46]

Thus Fuchs argued that moral theologians

> . . . know that they are under obligation to the People of God . . . For it is the moral theologian's task in the Church to identify the relationships between ethos and moral ordinance with the faith, to undertake the hermeneutic reading of the Bible in the awareness of moral questions, to read hermeneutically the moral traditions (and their history) that have grown up in the course of time, to deepen and develop moral values, to establish moral principles and norms credibly and contextually, to clarify the significance for correct moral behavior of the findings of other sciences, to tackle newly arising moral problems, etc.[47]

Fuchs illustrated his point by citing a now famous defense. 'In the notorious case of Savonarola, a cardinal publicly admonished the Master of the Sacred Palace, Pier Paolo Giannerini (a Dominican like Savonarola) not to defend Savonarola so energetically, but to defend the Holy See. He received the reply: "My commission is to fight for the truth, and in this way to safeguard the honor of the Holy See".'[48]

Fuchs not only changed the locus of moral competency but also democratized the process of determining the morally right. For at least the past five centuries, the laity sought moral guidance not in the manualists' particular norms but rather in the judgments of their confessors who interpreted the judgments of their moral theologians. With Fuchs the individual agent is herself understood to be more competent to judge specifically about the course of moral action that she should take. This competency is based on the agent's familiarity with the details of the task before her: to know herself, to grasp the situation, to understand the significance of particular circumstances, and to appreciate the way actions redound to the person of the agent and to those for whom the agent is responsible. Recognizing these factors leads to recognizing the agent as a competent person for determining moral action.[49]

This democratization of moral decision-making was not, then, based on an ecclesiological vision. Fuchs was not intellectually converted because he believed that a true Church invited each of her members to an originality in moral decision-making. Rather, he believed that married lay persons were in fact more competent to judge the moral liceity of birth control in their particular marriages. They understood the nature of their particular marriage, the demands that their marriage had, and the persons to whom they were responsible. They also understood the significance that particular actions had in the context of their relationship. Prior to his conversion, Fuchs located competency to determine moral rightness in the traditional unchanging norms and the judgments of moral theologians who were modest custodians and interpreters of those truths. Through the commission he recognized the competency of the laity to better articulate objectively right judgment.

Other moral theologians defended *Humanae Vitae* (1968) by arguing that any change in church teaching would destabilize the laity's dependency on the teachings of the magisterium. They were not interested in knowing whether birth control was morally wrong but rather in maintaining the laity's confidence in the Church's guidance. For instance, the Irish Jesuit Bartholomew Kiely doubted an ordinary person's capabilities to reason well: with some statistical evidence he contended that most people are not adequately free of conflicting, subjective needs so as to make an objective moral decision. Encouraging people to depend on their own resources, that is, to weigh values and disvalues, is misleading and harmful; better to endorse existing, functional steadfast rules that will keep people from doing more harm than might occur were they left to their own devices.[50]

Kiely admits that in the here and now the steadfast rule might not actually always be right, but allowing for that mistake is better than promoting a moral chaos resulting from the irresponsible presumption that each person can reason on her own.[51] Kiely sacrifices moral objectivity in order to maintain a general sense of moral order in the person and in the community. Commenting in the *Osservatore Romano* on the Vatican's opposition to artificial contraception, reproductive technologies, and homosexual activity, Kiely sees in each case that the long-standing wisdom of the Church's teaching supersedes both an individual's experience and her own moral discernment. While Kiely does not prove that prudence resides in the Church's teachers, he argues that it is not in its members.[52]

Many were angry at the encyclical's teaching and in turn they voted with their feet. This was particularly the case with John Ford. For many years, John Ford and Weston School of Theology were somewhat synonymous: he was the embodiment of moral theology at the Jesuit seminary in the Massachusetts town. Gracious, big-hearted, and opinionated, Ford was easily identified with the place. In 1968, when Ford returned from Rome, he found that the Jesuit students boycotted his classes in protest at his role in the formulation of *Humanae Vitae*.[53] In that same year, the Jesuit provincial decided to move the School of Theology from Weston to the city of Cambridge. In light of that decision, Ford resigned. Ford did not want to see the seminary away from its Catholic setting and was set against having Weston rent classroom space on the campus of Episcopal Theological Seminary (ETS, later Episcopal Divinity School), while participating as a member of the Boston Theological Institute (BTI). He did not want to see Jesuit students taking courses at ETS, or worse, at Harvard Divinity School and Boston University. In Ford's mind, ecumenical ventures were not pertinent to and in fact undermined Catholic priestly formation.

Ten years after John Ford's resignation, I began my Master of Divinity degree at Weston. The moral theology faculty at the time was Sr Mary Emil Penet, IHM, David Hollenbach, SJ, and Edward Vacek, SJ. Each of the two Jesuits had done their doctoral studies at American non-Catholic universities, Yale and Northwestern respectively. Sr Mary Emil, or SME as we called her, taught the fundamental moral theology course and had been trained by Josef Fuchs. In a sense, she brought Fuchs to Weston. The high point of any lecture was when she shared with us a moral conundrum, and would recount how she went and asked Fuchs what he thought. She would begin the narrative, 'So I asked Fuchs . . .' At Weston, in 1979, Fuchs was a legend, and Ford was simply in people's memory. Or, so it seemed.

The irony of this shift should not be lost on the reader. It is hard to imagine any senior moralist having greater influence in the writing of *Humanae Vitae* than John Ford. It is equally hard to imagine any senior moralist more influential than Fuchs in galvanizing cardinals and bishops to consider changing the teaching on birth control. In Fuchs' Rome, Ford won; in Ford's Weston, Fuchs did.

Had Ford come to Cambridge in 1969 and taught in the Weston classrooms, in all likelihood he would have encountered ETS's own moral theologian, Joseph Fletcher, the father of situation ethics, whose landmark book on the topic in 1966 sold ten million copies! What would Weston and ETS have been like in its first year together, if the 'father' of *Humanae Vitae*, who insisted on the absolute universal applicability of church teaching on birth control, met the 'father' of an ethics that denied the universal norms and insisted on the radical uniqueness of the particular situation? The two effectively represented the two extremes of moral logic.

History did not go in that direction. Though Ford resigned with considerable anger and resentment, it is noteworthy that the first book on John Ford, a praiseworthy work, was Eric Genilo's. Genilo was once a Weston student mentored by me, Josef Fuchs' last student. In 1991, I succeeded SME and assumed the very teaching position held by John Ford at Weston.

A contemporary work: John Paul II's *Veritatis Splendor* (1993)[54]

If we were to consider a turn to a contemporary expression of neo-manualism, the philosopher Germain Grisez's (1929–) massive *The Way of the Lord* (1983) would be a worthy choice.[55] In three volumes he goes from basic principles, to Christian living, to difficult issues.

In 1964, Grisez authored *Contraception and Natural Law*.[56] Since then, he has sustained the neo-manualist stance for more than 30 years, and, as a close collaborator of John Ford, he has had a deep appreciation for its claims. For many of those years, he and Richard McCormick were engaged in a series of polemical arguments, starting with birth control and expanding through a series of sexual and reproductive issues, but eventually dealing with fundamental premises for a moral theology.

Grisez is also well known for his basic-goods theory and its expression as a new natural law theory; he developed these insights with two other philosophers, John Finnis[57] and Joseph Boyle.[58] In 1987, they wrote an essay on moral principles and a manuscript on the defense of nuclear deterrence. From then on, they did a series of essays and books, with the theologians John Ford and William E. May occasionally joining the threesome.[59] Together they proposed their natural law theory as consisting of seven incommensurable goods. They have generated discussion, mostly among Catholic philosophers, with the best known defense coming from Robert George[60] and the most stinging critique from Russell Hittinger.[61]

Interestingly, while most moral theologians followed the revisionism of Häring and Fuchs, only a few became neo-manualists. For the most part, neo-manualists were, like Pope John Paul II, trained philosophers. Not surprisingly, they were mostly influential during the years of John Paul II and, aside from the Opus Dei moral philosopher Martin Rhonheimer, their influence seemed to be mostly in the United States and the United Kingdom.

Much more influential was their most sustained critic, the moral theologian Richard McCormick.[62] McCormick was interested in more than debate with the neo-manualists, however; he was internationally influential for moderating the discussions on the 'moral notes' from 1965 to 1984 in *Theological Studies*. In these twenty essays, McCormick provided a bridge for moral theologians from the United States and Europe to understand and exchange with each other – no easy task, when the former were much more inclined to practical outcomes, and the latter more interested in the foundational concepts in the field.

To complement these contributions, together with Charles Curran he edited a multi-volume series of collections of internationally distinguished essays on particular topics in moral theology: from moral norms, the proprium of moral theology and the magisterium, to feminism and the development of moral doctrine.[63] In both the series and the 'moral notes', McCormick promoted an ongoing literacy among bishops, priests, theologians, and laity regarding recent innovations in theology.

Like Ford and Kelly, McCormick kept readers in the United States aware of magisterial thoughts and teachings, but unlike them he brought an easy, pragmatic, and empirical critique to these teachings, asking whether or not they resonated with the better ideas available today. He especially entered into the fray over matters of bioethics.[64] But he also was probably the best known advocate for the form of moral reasoning known as proportionalism.[65]

McCormick was an opponent of neo-manualism. If we want a contemporary expression of neo-manualism, no work in the 1990s better advances the movement than Pope John Paul II's *Veritatis Splendor*.[66] Though it was not a manual *per se*, still it was a reflection on the 'whole of the Church's moral teaching', with particular attention to the problematic separation of human freedom from the essence of truth. Above all it was critical of the interpretations of many conceptual claims made by the revisionists. In making many critiques, the encyclical identified no moral theologian as the object of its scrutiny.

Reactions to the encyclical were of three general kinds. First, a hearty welcome by hierarchy and others who found in the encyclical a worthy challenge to the pervasive culture of contemporary moral relativism. Second, an argument, notably from Redemptorists, claiming the pope's fundamental compatibility with revisionists, while making corrections of a few of their misinterpretations. Third, a lament by revisionists that they were misrepresented.

The encyclical is divided into three chapters. The first is a sustained reflection on the question of the rich young man, 'Teacher, what must I do?' (Matthew 19.16). This scriptural–ethical reflection echoed the themes in Fritz Tillmann: the call to discipleship as a call to perfection for all Christians, who need to have an interior virtuous self to follow Christ's law. Neo-manualists, however, would also see here the summons to follow the commandments and their principles constantly taught by the Church, always recognizing that God does not ask the impossible. The chapter concluded with the urgent matter of addressing debates that might compromise church teaching on the relationship between freedom and truth.

> Precisely on the questions frequently debated in moral theology today and with regard to which new tendencies and theories have developed, the Magisterium, in fidelity to Jesus Christ and in continuity with the Church's tradition, senses more urgently the duty to offer its own discernment and teaching, in order to help man in his journey towards truth and freedom.[67]

The first section is in tone and substance innovative in its use of scripture, in its call to discipleship, and in its emphasis on virtue. With his typical sense of wit, Oliver O'Donovan, who calls this summons an 'evangelical proclamation' (see *VS* 107), states, 'Everyone has had a nice word to say about this first section.'[68]

Still, three very different responses arose from this chapter. First, the late

Servais Pinckaers praised the encyclical particularly for its first chapter and especially for its future orientation, its intrinsic development, its scriptural and Christological foundations, its emphasis on virtue and grace, and its insertion of the ten commandments into the perspective of virtue.[69] He argued that keeping the law but placing it within the context of virtue brought two historically compatible trends rightly together. Others agreed with him.[70] In fact, younger scholars saw in this chapter a great challenge for the revisionists, inviting them to further define their positions in keeping with the claims of discernible objective moral conduct.[71]

The late Herbert McCabe, however, believed that these goals were not and could not be accomplished. McCabe argued that, in the Thomistic framework, laws arise from virtue, and not vice versa; in the encyclical, because of its unwavering interests in articulating specific laws, virtues become no more than mere handmaidens of these norms. For all its attempts to discuss virtue, the scriptures, and the development of discipleship, still it reduced morality to an 'obedience to church teaching' model. He wrote:

> I think it fails because, despite its frequent references to St. Thomas, it is still trapped in a post-Renaissance morality, in terms of law and conscience and free will. Amongst Christians this commonly shows itself in attempts to *base* an account of Christian morality on the ten commandments, and this can only lead to a sterile polarization of 'legalism' or 'liberalism'. You cannot fit the virtues into a legal structure without reducing them to dispositions to follow rules. You can, however, fit law and obedience to law into a comfortable, though minor niche in the project of growing up in the rich and variegated life of virtue.[72]

Similarly, the Protestant New Testament scholar, Karl Donfried, expressed his disappointment in the encyclical because its first part suggested a forthcoming discipleship ethics based on a Christological vision. Such a vision would respect 'the freedom and dignity' of the disciple, while still calling the disciple to a moral life. Donfried expected an ethics of interiority; instead, the encyclical asserted the need for 'obedience to universal and unchanging moral norms'.[73] This perfunctory turn to norms for guiding external conduct prompts Donfried to offer the same final verdict of disappointment as William Spohn did: 'The encyclical promises a Christonomous ethics of discipleship but it cannot deliver because it reduces morality to a matter of rules and principles.'[74]

Third, the Lutheran ethicist Gilbert Meilaender, like other Protestants very sympathetic to the Pope's agenda, was concerned about the matter of faith in this first chapter. He noted that the purpose of the pericope of the rich young man is not to illustrate the call of Christ but rather to teach that, without faith, none of us are saved. Meilaender saw the first chapter as theologically difficult.[75]

The second chapter argued that we ought not to be conformed to this world (Romans 12.2) and focused on four themes: freedom and law, conscience and truth, fundamental choice, and the moral act. It began with a crucial and frequently cited passage acknowledging the need to correct certain misunderstandings about specific teachings of moral theology, without endorsing a particular moral theological system.[76]

> Within the context of the theological debates which followed the Council, there have developed *certain interpretations of Christian morality which are not consistent with 'sound teaching'* (2 Timothy 4.3). Certainly the Church's Magisterium does not intend to impose upon the faithful any particular theological system, still less a philosophical one. Nevertheless, in order to 'reverently preserve and faithfully expound' the word of God, the Magisterium has the duty to state that some trends of theological thinking and certain philosophical affirmations are incompatible with revealed truth.[77]

The Pope then made it clear that principles are the matter at hand in the corrections that need to be made: 'In addressing this Encyclical to you, my Brother Bishops, it is my intention to state *the principles necessary for discerning what is contrary to "sound doctrine"*, drawing attention to those elements of the Church's moral teaching which today appear particularly exposed to error, ambiguity or neglect.'[78]

He insisted on the inseparability of freedom and truth and that the latter belongs to the objective moral order; similarly the dignity of conscience derives always from the truth.[79] The section on fundamental choice highlighted the connection between the basic stance or option of a person (for or away from God) and how particular acts influence and define that fundamental option.[80] Finally, in the section on the morality of the act, the Pope critiqued the moral method of proportionalism, and in particular its denial of intrinsically evil actions.[81] To uphold objective morality which he argued is derived from the object of the act, he contended that intrinsically evil actions are of their own nature never referable to God, despite important circumstances or good intentions.

> Reason attests that there are objects of the human act which are by their nature 'incapable of being ordered' to God, because they radically contradict the good of the person made in his image. These are the acts which, in the Church's moral tradition, have been termed 'intrinsically evil' (*intrinsece malum*): they are such *always and per se*, in other words, on account of their very object, and quite apart from the ulterior intentions of the one acting and the circumstances. Consequently, without in the least denying the influence on morality exercised by circumstances and especially by intentions, the Church teaches that 'there exist acts which *per se* and in themselves, independently of circumstances, are always seriously wrong by reason of their object'.[82]

In the third part, the Pope instructed his brother bishops to uphold the teaching of the encyclical. 'In the end, only a morality which acknowledges certain norms as valid always and for everyone, with no exception, can guarantee the ethical foundation of social coexistence, both on the national and international levels.'[83]

He closed the encyclical with words reiterating an understanding of moral theology that is principle-based, universal, and inclusive of absolute prohibitions: 'Each of us can see the seriousness of what is involved, not only for individuals but also for the whole of society, with the *reaffirmation of the universality and immutability of the moral commandments*, particularly those which prohibit always and without exception *intrinsically evil acts*.'[84]

In its aftermath, a variety of moral theological commentaries on the encyclical appeared throughout Europe[85] and the United States.[86] The Cardinal Archbishop of Milan, Dionigi Tettamanzi, provided a lengthy introduction to the Italian translation of the text.[87] Raphael Gallagher gave a particularly helpful overview of the more significant responses, noting that the encyclical was 'treated with a notable seriousness by the theological community'.[88] Arguing that it was written neither to discredit moral theologians nor to restore the neo-scholastic period, Gallagher saw in the encyclical two important goals: to encourage moral theologians to pursue the reform project of moral theology that was offered in Vatican II's *Optatam Totius* 16 and to express concern regarding certain tendencies that moral theologians have taken in this reform.

Its reception in Germany serves as an indication of the wide range of theological sentiment that greeted the encyclical throughout Europe. For the most part, the bishops applauded it. The well-respected president of the German Bishops' Conference, Karl Lehmann, saw it as setting the boundaries of discourse over fundamental moral themes and urged theologians to clarify their positions in light of it, while, at the same time, making sure 'to shed light on, deepen and further develop' the teaching of the Church. Josef Spital, Bishop of Trier, saw it as 'a prophetic sign' in a time when moral truths are easily dismissed when they prove uncomfortable or inconvenient to follow. Reinhard Lettman, Bishop of Hildesheim, identified the central concern of the encyclical as being the need to assert the existence of absolute and universally valid moral norms to anyone – inside or outside of the Church – who might have doubted them.

German moral theologians like Johannes Gründel questioned whether the positions that were criticized 'were correctly understood'. Bruno Schüller had 'the impression that criticisms of moral theologians were rooted in misunderstandings'. Helmut Weber emphasized that there was nothing in it to preclude continued theological reflection. Volker Eid, however, reacted strongly to the encyclical by characterizing it as 'authoritarian and fundamentalist'; for him, the paucity of reflection undermined its authority to the extent that it cannot be taken seriously.[89] It was Häring, however, who probably best summed up the reactions of many of his fellow ethicists with his essay, 'A Distrust that Wounds'.[90]

A central question raised by many, apart from the discussion on intrinsic evil,[91] was: were the claims about the revisionists apparent or real? Were the depictions of their positions not what revisionists advanced but rather what others attributed to them?[92] In fact, could one argue that, like the Pope, the revisionists too were trying to articulate and promote moral objectivity in a world more interested in making one's choices than in the question of whether the choices were objectively moral? Gallagher captured that viewpoint of the world as a place 'of widespread acceptance of the inevitability of a relativistic interpretation of morality, the correctness of technological interventions in all areas of human life and of a belief that the only political system that can function in such an emerging culture is one where morality is left to the private choice of the individual'.[93]

These questions led to questions about the nature of the moral theologian's work. Basilio Petrà saw the moral theologian as called to be prophetic. In a rather refreshing grouping he referred to Bernhard Häring, *Veritatis Splendor*, Marciano Vidal, and liberation theologians as restoring the prophetic quality of church teaching.[94] For Petrà, the moralist looks at the world much as the Vatican does. Sabatino Majorano offered a different slant, arguing that the moralist today is called to service, and echoes the position of English theologian Kevin Kelly that the moralist is responsible for transmitting, developing, and presenting teaching culled from a variety of relationships within the Church.[95]

These depictions are somewhat illuminating; they underline the extraordinary shift that has occurred in the identity of moral theologians. Today, the moral theologian is responsible to serve humanity in leading persons of good will to understand the demands of moral conscience and moral truth. As Klaus Demmer noted years ago, both moralists and bishops have the triple obligation to call each person first, to heed her own conscience; second, to form her own conscience for right conduct; and third, occasionally to address particular concrete issues. Demmer also suggested that the more important first and second obligations were often overlooked when bishops spent too much time on the third obligation.[96] If bishops and theologians followed Demmer's argument, this would mean not giving the laity answers, but rather prophetically calling them to conscientious formation through virtues, values, and principles in general.

Veritatis Splendor served as a catalyst for moral theologians to see how their writings were being understood. Gallagher noted that many theologians showed a 'serious effort to both understand the precise purpose of the encyclical while not neglecting the search for theological systems of morality that could incorporate the substance of *VS* with other elements'.[97] Echoing Hans Rotter's belief that moral theologians would prefer communication with the Vatican rather than instruction from it, Gallagher demonstrated that moral theologians have continued on the way of the conciliar reform, while attempting to highlight that their own positions were in fact resonant with papal interests.[98] This accommodation is not as difficult as one may suspect, for, as Brian Johnstone noted, both *Veritatis Splendor* and the new Catechism are more personalist and less neo-scholastic than people might think.[99]

Moreover, the encyclical helped moral theologians recognize that a major moral challenge today is to determine how we can understand moral truth as mediating the relationship between the order of being and the ethical order of values: how is it that who we are determines what we are called to do?[100] Underlying this question is the relationship between freedom and truth: to what extent is freedom a condition for knowing the truth and to what extent is knowing the truth a condition of freedom?[101] This was, after all, the question that Pope John Paul II had in the first place.

Still, few moral theologians found the encyclical a hospitable acceptance of their work during the 25 years since *Humanae Vitae*. In one way the differences between Rome and the revisionists might have been, after all, how classicist was one with its universal, unchanging, absolute principles, and how historicist were the others in looking to the context in which objective moral judgments are made. Sometimes these presuppositions have kept bishops and theologians from understanding one another, prompting Daniel Finn to argue, in his presidential address at the Catholic Theological Society of America, that theologians share in the responsibility toward constructing a more reconciling relationship between the two.[102]

In conclusion, I would like to cite an example of a reconciling moment that tried to overcome these divisions. In spring 1994 the Cardinal Archbishop of London, Basil Hume, invited fifteen theologians and fifteen bishops to a three-day retreat to consider *Veritatis Splendor*. The moral theologians were the leading figures from the United Kingdom and Ireland: Enda McDonagh, Gerry Hughes, Jack Mahoney, Kevin Kelly, Patrick Hannon, and Bernard Hoose. Also there were new young scholars, most significantly Linda Hogan and Julie Clague. I was doing a fellowship in Edinburgh and was therefore the only 'foreigner' invited.

Moral theologians were quite angry about the encyclical, especially with the implicit charge that moral theologians were teaching moral relativism. Inasmuch as we search for moral truth, to suggest that we were advancing moral relativism is probably the most serious attack to be made on us. Moreover, the document continually depicted certain theological arguments (about goodness and rightness, the fundamental option, the erroneous conscience, etc.) in ways that moral theologians could not identify them as originating from any particular moral theologian. Theologians found these arguments caricatures of positions they held. Finally, *Veritatis Splendor* was for the most part a very lengthy philosophical document, written it seems mostly by philosophers. These philosophers were writing erroneously about the writings of moral theologians.

Cardinal Hume divided the agenda into six themes, two for each day. Each session began with a theme, with first a moral theologian speaking, followed by a bishop on the topic. I remember wondering what would happen at the first session and was surprised by how refreshing the exchange was. The first speaker, a moral theologian teaching in a regional seminary, stated quite emphatically how harmful the encyclical was to moral theologians. The bishop, on the other hand, spoke of his need to have greater clarity in teaching and lamented the distance in conversation between theologian and bishop. He added that the positions in the encyclical may not be from moral theologians, but they conveyed the positions held by many lay people today.

For the next three days we named and addressed misunderstandings and constructed ways for better discourse among bishops and theologians. A spirit of co-operation permeated the conference; it demonstrated how bishops and theologians could once again discern together.

Notes

1 Bernard Lonergan, *Insight: A Study of Human Understanding* (London: Longmans, Green and Co. and New York: Philosophical Library, 1957).

2 Bernard Lonergan, 'Christ as Subject: A Reply', in *Gregorianum* 40 (1959) 242–70; reprinted in Frederick Crowe, *Collection* (New York: Herder, 1967) 153–84; *The Subject* (Milwaukee: Marquette University, 1968).

3 Lonergan, 'Dehellenization of Dogma', *TS* 28 (1967) 336–51; reprinted in William Ryan and Bernard Tyrrell, eds, *A Second Collection* (Philadelphia: Westminster Press, 1975) 11–32; 'Transition from A Classicist World View to Historical Mindedness', *A Second Collection* 1–9; 'Theology in its New Context', *A Second Collection*, 55–67.

4 Phil Keane, 'The Objective Moral Order', *TS* 43 (1982) 260–78; Kenneth Melchin, *History, Ethics and Emergent Probability: Ethics, Society and History in the Work of Bernard Lonergan* (Lanham, MD: University Press of America, 1987); Richard Gula, *Reason Informed by Faith: Foundations of Moral Theology* (Mahwah: Paulist Press, 1989) 25–41; Thomas Kopfensteiner, 'Historical Epistemology', *Heythrop Journal* 33 (1992) 45–60; Mark Miller, *Living Ethically in Christ: Is Christian Ethics Unique?* (New York: Peter Lang, 1999).

5 Pius XI, *Casti Connubii* (31 December 1930) para. 56: http://www.vatican.va/holy_father/pius_xi/encyclicals/documents/hf_p-xi_enc_31121930_casti-connubii_en.html.

6 Ibid., 95.

7 Patrick, *Liberating Conscience.*

8 Joseph Fletcher, *Situation Ethics: The New Morality* (Philadelphia: Westminster Press, 1966).

9 John Paul II, *Ordinatio Sacerdotalis*, 22 May 1994, para. 4: http://www.vatican.va/holy_father/john_paul_ii/apost_letters/documents/hf_jp-ii_apl_22051994_ordinatio-sacerdotalis_en.html. Cardinal Ratzinger reiterated this teaching adding that it was infallible: Congregation for the Doctrine of the Faith, 'Reply to the *dubium* concerning the teaching contained in the apostolic letter *Ordinatio Sacerdotalis*', *Origins* 25 (30 November 1995) 401, 403.

10 John Ford, 'The Concept of Natural Law', Lecture notes, 11. As quoted in Eric Mercel Genilo, *John Cuthbert Ford, SJ: Moral Theologian at the End of the Manualist Era* (Washington, DC: Georgetown University Press, 2007) (hereafter *Ford*) 105–6.

11 Noonan, *Contraception.*
12 Gerald Kelly, 'The Duty of Using Artificial Means of Preserving Life', *TS* 11 (1950) 203–20, at 220; *Medico-Moral Problems* (St Louis: The Catholic Health Association of The United States and Canada, 1958).
13 John Ford, 'The Morality of Obliteration Bombing', *TS* 5.3 (1944) 261–309.
14 John Ford and Gerald Kelly, *Contemporary Moral Theology I: Questions in Fundamental Moral Theology* and *Contemporary Moral Theology II: Marriage Questions* (Westminster, MD: Newman Press, 1964).
15 Kelly, 'The Morality of Mutilation', *TS* 17 (1956) 322.
16 Ford and Kelly, *Contemporary Moral Theology*, I. 3.
17 Ibid., 111.
18 McCormick, 'Moral Theology 1940–1989: An Overview', *TS* 50 (1989) 3–24, at 5.
19 *Ford*, 38; 166–7.
20 Oliver Morgan, '"Chemical Comforting" and the Theology of John C. Ford, SJ: Classic Answers to a Contemporary Problem', *Journal of Ministry in Addiction and Recovery* 6 (1999) 29–66 at 60, in *Ford*, 29.
21 John Ford and Germain Grisez, 'Contraception and Infallibility', *TS* 39 (1978) 258–312. The article prompted considerable controversy. See McCormick's moderation of the debate, *Notes on Moral Theology 1965–1980* (Lanham: University Press of America, 1981) (hereafter *Notes*) 774–7; *Notes on Moral Theology 1981 through 1984* (Lanham: University Press of America, 1984) (hereafter *Notes 2*) 172–4.
22 Ford and Kelly, *Contemporary Moral Theology*, I. 29.
23 Ibid., I. 32.
24 Ibid., I. 20–1.
25 Daniel Callahan, 'Authority and the Theologian', *Commonweal* 30.11 (5 June 1964) 319–23.
26 David Kelly, *The Emergence of Roman Catholic Medical Ethics in North America* (New York: Edwin Mellen Press, 1979) 230.
27 See Peter Black and James F. Keenan, 'The Evolving Self-understanding of the Moral Theologian: 1900–2000', *Studia Moralia* 39 (2001) 291–327.
28 Josef Fuchs, *Natural Law: A Theological Investigation* (New York: Sheed and Ward, 1965) 56; *Lex Naturae. Zur Theologie des Naturrechts* (Düsseldorf: Patmos, 1955).
29 Ibid., 12.
30 Clearly the most important study of the debate is in Ambrogio Valsecchi, *Controversy: The Birth Control Debate 1958–1968* (Cleveland: Corpus Books, 1968).
31 Mark Graham, *Josef Fuchs on Natural Law* (Washington, DC: Georgetown University Press, 2002); Keenan, 'Josef Fuchs and the Question of Moral Objectivity in Roman Catholic Ethical Reasoning', *Religious Studies Review* 24, 3 (1998) 253–8.
32 Interview with Fr Jack Mahoney, London, 2 March 2007.
33 Robert McClory, *Turning Point* (New York: Crossroad, 1995), 109.
34 Robert Kaiser, *The Politics of Sex and Religion: A Case History in the Development of Doctrine 1962–1984* (Kansas City, MO: Leaven Press, 1985), 154.
35 Ibid., 161.
36 McClory, *Turning Point*, 127. See also Graham, *Josef Fuchs*, 83–114; *Ford*, 129–49.
37 John O'Malley, *What Happened at Vatican II* (Cambridge: Harvard University Press, 2008) 284.
38 *Ford*, 63–5.
39 *Ford*, 64.

40 John Ford, 'Response of Father John C. Ford to the Award of the Cardinal O'Boyle Medal', *Fellowship of Catholic Scholars Newsletter* 12.1 14 (1988), in *Ford*, 56–7.
41 Pope Paul VI, *Humanae Vitae* (1968) para. 6: http://www.vatican.va/holy_father/paul_vi/encyclicals/documents/hf_p-vi_enc_25071968_humanae-vitae_en.html. See Joseph Selling, 'Moral Teaching: Traditional Teaching and Humanae Vitae', *Louvain Studies* 7 (1978–9) 28.
42 *Humanae Vitae*, para. 11, 12, respectively.
43 Among the fullest narratives by a moral theologian, see Mahoney, *The Making of Moral Theology*, 267–301. See also the extended reporting and commentary in McCormick's *Notes on Moral Theology 1965 through 1980*; also Odozor, *Moral Theology in an Age of Renewal*, 44–77.
44 Joseph Fuchs, *Christian Ethics in a Secular Arena* (Washington, DC: Georgetown University Press, 1984), 137.
45 Ibid., 138.
46 See Gabriel Flynn, *Yves Congar's Vision of the Church in a World of Unbelief* (Farnham, Surrey: Ashgate, 2004).
47 Fuchs, *Christian Ethics*, 138–9.
48 Ibid., 140.
49 Fuchs, *Christian Ethics*, 100–13.
50 Bartholomew Kiely, *Psychology and Moral Theology: Lines of Convergence* (Rome: Gregorian University Press, 1980).
51 Kiely, 'The Impracticality of Proportionalism', *Gregorianum* 66 (1985) 655–86.
52 Kiely, 'The Pastoral Care of Homosexual Persons', *Osservatore Romano* 970.2 (1987) 6–7; 'Science and Morality', *Osservatore Romano* 983 (1987) 15, 20.
53 Genilo, *Ford*, 3.
54 John Paul II, *Veritatis Splendor* (6 August 1993): http://www.vatican.va/holy_father/john_paul_ii/encyclicals/documents/hf_jp-ii_enc_06081993_veritatis-splendor_en.html.
55 Germain Grisez, *The Way of the Lord: Moral Theology* (Chicago: Franciscan Press, 1983). See also with Russell Shaw, *Beyond the New Morality: The Responsibilities of Freedom* (Notre Dame: University of Notre Dame Press, 1988).
56 Germain Grisez, *Contraception and the Natural Law* (Milwaukee: Bruce Publishing, 1964).
57 John Finnis, *Natural Law and Natural Rights* (Oxford: Clarendon Press, 1980); *Moral Absolutes: Tradition, Revision, and Truth* (Washington, DC: CUA Press, 1991).
58 Joseph Boyle, 'Free Choice, Incomparably Valuable Options and Incommensurable Categories of Good', *The American Journal of Jurisprudence* 47 (2002) 123–41; Joseph Boyle, 'Free Choice, Incommensurable Goods and the Self-Refutation of Determinism', *The American Journal of Jurisprudence* 50 (2005) 139–63.
59 Germain Grisez, Joseph Boyle, and John Finnis, 'Practical Principles, Moral Truth, and Ultimate Ends', *American Journal of Jurisprudence* 32 (1987) 99–151; Finnis, Boyle, and Grisez, *Nuclear Deterrence, Morality and Realism* (Oxford: Oxford University Press, 1987); Finnis, Boyle, and Grisez, 'Incoherence and Consequentialism (or Proportionalism) – A Rejoinder', *American Catholic Philosophical Quarterly* 64 (1990) 271–7; Finnis, Grisez, and Boyle, "Direct" and "Indirect": A Reply to Critics of Our Action Theory', *The Thomist* 65 (2001) 1–44. In 1988 the three joined with John Ford and William E. May, *The Teaching of 'Humanae Vitae': A Defense* (St Ignatius Press, 1988); see also, Grisez, Boyle, Finnis, and May, 'Every

Marital Act Ought To Be Open to New Life: Toward a Clearer Understanding', *The Thomist* 52 (1988) 365–6. For more information see Christopher Tollefsen, 'The New Natural Law Theory', *Lyceum* 10 (2008) 1–19.

60 Robert George, *In Defense of the New Natural Law Theory* (Oxford: Clarendon Press, 1999).

61 Russell Hittinger, *A Critique of the New Natural Law Theory* (Notre Dame: University of Notre Dame Press, 1987).

62 For an excellent study, see Paulinus Ikechukwu Odozor, *Richard McCormick and the Renewal of Moral Theology* (Notre Dame: University of Notre Dame Press, 1995).

63 Each volume was entitled *Readings in Moral Theology* and then followed by the volume number and the specific sub-title of the volume. Their first was *Readings in Moral Theology No. 1: Moral Norms and Catholic Tradition* (Newark: Paulist Press, 1979).

64 Richard McCormick, *How Brave a New World: Dilemmas in Bioethics* (New York: Doubleday, 1981); *Critical Calling* (Washington, DC: Georgetown University Press, 2006).

65 See Richard McCormick and Paul Ramsey, eds, *Doing Evil to Achieve Good* (Chicago: Loyola University Press, 1978).

66 See Charles Curran, *The Moral Theology of Pope John Paul II* (Washington, DC: Georgetown University Press, 2005); Reinhard Hütter and Theodor Dieter, eds, *Ecumenical Ventures in Ethics: Protestants Engage Pope John Paul II's Moral Encyclicals* (Grand Rapids, MI: Eerdmans, 1997); Gerard Mannion, ed., *The Vision of John Paul II: Assessing His Thought and Influence* (Collegeville: Liturgical Press, 2008); Paulinus Odozor, 'Pope John Paul II on Postconciliar Moral Theology: An Epilogue and a Beginning', *Moral Theology in an Age of Renewal*, 304–25.

67 *Veritatis Splendor*, 27.

68 Oliver O'Donovan, 'A Summons to Reality', John Wilkins, ed., *Understanding Veritatis Splendor* (London: SPCK, 1994) 41–5, at 42.

69 Servais Pinckaers, *Pour Une Lecture de Veritatis Splendor* (Paris: Mame, 1995); 'An Encyclical for the Future: *Veritatis Splendor*', Augustine DiNoia and Romanus Cessario, eds, *Veritatis Splendor and the Renewal of Moral Theology* (Chicago: Midwest Theological Forum, 1999) 11–72; 'Scripture and the Renewal of Moral Theology', John Berkman and Craig Steven Titus, *The Pinckaers Reader: Renewing Thomistic Moral Theology* (Washington, DC: CUA, 2005) 47–53.

70 Réal Tremblay, 'Premier regard sur la "réception" de *Veritatis Splendor* à propos du rapport du Christ et de la morale', *Studia Moralia* 34 (1996) 97–120. Jacques Servais supports Tremblay and turns to the theology of Hans Urs von Balthasar, '"Si tu veux être parfait . . . viens, suis-moi". Le Christ, norme concrète et pleniere de l'agir humain', *Anthropotes* 1 (1994) 25–38; Sergio Bastianel, 'La chiamata in Cristo come tema e principio dell'insegnamento della teologia morale', *Seminarum* 34 (1994) 52–71.

71 See David Cloutier, 'Moral theology for Real People: Agency, Practical Reason, and the Task of the Moral Theologian', William Mattison III, ed., *New Wine, New Wineskins* (New York: Rowman and Littlefield, 2005) 119–42; Darlene Fozard Weaver, 'Intimacy with God and Self-relation in the World', ibid., 143–64.

72 Herbert McCabe, 'Manuals and Rule Books', *Understanding Veritatis Splendor*, 61–8 at 67–8.

73 Karl Donfried, 'The Use of Scripture in Veritatis Splendor', *Ecumenical Ventures in Ethics*, 38–59.

74 William Spohn, 'Morality on the Way of Discipleship: The Use of Scripture in

Veritatis Splendor', in Michael Allsopp and John O'Keefe, eds, *Veritatis Splendor: American Responses* (Kansas City: Sheed and Ward, 1995) 83–105, at 102. See also Gareth Moore, 'Some Remarks on the Use of Scripture in *Veritatis Splendor*', Joseph Selling and Jan Jans, eds, *The Splendor of Accuracy: An Examination of the Assertions Made by Veritatis Splendor* (Kampen: Kok Pharos, 1994) 71–98.

75 Gilbert Meilaender, 'Grace, Justification through Faith, and Sin', *Ecumenical Ventures*, 60–83.

76 Louis Vereecke, 'Magistère et morale selon *Veritatis Splendor*', *Studia Moralia* 31 (1993) 391–401, at 397.

77 *VS*, 29.

78 *VS*, 30.

79 *VS*, 63.

80 Josef Fuchs, 'Good Acts and Good Persons', *Understanding Veritatis Splendor*, 21–6.

81 *VS*, 79.

82 *VS*, 80.

83 *VS*, 97.

84 *VS*, 115.

85 Besides the literature already noted, from Italy: Sergio Bastianel, 'L'enciclica sulla morale: Veritatis Splendor', *Civiltà Cattolica* 144 (1993) 209–19; Dario Composta, 'L'enciclica "Veritatis Splendor" del Sommo Pontefice Giovanni Paolo II. Riflessioni sulla sua attualità', *Divinitas* 38 (1994) 9–22; George Cottier, 'Una lettura della Veritatis Splendor', *Rassegna di Teologia* 34 (1993) 603–14; Ramón Lucas, ed., *Veritatis Splendor Testo integrale e commento filosofico-teologico* (Milan: San Paolo, 1994); G. Russo, *Veritatis Splendor: Genesi, elaborazione, significato* (Rome: Dehoniane, 1995); Cataldo Zuccaro, 'La "Veritatis Splendor": Una triplice chiave di lettura', *Rivista di Teologia Morale* 25 (1993) 567–81. From France: Albert Chapelle, 'Les enjeux de "Veritatis Splendor"', *Nouvelle Revue Théologique* 115 (1993) 801–17; Leo Elders, 'Veritatis Splendor et la doctrine de Saint Thomas d'Aquin', *Doctor Communis* 47 (1994) 121–46. From Spain, Gerardo Del Pozo Abejón, ed., *Comentarios a la Veritatis Splendor* (Madrid: PPC, 1995); Marciano Vidal, *La propuesta moral de Juan Pablo II. Comentario teológico-moral de la encíclica 'Veritatis Splendor'* (Madrid: PPC, 1994). The moral teaching of the new catechism has been the subject of much commentary, also. See, for instance, Francesco Compagnoni and T. Rossi, 'La morale nel Catechismo della Chiesa Cattolica', *Rivista di Teologia Morale* 25 (1993) 157–95; Marciano Vidal, *La moral cristiana en el nuevo Catecismo* (Madrid: PPC, 1993); Albert Chapelle, '"La vie dans le Christ". Le Catéchisme de L'Église Catholique', *Nouvelle Revue Théologique* 115 (1993) 169–85, 641–57; Sante Raponi, 'Decalogo e vita critiana', *Studia Moralia* 32 (1994) 93–120; Louis Vereecke, 'La conscience morale selon le Catéchisme de L'Église Catholique', *Studia Moralia* 32 (1994) 61–74.

86 Besides *Veritatis Splendor and the Renewal of Moral Theology*, see Finnis and Grisez, 'Negative Moral Precepts Protect the Dignity of the Human Person', *L'Osservatore Romano*, English edn, No. 8 (1994) 6–7; William E. May, '*Veritatis Splendor:* An Overview of the Encyclical', *Communio* 21 (1994) 228–51; '*The Splendor of Accuracy*: How Accurate?' *The Thomist* 59.3 (1995) 467–83.

87 Dionigi Tettamanzi, *Guida alla lettura: Lettera Enciclica di S.S. Papa Giovanni Paolo II Veritatis Splendori* (Casale Monferrato: Edizioni Piemme, 1993) 5–56.

88 Raphael Gallagher, 'The Reception of Veritatis Splendor within the Theological Community', *Studia Moralia* 33 (1995) 415–35, at 435.

89 These are gathered from Reinhard Lettmann, 'Moral in der Spannung von Frei-

heit und Wahrheit', *Kirche und Leben*, 10 October 1993, 1 and 6; 'Grundlage, Mahnung, Hilfe: Reaktionen auf die Moralenzyklika "Veritatis Splendor"', *Kirche und Leben*, 17 October 1993, 3; Walter Kerber, 'Veritatis Splendor', *Stimmen der Zeit* 211 (1993) 793–4.

90 Häring, 'A Distrust that Wounds', *The Tablet* 247 (23 October 1993) 1378–9 Dietmar Mieth, ed., *Moraltheologie im Abseits? Antwort auf die Enzyklika 'Veritatis Splendor'* (Freiburg: Herder, 1994); Konrad Hilpert, 'Glanz der Wahrheit: Licht und Schatten. Eine Analyse der neuen Moralenzyklika', *Herder Korrespondenz* 47 (1993) 623–30; Peter Knauer, 'Zu Grundbegriffen der Enzyklika "Veritatis Splendor"', *Stimmen der Zeit* 212 (1994) 14–26.

91 On the encyclical's discussion of intrinsically evil acts: Bernd Wannenwetsch, '"Intrinsically Evil Acts"; or, Why Abortion and Euthanasia Cannot be Justified', *Ecumenical Ventures in Ethics*, 185–215; Jean Porter, 'The Moral Act in *Veritatis Splendor* and in Aquinas's *Summa Theologiae*: A Comparative Analysis', *Veritatis Splendor: American Responses*, 278–95; Martin Rhonheimer, '"Intrinsically Evil Acts" and the Moral Viewpoint: Clarifying a Central Teaching of *Veritatis Splendor*', *The Thomist* 58 (1994) 1–39.

92 For instance, see Joseph Selling, 'The Context and Arguments of *Veritatis Spendor*', *The Splendor of Accuracy*, 11–70.

93 Gallagher, ibid., 420.

94 Basilio Petrà, 'Le sfide del teologo moralista, oggi', *Studia Moralia* 33 (1995) 5–20. See also Carla Rossi Espagnet, 'Magistero e teologia morale in "Veritatis Splendor"', *Anthropotes* (1994) 145–59.

95 Sabatino Majorano, 'Il teologo moralista oggi', *Studia Moralia* 33 (1995) 21–44; Kevin Kelly, 'The Role of the Moral Theologian in the Life of the Church', in Raphael Gallagher and Brendan McConvery, eds, *History and Conscience* (Dublin: Gill and Macmillan, 1989) 8–23.

96 Klaus Demmer, 'La competenza normativa del magistero ecclesiastico in morale', in Klaus Demmer and Bruno Schüller, *Fede cristiana e agire morale* (Assisi: Cittadella, 1980) 144–72.

97 Gallagher, 426.

98 Hans Rotter, 'Instruktion oder Kommunikation?', *Moraltheologie im Abseits?*, 194–202.

99 Brian Johnstone, 'Faithful Action: The Catholic Moral Tradition and *Veritatis Splendor*', *Studia Moralia* 31 (1993) 283–305; 'Personalist Morality for a Technological Age: *The Catechism of the Catholic Church* and *Veritatis Splendor*', *Studia Moralia* 32 (1994) 121–36.

100 Juan Luis Ruiz de la Peña, 'La verdad, el bien y el ser. Un paseo por la ética, de la mano de la *Veritatis Splendor*', *Salmanticensis* 41 (1994) 37–65.

101 Jean-Yves Calvez, 'Liberté et vérité', *Études* 379 (1993) 657–60.

102 Daniel Finn, 'Power and Presence in Catholic Social Thought, the Church and the CTSA', *CTSA Proceedings* 62 (2007) 62–77.

7

New Foundations for Moral Reasoning, 1970–89

Genuine theology leads to a fundamental change in our way of thinking.[1]

The aftermath of *Humanae Vitae* was marked by great personal and social upheaval in the Church. In the industrialized world, Catholics found in the bishops of Canada, France, Germany, and Holland a variety of responses that encouraged them to follow their consciences. In the English-speaking world and in the developing world, many found themselves facing a hierarchy in strong solidarity with the Vatican.[2]

Moral theologians had a protracted battle with hierarchical authority about the competency of the moral magisterium. They joined with systematic theologians to reflect theologically on the Episcopal responsibility for moral teaching. They argued that bishops were not simply called to instruct on a given teaching, but to mediate the unity of the Church and to demonstrate to the laity how church teaching moved the Church eschatologically to a place closer to Jesus Christ and the kingdom.[3]

Whereas earlier moralists decided what was right or wrong in every area of life, the contemporary moralist was more interested in helping persons to rightly realize their moral truth. In that sense moralists looked to work with the hierarchy at the service of the Church.

In the twenty years after *Humanae Vitae*, for the most part, moral theologians engaged in the re-examination and renovation of moral concepts. There was a scholastic, scientific tone to these investigations, and their highly conceptual discussions were arguably the most productive of the last century. Theological ethicists, as they came to be known, were no longer lone revisionists; they were now participants in a clear movement looking to establish basic fundamental concepts for the moral theology of the contemporary Church, and despite *Veritatis Splendor*'s later critique, most theological ethicists acquitted themselves of the relativism with which they were tarnished.

1. Mentoring to new foundations

The clerical nature of theological ethics became less and less evident as lay people entered the field of theological ethics and pursued doctoral degrees. Margaret Farley studied with James Gustafson and finished her dissertation at Yale University in 1973.[4] Dietmar Mieth studied with Alfons Auer at Tübingen and concluded his habilitation in 1974. Lisa Sowle Cahill was also mentored by James Gustafson at the University of Chicago and was influenced by the writings of Richard McCormick; she completed her dissertation in 1976. Under the supervision of Louis Janssens, Joseph Selling completed his dissertation on the reception of *Humanae Vitae* at the Katholieke Universiteit Leuven in 1977.

Mentoring was central. Persons were no longer choosing simply to study in Rome. Rather, as Mieth found in Auer, Farley and Cahill in Gustafson, and Selling in Janssens, the mentor, more than the university itself, was the object of a discerning student's choice. These mentors were the architects of the new theological ethics.

As critical as they were of manualism and neo-manualism, they were critical of themselves. They recognized that, animated by the vision of Christ on the horizon of our expectations, theological ethics and its theologians are always in need of re-examination and reformation. Assessing his contribution to moral theology, Richard McCormick called it 'Self-assessment and Self-indictment'.[5] In one albeit limited way, the moral theologians' search for moral truth became a bit of an autobiographical journey. Enda McDonagh offered this perspective implicitly in his aptly named work, *Doing the Truth: The Quest for Moral Theology*.[6] If we are calling moral subjects to discover Christ and to realize the truth from within, then moral theologians are even more responsible for doing that for themselves.

Each of these mentors had their histories as well. Josef Fuchs' 400 books and essays shaped contemporary Roman Catholic moral theology since he first began writing in 1940. His influence is peculiarly striking inasmuch as before 1968 he was among the most articulate proponents of the classical Roman Catholic paradigm of moral objectivity and after 1968 its most ardent and astute critic.[7]

Fuchs was originally trained not in moral theology, but in ecclesiology. His dissertation in 1940 investigated the nature of the Church's teaching authority; there he reflected on the roots of the triple self-understanding of the Church as teacher, minister, and ruler, a predilection to Vatican II's Dogmatic Constitution *Lumen Gentium* which described the Church as priest, prophet, and king. This confidence in the Church's magisterial authority served as a firm ground for the young German Jesuit who was assigned to teach moral theology at the Gregorian University only a few years after finishing his dissertation.

Fuchs' earliest works in ethics focused on Aquinas' writing on the ends of marriage and sexual ethics.[8] Shortly after that, in 1952, he wrote a book and several major essays on the question of situational ethics.[9] Then in 1955 he published his work on the natural law.

After his 'conversion' experience on the papal commission, Fuchs went in search of new theological and philosophical foundations. He was inspired and guided by the contributions of Dom Odon Lottin. Though a classicist in the 1950s, still from 1949 to 1955 Fuchs wrote seven favorable reviews of Lottin's works.[10] From Lottin, Fuchs developed self-determination and integrated Rahner's transcendentalism into it, so as to articulate a natural law ethics based on the right-realization of the person.[11]

In articulating his new positions, Fuchs did not produce myriad positions overnight. From 1968, he was constantly developing his positions, always in the form of discreet essays, and often rather critical of underlying presuppositions that animated magisterial and neomanualist thought, as well as occasionally the writings of fellow revisionists, whether Alfons Auer or Richard McCormick.

During the 1980s I asked Fuchs why he wrote on so many different topics in essay form and no book-length work. He said he liked watching how a variety of arguments was initiated by others and how in time those initiatives became debates and discussions. In the middle of these discourses, he said, he liked to enter with his own contribution; through these exchanges, he developed his thought.

Fuchs mentored many. His most famous students were Klaus Demmer (1921–) and Bruno Schüller (1925–2007). Demmer taught for 30 years at the Gregorian University; Schüller taught at Münster.[12] The methodological foundations for their theological ethics were remarkably different. Schüller discovered English analytical philosophy, particularly in the writings of C. D. Broad,[13] and brought to moral theology a critical reading of the concepts that were used, constantly distinguishing one from another, as in the case of the general distinction between direct and indirect killing.[14]

Demmer operated with a methodology based on hermeneutics. Rather than making clear distinctions, Demmer's approach was constantly engaging presuppositions, understanding contexts, and working out differences through a dialect of mutual defining concepts.[15] If two people could be different in fundamental methodologies and their approaches to moral theology, they were Demmer and Schüller. If Schüller's work looked linear, Demmer's was like a spiral.

One illustration helps highlight how differing methods led to different claims, and how, as a result, revisionists were able to make this a time of rigorous debate. Schüller promoted the distinction between the genesis (*Genese*) and the validity (*Geltung*) of moral insight,[16] offering the example of the student who

> . . . does his sums and writes: 2 + 2 = 5. We may ask whether this arithmetical computation is true or false . . . Then we are dealing with the truth-value (validity) of arithmetical computation. But we can also ask how the pupil came to make such a mistake . . . Then we are asking for a genetic explanation of an erroneous arithmetical computation.[17]

Applied to moral insights, the distinction has great significance. According to Schüller, the origin of a norm does not bear on its validity. This separation not only de-historicized norms, it also de-Christianized them. A norm's origin deriving from a faith community, for instance, was not cause for its contemporary validity. Validity was a categorically singular issue. Moreover, in this context, faith does not add to our knowledge in the moral sphere. The norm might derive from the Gospels, but its validity today is independent of them.

For those in the hermeneutical context, the validity of moral insight is derived from its genesis.[18] The need to articulate a norm at some point in time animates the meaning of the norm as well as its legitimacy. When Demmer looked to the relationship between norms founded on faith and contemporary norms, he took seriously the immediacy of God's presence (building on the Augustinian insight that God is closer to us than we are to ourselves)[19] and aimed to draw the ethical implications of faith. While moral truths cannot be deduced from truths of faith, faith provides an orientation to all of reality. Faith is not an independent reality alongside moral reasoning; nor does faith diminish our interest in the universal community of communication. Faith exerts a maieutic function on reason and allows the believer to 'draw on sources that are not accessible to everyone'. [20] For Demmer, then, when faith and reason are dialectically related, the context of 'genesis is not only manifested in but constitutive of moral truth'.[21]

While Fuchs stressed fundamental moral theology by writing on such diverse topics as the specificity of moral theology, the historicity of the person, the primacy of the conscience, and the role of the magisterium, and while Häring later promoted a moral theology integrated into a pastoral framework in *Free and Faithful in Christ*,[22] Louis Janssens (1908–2001) developed a personalistic ethics, espousing the freedom of conscience and religious liberty, revisioning Aquinas, and proposing the concept of ontic evil which later will be a constitutive insight in the foundation of proportionalism.[23]

In 1934 he enrolled for doctoral studies at the Faculty of Theology at Louvain, and, like Fuchs, Janssens did his dissertation in theology, specializing in patristics, with a dissertation (defended, 1937) on Cyril of Alexandria. He first taught at Mechelen seminary from 1939 to 1942 during the Nazi occupation of Belgium and later became a full-time professor at Leuven University in 1942. There he lectured first in dogmatic theology, but from 1945 until his retirement in 1978 he concentrated on moral theology.[24]

Above all, Janssens asked us to reflect on the 'subject adequately considered' and outlined the key components of such a person: a corporeal subject in relationship to the world, others, social groups, and God, historically developed, and fundamentally equal to all other human beings though uniquely original.[25] Until the person is adequately considered, we cannot ascertain whether the claims for a particular judgment are adequately considered.[26] This consideration of the person marks, as Brian Johnstone notes, the full departure from the naïve essentialism of the manuals and the full turn to the subject who so animates the revisionist agenda.[27]

When Louis Janssens died on 19 December 2001, *Louvain Studies* published several essays on him in spring 2002. Roger Burggraeve wrote touchingly about Janssens' 'personalist calling' and his 'ethics for concrete people'.[28] Selling provided a strong argument for the lasting impact of Janssens' work for fundamental moral theology.[29]

There were other great scholars at the time: Franz Böckle (1921–91) was for more than twenty years the professor of moral theology at the University of Bonn.[30] Alfons Auer (1915–2005) was at Tübingen training not only Dietmar Mieth but also Antonio Autiero. Auer championed an autonomous ethics and fought vigorously against a naïve essentialism that could take us away from the turn to the subject. Among the 65 editions of his books, three are particularly noteworthy. In 1960 he published his work promoting a lay spirituality for life in the world with Christ.[31] In the 1990s he developed a very popular environmental ethics.[32] His longstanding contribution remains his work on autonomous morality.[33]

Others were less inclined to have simply an academic appointment and provided sustained guidance to the laity through their own pastoral experiences. While teaching in Florence's theological faculty, Enrico Chiavacci (1926–) has been the pastor of the same Florentine parish since 1961. Over the course of thirteen years (1977–1990) he published his four-volume study in moral theology that covered fundamental morals as well as social, economic, and political challenges. He has recently revisited this project nearly 30 years later to offer, in a singular volume, a fundamental moral theology that includes rather than distinguishes itself from a social ethics.[34] In England, Kevin Kelly (1933–) started teaching in a seminary (1965–75) then directed an institute for adult education (1975–81), then worked in team ministry (1981–85) and eventually became pastor of a parish (1985–), while also lecturing at universities around the world. His many books have offered new directions in moral theology, sexual ethics, marriage, and parish life.[35] In Ireland, Enda McDonagh (1930–) has been teaching at St Patrick's College in Maynooth for 50 years and has developed a moral theology rich in ascetical as well as social claims. He locates his work between poetry and politics, having published over sixteen books on topics from HIV/AIDS to vulnerability.[36]

The development of moral theology from the late 1960s to 1980 was largely guided by these dedicated priests whose work in moral theology prompted others to participate in a reconstruction of the field. As we will see, ministering pastorally to the laity especially in the face of classical church teachings on birth control, masturbation, divorce, remarriage, and homosexuality, these priests first offered pastoral adaptations to resolve the gulf between the Church's norms and the experience that the laity lived. In time, they realized that their task was not to offer pastoral adaptations, which after all often upheld the norms. Rather, they needed to determine what indeed made a moral decision an objectively right one.

2. Moral norms and pastoral adaptation

In 1967, anticipating the papal encyclical *Humanae Vitae*, the Sulpician Peter Chirico proposed a 'tension morality' which

> . . . recognizes that man is continuously facing obligations that he cannot immediately fulfill but toward which he must ever move. There is always a tension between what one is called to do and what he can actually do in the here and now. In attempting to affirm in the external world all the personal moral values necessary to his growth, man will encounter many circumstances in which he may find it impossible to live up to the total range of demands of the moral order.[37]

Chirico added two points. First, God does not ask the impossible. Second, he commented on a certain win/win situation: 'the tension situation must be seen as a challenge to grow. If the Christian realizes the challenge in his situation he will avoid two extremes: either to despair of salvation because he cannot in the here and now fulfill the whole law, or to fall into dishonesty by declaring the law to be non-existent.' [38]

While Chirico believed that a universal law does not immediately apply to every decision, the law still stands; he did not ignore the law nor suggest that the law was non-existent. Chirico acknowledged the law, but he contended against the law's immediate, exclusive, and direct universal applicability in every instance. The total range of demands needs to be considered. This led him to see that concrete acts are not simply right or wrong. They are complex, and their moral nature must be differentiated if one is properly to evaluate them and place them within the context of Christian growth.

The promulgation of *Humanae Vitae* prompted moral theologians and bishops to reflect on what to do with so many sincere and earnest Catholics who were not adhering to the law of the Church. To address the gulf between the teaching and the couples' discernment, theologians and bishops came up with a variety of models. In France, the bishops saw the encyclical as posing a veritable 'conflict of duties'.[39] Charles Robert took that claim and developed it: 'conflict situation' solutions could apply not only for contraception but also for divorce and remarriage.[40] Their 'conflict' was not far from Chirico's 'tension'.

From South Africa, Durban's Archbishop Denis Hurley developed a so-called 'principle of the overriding right' for trying to appreciate the fact that one could not directly apply a universal norm immediately to a situation without recognizing the other claims that were present.[41] Hurley, Chirico, and the French Bishops had much in common in addressing the divide. In each case, they upheld the Church's teaching but they also acknowledged the complexity of the laity's experience and recognized the tension, conflict, and the overriding duties.

In 1965 the journal *Concilium* appeared, championing the best of the new theology celebrated at Vatican II. Each issue took a theme: morality, systematics, liturgy, etc. and each volume appeared in six editions in six languages. In its premier issue on morality, the Dutch theologian Conrad van Ouwerkerk raised the question of compromise.[42] Two German scholars, Helmut Weber and Klaus Demmer, similarly raised the same question.[43] Finally, Charles Curran examined the concept and argued that some situations manifest the presence of sin in the world to such an extent that even a best possible solution cannot be called good, but is tolerated simply because it is the best compromise that could be achieved.[44] Curran resisted calling some actions, like an abortion to save a mother's life, good; similarly, he did not call such compromises sinful. Instead, Curran acknowledged the sinfulness of the world and provided a moral category between the right and the wrong, the compromise that we can tolerate.

The ambiguity of compromise, however, did not sit well with Catholics who prefer some clarity even when there is ambiguity.[45] Curran's defense prompted a host of questions, from, among others, Richard McCormick and Josef Fuchs, and even a doctorate dissertation by the Maltese moral theologian Mark Attard.[46]

Two other concepts have had longer lives than compromise. The first concerned Catholics who acknowledged the rightness of the Church's teaching, but who strove unsuccessfully to obey it. They found that the Church's teaching was compelling but they could not realize it in their lives. These people were confessing, with great frequency, but still asking: were they sinners each and every time they practiced birth control, even though they tried to adhere to the Church's teaching without excuse? In particular, they wanted to know were they to absent themselves from Communion, even though it could help them grow in the moral life?

Confessors and pastors responded, recommending the practice known as the law of graduality. Through this law, confessors encouraged the laity to understand that gradually they would make the law a reality in their lives and that in the meantime the sacraments could accompany them along the journey.

In 1981, nearly 25 years after *Humanae Vitae*, Pope John Paul II published *Familiaris Consortio*, and therein acknowledged the problems married Catholics had in following the teaching on birth control. He argued that the Church as teacher also had to be a compassionate mother and in the latter role referred to the law of graduality favorably.[47] He differentiated the practice from the gradualization of the law, that is, moderating the universality and/or force of the law itself. The law had already expressed itself; it was for the laity to gradually adhere to it.

Two years later, in 1983, the Italian moral theologian Dionigi Tettamanzi explicated the teaching by way of commentary in *L'Osservatore Romano*.[48] In

1997, Cardinal López Trujillo at the Lateran's Pontifical Council for the Family issued a statement, 'Vade Mecum for Confessors Concerning Some Aspects of the Morality of Conjugal Life', again endorsing the law of graduality.[49]

In 1997 Tettamanzi returned to *L'Osservatore Romano* with the law of graduality, this time in discussing the matter of homosexuality. The homosexual person trying to adhere to church teaching on the celibate call could be counseled by her or his confessor through the law of graduality.[50] More recently the Argentinian moralist Gustavo Irrazabal returned to it for the law's general usefulness. In a manner of speaking, his claims were not far from Chirico's 40 years earlier:[51] the law on birth control as a goal provides a maturing tension for the striving Christian; the practice affirms the objective truth of the law; compassionately acknowledges human experience; and is pastorally sensible.

Still, Josef Fuchs asked where was moral objectivity in all this? If the demands of a couple's marriage meant that they 'had' to practice birth control, then the morally right act would be to use birth control. Pope John Paul II and Tettamanzi had argued that using birth control was always in itself wrong and that failure to acknowledge the truth of the teaching would 'gradualize', that is, 'relativize', the Church's law. Fuchs denied the claim; he argued that in determining the moral law in the concrete, many claims had to be considered. Just as Chirico did, he acknowledged assuredly that there was a universal undifferentiated law in the encyclical. But in determining the actual moral law regarding procreation and sexual relations in the specific marriage, there were other claims on the couple as well. Fuchs was not relativizing the law, he retorted; he was recognizing the couple's responsibility to make a morally, objectively right decision in light of *Humanae Vitae* and the demands of their marriage.[52]

We will return to Fuchs' question about moral objectivity shortly, but we need to appreciate another pastoral adaptation that was long held before *Humanae Vitae* and well used in the aftermath of its teaching: the distinction between objectively grave matter and subjective non-culpability.

We saw earlier that the laity found consolation in the confessional where the confessor took into account a variety of circumstances affecting their experience. Though the hierarchy publicly proclaimed a moral norm as foundational to church teaching, pastoral adaptations in the confessional did not simply absolve confessing laity, but tended to dissolve them of any guilt in the first place. For instance, many laity confessed the sin of masturbating. Confessors could treat penitents in one of three ways: absolve penitents of the practice as sinful, urging them to return to the confessional before approaching the Eucharist if they should sin again; counsel the law of graduality, encouraging them to understand the rightness of the teaching and the poverty of their weakness, but urging them to see this in a context of maturation where the frequent reception of confession and Communion can help them overcome the practice; or invoke the distinction between objectively sinful and subjectively non-culpable where the gravity of masturbation is recognized, but the circumstances of the penitents are such that there was little or no moral culpability in their action.

This third practice stretched the divide between church teaching and pastoral practice, for it gave us sins without sinners. Still, it derived its logic from the manualists. We saw that, from Slater to Jone, there was a progressive willingness by moralists to find more and more extenuating circumstances in the lives of the laity that effectively extended the grounds of their non-culpability. By distinguishing the objectively grave from the subjectively non-culpable, manualists taught that the teaching of the Church remained intact, but kept the laity from thinking of themselves as sinners.

While manualists were offering their probabilistic decisions to pastors, penitents were searching for which priests were more 'understanding' in the confessional, and were surprised to learn that sometimes the more understanding confessor was the vocal preacher who robustly defended from the pulpit the objective truthfulness of a church teaching. This was Catholic accommodation from the manuals. Bishops and confessors found it as useful as the laity found it helpful.

The revisionists had their doubts. If the confessor found the laity to have compelling grounds for their action, such that they were exonerated from any guilt, was the action actually objectively wrong in the first place? Charles Curran asked it this way: 'Does the confessional experience of a frequent lack of subjective guilt indicate that the matter itself might not be objectively grave?'[53]

The distinction between objectively grave and subjectively non-culpable became less and less credible. Married couples began asking: should they be confessing as sinful something that they were less and less certain actually was sinful? And what about the confessor? Should he be insisting that married couples were objectively sinful because of their use of birth control, but subjectively not-culpable even though the couple was convinced in conscience that the action was not sinful *and* he believed them? To these questions, the revisionists argued that the problem was not the laity's weakness but the narrowness of the specific teaching on birth control.

A few years after *Humanae Vitae*, the distinction regarding moral objectivity and pastoral solutions arose again, this time concerning homosexual actions. In 1971, an editorial in the *Christian Century* called for the 'complete acceptance' of homosexuals.[54] The editorial launched extensive discussion and Richard McCormick argued that theological ethicists had a responsibility to consider the rightness or wrongness of *Christian Century*'s proposal. Toward this end he presented several contemporary Catholic positions including those of Lisa Sowle Cahill, Phillip Keane, and Charles Curran in his 'moral notes'.[55]

Cahill argued that 'heterosexual marriage is the normative context for sexual acts' but saw the 'exception situation, including that of the confirmed homosexual' wherein it would be possible to judge sexual acts as 'non-normative but objectively justifiable'. She described homosexual acts as pre-morally wrong, but in the case of the homosexual person this sexual activity would not be objectively wrong if were there sufficient reason. McCormick noted that Philip Keane argued similarly.[56] Cahill's and Keane's position created space for a moral exceptionalism; the homosexual could be considered objectively right in a sexual relationship; but the particular case was not normative. Their solution begged the question: how could an action be objectively justifiable yet still non-normative?

Charles Curran argued differently. He examined the pastoral solution proposed by some that, though homosexual activity was objectively wrong, it may not be considered subjectively sinful. Curran noted that this solution did not go 'quite far enough' and proposed instead the theory of compromise, which acknowledged that heterosexual marital relations were the ideal, but that in the world as it is, homosexual activity and unions are often the only morally viable solution for gay and lesbian persons.[57] In a later work of Curran, he called these actions of actual homosexuals morally right.[58]

McCormick's position was to use the distinction between moral norm and pastoral adaptation, and remarked that heterosexual intercourse was normative and that homogenital acts 'always depart from the ideal or the normative'.[59] Still he offered a 'modest proposal' for one who is 'irreversibly' homosexual and not called to celibacy (the judgments about both conditions being the 'responsibility of the individual before God'). He distinguished between specific and individual rectitude, where the former is a general assessment and the latter considers the agent's own personal circumstances. But he specifically added that this approach would not put these homosexual acts 'on a par with heterosexual acts' nor would it 'give legitimacy to those actions'.[60]

Like Cahill and Keane, McCormick's proposal left the matter unresolved. If homosexual actions 'always depart' from the normative, why counsel someone to pursue the non-normative?[61] Without an assertion regarding normativity, McCormick left the gay or lesbian person with an individual judgment that was pastorally permitted but not morally acceptable. McCormick's position resonated with those before him: teach the norm, but practice the pastoral adaptation, which was nothing short of disbanding the norm for this particular homosexual person. McCormick's position was echoed elsewhere.[62]

Years later, several moral theologians revisited these arguments. Cristina Traina saw these positions as ecclesial solutions to an intransigent situation; they had no other choice but to offer these casuistic pastiches: 'The roots of this ambivalence may well be political . . . Aware that most members of the Roman Catholic church hierarchy hold many traditional moral norms to be unalterable, he [McCormick]has adopted the strategy of pledging allegiance to these norms but . . . arguing painstakingly for the acceptability in particular circumstances of many acts the norms had been assumed to proscribe.'[63]

William George approached the homosexual question much as Curran and Fuchs approached birth control. He basically asked what is the morally right norm for conduct in light of the experience and discernment of the acting person? If a homosexual proposed her or his position to a pastor who found the person's judgment compelling, does this prompt in turn a reconsideration of the specific norm? He wrote that:

> . . . a hesitancy to revise the starting norm in light of the judgments reached by individuals leaves the unhappy impression that individual rectitude . . . will inevitably be less than that to which the human species as a whole is invited. Gays and lesbians will, at best, be regarded as trying to approximate the morality of the species.[64]

The moralists' responsibility to reflect on homosexual conduct meant an examination not only of homosexual lives, but also of our norms. Against McCormick's pastoral adaptation, George offered the virtue of prudence to formulate individual judgments, and, in light of those, to examine the enduring validity of the Church's specific norms, and, if necessary, to articulate more correct expressions of them.

By the mid-1970s revisionists and neo-manualists were at opposite ends of the spectrum, not on the sinfulness of the laity but on moral objectivity: for revisionists, a competent judgment was the source of moral objectivity; for the neo-manualists, a promulgated universal law was.

3. Intrinsic evil, universal validity, and the moral absolute

The debate between the revisionists and neo-manualists was not over every teaching that the Church ever held or every ethical decision a Catholic made. In fact, Catholics were making (as they always had) plenty of ethical decisions, and the Church's hierarchy was not offering universally valid norms for these matters: regarding neighborliness and friendship; truth-telling and promise-keeping; child-raising and home-purchasing; schooling and careers; voting and zoning.

In these ethical decisions moral theologians like Tillmann and Häring, as well as Slater and Jone, all urged Catholics to consider adequately all the demands that they had to entertain in order to make a good decision. Indeed, on this, moral theologians, hierarchy, and the laity were agreed: know what you should know; decide rightly; act responsibly.

The teachings that revisionists questioned were those that the Church had taught were 'intrinsically evil'. That is, those which, in effect, pre-empted full moral decision-making. To call an object of activity intrinsically evil (a concept that derives from the fourteenth-century anti-Thomist, Durandus of St Pourcain)[65] means that no other claim, no intention and no circumstances can possibly redeem the wrongness of the object; it is so clearly, unalterably wrong that it could never be considered a right action.

M. Cathleen Kaveny explains that actions that were classified as intrinsically evil were not identified always with grave moral actions. Actions like extensive collateral damage in war or wrongful entry into war were morally grave, but not intrinsically evil. Ejaculating into a receptacle to test for sexual potency was not grave but it was an intrinsically wrong action.[66]

The teaching on intrinsically evil actions has had an *a priori* significance by claiming that such actions could never be admitted to moral judgment.[67] Actions like masturbation, divorce, homosexual activity, and birth control were not simply wrong, but intrinsically wrong. No Catholic in making any decision about responsible parenting, for instance, could entertain birth control, even though they were being called to adequately consider all the claims on them.

Aside from the teaching on direct killing of the innocent, many of these intrinsically wrong actions focused on sexual and reproductive activity. One reason for the decisive wrongness of these activities was the long-held insistence that all sexual matters were grave and admitted no lightness or parvity of matter.[68]

Moral theologians asked: did the Church always teach these actions to be wrong? A host of works on the history of church teaching on sexuality demonstrated convincingly that these teachings lacked a good deal of consistency and continuity.[69]

But what about the concept of intrinsic evil itself? Was it valid to say that an act of masturbation, birth control or divorce could never be right? Johannes Gründel looked at the case of sterilization to argue precisely against its status as an intrinsic evil,[70] while James Murtaugh provided an exhaustive study of the term's use.[71]

In 1971, Josef Fuchs published a landmark article entitled 'The Absoluteness of Moral Terms'.[72] At the outset, he established the concept of the moral absolute as the foundational aim of all who seek moral objectivity: 'Absoluteness in moral imperatives is directly opposed, obviously, to all arbitrary judgment and to all relativism, and thereby positively affirms the objectivity, grounded in human reality itself.' This assertion led him to ask whether the association of universally valid norms with absoluteness might have compromised our ability to realize the objective truth: 'The real problem, we repeat, lies in determining to what degree the absolute, in the sense of the non-arbitrary but objective, is comprehensible and guaranteed in the case of universally valid norms.'[73] He asked, then, whether 'universally valid norms' have obfuscated our ability to recognize the absolute in the here and now.[74]

Looking to the scriptures, Fuchs argued that absoluteness superseded the universally valid. Often, in the scriptures, the call to act in certain ways was specific to the individual; the absolute requirements for those summoned in the scriptures were hardly universal: 'The moral behavioral norms in scripture are directed to actual persons of a definite era and culture. Hence their character of absoluteness would not signify primarily universality, but objectivity.'[75]

Fuchs then made a claim: the absolute is the morally objective. 'The absoluteness of moral norms is constituted primarily by their objective effectiveness vis-à-vis the given reality.'[76] Seeking the morally objective action,

Fuchs saw it in the *de facto* norm at which the agent arrives in answer to the question: what should one do in this context of given reality? A person's task in answering this question is to consider adequately the multitudinous claims on her/him and then to make a moral judgment; that judgment bears in itself the immediate moral norm for action.

Fuchs also argued against reducing the sources of a moral judgment to a singular consideration of the object, which in these magisterial teachings is always necessarily the object in the abstract. In considering the adequacy of a moral judgment, with its attention to circumstances and intention, Fuchs explained: 'The norm for concrete action is constituted by the *one* moral judgment of the whole complex (the action *in abstracto*, circumstances, intention) and not by the moral judgment of an action *in abstracto and* the added judgment of circumstances and intention.'[77]

Establishing the judgment in conscience as the absolute moral norm, he then contested the concept of intrinsic evil. Regarding intrinsic evil, viewed theoretically, 'there seems to be no possibility of norms of this kind for human action'. He explained: 'The reason is, that an action cannot be judged morally at all, considered purely in itself, but only together with all the circumstances and the intention.' Only when the action is fully considered can we arrive at the absolute moral judgment. Moreover, we do not have the omniscience to anticipate all the circumstances and intentions that might accompany the object of an act. Fuchs entertained the question: can we say definitively that we know that this object could never be used? He answered: 'A behavioral norm, universally valid in the full sense, would presuppose that those who arrive at it could know or foresee adequately *all the possible combinations* of the action concerned with circumstances and intentions, with (pre-moral) values and non-values (*bona* and *mala physica*).' Fuchs concluded his critique with this very clear assertion: '*A priori*, such knowledge is not attainable.'[78]

In this article, Fuchs undid not only the credibility of the concept of intrinsic evil, but also the claims of any metaphysical *a prioris* that could diminish the range of consideration necessary to make a prudential judgment. Despite his work, Fuchs acknowledged in a later article that since *Casti Connubii* (1930) the 'formulation "intrinsic evil" has been employed more frequently in Roman documents, but never so frequently as in the document *Persona Humana* (1975) on some questions concerning sexual ethics, at the very time when reflection and discussion on the concept of "intrinsic evil, had become very explicit".'[79]

4. Democratizing *Epikeia*

The virtue of prudence becomes the very foundation for the moral objectivity of human judgment. This virtue needs to understand ethical claims, weigh their urgency and relevance, and understand the effects that certain courses of action may have. Prudence helps us to understand ourselves and our capabilities as moral agents, as well as the context in which we find ourselves. As the virtue of practical reason, it guides us in making the actual judgment and in determining the appropriate means for realizing well our decisions.[80] Without prudence there is no right moral judgment, no right moral action, and no right moral living.

Of course, prudence does not function robotically. In order to entertain all moral possibilities, it needs to be imaginative. Philip Keane argued that theological ethics needs the imagination in order for the decision-maker to be fully prudential.[81] Likewise, William Spohn argued for the analogical imagination so as to grasp more fully (and hermeneutically) the ethics of the scriptures.[82]

Beyond the imagination, we need a virtue that belongs to the field of justice: the virtue of *epikeia* allows us to interpret the law and the validity of claims made on us.[83] Earlier, *epikeia* was a dispensation from the law by the one competent to grant that dispensation, whether manualist or priest-confessor; it was and is the virtue of those who correctly understand and interpret and apply the moral law.[84] As such it is a 'higher rule of action'.[85]

As moral theologians recognized moral truth more in the lives of individual Christians than in particular propositions, the process of applying the moral truth moved from a cognitive process of deducing judgments from principles to discerning the correct way of living out one's call to discipleship. In this shift, one's prudential conscience by virtue of *epikeia* not only directs one to apply norms, but actually to recognize the more urgent ones.[86] Eventually *epikeia* provides the moral agent with self-direction,[87] just as earlier it provided the moral theologian's competency to provide direction to priests in their confessional and pastoral ministries to the laity.[88]

The laity, like moral theologians before them, realized that norms are constantly being reinterpreted, modified, and edited. They look, therefore, to the wisdom of the tradition going forward in these norms, appreciating their limits and their historical context. In conscience they examine the applicability of these norms and finally shape their thinking through *epikeia* through which a well-articulated judgment emerges. Effectively they translate norms into action in the appropriate situation, and, hopefully, move through their decisive action into greater personal freedom to serve better.[89]

Fuchs expanded on the notion of *epikeia*. With an Aristotelian appreciation that *epikeia* helps not only to apply, but also to mediate between norms and concrete reality, Fuchs saw competent moral agents recognizing that existing norms might not express adequately the values that are at stake in a particular area of concern.

> If problems previously unknown arise today because of new knowledge – for example, in the fields of embryology or genetics – can these problems be resolved by means of principles or norms that were established without this knowledge, that is by norms that were not truly formulated for our new problems. If norms are frequently formulated in an inadequate manner without taking account of certain realities, and if they are

> seemingly unable to give a sufficient answer to the problem – then ought we not reformulate the norm, at least in part to make it more adequate?[90]

Epikeia helps us realize the capacity to re-formulate moral norms.

Klaus Demmer also took *epikeia* to the world of moral norms that look less like the static and closed systems of modern manualism and more like dynamic, open, and evolving systems of contemporary science. He is quick to point out that this historical understanding of moral norms has nothing to do with relativism as an essentialist metaphysics would imply; taking the historicity of moral norms seriously means, rather, maintaining a vigilance regarding the adequacy of their proper expression. In sum, this historical process encourages the mutual conditioning of theory and praxis.[91]

The Christ-event is an example of divine *epikeia*, the new dispensation.[92] Demmer sketched a unique theological conception of *epikeia* by placing it in the context of New Testament casuistry, specifically the secondary antithetic statements of the Sermon on the Mount that exemplify the 'better righteousness' of the Christian (Matthew 5.20). For Demmer, casuistry was no longer controlled by the essentialist metaphysics of the neo-manualists which subsumed particular cases under universal principles. In a hermeneutical context, moral reasoning is characterized as the art of the possible (*Kunst des Möglichen*); it is marked by the ability to discover new and better alternatives of acting and it translates the radical message of the gospel into feasible ways of acting. In this way, the Christian steers the often narrow middle course between the minimalist tendencies of laxism and the legalistic tendencies of rigorism.[93]

The virtue of *epikeia* preserves, then, the personal character of moral action. It safeguards the proper autonomy of moral reasoning and reflects the 'freedom, creativity, and responsibility' of the person.[94] The retrieval of the virtue of *epikeia* reminds us that the application of a norm is a continual historical accomplishment which depends on experience and insight. *Epikeia* underlines the hypothetical or indeterminant character of our moral norms: it is a means to show how a norm's application always stands between tradition and contemporary reality. *Epikeia* is, then, the virtue of freedom that reflects our willingness to occasionally go beyond traditional applications of a norm and to introduce an element of newness to a moral tradition.[95]

5. Pre-moral evil, principle of double effect, proportionalism

If the moral judgment is the moral norm for a course of action, what do we call the traditional 'moral' norms about abstract intrinsically evil objects? We could say that the moral judgment itself is the specific realization of the universal norm in context, something that both Chirico and Fuchs argued for earlier. Similarly we could say that 'moral' norms in the tradition are only descriptively so, but then why call them norms?

Fuchs insisted that the abstract object cannot sufficiently lead us to a moral judgment: we need the object, the end or intention, and the circumstances. Only when the full complexity is adequately considered can we attain the objective moral judgment. Still, Fuchs recognized that these norms had some claim on us and he therefore referred to them as 'pre-moral evil'.[96] This description was not far from that of the philosopher W. D. Ross who distinguished between general *prima facie* duties and the actual duty to be done. The former attributed to an object of activity a moral relevance but not an immediate or an exclusive one.[97]

Major revisionists like McCormick and Janssens were early followers of Fuchs' initiative.[98] Only Fuchs' student, Schüller, argued that such norms should more appropriately be called 'non-moral'.[99] Still, by naming these norms pre-moral, Fuchs accomplished two things: he diminished the immediacy of the moral teaching on these exceptionless norms but also affirmed that these norms were not neutral or free of any moral consideration.

Over the course of some seven years an important debate emerged which Richard McCormick moderated in the *Notes on Moral Theology*.[100] The first issue to occur is that another revisionist, Gustav Ermecke, assailed Fuchs' proposal with what Richard McCormick called 'a rather free-swinging theological attack'.[101] Ermecke's major objection seemed to be that Fuchs diminished the centrality of the object in the moral sources and replaced it with the intention and circumstances. Fuchs responded that he was not replacing anything; the entire action, with all three sources, was the basis for moral judgment.[102]

At the same time Louis Janssens entered the debate and made four significant claims in a memorable article on ontic and moral evil. First, he argued that a moral judgment is possible when we consider the totality of the action.[103] Second, the matter of material norms concerns ontic evil, not moral evil. Janssens defined ontic evil 'as a lack of perfection which impedes the fulfillment of a human subject'. As such, ontic evil is inevitably involved in all our activity.[104] Third, when we act, we ought to seek to reduce as much as possible the presence of ontic evil in the world.[105] If the universal norms are about ontic evil, then as such they are about ideals: in the limited historical framework in which we live, we will never be free of the ontic evil that we encounter.[106] Constitutive of the rightness of moral activity is not only the responsibility to diminish ontic evil and to adequately engage all claims, but also to mind the due proportionality between what we intend to do and the means for realizing that intention.[107]

Fuchs and Janssens became critical targets of those who believed that church teaching was being abandoned by the revisionists. For instance, John Connery argued that Fuchs' proposal was basically a morality of consequences that undermined the claims of the longstanding moral teachings.[108] Bruno Schüller and others responded that Catholic ethics has been in its history fundamentally teleological, but it was not a form of consequentialism or utilitarianism.[109] Both Aristotle's and Thomas Aquinas' ethics were clearly teleological, aiming for the end of happiness, but neither was an endorsement of consequentialism.

Of all the reforms claimed by the revisionists, nothing alarmed conservatives more than naming universal moral norms as pre-moral. Ermecke wrote again, lamenting that moral theology was at a crossroad.[110] Janssens responded, describing pre-moral norms as located between the non-moral and the moral.[111] Enrico Chiavacci defended the teleology of contemporary revisionism as belonging to the longstanding Catholic tradition, which is founded on charity seeking its expression.[112]

At the same time, an article by a young German theologian, Peter Knauer, gained a great deal of currency. Originally written in 1965, but reappearing in later editions in different languages, Knauer argued that the principle of double effect was 'the fundamental principle of all morality'.[113] He then contended that, in the absence of intrinsic evil, an action can only be considered as a directly willed evil if it lacked commensurate or proportionate reason between the intention and the actually executed action. This controlling insight about proportionality became the measure of morality, for Knauer and for Janssens, who wrote that 'Knauer pointed out very well that the axiom of the *debita proportion* or of the unwarrantableness of the inner contradiction between means and ends is the central norm of each human act.'[114]

Several critical responses arose. Interestingly, the revisionist Bruno Schüller wrote a blistering essay contending that the principle of double effect was hardly historically representative of Catholic thought. Moreover, in making the claim, Knauer reduced the complexity of church teaching to a rather naïve teleology.[115] Schüller's doctoral student, the Nigerian Lucius Iwejuru Ugorji, substantiated his mentor's claim by reviewing the principle as it was used in the moral manuals and by twentieth-century moralists.[116] More recently, Brian Johnstone raised questions as to whether proportionalism, like other methods of contemporary reasoning, made a false dichotomy between the agent and the action. Joseph Selling took up the critique, defending proportionalism as a method for a more integrated understanding of human action.[117]

Other essays came from more conservative quarters. In the early 1980s, both Servais Pinckaers and John Connery criticized Knauer and Janssens, grouping Fuchs, Schüller, and McCormick with them and calling them 'proportionalists'. Each critic believed that the centrality of the moral object had been diminished, that the absolutes attributed to it had been abandoned, and that Catholic moral reasoning had been treated reductively by revisionism, whence they dismissed the authors by the term 'proportionalists'.[118]

The appellation was striking and itself reductive: Connery and Pinckaers believed that their opponents' argument could be grasped by understanding a single word. Still, before Connery and Pinckaers used the phrase, Richard McCormick had already made the attribution by referring to Fuchs, Janssens, Knauer, and others as '"proportionalists" in their understanding of moral norms'.[119]

Many of the Europeans scoffed at the idea of being corralled together, and, aside from Janssens, few developed the notion of commensurate or proportionalist reason.[120] Most Europeans like Fuchs thought of themselves, instead, as critiquing early manualists and as building the foundations of a new morality. They were interested in matters especially of the philosophical and theological foundations for a moral epistemology and were hardly inclined to name their project as if it were complete. Europeans were more inclined to being known as revisionists and later as proponents of either an autonomous ethics or an ethics of faith. For this reason, in his expansive and clearly definitive study on proportionalism, Bernard Hoose notes that the debate over proportionalism was founded on European critical investigations but developed by the Americans themselves.[121]

Proportionalism was basically a transitional phase in Catholic theological ethics. In trying to establish a method for moral judgment as an alternative to the moral manuals, proportionalism was simply the logic of the moral manuals without the overriding absolute moral norms. Moreover, it normally addressed prohibitive norms regarding contraception, sterilization, divorce, homosexual acts, etc. With a focus on pre-moral evil, proportionalism never developed a positive agenda that could be seen as the methodological extension of the robust moral theology proposed by Häring and his predecessors. Worse still, there was no fundamental context for proportionalists: against what do we weigh pre-moral values? Toward what end do we pursue the good? In time, most theological ethicists moved on in search of a context for developing arguments on moral reasoning and moral living.[122] In answer to her question, 'Where have all the proportionalists gone?',[123] Aline Kalbian answered that theological ethicists turned to feminism, virtue ethics, and other contexts for developing a thicker and more enduring notion of Catholic ethics. As a kind of final word on the topic, Curran too remarked recently, 'By the later part of the twentieth century the defense of proportionalism was no longer a major topic in moral theology.'[124]

These debates demonstrate theological ethicists' deep commitment to intellectual inquiry, moral objectivity, and respect for the teachings of the tradition. Trying to maintain a critical fidelity to church teaching while honoring the experiences of the laity, theological ethicists labored mightily to re-establish the *proprium* of moral theology. Though occasionally ethicists did not fairly represent their opponents' viewpoints, the vigor of the exchanges conveyed the passion as well as the resources of the Catholic tradition. It is remarkable, then, that in the middle of these discussions, the American Timothy O'Connell published the first textbook of the work of mostly revisionists. In 1976 O'Connell not only provided summary claims of the discussions, but he contextualized the developments into a trajectory of moral reasoning and moral living. His book, which 30 years later reads as well as when it was first published, assured us that, as fragmented as the debates were, they were undoubtedly comprehensive in their scope and vision.[125]

A Contemporary Work: Albert Jonsen and Stephen Toulmin, *The Abuse of Casuistry: A History of Moral Reasoning*

If there is one book that bridged the world of the 1970s and 1980s with the twenty-first century on the topic of Catholic moral reasoning, it was *The Abuse of Casuistry* by Albert Jonsen and Stephen Toulmin.[126] Toulmin was a philosopher of moral epistemology; Jonsen a moral theologian-turned-historian of bioethics. Together they worked to study high casuistry.

Their retrieval of high casuistry is riddled with irony. First, if one area of moral reasoning was consistently dismissed by the revisionists, it was casuistry, the deductive application of a principle to a case. Before them, many major Protestant scholars were also outspoken critics of casuistry. Karl Barth (1886–1968), Dietrich Bonhoeffer (1906–45), and Helmut Thielicke (1908–86) saw casuistry as nothing more than a mechanical logic that pretended to have a self-sufficiency in its simplistic method of applying a principle to a case.[127]

Still, while Catholics also repudiated casuistry, some Protestants summoned a new, positive turn to it. In 1948, the Anglican Bishop of Oxford, Kenneth Kirk, argued that, as Paul did casuistry, so should we: it was the abuse of casuistry and not casuistry itself that was at fault.[128] Edward Long argued that casuistry was needed to apply the absolute ideal of love to the concrete.[129] Later, Paul Ramsey argued similarly and endorsed casuistry.[130] More recently both Nigel Biggar[131] and Stanley Hauerwas have favorably reviewed casuistry. Hauerwas writes, 'Casuistry is the mode of reflection a community employs to test imaginatively the often unnoticed and unacknowledged implications of its narrative commitments.' Into his theology of Christian narrative, he sees casuistry as 'a necessity because it provides the means by which we learn to check our particular telling of the story of God with the way our community is'.[132]

At the same time, Protestant English historians were investigating, again positively, sixteenth- and seventeenth-century casuistry.[133] Later, Catholic historians too began studying casuistry anew, particularly as it related to the confessional.[134]

In time, a few European Catholic ethicists began returning to casuistry. Both Jean-Marie Aubert and Klaus Demmer explored the foundations of casuistry as germane to the revisionist project. Aubert saw casuistry as providing the mediation between law and liberty;[135] Demmer noted that casuistry calls us to recognize the historicity of truth in moral reasoning.[136] For Demmer, every time a principle was applied to a new case, the principle itself was being reinterpreted: the hermenutics of the application of casuistic principles to cases was a sure guarantee for the historical development of doctrine. Later, Demmer's student Thomas Kopfensteiner advanced the position that casuistry was used to liberate institutions from normative determinations that did not keep pace with other developments.[137] John Noonan studied the mutation of old rules by the introduction of new cases that shape both the meaning and the application of the rule. After a lengthy process of application and development, new prescriptions are even articulated.[138]

In 1988, in *The Abuse of Casuistry*, Albert Jonsen and Stephen Toulmin proposed and differentiated two forms of casuistry. The first is familiar: it is theoretical and finds its prototype in geometry; its arguments are idealized, atemporal, and necessary; and an axiom underpins the particular conclusion. A typical deductive application of a principle to a case is one clear representation of this geometric logic. Practical reasoning, on the other hand, uses experience gathered from a variety of cases as a guide for future action. Its arguments are concrete, temporal, and presumptive. It employs 'a detailed and methodological map of significant likenesses and differences' between related cases. The authors call this instrument 'taxonomy', and, in this case, a 'moral taxonomy'.[139] Contrary to contemporary assumptions, Jonsen and Toulmin argue that the history of practical reasoning is predominantly a history of taxonomic and not geometric methods. From antiquity, Aristotle's *Rhetoric*, Cicero's *De Inventione*, and the Rabbinic *Halakhah* demonstrate that the resolution of moral problems occurred through the comparison of cases. Rather than applying a particular rule to a concrete situation, the contours of one case were compared, contrasted, and evaluated against other cases that were already held as successfully resolved.[140]

Moral teachers and rabbis, not set prescriptive or prohibitive principles, resolved moral problems. Through their experiential, practical wisdom, they could recognize whether a particular case related to one set of cases or another. Though certain time-honored maxims were invoked, for the most part it was the prudence of the wise that resolved arguments through comparing cases. Their primary wisdom was in the ability to recognize to which set of cases a new case with a new moral problem ought to be compared and measured.[141]

These cases Jonsen and Toulmin call 'paradigm' cases.[142] The paradigm case would set the standard of the correct prudential insight and other cases would be measured against the paradigm. Congruency with a paradigm case, then, highlighted or revealed the fact that the moral logic in the new case was equally correct; congruency made apparent the new case's internal certitude. Moral theologians gave it external certitude by listing the new case within their canons. Jonsen and Toulmin name this method 'high casuistry'.[143]

Jonsen and Toulmin note that, in some historical periods, high casuistry was replaced by more structured, abbreviated expressions of moral reasoning. On those occasions, a shortage of teachers led to the formulation of such rules to guide the judgments of the less skilled and the less experienced. For instance, classical Roman society went from an arbitrating society to a more rule-based one, from pontiffs to statutes. As Rome expanded, so did the case-load, and less experienced judges had to settle disputes. Since their judgments were not always trusted, rules were articulated to measure the correctness of their decisions. Second, since rules were needed, law schools were established that found the teaching of rules more expeditious than the formation of prudential character. Third, the entrance of non-Romans into Roman society required a concordance between the laws of the new peoples and Roman law itself. Fourth, as the empire grew, so did its bureaucracy, and its operating procedures made further appeal to rules a form of life.[144]

Still, Jonsen and Toulmin narrate how often the Greeks, Romans, and Jews preferred to depend on the judges' prudential verdicts; only when they lacked such leadership did they put into stone specifically worded laws.[145] The turn to written law is often, then, a temporary turn away from the exercise of human prudence.[146]

Their work generated enormous interest in the field of moral reasoning and certainly restored the credibility of casuistry.[147] Moreover, they gave a refreshingly contemporary understanding to high casuistry, distancing it from the old, deductive model.

Today they have become casuistry's ardent defenders. Toulmin claims that high casuistry returns ethics to the realm of practical science.[148] The analogical vocation for the casuist is no longer the speculative geometer with theorems and axioms, but rather the attending physician with practical problems all about. Against advocates of principle based moral logic, the principlists, who have their point of departure in theory, the casuist is at home with the categorical.[149]

Toulmin believes that our society today relies too heavily and mistakenly on principles: 'In law, in ethics, and in public administration alike, there is nowadays a similar preoccupation with general principles and a similar distrust of individual discretion.' He recommends that, by being like the physician, the casuist could consider first the concrete problems at hand through a variety of resources and not singularly the principles that so often 'glide over the facts'. [150] Toulmin notes the casuists 'reverse the relationship between theory and practice'.[151]

Jonsen agrees, 'Justification of any particular moral claim comes rarely from a single principle, as many theories would like, but usually from the convergence of many considerations, each partially persuasive but together convincing with plausible probability . . . The weight of any ethical considerations comes, not from the principles or maxims invoked, but from the more fact-like considerations that are piled onto practical judgment.'[152]

Jonsen believes that our present reliance on principles to determine morally right conduct is entrenched in Puritan and Jansenist thought: 'Moralism is absolutist in the etymological sense, namely, it tends to remove (*absolvere*) a moral problem from the actual circumstances of moral action.'[153] Despite that distrust of principles censoring moral data, Jonsen described casuistry as an imaginary building where the frame is set in principles, but the entire make-up of the house, from mortar to furniture, is constituted by circumstances. He adds, 'Principles and circumstances are complementary in a complex and subtle way.'[154]

The real issue of casuistry, however, is not its relationship to principles or their abbreviated and less demanding maxims, but its claim to be 'pre-theoretical'.[155] In the concrete world, where theory is neither known well nor used much, people deliberate morally, inductively, attentive to circumstances.

Because casuistry is concrete and pre-theoretical, it is context-dependent.[156] Casuistry works formally, needs further definition, and functions well in a variety of cultures. Kevin Wildes notes that casuistry cannot operate in a vacuum; it requires context.[157] Hauerwas agrees: 'Casuistry is, therefore, unintelligible as an activity separated from its communal context.'[158]

This combination of turning to the concrete and away from theory, while being context-dependent, has attracted feminist comment.[159] It has also prompted Jonsen and Toulmin to modify some of their earlier claims that casuistry can operate free of the differing presuppositions that animate and distinguish individual cultures.[160] Casuistry engages ourselves, our circumstances, and our cultures.

While casuistry has grown ever more popular, so have the historical investigations into the work of the sixteenth- and seventeenth-century high casuists. The list of works is rather stunning inasmuch as, prior to the 1990s, no one but Louis Vereecke and John Noonan wrote on casuists, but since then ethicists have studied the following: Duns Scotus (1266–1308),[161] William of Ockham (1280–1349),[162] Jean Gerson (1363–1429), [163] Bernardino of Siena (1380–1444),[164] Giovanni da Capestrano (1386–1456),[165] Adrian of Utrecht (1459–1523),[166] John Mair (1470–1550), [167] Francisco de Vitoria (1483–1546),[168] Bartolomé de las Casas (1484–1566),[169] Juan Gines de Sepulveda (1494–1573),[170] Francesco de Toledo (1532–96),[171] Francisco Suárez (1548–1617),[172] Leonardus Lessius (1554–1623),[173] Juan Caramuel (1606–82),[174] Frederich Spee (1591–1635),[175] and Francois Genet (1640–1702).[176]

Notes

1 Klaus Demmer, 'Die autonome Moral – einige Anfrage an die Denkform', 262.

2 John Horgan, *Humanae Vitae and the Bishops* (Dublin: Irish University Press, 1972).

3 Curran and McCormick, eds, *Readings in Moral Theology, No. 3: The Magisterium and Morality* (Mahwah: Paulist Press, 1982).

4 An excellent collection of essays, James Gustafson, *Moral Discernment in the Christian Life: Essays in Theological Ethics* (Louisville: Westminster John Knox, 2007).

5 Richard McCormick, 'Self-assessment and Self-indictment', *Religious Studies Review* 13 (1987) 37–9.

6 Enda McDonagh, *Doing the Truth: The Quest for Moral Theology* (Notre Dame: University of Notre Dame Press, 1979) 12–13.

7 See Keenan, 'Josef Fuchs at Eighty', *Irish Theological Quarterly* 59 (1993) 204–10. Reprinted in *Theology Digest* 42 (1995) 137–40; 'Josef Fuchs and the Question of Moral Objectivity in Roman Catholic Ethical Reasoning', *Religious Studies Review* 24.3 (1998) 253–8; 'Champion of Conscience', *America* (4 April 2005) 6.

8 Josef Fuchs, *Die Sexualethik des heiligen Thomas von Aquin* (Köln: Bachem, 1949); see *De Castitate et Ordine Sexuali* (Rome: Gregorian University Press, 1963).

9 Fuchs, *Situation und Entschiedung: Grundfragen Cristlicher Situationethik* (Frankfürt: Knecht, 1952).

10 See Fuchs' bibliography: Fuchs, *Für eine menschliche Moral* (Freiburg: Herder, 1997) 219–64.
11 See Mark Graham, *Josef Fuchs on the Natural Law* (Washington, DC: Georgetown University Press, 2002) 117–24.
12 Bruno Schüller, *Gesetz und Freiheit* (Düsseldorf: Patmos, 1966); *Die Begründung sittlicher Urteile. Typen ethischer Argumentation in der katholischen Moraltheologie* (Düsseldorf: Patmos-Verlag, 1973); *Der menschliche Mensch. Aufsätze zur Metaethik und zur Sprache der Moral* (Düsseldorf: Patmos, 1982), translated into *Wholly Human: Essays on the Theory and Language of Morality* (Washington, DC: Georgetown University Press, 1986).
13 C. D. Broad, *Five Types of Ethical Theories* (London: Routledge, 1930). See Todd Salzman's very fine and extensive discussion on Broad and then on Schüller, *Deontology and Teleology: An Investigation of the Normative Debate in Roman Catholic Moral Theology* (Leuven: Leuven University Press, 1995) 3–183; *What Are They Saying About Catholic Ethical Method* (Mahwah: Paulist, 2003).
14 Schüller, 'Direct Killing/Indirect Killing', Charles Curran and Richard McCormick, eds, *Readings in Moral Theology No. 1: Moral Norms and Catholic Tradition* (Mahwah: Paulist Press, 1979) 138–57 (hereafter, *Moral Norms*); see also Albert Di Ianni, 'The Direct/Indirect Distinction in Morals', *Moral Norms*, 215–43; Richard McCormick and Paul Ramsey, eds, *Doing Evil to Achieve Good: Moral Choice in Conflict Situations* (Chicago: Loyola University Press, 1978). Probably the most insightful writing on the topic is Franz Scholz, 'Possibilità e impossibilità dell'agire indiretto', *Fede Cristiana e Agire Morale*, 289–311.
15 See William O'Neill, *The Ethics of Our Climate: Hermeneutics and Ethical Theory* (Washington, DC: Georgetown University Press, 1994).
16 Bruno Schüller, 'The Debate on the Specific Character of a Christian Ethics: Some Remarks', *Wholly Human*, 32–42.
17 Schüller, 'The Debate', 37–8.
18 Demmer, 'Die autonome Moral'. See Thomas Kopfensteiner, 'The Metaphorical Structure of Normativity', *TS* 58 (1997) 331–46.
19 Augustine, *Confessions* III 6, 11; *PL* 32, 683.
20 Demmer, 'Die autonome Moral', 261. See Jan Jans, 'Divine Command and/or Human Ethics? Exploring the maieutical dialectics between Christian Faith in God and Responsibility', in Jan Jans, ed., *Für di Freiheit verantwortliche, Festschrift für Karl-Wilhelm Merks zum 65 Geburtstag* (Freiburg: Herder, 2004) 35–49.
21 Klaus Demmer, *Deuten und handeln: Grundlagen und Grundfragen der Fundamentalmoral,* (Freiburg: Herder, 1985) 17; *Gottes Anspruch denken: Die Gottesfrage in der Moraltheologie* (Freiburg: Herder, 1993) 160–2.
22 Häring, *Free and Faithful in Christ: Moral Theology for Clergy and Laity* (New York: Seabury Press, 1981).
23 Louis Janssens, *Liberté de conscience et liberté religieuse* (Paris: Desclée de Brouwer, 1964) (in English: *Freedom of Conscience and Religious Freedom*) (New York: Alba House, 1966). Among his more significant essays, 'Personalist Morals', *Louvain Studies* (1970–1) 5–16; 'Ontic Evil and Moral Evil', *Louvain Studies* 4 (1972–3) 115–56; 'Norms And Priorities in a Love Ethics', *Louvain Studies* 6 (1976–7) 207–38; 'Saint Thomas Aquinas and the Question of Proportionality', *Louvain Studies* 9 (1982–3) 26–46; 'Ontic Good and Evil: Premoral Values and Disvalues', *Louvain Studies* 12 (1987) 62–82. Janssens, 'Personalism in Moral Theology', in Curran, ed. *Moral Theology: Challenges for the Future*, 94–107.
24 Michael Fahey, 'From the Editor's Desk', *TS* 63 (2002) 1–2.

25 See Louis Janssens, 'Artificial Insemination: Ethical considerations', *Louvain Studies* 8 (1980) 3–29; 'Particular Goods and Personalist Morals', *Ethical Perspectives* 6 (1999) 55–9; also Jan Jans, 'The Foundations of an Ethics of Responsibility', *Ethical Perspectives* 3 (1996) 148–56; Salzman and Lawler, *The Sexual Person*, 102–3.

26 Dolores Christie, *Adequately Considered: An American Perspective on Louis Janssens' Personalist Morals* (Leuven: Peters Press, 1990); see the festschrift, Joseph A. Selling, ed., *Personalist Morals: Essays in Honor of Professor Louis Janssens* (Leuven: Peeters, 1988), esp. Jan Jans, 'Some Remarks on the Work of Professor Emeritus Louis Janssens', 319–28.

27 Brian Johnstone, 'From Physicalism to Personalism', *Studia Moralia* 30 (1992) 71–96; Joseph Selling, 'The Human Person', in Bernard Hoose, ed., *Christian Ethics: An Introduction* (London: Cassell, 1998) 95–109.

28 Roger Burggraeve, 'The Holistic Personalism of Professor Magister Louis Janssens', *Louvain Studies* 27.1 (2002) 29–38.

29 Joseph A. Selling, 'Proportionate Reasoning and the Concept of Ontic Evil: The Moral Theological Legacy of Louis Janssens', *Louvain Studies* 27.1 (2002) 3–28; 'Louis Janssens' Interpretation of Aquinas: A Response to Recent Criticism', *Louvain Studies* 19 (1994) 65–74.

30 Dewi Maria Suharjanto, *Die Probe auf das Humane: Zum theologische Profil der Ethik Franz Böckle* (Bonn: Bonn University, 2005).

31 Alfons Auer, *Weltoffener Christ* (Düsseldorf: Patmos, 1960) (in English, *Open to the World*) (Baltimore: Helicon Press, 1966).

32 Auer, *Umweltethik* (Düsseldorf: Patmos, 1994).

33 Auer, *Autonome Morale und christlicher Glaube* (Düsseldorf: Patmos, 1971, 1995.)

34 Enrico Chiavacci, *Teologia Morale* (Assisi: Cittadella Editrice, 1977, 1980, 1985, 1990); *I. Morale Generale* (1977); II *Complementi di Morale Generale* (1980); III.1 *Teologia Morale e Vita Economica* (1985) III.2; *Morale della Vita Economica, Politica, di communicazione* (1990); *Teologia Morale Fondamentale* (Assisi: Cittadella Editrice, 2007).

35 Bernard Hoose, Julie Clague, and Gerard Mannion, eds, *Moral Theology for the Twenty-First Century: Essays in Celebration of Kevin Kelly* (London: T&T Clark, 2008) provides a bibliography of Kelly's works, 293–5.

36 Emblematic of McDonagh's recent work, *Vulnerable to the Holy: In Faith, Morality and Art* (Dublin: Columba Press, 2004); Linda Hogan and Barbara FitzGerald, eds, *Between Poetry and Politics, Essays in Honour of Enda McDonagh* (Dublin, Columba Press, 2003). In this volume is a bibliography (228–32) and two fine biographical essays: Kevin Kelly, 'It's Great to be Alive', 191–204; Charles Curran, 'Enda McDonagh's Moral Theology,' 206–26.

37 Peter Chirico, 'Tension, Morality and Birth Control', *TS* 28 (1967) 258–85; Tension, 'Morality and Birth Control', in *Theology Digest* 16 (1968) 104–10, 107.

38 Ibid.

39 Charles Robert, 'La situation de "conflit": Un theme dangereux de la theologie morale d'aujourd'hui', *Revue des sciences religieuses* 44 (1970) 190–213. See also, Nicholas Crotty, 'Conscience and Conflict', *TS* 32 (1971) 208–32. The concept of conflict in theological situations derives from the Protestant Helmut Thielicke, *Theological Ethics* (Philadelphia: Fortress Press, 1966–9). See Rainer Mayer, *Moral und christliche Ethik* (Stuttgart: Calwer Verlag, 1976).

40 Charles Robert, 'Est-il encore opportun de priver les sacrements de la reconciliation et de l'eucharistie indistinctment tous les divorcés remarries?', *Revue de droit canonique* 24 (1974) 152–76.

41 Denis Hurley, 'A New Moral Principle: When Right and Duty Clash', *Furrow* 17 (1966) 619–22.
42 Conrad van Ouwerkerk, 'Gospel Morality and Human Compromise', *Concilium* 7 (May 1965) 5–12.
43 Helmut Weber, 'Il Compromesso Etico', *Problemi e Prospettive di Teologia Morale*, 199–220; Demmer, 'Entscheidung und Kompromiss', *Gregorianum* 53 (1972) 323–51.
44 Charles Curran, 'Dialogue with Joseph Fletcher', *A New Look at Christian Morality* (Notre Dame, Indiana: Fides Press, 1968) 159–73.
45 Richard McCormick, *Ambiguity in Moral Choice* (Milwaukee: Marquette University Press, 1973).
46 McCormick, *Notes*; Mark Attard, *Compromise in Morality* (Rome, Gregorian University, 1976) STD dissertation.
47 John Paul II, *Familiaris Consortio* (22 November 1981) para. 34: http://www.vatican.va/holy_father/john_paul_ii/apost_exhortations/documents/hf_jp-ii_exh_19811122_familiaris-consortio_en.html.
48 Dionigi Tettamanzi, '*Verita ed Ethos*', *Osservatore Romano* (28 September 1983) 1.
49 A. López Trujillo, '*Vade Mecum* for Confessors Concerning Some Aspects of the Morality of Conjugal Life', *Origins* 26 (1997) 617, 619–25: http://www.vatican.va/roman_curia/pontifical_councils/family/documents/rc_pc_family_doc_12021997_vademecum_en.html.
50 Dionigi Tettamanzi, 'Christian Anthropology and Homosexuality', *L'Osservatore Romano* (12 March 1997) 5.
51 Gustavo Irrazabal, 'La ley de la gradualidad como cambio de paradigma', *Moralia* 27 (2004) 167–90.
52 Josef Fuchs, 'The Law of Graduality and the Graduality of the Law', *Christian Morality: The Word Becomes Flesh* (Washington, DC: Georgetown University Press, 1987) 33–7.
53 Curran, *A New Look at Christian Morality*, 203.
54 'To Accept Homosexuals', *Christian Century* 88 (1971) 275.
55 Richard McCormick, *Notes*, 393–4.
56 Lisa Sowle Cahill, 'Moral Methodology: A Case Study', *Chicago Studies* 19 (1980) 171–87, at 186; Philip Keane, *Sexual Morality* (New York: Paulist Press, 1977) 71–91.
57 Charles Curran, 'Dialogue with the Homophile Movement', *Catholic Moral Theology in Dialogue* (Notre Dame: University of Notre Dame, 1976) 184–219.
58 Curran, *Critical Consensus in Moral Theology* (Notre Dame: University of Notre Dame, 1984) 93.
59 Richard McCormick, 'Homosexuality as a Moral and Pastoral Problem', *The Critical Calling*, 289–314, at 312.
60 McCormick, 'Homosexuality', 309.
61 Paul Ramsey called into question an exception without any normative guidance. Paul Ramsey, 'The Case of Curious Exception', Gene H. Outka and Paul Ramsey, eds, *Norm and Context in Christian Ethics* (New York: Scribner's, 1968) 67–135.
62 See Jan Visser's solution in John Coleman, 'Two Unanswered Questions', in Jeanine Gramick, *The Vatican and Homosexuality* (New York: Crossroad Publishing Company, 1988) 59–65, at 62; Elio Sgreccia, *Manuale di bioetica* (Milano: Vita e Pensiero, 1991) 141; Jose Vico Peinado, 'Misericordia en los juicios', *Sal terrae* 90 (2002) 115–28. On the disconnect between moral norms and pastoral adaptation,

Jorge Humberto Pelaez, 'Reflexiones teologico pastorales en torno a la homosexualidad', *Theologica Xaveriana* 35 (1985) 187–210.

63 Cristina Traina, *Feminist Ethics and Natural Law: An End to the Anathemas* (Washington, DC: Georgetown University Press, 1999) 217.

64 William George, 'Moral Statement and Pastoral Adaptation: A Problematic Distinction in McCormick's Theological Ethics', *The Annual of the Society of Christian Ethics* (Boston: Society of Christian Ethics, 1992) 135–56, 142–3. Edward Vacek proposed an 'ethic of proportionality' in his much cited, 'A Christian Homosexuality?', *Commonweal* 107 (3 December 1980) 681–4.

65 John Dedek, 'Intrinsically Evil Acts: The Emergence of a Doctrine', *Recherches de theologie ancienne et medievale* 50 (1983) 191–226.

66 M. Cathleen Kaveny, 'Intrinsic Evil and Political Responsibility: Is the Concept of Intrinsic Evil Helpful to the Catholic Voter?' *America* 199.13 (27 October 2008) 15–19. Myles Reareden, 'Grave Matter: Humanae Vitae Thirty-five Years Later', *Irish Theological Quarterly* 68 (2003) 155–9.

67 On intrinsic evil, see Curran, 'Absolute Moral Norms', *Christian Ethics*, 72–83; Franz Scholz, 'Problems on Norms Raised by Ethical Borderline Situations: The Beginnings of a Solution in Thomas Aquinas and Bonaventure', *Moral Norms*, 158–83; James Bretzke, 'The Debate Over Intrinsically Evil Acts', *A Morally Complex World: Engaging Contemporary Moral Theology* (Collegeville: Liturgical Press, 2004) 69–77.

68 Patrick Boyle, *Parvitas Materiae in Sexto in Contemporary Catholic Thought* (Lanham: University Press of America); James Brundage, *Law, Sex and Christian Society in Medieval Europe* (Chicago: University of Chicago Press, 1987); James A. Brundage and Vern Bullough, eds, *Handbook of Medieval Sexuality* (New York: Garland Publishing, 1996); Margaret Farley, 'Sexual Ethics', in Warren Reich, ed., *Encyclopedia of Bioethics,* revised edn (New York: Simon Schuster Macmillan, 1995) V, 2363–75; James Keenan, 'Catholicism, history', in Alan Soble, ed., *Sex from Plato to Paglia: A Philosophical Encyclopedia* (Westport, CN: Greenwood Press, 2006) I. 143–53; Hubertus Lutterbach, 'Die Sexualtabus in den Bussbüchern.', *Saeculum* 46 (1995) 216–48; Ibid., *Sexualität im Mittelalter. Eine Kulturstudie anhand von Bussbüchern des 6. bis 12. Jahrhunderts* (Köln: Böhlau Verlag, 1999); Pierre Payer, *Sex and the Penitentials: The Development of a Sexual Code, 550–1150* (Toronto: Toronto University Press, 1984); Payer, *The Bridling of Desire: Views of Sex in the Later Middle Ages* (Toronto: University of Toronto Press, 1993); Payer, 'Confession and the Study of Sex in the Middle Ages', in *Handbook of Medieval Sexuality*, 3–32.

70 Johannes Gründel, 'Zur Problematik der operativen Sterilisation in katholischen Krankenhaüsern', *Stimmen der Zeit* 199 (1981) 671–7.

71 James Murtaugh, *Intrinsic Evil: An Examination of This Concept and its Place in Current Discussions on Absolute Moral Norms* (Rome: Gregorian University Press, 1973).

72 Josef Fuchs, 'The Absoluteness of Moral Terms', *Moral Norms*, 94–137. The article originally appeared in *Gregorianum* 52 (1971) 415–58.

73 Ibid., 96.

74 Ibid., 94.

75 Ibid., 100.

76 Ibid., 116.

77 Ibid., 124.

78 Ibid., 124.

79 Josef Fuchs, 'An On-Going Discussion in Christian Ethics: "Intrinsically Evil Acts"?', *Christian Ethics in a Secular Arena* (Washington, DC: Georgetown Univer-

sity Press, 1984) 74. He concluded with this observation: 'Moral theologians today are concerned with greater objectivity as opposed to abstract and therefore insufficient moral judgments.' At 86.

80 Josef Endres, 'Anteil der Klugheit am Erkennen des konkreten Wahren und an dem Wollen des Wahrhaft Guten', *Studia Moralia* 1 (1963) 221–53; Giuseppe Gullo, *Prudenza e Politica* (Naples: Edizioni Domenicane Italianae, 1974); A-M Henry, ed., *Prudence chrétienne* (Paris: Cahiers de la vie spirituelle, 1948); Thomas Hibbs, 'Principles and Prudence', *New Scholasticism* 61 (1987) 271–84; James Keenan, 'Distinguishing Charity As Goodness and Prudence As Rightness: A Key to Thomas', *Pars Secunda, The Thomist* 56 (1992) 407–26; Keenan, 'The Virtue of Prudence (IIa IIae 47–56)', *The Ethics of Aquinas*, 259–71; Wolfgang Kluxen, *Philosophische Ethik bei Thomas von Aquin*, 2nd edn (Hamburg: Felix Meiner Verlag, 1980); Daniel Mark Nelson, *The Priority of Prudence: Virtue and Natural Law in Thomas Aquinas and the Implications for Modern Ethics* (University Park, PA: The Pennsylvania State University Press, 1992); Josef Pieper, *Prudence* (New York: Pantheon Books, 1959); Yves Simon, *Practical Knowledge* (New York: Fordham University Press, 1991); Conrad van Ouwerkerk, *Caritas et Ratio: Etude sur le double principe de la vie morale chretienne d'apres S. Thomas d'Aquin* (Nijmegen: Drukkerij Gebr. Janssen, 1956); Daniel Westberg, *Right Practical Reason: Aristotle, Action, and Prudence in Aquinas* (Oxford: Oxford University Press, 1994).

81 Philip Keane, *Christian Ethics and Imagination* (Ramsey, New Jersey: Paulist Press, 1984).

82 William Spohn, 'The Analogical Imagination', *Go and Do Likewise*, 50–71.

83 Background essays include: O. Robleda, 'La "Aequitas" en Aristóteles, Cicerón, Santo Tómas y Suárez', *Miscelanea Comillas* 15 (1951) 241–79; Lawrence Riley, *The History, Nature, and Use of Epikeia in Moral Theology* (Washington, DC: Catholic University of America Press, 1948); Edouard Hamel, 'L'usage de l'epikie', *Studia Moralia* 3 (1965) 48–81; Roger Couture, 'The Use of Epikeia in Natural Law: Its Early Developoments', *Eglíse et Théologie* 4 (1973) 71–103.

84 Josef Fuchs, 'Epikeia Applied to Natural Law', *Personal Responsibility and Christian Morality* (Washington, DC: Georgetown University Press, 1983) 185–99.

85 Thomas Aquinas, *Summa Theologiae*, II.II. 120.1c.

86 Fuchs, 'The Questions Addressed to Conscience', ibid., 216–28.

87 Fuchs, 'Ethical Self-Direction', *Moral Demands and Personal Obligations* (Washington, DC: Georgetown University Press, 1993) 181–8.

88 See Steven O'Hala, *Epieikeia and Contemporary Moral Theology in the Light of Hans-Georg Gadamer's Philosophical Hermeneutics* (Rome: Pontificia Universitas Gregoriana, 1997).

89 Josef Fuchs, *Für eine menschliche Moral*, 184–92.

90 Fuchs, 'Historicity and Moral Norm', *Moral Demands*, 91–108, at 106; see also *Für eine*, 193–204.

91 Demmer, *Die sittliche Persönlichkeit*, in Wilhelm Ernst and K. Feiereis, eds, *Moraltheologie im Dienst der Kirche* (Leipzig: Benno, 1992) 102–14, at 106.

92 Demmer, *Gottes Anspruch denken. Die Gottesfrage in der Moraltheologie* (Freiburg, Herder, 1993) 151–2.

93 Demmer, *Die sittliche Persönlichkeit*, 112.

94 J. Fuchs, '*Epikie* – Der praktizierte Vorbehalt', *Stimmen der Zeit* 214 (1996) 749–58.

95 Thomas Kopfensteiner helped me to see the importance of *epikeia* when we were writing 'Moral Theology out of Western Europe', *TS* 59 (1998) 107–35.

96 Fuchs, 'The Absoluteness of Moral Terms', 122–6.
97 W. D. Ross, *The Right and the Good* (Oxford: Oxford University Press 1965) 18–36.
98 See also Richard Gula, *What are They Saying about Moral Norms?* (Ramsey, New Jersey: Paulist Press, 1982).
99 See Schüller, *Wholly Human*, 164–6; McCormick, *Notes*, 688.
100 See Odozor, 'The Debate on Moral Norms', *Moral Theology in an Age of Renewal*, 209–46.
101 McCormick, *Notes*, 528–51, at 530; Gustav Ermecke, 'Das Problem der Universaliltät oder Allgemeingültigkeit sittlicher Normen innerweltlicher Lebensgestaltung', *Münchener theologische Zeitschrift* 24 (1973) 1–24.
102 Fuchs, 'Sittliche Normen – Universalien und Generalisierungen', *Münchener theologische Zeitschrift* 25 (1974) 18–33.
103 Janssens, 'Ontic Evil and Moral Evil', 73.
104 Ibid., 67.
105 Ibid., 79.
106 Ibid., 84.
107 Ibid., 41–59.
108 John Connery, 'Morality of Consequences: A Critical Appraisal', *TS* 34 (1973) 396–414.
109 Bruno Schüller, 'Neuere Beiträge zum Thema "Begrundung sittlicher Normen"', in Franz Furger, ed., *Fragen christlicher Ethik* (Zurich: Benziger, 1974) 109–81. See McCormick's discussion, *Notes in Moral Theology*, 536–43; Lisa Sowle Cahill, 'Teleology, Utilitarianism, and Christian Ethics', *TS* 42 (1981) 601–29; Edward Vacek, 'Proportionalism: One View of the Debate', *TS* 46 (June 1985) 287–314; Todd Salzman, *Deontology and Teleology*. Bernard Hoose provides a very helpful summary of the teleology debate, *Proportionalism: The American Debate and Its European Roots* (Washington, DC: Georgetown University Press, 1987) 69–100. See also, Brian Mullady, *The Meaning of the Term 'Moral' in St. Thomas Aquinas* (Vatican City: Libreria Editrice Vaticana, 1986).
110 Gustav Ermecke, 'Katholische Moraltheologie am Scheideweg', *Münchener theologische Zeitschrift* 28 (1977) 47–54; William May, 'Contraception, Abstinence and Responsible Parenthood', *Faith and Reason* 3 (1977) 34–52.
111 Janssens, 'Norms and Priorities in a Love Ethic', *Louvain Studies* 6 (1977) 207–38. See also Curran, 'Utilitarianism and Contemporary Moral Theology: Situating the Debates', *Louvain Studies* 6 (1977) 239–55.
112 Enrico Chiavacci, 'The Grounding of the Moral Norm in Contemporary Theological Reflection', *Readings in Moral Theology No. 2*, 270–304.
113 Peter Knauer, 'The Hermeneutic Function of the Principle of Double Effect', *Readings in Moral Theoology No. 1*, 1–39, at 1. The first appearance of this article is 'La détermination du bien et du mal par le principe du double effet', *Nouvelle Revue Théologique* 87 (1965) 356–76.
114 Janssens, 'Ontic Evil', 72.
115 Bruno Schüller, 'The Double Effect in Catholic Thought: A Re-evaluation', *Doing Evil to Achieve Good*, 165–92.
116 Lucius Iwejuru Ugorji, *The Principle of Double Effect: A Critical Appraisal of its Traditional Understanding and Its Modern Reinterpretation* (Frankfurt Am Main: Peter Lang, 1985); Haig Khatchadourian, 'Is the Principle of Double Effect Morally Acceptable?', *International Philosophical Quarterly* 28 (1988) 21–30; Keenan, 'Taking Aim at the Principle of Double Effect: Reply to Khatchadourian', *International Philo-*

sophical Quarterly 28 (1988) 201–5; Keenan, 'The Function of the Principle of Double Effect', *TS* 54 (1993) 294–315; Christopher Kaczor; 'Double-Effect Reasoning from Jean Pierre Gury to Peter Knauer', *TS* 59 (1998) 297–316.

117 Brian Johnstone, 'Objectivism, Basic Human Goods, and Proportionalism', *Studia Moralia* 43 (2005) 97–126; 'Intrinsically Evil Acts', *Studia Moralia* 43 (2005) 379–406; Joseph A. Selling, 'Distinct But Not Separate: The Subject–Object Relation in Contemporary Moral Theology', *Studia Moralia* 44 (2006) 15–40; Brian Johnstone, 'The Subject Object Relation in Contemporary Moral Theology: A Reply to Joseph A. Selling', *Studia Moralia* 44 (2006) 41–62; Werner Wolbert, 'Proportionalismus und die in sich schlechten Handlungen', *Studia Moralia* 45 (2007) 377–99. Wolbert developed a series of questions regarding killing in *Du solst nicht töten; Systematiche überlegungen zum Tötungsverbot* (Freiburg: Herder, 2000). More recently, *Was sollen wir tun?* (Freiburg: Herder, 2005).

118 John Connery, 'Catholic Ethics: Has the Rule for Norm-Making Changed', *Theological Studies* 42 (1981) 232–50. Servais Pinckaers, 'La question des actes intrinsèquement mauvais et le "proportionalisme"', *Revue Thomiste* 82 (1982) 181–212; see also William May, 'Aquinas and Janssens on the Moral Meaning of Human Acts', *The Thomist* 48.4 (1984) 566–616; Christopher Kaczor, *Proportionalism and the Natural Law Tradition* (Washington, DC: Catholic University Press, 2000).

119 McCormick, *Notes*, 709.

120 For instance, in Rome in the 1980s, on any number of occasions, Fuchs and Demmer remarked to their students that they never welcomed the title proportionalist.

121 Hoose, *Proportionalism.*

122 See my contentions in 'The Moral Agent: Actions and Normative Decision Making', *A Call to Fidelity*, 37–54.

123 Aline Kalbian, 'Where Have All the Proportionalists Gone?', *Journal of Religious Ethics* 30 (2002) 3–22.

124 Curran, *Catholic Moral Theology in the United States*, 109.

125 Timothy O'Connell, *Principles for a Catholic Morality* (Minneapolis: Seabury Press, 1976). Earlier, Albert Jonsen published a striking handbook reporting on the work of the revisionists: *Christian Decision and Action* (New York: The Bruce Publishing, 1970).

126 Albert Jonsen and Stephen Toulmin, *The Abuse of Casuistry: A History of Moral Reasoning* (Berkeley: University of California Press, 1988) (hereinafter *Abuse*).

127 Karl Barth, *Church Dogmatics* III, 4, 7ff; Nigel Biggar, 'Barth's Trinitarian Ethics', in John Webster, ed., *Cambridge Companion to Karl Barth* (New York: Cambridge University Press, 2000) 212–28, esp. 220–2.

128 Kenneth Kirk, *Conscience and Its Problems: An Introduction to Casuistry* (London: Longmans, 1948).

129 Edward Long, *Conscience and Compromise: An Approach to Protestant Casuistry* (Philadelphia: Westminster Press, 1954).

130 Ronald Carson, 'Paul Ramsey, Principled Protestant Casuist: A Retrospective', *Medical Humanities Review* 2 (1988) 24–35.

131 Biggar, 'A Case for Casuistry in the Church', *Modern Theology* 6 (1989) 29–51.

132 Stanley Hauerwas, 'Casuistry as a Narrative Art', *Interpretation* 37 (1993) 377–88, at 381 and 377, respectively.

133 Henry McAdoo, *The Structure of Caroline Moral Theology* (London: Longmans, 1949); Elliot Rose, *Cases of Conscience: Alternatives Open to Recusants and Puritans Under Elizabeth I and James I* (New York: Cambridge University Press, 1975);

Thomas Wood, *English Casuistical Divinity during the Seventeenth Century* (London: SPCK, 1952).

134 John O'Malley, *The First Jesuits* (Cambridge: Harvard University Press, 1993) 136–52; Thomas Tentler, *Sin and Confession on the Eve of the Reformation* (Princeton: Princeton University, 1977); Miriam Turrini, *La coscienza e le leggi. Morale e diritto nei testi per la confessione della prima Età moderna* (Bologna: Società editrice il Mulino, 1991).

135 Jean-Marie Aubert, 'Morale et Casuistique', *Recherches de Science Religieuses* 68 (1980) 167–204.

136 Demmer, 'Erwägungen über den Segen der Kasuistik', *Gregorianum* 63 (1982) 133–40.

137 Thomas Kopfensteiner, 'Science, Metaphor, and Casuistry'.

138 John T. Noonan, Jr, 'Development in Moral Doctrine'.

139 *Abuse*, 14.

140 Ibid., 47–74.

141 Ibid., 250–66.

142 Ibid. 252.

143 See also, Keenan, 'Casuistry', *Oxford Encyclopedia of the Reformation* (New York: Oxford University Press, 1995) I: 272–4; Bretzke, 'Navigating a Morally Complex World: Casuistry with a Human Face', *A Morally Complex World*, 169–90

144 *Abuse*, 54.

145 *Abuse*, 47–88.

146 See John Treloar, 'Moral Virtue and the Demise of Prudence in the Thought of Francis Suárez', *American Catholic Philosophical Quarterly* 65 (1991) 387–405.

147 Edmund Leites, ed., *Conscience and Casuistry in Early Modern Europe* (New York: Cambridge University Press, 1988); Richard Miller, *Casuistry and Modern Ethics: A Poetics of Practical Reasoning* (Chicago: University of Chicago Press, 1996).

148 Toulmin, 'The Recovery of Practical Philosophy', *The American Scholar* 57 (1988) 337–52.

149 Toulmin, 'Casuistry and Clinical Ethics', Edwin DuBose et al., eds, *A Matter of Principles?* (Valley Forge: Trinity Press International, 1994) 310–20, at 314.

150 Toulmin, 'The Tyranny of Principles', *The Hastings Center Report* 11 (1981) 31–9, at 34.

151 Toulmin, 'Casuistry and Clinical Ethics', 310.

152 Jonsen, 'Of Balloons or Bicycles – or – The Relationship between Ethical Theory and Practical Judgment', *Hastings Center Report* 21 (1991) 14–16, at 15.

153 Jonsen, 'American Moralism and the Origin of Bioethics in the United States', *Journal of Medicine and Philosophy* 16 (1991) 113–30, at 120.

154 Jonsen, 'Casuistry: An Alternative or Complement to Principles', *Kennedy Institute of Ethics Journal* 5 (September 1995) 237–51, at 249.

155 Toulmin, 'Casuistry and Clinical Ethics'. See also his account of the importance of casuists causing confusion with the profusion of circumstantial issues in sixteenth century Europe, *Cosmopolis* (Chicago: University of Chicago Press, 1990) esp. 5–44.

156 The argument of our book, *Context of Casuistry*.

157 Kevin Wildes, 'The Priesthood of Bioethics and the Return of Casuistry', *Journal of Medicine and Philosophy* 18 (1993) 33–49, at 45; James Tallmon, 'How Jonsen Really Views Casuistry: A Note on the Abuse of Father Wildes', *Journal of Medicine and Philosophy* 19 (1994) 103–13; Wildes, 'Respondeo: Method and Content in Casuistry', *Journal of Medicine and Philosophy* 19 (1994) 115–19.

158 Hauerwas, 'Casuistry as Narrative Art', 387.

159 See Cristina Traina, *Feminist Ethics and the Natural Law*; Marcia Sichol, 'Women and the New Casuistry', *Thought* 67 (1992) 148–57; A. Cheree Carlson, 'Creative Casuistry and Feminist Consciousness: The Rhetoric of Moral Reform', *Quarterly Journal of Speech* 78 (1992) 16–32; Dena Davis, 'Abortion in Jewish Thought: A Study in Casuistry', *Journal of the American Academy of Religion* 60 (1992) 313–24; Kathy Rudy, 'Thinking Through the Ethics of Abortion', *Theology Today* 51 (1994) 235–48.

160 *Abuse*, 1–20.

161 Antonio Poppi, 'La Fondazione dell'etica nel pensiero di Giovanni Duns Scotus', *Studi sull'Etica della Prima Sculoa Francescana* (Padova: Centro Studi Antoniani, 1996) 59–80; Thomas A. Shannon, 'Method in Ethics: A Scotistic Contribution', *Context in Casuistry*, 3–24; Alan Woolter, 'Introduction', William Frank, ed., *Duns Scotus on the Will and Morality* (Washington, DC: Catholic University Press of America, 1997) 1–124.

162 Marilyn McCord Adams, 'The Structure of Ockham's Moral Theory', *Context*, 35–51.

163 Brian McGuire, 'In Search of Jean Gerson', Brian McGuire, ed., *A Companion to Jean Gerson* (Boston: Brill, 2006) 1–40.

164 Franco Mormando, '"To Persuade is a Victory": Rhetoric and Moral Reasoning in the Sermons of Bernardino of Siena', *Context*, 55–84.

165 Poppi, '"Veritas et Iustitia" nello *Speculum conscentiae* di Giovanni da Capestrano', *Studi sull'Etica della Prima Sculoa Francescana*, 145–64.

166 Martin Stone, 'Adrian of Utrecht and the University of Louvain: Theology and the Discussion of Moral Problems in the Late Fifteenth Century', *Traditio* 61 (2006) 247–87, at 286–7.

167 Keenan, 'The Casuistry of John Major, Nominalist Professor of Paris (1506–1531)', *Annual of Society of Christian Ethics*, 1993, 205–22; reprinted in *Context*, 85–100.

168 Francisco de Vitoria, *Political Writings*, in Anthony Pagden and Jeremy Lawrence, eds (Cambridge University Press, 1992); G. Scott Davis, 'Conscience and Conquest: Francisco de Vitoria on Justice in the New World', *Modern Theology* 13 (1997) 475–500; Roger Ruston, 'Part II: Salamanca: Francisco de Vitoria', *Human Rights and the Image of God* (London: SCM Press, 2004) 65–118; Julia Fleming, 'When "Meats Are Like Medicines": Vitoria and Lessius on the Role of Food in the Duty to Preserve Life', *Theological Studies* 69 (2008) 99–116.

169 Ruston, 'Part III: 'Mexico and Peru: Bartolomé de las Casas', *Human Rights*, 119–90; Thomas O'Meara, 'The Dominican School of Salamanca and the Spanish Conquest of America: Some Bibliographical Notes', *The Thomist* 56.4 (1992) 555–82.

170 G. Scott Davis 'Humanist Ethics and Political Justice: Soto, Sepulveda, and the "Affair of the Indies"', *Annual of the Society of Christian Ethics* (1999) 193–212. See also his *Warcraft and the Fragility of Virtue* (Moscow, Idaho: University of Idaho, 1992).

171 Keenan, 'The Birth of Jesuit Casuistry'.

172 Martin Stone, 'Scrupulosity and Conscience: Probabilism in Early Modern Scholastic Ethics', *Contexts of Conscience*, 1–16. See also Philip Schmitz, 'Kasuistik: Ein wiederentdecktes Kapitel der Jesuitenmoral', *Theologie und Philosophie* 67 (1992) 29–59.

173 Toon van Houdt, 'Money, Time, and Labour: Leonardus Lessius and the Ethics of

Lending and Interest Taking', *Ethical Perspectives* 2 (1995) 18–22; 'Tradition and Renewal in Late Scholastic Economic Thought: The Case of Leonardus Lessius (1554–1623)', *Journal of Medieval and Early Modern Studies* 28 (1998) 51–75; with Martin Stone, 'Probabilism and its Methods: Leonardus Lessius and his Contribution to the Development of Jesuit Casuistry', *Ephemerides Theologicae Lovanienses*, 75 (1999) 359–94.

174 Julia Fleming, *Defending Probabilism: The Moral Theology of Juan Caramuel* (Washington: Georgetown University, 2006). Peter Dvorák and Jacob Schmutz, eds, *Juan Caramuel Lobkowitz: The Last Scholastic Polymath* (Prague: Institute of Philosophy, 2008). Here Fleming has another essay, 'Distinctions without Practical Effect: Caramuel's *Apologema* and *Dialexis de Non-Certitudine* on the Standard Classifications of Probable Opinions', 87–98.

175 Frederich Spee, 'Cautio Criminalis', John Patrick Donnelly, ed., *Jesuit Writings of the Early Modern Period* (Indianapolis: Hackett, 2006) 198–204.

176 James Pollock, *Francois Genet: The Man and His Methodology* (Rome: Gregorian University, 1984).

8

New Foundations for a Theological Anthropology, 1980–2000

Ethics can be defined as 'normative anthropology'.[1]

In the aftermath of *Humanae Vitae*, theological ethicists pursued the notions of moral reasoning and objective moral truth during the next twenty years. This sustained investigation culminated ironically in its critical treatment in *Veritatis Splendor* (1993).

Besides arguing that their works were misrepresented in the encyclical and therefore that they were innocent of the charges of relativism, many theological ethicists, in responding to the encyclical, realized that they had achieved a consensus among themselves in terms of revisionism in general. In particular, they also stood together on the matter of conscience and the notion that moral truth is articulated in the judgment of the agent who has adequately considered all moral claims (in classical terms, the object, circumstances, and intention).

What distinguished the revisionists from the magisterium were philosophical issues. Naming this difference as philosophical is important: as Gallagher and others have been at pains to convey, philosophical claims, not theological ones, separate ethicists and the magisterium in *Veritatis Splendor*. Their disagreements concerned method in general and intrinsic evil in particular. As Fuchs recognized years ago, intrinsic evil is the emblem of the classical, deductive mode of moral reasoning that expresses the fundamental negativity of the moral manuals. Intrinsic evil represents that geometric, theoretical form of moral logic that resides in the manuals and their teachers, and not in the experiential, pre-theoretical reasoning of the ordinary, morally-obliged lay person.

Re-examining the natural law

The beginning of all investigations into a new theological anthropology is the revision of the natural law and the development of an autonomous ethics.

After the high casuistry of the sixteenth and seventeenth centuries, theological ethics settled into a highly classical format of the 'moral manuals'. In these manuals, human nature and moral reasoning became reified and the dynamism that animated both high casuistry and the natural law which provided casuistry with its context came to a halt. Natural law from the eighteenth to mid-twentieth century became a set of unalterable prescriptions and prohibitions: no abortion, no divorce, no masturbation, no birth control, etc. Moreover, they were universal teachings: they pertained to every human being in every local culture. Additionally, the claim was made that the teachings were unchanging throughout history. For this reason they often introduced their teachings, with the phrase, 'As we have always taught.'

Finally, these teachings were rooted in a notion that everything had an essence with a fixed immutable teleology. Thus the nature of human genitals was to reproduce and the use of the genitals for something other than procreation was a violation of the natural law. These unchanging laws of nature were seen then as manifestations of the divine will of the Creator.[2] But this eighteenth-century foundational presupposition of being able to specify the nature of a thing was later recognized in the twentieth century as no more than a naïve essentialism.[3]

Most people today, when they hear the phrase 'natural law', think of these fixed teachings with an established set of ends. Theological ethicists think otherwise. In 1996, the German Eberhard Schockenhoff wrote an apology for a contemporary understanding of the natural law. Explaining the impact that historicist thinking has had on the natural law, Schockenhoff, a student of Demmer, wrote: 'Historical thinking shattered the assumption that the human person had an essential nature which was the same, untouched by the passage of time.' He added, 'The totality of human nature in its whole richness, with its potential and capacities which are yet to be awakened, can be grasped only in history, not by an aprioristic affirmation about its essence or by a perception of its substance which remains limited to the consciousness.'[4]

Schockenhoff explained that since human nature is 'so fortunately imperfect', we need to understand human nature within the context of history in all its incompleteness.[5] Thus the 'natural law affirmations remain in a "preliminary sphere" which points beyond itself to "the fullness of the basis of life".'[6] This more modest assertion of our understanding of nature in an historical context is shared today by most theological ethicists.[7] The claim that the natures of the human and the world have fixed essences is more about a teaching of an era that has passed. In fact, many believe that the eighteenth-century notion of the natural law is simply a contradiction of what the scholastics of the high Middle Ages were arguing.[8]

In order to overcome essentialism and to retrieve a truer understanding of the natural law, we need an interdisciplinary approach to understanding nature and its role in moral reasoning. Nature is no longer understood as the pure object that we engage and examine, as something distant and apart from the human being. Nature is not seen as an object as it was in essentialism; rather, nature is a complex and unfolding system whose finality, development and ways of interacting are grasped only partially – though not arbitrarily – by human insight.

This interdisciplinary understanding of nature offers the possibility of a reintegration of humanity and nature. We cannot separate humanity and nature: we cannot talk about nature without humanity, nor of humanity without nature. The dialogue with contemporary sciences has important implications for ethics. The normative meaning of nature is not found in nature itself. Nature, instead, is an evolving and open source of normativity.[9] Not only is our knowledge of nature and all its complex structures partial, relative, and open to revision, but because the human knowledge process is interactive, as we learn more about nature we gain new perspectives from which to interact with it.[10] The better we understand ourselves, the better we understand nature.

The capacity for understanding is dependent on human reason. Years ago, Wilhelm Korff explored the relationship of the natural law to human reason by asking whether nature or reason is the foundation for the universality of moral judgments. This dichotomy had been the subject of debate for decades.[11] But Korff answered decisively:

> Whatever recognizable or even hidden pre-existing elements of nature may be at the disposal of the rational processes of decision with regard to moral behavior, the principle of moral action nevertheless remains not nature but reason. It is reason alone that puts man in a position to distinguish between good and evil. This ability belongs to reason of its nature and is specific to it in just as elementary a fashion as the ability to distinguish between true and false.[12]

Human reason depends on human experience as an important foundation for theological ethics. The turn to the subject leads us to human experience which in turn replaces eighteenth-century essentialism.[13] Still, experience is a fluid concept, and, though integral to contemporary theological ethics, is not free from prompting further debate. Cristina Traina observes: 'Experience is perhaps both the most-cited factor and wildest variable in debates over methods and questions in ethics.'[14]

A renewed understanding of nature does not mean, then, that humanity is passive before the processes of nature. On the contrary, a continuum through every notion of the natural law has been the enduring assumption of the rationality of moral insight and the legitimacy of plausible arguments. The reintegration of humanity and nature does not diminish, then, our ability to reflect on our place in nature and the possibilities we have of consciously intervening and directing it.[15] Still, we are a part of nature's process of development, are carried along within it, and, in part, are determined by it. Our interventions into nature reflect therefore both our responsibility for nature of which we are always a part and our ability to mold nature in light of human purposes.[16] As Enrico Chiavacci and Antonio Autiero point out, an appreciation of our being part of nature is at the heart of environmental concerns.[17]

The interpretation of natural law norms is an ongoing process. As Korff wrote, 'Ethical norms are not properties of nature but the results of interpretation by reason.'[18] As such, the laws change according to our understanding of where and how human flourishing can be realized. This can only be done by interdisciplinary investigations: we cannot know what humanity is responsible for until we have the data outlining the challenges and possible approaches to be taken.[19] In this way we are constantly realizing the natural law.[20]

Still other presuppositions animate our understanding of the natural law. Some believe that a particular teaching or a particular interpretation of the natural law is something shared with all cultures without difference, because it has an a-religious source and meaning to it. Jean Porter notes, however, that the natural law emerges precisely from and as a religious tradition: it is not free of local cultures or histories but rather formed by them.[21] This might seem a rather problematic claim 'if we assume that rational inquiry must be purified of all historical and cultural contingencies'. But is the nature of human reasoning not dependent on human experience? Can we 'purify' our inquiry? Porter argues against the stripping away of natural law assumptions that are suspected of specific theological or local cultural claims. On the contrary, the theory provides 'a way of thinking about the theological significance of human nature and the moralities stemming from that nature'.[22]

Porter's claim that the natural law, like all normative claims, arises out of local cultures, could suggest the impossibility of ever reaching universal moral consensus. In fact, she writes: 'The claim that all moral traditions share a fundamental core, which amounts to a universally valid morality, appears to me to be defensible only if the core in question is described at such a high level of generality as to be virtually empty, and even then, it is difficult to arrive at a statement of principles that would be universally acceptable.'[23] Elsewhere she argues: 'In my view the cumulative weight of arguments against a strong universalist view of morality is by now overwhelming. Too many considerations point to the conclusion that moral systems are dependent in a variety of ways on the particular convictions and practices of the communities out of which they emerge.'[24]

Lisa Sowle Cahill responded critically to Porter by exploring 'actual intercultural moral and policy consensus and the character of practical reason, in order to nuance the idea of a global common good and to strengthen the prospect of finding global ethics'.[25] Reflecting on the universally consensual achievement of human rights, Cahill notes:

> More credence need not be given to postmodern agnostic theory about the possibility of a common morality, than to the evidence of a remarkable convergence of ethically-motivated action in the present global system . . . The most important and visible areas of change – human

rights, women's rights and the environment – display a unity of moral vision, a common commitment to redressing imbalance of power and well-being so that marginal persons, groups, and nature can flourish. Inclusiveness, equality and solidarity are uniting values.[26]

The claims of universality as an achievement instead of as a metaphysical given does not deny Porter's statement that all moral claims have historical roots rules in particular cultures. Still, Cahill is inviting her readers to ask whether the theological ethical agenda ought to be fixed on the source of morality or on its purpose.

Before Porter's work on natural law, Brian Tierney argued that the very idea of natural rights derives not from the Enlightenment and its universal claims but rather from the Church's desires in the eleventh century to determine the proper roles of the pope and bishops, not as free-standing individuals, but rather as being deeply interconnected with the communities they shepherded. In articulating their rights, canonists saw rights not as privatizing privileges that distanced an individual away from the community but rather as sanctions necessary for and embedded in the community precisely to safeguard the common good.[27]

Stephen Pope reminds us of two other insights regarding the natural law. First, in an essay about homosexuality, he compares the claims both of scientists who argue that homosexuality is constitutively natural and of religious leaders who argue against it.[28] Pope contends that Thomas Aquinas uses the word 'natural' not in a biological sense but rather in a teleological and therefore normative sense: the natural is not primarily what we are given, but rather what we are called to become. This issue of becoming points to the teleological view of human flourishing.

According to Pope, then, the context for considering 'naturalness' is overlooked by both sides: 'moral assessment of any pattern of human conduct turns not on its naturalness but on its relation to human flourishing'. He adds: 'The central moral issue, then, is not genetic or statistical naturalness but rather whether homosexuals can respond (at least, that is, as well as heterosexuals) to the universal challenge to train and habituate their sexual passions – naturally oriented to various goods but existentially disordered by concupiscence – in a way that contributes to their flourishing.'[29]

The issue of human flourishing is not a simple, private matter. Each person's good is dependent on social notions of the common good.[30] Thus the natural law question on homosexuality asks: whether in realizing their orientation(s), gay and lesbian persons contribute to their own betterment as well as all of society's. Elsewhere, Pope proposes to shape the future course of the natural law tradition for a globalized world. Since the eighteenth-century notion of natural law presumed a classical teleology, those who still adhere to it display complete disinterest in evolutionary theory. Pope, however, uses the more historicist interpretation to provide an apologia for evolutionary theory. His stance places him with many whom we have already cited: Antonio Autiero, Franz Böckle, Enrico Chiavacci, Klaus Demmer, Marciano Vidal, and other European theological ethicists who have for the past twenty years been developing a deep and abiding interest in the hermeneutical compatibility of reason, tradition, and the evolutionary nature of creation.[31]

Autonomous ethics, an ethics of faith, and a middle position

In 1999, Franz-Josef Bormann published a study of the natural law according to Thomas Aquinas. He made his study in the context of an earlier debate, one between an ethics of faith and an autonomous ethics. Along the way he managed to avoid the corresponding pitfalls of the naturalistic fallacy on the one hand and a vague moral minimalism emanating from autonomous reason on the other. At the end, Bormann concluded that the natural law must be resituated in an historical perspective. He noted an 'antinaturalism' in Thomas and found in the practical reason, and especially through prudence, the way for making moral judgments in a natural law context.[32] Like the Congolese professor at Fribourg, Bénézet Bujo, he finds a clear compatibility between Thomas and the critical claims of an autonomous ethics.[33]

Thirty years earlier, Alfons Auer proposed an autonomous ethics, offering a number of ways of understanding it. As an *ethical* thesis, the autonomy of moral reasoning refers to the rational character of moral statements. As a *theological* thesis, the autonomy of moral reasoning protects the *proprium* or specificity of Christian ethics from being reduced to particular material content. For Auer, faith provides a new horizon of meaning. Norms are not naively derived from faith; faith does not replace the responsibility of human reason, but it exerts an integrating, criticizing, and stimulating effect on the reasoning process. He denies that the specificity of Christian ethics depends, then, on any material norm or content in Christian theological ethics. Rather, all Christians share with all people the same norms. What distinguishes Christian ethics is above all the motivation for being moral in the first place: the call of Christ summons us to love him and therefore to use our reason to discover the categorical norms for human action. As a thesis about *church teaching*, the autonomy of moral reasoning helps protect the moral norm from being imposed heteronomously by any outside authority in general, or by the magisterium in particular.[34] The Church's teaching must be made plausible not by simple imposition but by dialogue and rational argument with all people of good will.

The fundamental assertions of an autonomous ethics are: the primacy of the conscience of every individual; the right to exercise oneself responsibly in freedom; the belief that no person is denied access through human reason to the same moral norms but that these are shared through rational argument; and that the source of moral understanding derives from the moral subject. In turn, Christian faith provides to an autonomous morality: a community of faith that supports each member of conscience, a religious motivation for moral living that is rooted in the redemptive love of Christ, and the ultimate goal of eventually being in union with God. In sum, faith provides to the autonomous Christian the communal context, the motivation, and the last end, but not any specific teachings from Scripture, the tradition, or the contemporary magisterium.[35]

In a manner of speaking, Christian faith provides the form for ethics; the rational moral agent provides the matter of ethics. But can the matter of morality be hermetically sealed from its formal foundations?

This proposal, clearly an extension of the earlier claims for human freedom and responsibility from Häring and Fuchs, became foundational for many Catholic theological ethicists. Likewise, Vatican II in *Gaudium et Spes* affirmed the function of autonomy in Christian ethics: 'If by the autonomy of earthly affairs we mean that created things and societies themselves enjoy their own laws and values which must be gradually deciphered, put to use, and regulated by men, then it is entirely right to demand that autonomy.'[36] Among others, Dietmar Mieth[37] and Bruno Schüller[38] became ardent defenders of the theological foundations of such a morality.

Auer's contribution cannot be overlooked.[39] In this book, we have seen how Catholic theological ethics has been shaped by Lottin on history, Tillmann on Scripture, Gilleman on charity, Häring on a comprehensive, theologically integrated ethics of responsibility, Fuchs on moral objectivity and the critique of intrinsic evil, and Janssens on personalism. Auer's work ranks among these others in definitively shaping the history of moral theology in the twentieth century.

Auer put conscience front and center. He built the foundations of a contemporary theological anthropology on the assertion that the domain of theological ethics is the moral subject called by God in conscience to realize through critical reason a morally upright life responsible to God, the self, the neighbor, and the world. That foundation today remains integral to the ongoing project of theological ethics.

Some resisted Auer's initiative. Joseph Ratzinger, Hans Schürmann, and Hans Urs von Balthasar issued a robust salvo.[40] They saw in Catholic theological ethics a specificity founded not only formally, but also materially: the faith teachings of the tradition were normative and gave Christian ethics its identity and its understanding of Catholic moral truth. Their argument highlighted the need to continue the work of the apostolic Church by consistently proclaiming the teaching of Christ. They offered an ethics of faith that purifies and deepens reason. They also criticized the epistemology of the autonomists; Ratzinger, in particular, charged that they had a naïve understanding of human reason: 'This entire problem, it seems to me, lies in the abstract neutrality of the concept of reason, which actually presides over the discussion in too unreflected a way.'[41]

Though they insisted that they were describing how faith and revelation not only illuminate our understanding but actually inform it with very substantive claims, with the exception of Schürmann they were identifying matters of faith with the traditional teachings of the magisterium on abortion, homosexuality, etc. Others, notably Philippe Delhaye and Dionigi Tettamanzi, developed their criticisms of autonomous ethics.[42] Still others took a more aggressive stance: Gustav Ermecke and Bernhard Stoeckle made a variety of accusations against the autonomous advocates, including their abandonment of the moral tradition. Ermecke wrote: 'How far have some moral theologians already deviated from the ecclesial moral tradition, one never refuted by anyone up to now! There is total silence about binding Church teaching! The moral confusion in theory and practice is in our time almost complete.'[43]

Three very different kinds of responses from the autonomists followed. For the most part, they argued that imposing norms from the magisterium onto the Christian conscience was a heteronomous action, and therefore compromised the conscience and diminished the call to autonomy. Second, some began asking what could be asked morally of a Christian that would not be moral for another person. Referring to Stoeckle, McCormick complained: 'He would do well to give us a single example of a concrete act at the essential level that is in principle unavailable to human insight and demands faith.'[44] Third, more radically, some doubted whether anything from the tradition should be normative for contemporary Christians. Karl-Wilhelm Merks contended that the tradition could not promote an independent ethical truth criterion by which it is held accountable, though it needs to be.[45] In response, Brian Johnstone acknowledged that, while the tradition provides a guarantee for a community's historical identity, we still need to and can ask whether specific teachings from the tradition are ethically right. Johnstone then offered two key insights: critical reason must be constitutive of tradition's truth-claims, and, subsequently, any tradition must endorse those virtues that make possible the exercise of critical reason within the community. Critical reason and not consistency is the criterion by which the correctness of the tradition's claims is established.[46] In defending the tradition, Johnstone at once upheld the autonomous conscience.

Eventually, other ethicists began trying to break the stalemate between advocates of autonomous ethics and an ethics of faith. From the Netherlands, Frans Vosman noted the overall secularity of contemporary ethical conversations which forces theologians to leave God, scripture, tradition, and magisterial authority outside the discourse. Vosman argues that Catholics surrender too much. He proposed a more modest autonomous morality. First, he stressed an anthropological self-understanding that sees the human as being-related (to one another and to God) before being an autonomous individual. Then he turned to the ascetical tradition in which we find two apparently conflicting methods alive and well and enhancing one another: prayer of supplication and prayer of abandonment. Within one tradition we speak freely to God and yet protect the mystery of God. Theological ethicists could employ such an accommodating insight into their debates, by living with both an ethics of faith and an autonomous ethics.[47] Vosman's colleague, Carlo Leget, agreed and similarly opposed the contrasting of autonomous morality and an ethics of faith as well as human autonomy with God's heteronomy.[48]

In Belgium, Éric Gaziaux constructively engaged the positions of Philippe Delhaye and Josef Fuchs. Using Fuchs as Delhaye's alter-ego, Gaziaux highlighted Delhaye's development of a distinctive Christian ethics not in a natural-law-based ethics, but in a scripturally based one. Later, he interpreted magisterial teachings more to his own (more tolerant) way of thinking, combining a strong belief in the uniqueness of Christian morality with a realistic appreciation for mediating conflicting claims. Fuchs, on the other hand, believed that the response to the call of Christ needed to be distinguished transcendentally and categorically.[49] The former concerned matters of faith, grace, and charity; the latter required the natural law which, in the post-conciliar writings of Fuchs, is clearly identified as right reason. With these foundations described, the reader could see merits on both sides of the debate.[50]

At its most basic level, the debate over the autonomy of moral reasoning was about the relationship between faith and reason. Yet that debate was within the context of neo-scholasticism. Though earlier proponents of the autonomy thesis incorporated the transcendental language of Kant, its thesis derives from the same presuppositions found in the moral manuals. Like the American method of proportionalism, autonomous ethics was, in part, a response to the neo-manualists and therefore shared in many of their assumptions.[51]

The autonomous school sometimes had, especially when they were resisting their opponents, an understanding of faith that, like those who advocated for an ethics of faith, seemed to be a set of norms to which Christians attest. On both sides, faith seemed a competitor of human reason, offering its morality against human reason. What the ethics of faith proponents embraced was what the autonomous supporters resisted, but with such a shared preoccupation over magisterial teachings, faith was rarely understood as primarily a shared, communal belief in the Triune God who created, redeemed, and now sanctifies us.

Sooner or later, theological ethicists, while upholding the autonomous agenda of our fundamental responsibility to a formed conscience, would also acknowledge that, if faith was the foundation for the moral life of a Christian subject, it could not be so categorically kept out of the matter of morality. Furthermore, the subject's faith would not be so easily identified with magisterial teaching, but rather with the experience of faith informed by revelation itself.

Inevitably, autonomous ethics would undergo a significant shift.[52] Among the many contributors to the development of this more relational understanding of autonomous subjects who think out of their faith are: Sergio Bastianel, who dedicated two books to the topic, focusing largely on moral experience being informed by faith in Jesus Christ;[53] Enrico Chiavacci, who turned to the conscience as in its nature autonomous but whose whole foundation depends on God as creator;[54] Josef Römelt, who wrote about the ethical relationship with the Church;[55] Karl-Wilhelm Merks, who explored the nature of God as the foundation of Christian morals;[56] the Australian, Robert Gascoigne, who through solidarity brings autonomy and community together;[57] and Hans Rotter, whose attempt at mediating the two led Schüller into a rather remarkable critique of Rotter's attempts.[58] Two who deserve further attention are Klaus Demmer and Franz Böckle.

Klaus Demmer championed a more hermeneutical way of thinking about the relationship between faith and reason. A hermeneutical context opened the way for a dialectical understanding of faith and reason: the 'autonomy' of reason does not eliminate or diminish the role of faith, nor does faith handicap or cripple reason.[59]

Demmer wondered whether each side of the debate was defining faith and reason as two different sources of human wisdom, with anthropological assumptions that were classically neoscholastic, where faith and reason played dichotomous roles. For those involved in hermeneutics, dialects replace dichotomy.

Looking at the anthropological implications of faith, Demmer contended that between faith and moral insight there is a fittingness or a *convenientia*.[60] Exploring how God informs the theological nature of moral argument,[61] Demmer invoked the Augustinian insight that God is closer to us than we are to ourselves.[62] As believers, we think, judge, and act. Faith is not subsequent to or in competition with reason, rather it is in the depths of the person who is called to be fully human.[63]

For more than twenty years as the professor of moral theology at the University of Bonn where he was also University President, Franz Böckle (1921–91) developed a more integrated approach to autonomous ethics, which he called 'theonomous autonomy'.[64] This meant that the competency in and responsibility for our autonomy derives from God as Creator: 'It is a simple matter of course for theological ethics that the ultimate basis of man's moral obligation is found in God's radical claim imposed on man. But everything depends on the way we understand this divine claim.'[65] Böckle argued that the Catholic autonomous ethics presupposes a radical dependency on God and that this dependency did not negate the claims and responsibility for autonomy.

We do not need to presuppose God in order to impose commandments and or prohibitions, but we are convinced that a recognition of creation and a knowledge of our own state as creatures are the basis of our duty to exercise our freedom rationally. We also fear that without this – therefore, in the last resort, without God – everything would be the same to the autonomous will. And that would be a threat from within to autonomy.[66]

Böckle answers the query of those who wonder whether reason is compromised by his assertion of its foundation in the creative will of God. 'The structure of human reason itself is not changed by the attempt to trace reason back to its ultimate transcendental ground. What does in fact happen is that the claim to rational self-realization acquires an unconditioned character by being founded on the *lex aeterna*.'[67]

As Demmer noted that faith and reason are not running in distinctive tracks as sources of moral guidance, similarly Böckle wrote that:

> God and man are not in competition with each other in the same sphere of activity. God's creative activity transcendentally embraces the whole categorical evolution of the world, and man and the world are borne up in the sovereign and creative freedom of God in such a way that God himself is in no sense dependent on the world. On the other hand, the world cannot hold anything that is independent of God, but this is because he founds the world and man on their being themselves and on their own activity.[68]

Like Fuchs and Häring before him, Böckle emphasized the call to freedom and to self-realization in discipleship. Freedom is not discovered in a choice between objects. Rather, freedom expresses itself in our task of self-realization. This call to freedom ought not to be seen as a threat to God or the erection of an idolatrous construct. The fundamental obligatory claim for the moral life is 'understood as a total dependence (the creatural state) in the independence of self-determination (the personal state)'.[69] Böckle's words echoed again *Gaudium et Spes*: 'For though the same God is Savior and Creator, Lord of human history as well as of salvation history, in the divine arrangement itself, the rightful autonomy of the creature, and particularly of man is not withdrawn, but is rather re-established in its own dignity and strengthened in it.'[70]

The Indonesian theologian Dewi Maria Suharjanto notes that Böckle was always interested in the 'whole' ('*Das Ganze im Blicke*'). He had a full interest so that he could speak completely about the '*humanum*'. In this sense he would take from both sides of the autonomy debate the merits of each and look to root it in an unmistakably autonomous ethics.[71]

Let us close with Demmer who clearly resonated with Böckle's contributions:

> Autonomy must be conceived of as a 'relational' or 'theonomous' autonomy. Moreover, autonomy and theonomy, rather than excluding each other, stand in a relation of reciprocity in which one conditions the other. This statement is simply good Catholic theology, grounded on the classical doctrine of a theology of being; with it stands or falls the entire edifice of Catholic theology.[72]

Goodness and rightness, sin, and fundamental option

The distinction between goodness and rightness belongs to any type of moral methodology: deontology, proportionalism, responsibility ethics, virtue ethics, etc. The distinction shapes every moral method. Goodness describes the fundamental operative motivation out of which a human subject acts.

Rightness describes whether an intention and a choice, that is, whether an intended action and a realized one, attain the standards of moral objectivity. In all systems the good motivation seeks to express a morally right intention and action. That is, these descriptions are not separable: a good motivation is one that precisely seeks right living. Still, these systems acknowledge that a right action cannot necessarily deductively indicate a good motivation, nor can a good motivation guarantee the attainment of moral rightness.

Philosophers have been using this distinction for centuries. Democritus, for instance, argued that an agent cannot be called good unless the agent perform the good action and wanted to perform it as good.[73] Kant, in the *Foundation of the Metaphysics of Morals*, argued that only the will is good and made the distinction between a dutiful act (*pflichtmässiges Handeln*) and an act done out of duty (*Handeln aus Pflicht*). The first indicates that an act fulfills what is required, and therefore pertains to rightness; the second indicates that it is done precisely because it is dutifully required, and therefore pertains to goodness. For Kant, when the will acts out of duty, it is good. In keeping with philosophical skepticism, he added that a dutiful act is not by necessity an act done out of duty.[74]

George E. Moore acknowledged that the best motives are no guarantee for perceiving the right act. Similarly, a person acting out of selfishness might still find her interests met by calculating and performing the right act. With this possibility in mind, Moore concluded with a 'paradox': 'A man may really deserve the strongest moral condemnation for choosing an action which actually is right.'[75] Later, Richard Hare and W. D. Ross each wrote on the distinction as well.[76]

In contemporary theological ethics, Bruno Schüller[77] was an early advocate of it. Josef Fuchs,[78] Louis Janssens,[79] Klaus Demmer,[80] and Richard McCormick[81] also championed it. The English theological ethicist Bernard Hoose[82] and I[83] have each provided our own thoughts on it.

In theological ethics, the distinction stems from an understanding of the conscientious life. Through conscience we are called to love God, neighbor, and ourselves; the call to love is the call to love rightly.[84] Acting out of conscience or out of love (goodness), one strives to attain right ways of expressing that love.[85] Rightness, then, serves the goodness of the person in realizing this love, while goodness makes itself responsible for that realization.[86]

Antecedent to any action, goodness expresses whether the agent responds to the initiative of grace to love. Every yes to grace, every response that strives for greater union with God, is an expression of moral goodness. Goodness conveys whether we are responding to the invitation of Christ to seek Christ and neighbor.[87]

Goodness in the Christian tradition is expressed by love, the first movement. Whether one loves is alone the question of goodness.[88] Of course, from the scriptures both John and Paul made this clear: not only was love the sufficient cause of goodness, but even to die for the faith would not be an expression of goodness unless done out of love.

Love as antecedent is found in the expression 'out of love'. The phrase 'out of' appears to cross linguistic frontiers. Thomas, for instance, used it only when talking about charity. Unlike the other virtues, only charity is expressed as antecedent to all the other virtues,[89] working formally,[90] as the source of all moral expression. Thus while Thomas discussed the other virtues by the word '*de*'; that is, 'about', as in '*de temperantia*', he described the object of charity as that which is loved out of charity using the phrase '*ex caritate*' 66 times in the question in the *Summa Theologiae*[91] and 49 times in the parallel question in *On Charity*.[92] For Thomas, 'out of charity' defines the acting person as good. Germans too take to this primary expression. Kant used '*aus Pflicht*' to describe the good will and after him Schüller described goodness as acting 'out of the original moral insight', '*aus der sittlicher Ureinsicht*'.[93]

That primary self-movement is understood in context: goodness is descriptive of individuals insofar as they are able to respond. Thomas held that charity is loving as much as one can.[94] Philip Keane argued that goodness is measured by one's ability.[95] Schüller expresses well the fundamental insight here with his frequent reminder that 'ought implies can'.[96]

Goodness therefore describes a person striving as much as they can for the right out of love (or for Kant, out of duty). Badness or sin is the failure to express love by the failure to strive.

Unlike the classical method of moral description of beginning with the act and retreating into the subject, the historical method begins with the person's goodness in motivation and from there pursues the questions of rightness belonging to intention and choice. This point of departure raises new questions. In the classical model, the overriding presumption was that rightness solely concerned particular acts; in the historical model, the realm of rightness is much more extensive. Wanting to love rightly requires, then, not only the striving to perform right actions, but, more importantly, to live rightly.

In terms of a concept distinguishing goodness from expressions of rightness, 'motivation' is often used. Unlike 'intention', which describes an end which one seeks, 'motivation' describes an end out of which one acts. The earlier scholastic distinction here between the *terminus a quo*, that is, the end out of which we act, and the *terminus ad quem*, that is, the end which we seek, underlines the contemporary distinction between motivation and intention. This distinction has already been adopted by Fuchs,[97] Demmer,[98] and Schüller.[99]

Getting choices right is far more difficult than having right intentions. Because choices are concerned with concrete particulars, they demand greater wisdom, experience, and foresight than intentions do. Parents, for instance, may be right in intending greater strictness for one child and greater leniency for another, but the chances that all their subsequent choices will be right are less likely. Good people may have right intentions but still fall short in realizing them as right choices.

If goodness is striving out of love as much as one can for the right in intention and deed, then badness or sin is the failure to strive to love. Badness as failure underlies the fundamental concept of sin in the Gospels.[100] In Matthew 25, the saved are separated from the damned because the latter did not bother to respond to Christ who needed to be fed or clothed. The rich man failed to respond to Lazarus at his gate. The sinners in the Good Samaritan parable are not the thieves who assault the pilgrim, but the priest and Levite who did not bother to stop. In the same vein, the Pharisee is ridiculed for not bothering to know himself as the publican did. The foolish virgins, the man with the talent, and the rich young man are each types who simply do not bother to try to do what they have been called to do. Jerusalem itself failed to recognize Jesus just as it failed to recognize the prophets.

Some may argue that malice is a source of sin,[101] but malice is more a development of sin: malice results from hearts hardened by their failure to love. Thus, the malice of killing the prophets is like the malice behind those who wanted the Baptist dead: their malice derives from their failure to bother to recognize the prophets in the first place.

Failure as descriptive of sin is often considered by others to be inadequate. Often, personifications of evil, like Hitler and Stalin, are cited to demonstrate that badness is more than failure because it causes positive harm. But our argument does not deny that; rather, it asserts that antecedent to a malicious mind is a heart and will that has failed to love. This same insight governs Karl Menninger's assertion that the sin of indifference, *acedia*, is 'the Great Sin; the heart of all sin'.[102] Neither pride nor malice but indifference, the sin of not bothering, is the source of all sin.

Sin, therefore, is not really the choosing of the wrong or even the failure to choose the right. Antecedent to choice, sin is the failure to be bothered, which often results in wrong intentions and wrong choices. St Ignatius made this point well in *The Spiritual Exercises*. In the colloquy with the crucified Jesus, the exercitant is asked to consider three questions: 'What have I done for Christ?', 'What am I doing for Christ?', 'What ought I to do for Christ?' The questions are not between what right things one ought to do versus what wrong actions one ought to avoid. Rather, the questions concern whether one is acting or not: is one bothered about Christ or not?

Two final comments on sin merit our attention. Darlene Fozard Weaver discusses in two articles the importance of not just defining sin, but identifying sins, so as to appreciate the concrete ways in which we alienate ourselves.[103] Böckle identified sin as act, power, and symbol, and insisted that the deceptive nature of sins eludes us until we finally attempt to confess them.[104]

Finally, within the concept of moral goodness is the concept of fundamental option. This concept derives from a variety of attributions and sources. Michael Fahey held that 'according to his late Flemish colleague, Piet Fransen, S.J., Janssens was also the originator of the concept of fundamental option'.[105] Thomas Kopfensteiner claims it is Fransen himself who originated it.[106] Others name Häring, Rahner or Fuchs.

Though Häring described it as transcendental, its engagement with daily life makes it realized in a wholistic and even accessible way. He wrote: 'The fundamental option is for good and for God when the person does the truth in love in a way that he or she speaks firmly out of his truth of life in facing life's responsibilities. In the fundamental option, seen in a wholistic vision of growth and or regression, there is a kind of transcendental experience of bringing one's own existence into conformity with the reign of good or making oneself a part of evil.'[107]

Böckle saw the option as so radically prior to human action that it is unknowable. 'This original opening of oneself, this consent or original desire, is what is meant by the concept of transcendental freedom.'[108] Developing Rahner, Fuchs held that goodness is our experience of a transcendent call and our response to God's invitation in that call.[109] Fuchs sometimes called this our vertical relationship with God; other times he refers to it as the athematic; still other times, the subjective side of conscience. In each instance, it deals with moral goodness. The basis of our moral goodness is the fundamental option, 'basic freedom',[110] which describes whether, prior to all other decisions, the agent is open to the love of God. Though conceptually described, the fundamental option (*Urentscheidung*) remains athematic.

Mark Graham shows that the notion of fundamental option derives from Fuchs' desire to establish the basis of all moral choices on an option for God, in light of the soteriological design of God.[111] Probably the finest exposé of fundamental option is by Thomas Kopfensteiner, who writes, 'Behind the theory is the classical axiom that grace presupposes and perfects nature. The theory of the fundamental option originated in a psychology of grace which was meant to explain the inner operation of grace and the experience it begets.' Kopfensteiner adds, 'The theory refers to the instinct of grace that projects us toward God as the fulfillment of all our longings. Entailed in the theory of the fundamental option, then, is the anticipation of our eternal destiny and fulfillment; it designates our immanent and dynamic orientation to all of reality.'

Kopfensteiner upholds the transcendental athematic nature of the option. This is a point that has caused both Graham[112] and Jean Porter[113] to wonder whether the option is at all integrated into a moral action theory. Kopfensteiner retains the transcendental dimension of the option but assures us that its proponents in general and Fuchs in particular saw the option as functioning in every moral decision. 'It remains on a pre-reflexive or athematic level. The fundamental option can only be grasped asymptomatically in individual decisions and actions. Being a transcendental category, however, does not lessen the fundamental option's efficacy in individual decisions and actions. The fundamental option eludes a fully thematic awareness or reflexive apprehension because human existence is finite and contingent.' He concludes thus, 'Fuchs asserts that 'the fundamental option is not itself a single act of self-disposition, though it is always felt in particular acts of deciding'.[114] The fundamental option remains the nucleus of all our moral decisions. Every decision is sustained by it and every decision substantiates it.'[115]

Later, Kopfensteiner discusses the complaint of *Veritatis Splendor*, which suggests that the distinction between goodness and rightness is one of two separate descriptives.[116] We have seen above, however, that goodness can only be described in terms of pursuing the right (or else it is solipsistic). Kopfensteiner too comments: 'There is no separation between goodness and rightness or person and act. To separate the fundamental option from individual decisions is to risk falling into pure abstractions and to somehow forget that individual decisions have repercussions – in either a positive or negative sense – on the fundamental option.'[117]

While misinterpreting theologians on goodness and rightness, *Veritatis Splendor* was more supportive on a fundamental option: 'There is no doubt that Christian moral teaching, even in its Biblical roots, acknowledges the specific importance of a fundamental choice which qualifies the moral life and engages freedom on a radical level before God.'[118]

Kopfensteiner's insistence on the interactive relationship between option and human action is also important. Darlene Fozard Weaver wondered whether advocates of the option appreciated the reflexive character of acting. She noted that, while many revisionists describe how 'actions ferry the fundamental option into the categorical realm . . . [t]he ferry ride, as it were, does not appear to make a return trip'.[119] As one advocate, Kopfensteiner understands that a good or bad action affects the fundamental option. Demmer too writes:

> Although the fundamental decision normally remains in the background of consciousness and, as such, precedes reflection, it is nevertheless real. The fundamental decision is not a mechanism. Gushing out of freedom, it can be destroyed by sin, slowly but surely dissolving and relinguishing its dynamism. On the other hand, when the fundamental decision is put in the condition of activating an effectual history, it lets each moral decision come forth as its own interpretation and ratification in the facticity of space and time.[120]

Finally, Enda McDonagh and Mark Graham raised questions about whether moral goodness is reducible to, identified with, and exhausted by fundamental option. McDonagh had focused on the historicity of one's relational growth with the neighbor as constitutive of goodness. Goodness is more than a personal option.[121] Graham suggests identifying goodness with consistent patterns of striving to realize morally right activity.[122] Each counsels against overlooking the complexity of the history of one's striving out of love for the right.

A contemporary work: Cristina Traina, *Feminist Ethics and Natural Law: The End of the Anathemas*

Cristina Traina has argued in her groundbreaking work that the foundations of feminism resonate not with unchanging, essentialist claims of neo-scholastic natural law, but with the more historical and contextual approach. In fact, she argues, feminism needs the natural law so as retrieve its earlier claims that are now lost in the wake of feminist deconstructionism. Conversely, as the natural law continues to be re-examined and reinterpreted, she believes that, in order for it to be truly a contemporary natural law, it must appropriate into its normative structure basic feminist assumptions about gender, the body, and equity.[123]

Traina sees that the claims of contemporary feminism 'depend on the possibility of making some authentically common claims, rooted in commonly held visions of women's flourishing'.[124] She turns to the Catholic natural law tradition because of what she learns from Lisa Sowle Cahill, whom she refers to as an exemplar of natural law feminism. Cahill argues that Catholicism's 'characteristic confidence in moral objectivity and universal values opens onto the sort of inductive and communal mode of reasoned moral insight needed to re-establish public discourse after the post-modern critique'. To this, Traina adds, 'and thus also save feminism from morally debilitating relativism'.[125]

Traina argues that feminism's tendency to reject systematic foundations concerns essentialism and not natural law. The former, not the latter, is the true object of its hermeneutic of suspicion. She aims then 'to show that central natural law claims, critically corrected by feminism, meet the requirements of contemporary moral reflection by balancing novelty, variety, and creativity with claims about continuity and universality'.[126]

Traina examines three figures from the natural law tradition: Josef Fuchs, Richard McCormick, and Gustavo Gutiérrez. In each instance, she examines their theological anthropology, their use of the natural law, and their success as an integrative thinker. Regarding Fuchs, she underlines his anthropology, particularly on goodness and rightness, fundamental option, transcendental personalism, and in particular his work on the relationship between the human Christus and the Christian *humanum*. Concerning McCormick, she turns to his moral reasoning, in particular proportionalism and autonomous morality. Finally, on Gutiérrez, she sees the resources in his work in liberation theology and his reflection on the irruption of the poor and our summons to take a preferential option for the poor. To each of these theologians she appends an evaluation: first, how their contributions can help the feminist agenda; second, how the feminist agenda can improve their own claims.

By the end of the twentieth century, the foundations of theological ethics were well established in a natural law that secures the conscience of the moral subject as a relational, embodied person in an historical world. Its theological anthropology continues to develop in our understanding of it. But placing it at the service of feminism liberates it to ring true to a fuller grasp of human experience.

Notes

1 Franz Scholz, 'Problems on Norms Raised by Ethical Borderline Situations: The Beginnings of a Solution in Thomas Aquinas and Bonaventure', *Moral Norms*, 158.

2 Antonio Autiero, 'Zwischen Glaube und Vernunft. Zu einer Systematik ethischer Argumentation', Klaus Arntz and Peter Schallenberg, eds, *Ethik zwischen Anspruch und Zuspruch. Gottesfrage und Menschenbild in der katholischen Moraltheologie* (Freiburg: Herder, 1996) 41–2.

3 Stephan Lehrer, *Begründung ethischer Normen bei Viktor Cathrein und Wahrheitstheorien der Sprachphilosophie* (Innsbruck: Tyrolia, 1992); Peter Schallenberg, *Die Entwicklung des Theonomen Naturrechts der späten Neuscholastik im deutschen Sprachraum (1900–1960)* (Münster: Aschendorff, 1993).

4 Eberhard Schockenhoff, *Naturrecht und Menschenwürde: Universale Ethik in einer geschichtlichen Welt* (Mainz: Matthias-Grünewald Verlag, 1996), translated: *Natural Law and Human Dignity: Universal Ethics in an Historical World*, trans. Brian McNeil (Washington, DC: Catholic University of America Press, 2003), 128–9.

5 Ibid.

6 Ibid., 290–1. See also Jean Porter's remarks on the 'underdetermination' of human morality by human nature, *Nature as Reason*, 45–52.

7 On the development of the natural law tradition, see Michael Crowe, *The Changing Profile of the Natural Law* (The Hague: Martinus Nijhoff, 1977).

8 Klaus Demmer, 'Optionalismus – Entschiedung und Grundentscheidung', *Moraltheologie im Abseits?* 70, note 3; see in the same collection, Marciano Vidal, 'Die Enzyklika "Veritatis Splendor" und der Weltkatechismus: Die Restauration des Neuthomismus in der katholischen Morallehre' 267. Also Vidal, 'La enciclica 'Veritatis Splendor, y su marcado acento tomista', *Miscelánea Comillas* 52 (1994) 23–38.

9 Chiavacci, 'Für eine Neuinterpretationen des Naturbegriffs', 110–28; Karl-Wilhelm Merks, 'Autonome Moral', *Moraltheologie im Abseits?*, 59–60; see also Philip Schmitz, 'Natur im ökosystemischen Denken', in Bernhard Fraling, ed., *Natur im ethischen Argument* (Freiburg: Herder, 1990) 110–12.

10 Chiavacci, 127.

11 See some accounts of the philosophical debates in Anthony Lisska, *Aquinas's Theory of Natural Law: An Analytic Reconstruction* (New York: Oxford University Press, 1998).

12 Wilhelm Korff, 'Nature or Reason as the Criterion for the Universality of Moral Judgments', *Christian Ethics: Uniformity, Universality, Pluralism, Concilium* 10 (1981) 82–8, at 87. Also his, *Norm und Sittlichkeit* (Freiburg: Alber, 1985).

13 John Mahoney, 'Reflections on Experience as a Source of Moral Theology', *Personalist Morals* 25–44; see Roberto Dell'Oro, *Esperienza Morale e Persona: Per una reinterpretazione dell'etica fenomenologica di Dietrich von Hildebrand* (Rome: Georgian University Press, 1996).

14 Cristina Traina, 'Papal Ideals, Marital Realities: One View from the Ground', in Patricia Beattie Jung, ed., *Sexual Diversity and Catholicism: Toward the Development of Moral Theology* (Collegeville: Liturgical, 2001) 269–88, at 270.

15 Franz Böckle, 'Nature as the Basis of Morality', *Personalist Morals*, 45–60; for a more classical defense, see Martin Rhonheimer, *Natur als Grundlage der Moral: Eine Auseinandersetzung mit autonomer und teleologischer Ethik* (Innsbruck: Tyrolia Verlag, 1987); John Goyette, Mark S. Latkovic, and Richard S. Myers, eds, *St Thomas Aquinas And The Natural Law Tradition: Contemporary Perspectives* (Washington, DC: CUA, 2004).
16 See Demmer, 'Natur und Person: Brennpunkte gegenwärtiger moraltheologischer Auseinandersetzung', *Natur im ethischen Argument*, 64–70.
17 Chiavacci, 122; Antonio Autiero, 'Sozialethische Provokationen an eine anthropozentrische Moral. Das Beispiel der Umweltethik', *Theologie und Glaube* 37 (1994) 97–106.
18 Korff, 86.
19 Joseph Selling, 'Evolution and Continuity in Conjugal Morality', *Personalist Morals*, 243–64.
20 Thomas Kopfensteiner, 'Historical Epistemology and Moral Progress', *Heythrop Journal* 33 (1992) 45–60.
21 Jean Porter, *Nature as Reason*. Earlier she wrote, *Divine and Natural Law* (Grand Rapids: Eerdmans, 2005).
22 Porter, *Nature as Reason* at 29, 327 respectively.
23 Jean Porter, 'The Search for a Global Ethic', *TS* 62 (2001) 105–1221, at 120.
24 Jean Porter, 'A Tradition of Civility: The Natural Law as a Tradition of Moral Inquiry', *Scottish Journal of Theology* 56 (2003) 27–48, at 29.
25 Lisa Sowle Cahill, 'Toward Global Ethics', *TS* 63 (2002) 324–44, at 326–7.
26 Cahill, 342–3, 344.
27 Brian Tierney, *The Idea of Natural Rights* (Atlanta: Emory, 1997).
28 Stephen J. Pope, 'Scientific and Natural Law Analyses of Homosexuality: A Methodological Study', *Journal of Religious Ethics* 25 (1997) 89–126.
29 Ibid., 110–11.
30 Also, Stephen Pope, 'Reason and Natural Law', *Oxford Handbook of Theological Ethics*, 148–67.
31 Pope, *Human Evolution and Christian Ethics* (New York: Cambridge University, 2007). See earlier ideas in *The Evolution of Altruism and the Ordering of Love* (Washington, DC: Georgetown University Press, 1994).
32 Franz-Josef Bormann, *Natur als Horizont sittlicher Praxis: Zur Handlungstheoretischen der Lehre vom natürlichen Sittengesetz bei Thomas von Aquin* (Stuttgart: Kohlhammer Verlag, 1999).
33 Bénézet Bujo, *Moralautonomie und Normenfindung bei Thomas von Aquin* (Vienna: Schöningh, 1979).
34 Auer, *Autonome Moral und christlicher Glaube*, also 'Die Bedeutung des Christlichen bei der Normfindung', in Josef Sauer, ed., *Normen im Konflikt* (Freiburg: Herder, 1977) 29–55; 'Die Autonomie des Sittlichen nach Thomas von Aquin', *Christlich Glauben und Handeln*, 31–54. His interest in the thesis from an ecclesiological perspective stems from an early article 'Nach dem Erscheinen der Enzyklika "Humanae vitae" – Zehn Thesen über die findung sittlicher Weisungen', *Theologische Quartalschrift* 149 (1969) 78–85.
35 Richard Gula provides a brief but compelling summary of the debate in *Reason Informed by Faith*, 47–8; see also Odozor, *Moral Theology in an Age of Renewal*, 101–34; Vincent MacNamara, *Faith and Ethics* (Washington, DC: Georgetown University Press, 1985); Lucien Richard, *Is there a Christian Ethics?* (Mahwah: Paulist Press, 1988). In their first two volumes of *Readings in Moral Theology* (*Moral Norms*

and Catholic Tradition and *The Distinctiveness of Christian Ethics*), Curran and McCormick provide translations of most of the major essays in the debate.

36 *Gaudium et Spes*, 36.

37 Dietmar Mieth, 'Autonome Moral im christlichen Kontext', *Orientierung* 40 (1976) 31–4; ibid., 'Norma Morale e Autonomia dell'uomo', in Tullo Goffi, ed., *Problemi e Prospettive di Teologia Morale* (Brescia: Queriniana, 1976) 172–97.

38 Bruno Schüller, 'The Debate on the Specific Character of Christian Ethics'.

39 See Paolo Carlotti, *Storicità e morale: Un'indagine nel pensiero di Alfons Auer* (Rome: LAS, 1989); *Autonome Moral in christlichen Glauben: Reden zum 90. Geburtstag von prof. A. Auer* (Tübingen: Universitätts Verlag, 2005).

40 Heinz Schürmann, Joseph Ratzinger, and Hans Urs Von Balthasar, *Principles of Christian Morality* (San Francisco: Ignatius Press, 1986).

41 Joseph Ratzinger, 'Magisterium of the Church, Faith and Morality', *Readings in Moral Theology No. 2*, 174–89, note 13, at 189.

42 Philippe Delhaye, 'Questioning the Specificity of Christian Morality', *Readings in Moral Theology No. 2*, 234–69; Dionigi Tettamanzi, 'Is there a Christian Ethics', ibid., 234–69.

43 Quoted in McCormick, *Notes*, 689, from Gustav Ermecke, 'Katholische Moraltheologie am Scheideweg', *Münchener theologische Zeitschrift* 28 (1977) 47–54, at 54. Bernhard Stoeckle, 'Flucht in das Humane', *Internationale katholische Zeitschrift* 6 (1977) 312–25. McCormick provides, in turn, a devastating critique of their claims, *Notes*, 688–93.

44 McCormick, *Notes*, 693.

45 Karl-Wilhelm Merks, 'De Strenenzang van de tradities'.

46 Brian Johnstone, 'Can Tradition be a Source of Moral Truth?'; Merks, 'Tradition und moralische Wahrheit. Eine Antwort an Brian V. Johnstone', *Studia Moralia* 38 (2000) 265–78.

47 Frans Vosman, 'Tussen debat en gebed: De moraaltheologie in de openbare morele discussie', *Tijdschrift voor Theologie* 43 (2003) 323–45; 'Darf Gott Herrscher sein? Zur politischen Theologie der autonomen Moral', *Für di Freiheit verantwortliche*, 94–106.

48 Carlo Leget, 'Met heel u hart, heel u ziel, heel uw verstand: Thomas van Aquino's bijdrage aan een kritisch begrip van autonomie', *Tijdschrift voor Theologie* 43 (2003) 346–61.

49 On Fuchs and autonomous morality, see two very different themes: 'Is There a Distinctively Christian Morality?' and 'Is there a Normative Non-Christian Morality?', *Personal Responsibility and Christian Morality* (Washington, DC: Georgetown University Press, 1983) 51–68, 69–83. See also, 'Autonomous Morality and Morality of Faith', ibid., 84–112. In addition to Graham's work on Fuchs, see Donatella Abignente, *Decisione Morale del Credente: Il Pensiero di Josef Fuchs* (Casale Monferrato: Piemme, 1987).

50 Éric Gaziaux, *Morale de la Foi et Morale Autonome: Confrontation entre P. Delhaye et J. Fuchs* (Leuven: Peeters, 1995); *L'autonomie en morale: Au croisement de la philosophie et de la théologie* (Leuven: Leuven University Press, 1998).

51 Thomas Kopfensteiner, 'Historische Erkenntnistheorie und sittlicher Fortschritt', Franz Furger, *Ethische Theorie praktisch* (Münster: Aschendorff, 1991) 2–18.

52 See Franz Furger, 'Christlich-theologische Ethik-angefragt und in Frage gestellt', *Theologie der Gegenwart* 39 (1996) 209–34; James Keenan and Thomas Kopfensteiner, 'Moral Theology out of Western Europe', *Theological Studies* 59 (1998) 107–35.

53 Sergio Bastianel, *Il carattere specifico della morale cristiana*, (Assisi: Citadella Editrice, 1975); *Autonomia Morale del Credente* (Brescia: Morcelliana, 1980).

54 Enrico Chiavacci, *Teologia Morale Fondamentale* (Assisi: Cittadella Editrice, 2008) 81–108.

55 Josef Römelt, 'Glaube, Kirche, Ethik: Autonome Strukturen eines differnzierten Beziehungsgeflechts', Antonio Autiero, ed., *Endliche Autonomie: Interdisziplinäre Perspektiven auf ein theologisch-ethisches Programm* (Münster: Lit Verlag, 2004) 49–74.

56 Karl-Wilhelm Merks, *Theologische Grundlegung der sittlichen Autonomie* (Düsseldorf: Patmos Verlag, 1978); Merks, 'Sittliche Autonomie: Wissenssoziologische Studie zu Gencse und Bedeutsamkeit eines Begriffs', *Endliche Autonomie*, 11–48; Merks, 'Gott in der Moral', in Thomas Laubach, ed., *Angewandte Ethik und Religion* (Tübingen: Franke, 2003) 39–60. See also the essay in his festschrift, Hans Halter, '"Gott und die Moral", Karl-Wilhelm Merks und die Moral Eine kleine Laudatio', *Für di Freiheit verantwortliche*, 9–19.

57 Robert Gascoigne, 'Reconciling Autonomy and Community', *The Public Forum and Christian Ethics* (New York: Cambridge University Press, 2008) 212–34.

58 Hans Rotter, 'Christlicher Glaube und geschechtlichen Beziehungen', in Karl Golser, ed., *Christlicher Glaube und Moral* (Innsbruck: Tyrolia Verlag, 1986) 43–67; Bruno Schüller, 'Autonomus Ethics Revisited', *Personalist Morals*, 61–70. See Rotter, 'Naturrecht und Offenbarung', *Stimmen der Zeit* 179 (1967) 283–92.

59 The profound effects of hermeneutical studies on fundamental moral theology have been detailed in an early article by Klaus Demmer, 'Hermeneutische Probleme der Fundamentalmoral', in Dietmar Mieth and Francesco Compagnoni, eds, *Ethik im Kontext des Glaubens* (Freiburg: Herder, 1978) 101–19. He details the hermeneutical relationship between faith and reason in *Moraltheologische Methodenlehre* (Freiburg: Herder, 1989) 71–4.

60 Klaus Demmer, 'Die autonome Moral – einige Anfrage an die Denkform', 261–76; *Gottes Anspruch denken*, 160–2.

61 Demmer, 'Gott in der Moral: Überlegungen zur Identiät der Moraltheologie', *Gregorianum* 84.1 (2003) 81–101; *Shaping the Moral Life: An Approach to Moral Theology* (Washington, DC: Georgetown University Press, 2000) 3–4, 15–16, 83–4; see also his *Die Wahrheit leben Theorie des Handelns* (Freiburg: Herder, 1991).

62 Augustine, *Confessions* III 6, 11; PL 32, 683.

63 Demmer, 'Die autonome Moral', 261.

64 Franz Böckle, 'Theonome Autonomie: Zur Aufgabenstellung einer fundamentalen Moraltheologie', in J. Gründel, F. Rauh, V. Eid, eds, *Humanum: Moraltheologie im Dienst des Menschen. Festschrift für R. Egenter* (Düsseldorf: Partmos, 1972), 17–46.

65 Franz Böckle, *Fundamental Moral Theology* (Dublin: Gill and Macmillan, 1980) 5.

66 Ibid., 6.

67 Ibid., 63.

68 Ibid., 54.

69 Ibid., 63.

70 *Gaudium et Spes*, 41.

71 Suharjanto, *Die Probe auf das Humane*; Francisco Jose Marin-Porgueres, *La moral autonoma: Un acercamiento desde Franz Böckle* (Pamplona: Ediciones Universidad de Navarra, 2002).

72 Demmer, *Shaping the Moral Life*, 6.

73 Democritus, *Fragmenta Moralia*, no. 109. Cited in Stephen Toulmin, *An Examination of the Place of Reason in Ethics* (Cambridge: University Press, 1958) 170.

74 Immanuel Kant, *Foundation of the Metaphysics of Morals* (Indianapolis: Bobbs-Merrill, 1969). Kant envisions the cool virtuous villain on pp. 11–12.

75 George E. Moore, *Ethics* (London: Thornton Butterworth, 1912) 193–5.

76 Richard M. Hare, *The Language of Morals* (Oxford: Oxford University Press, 1952) 113–34, 151–2, 186; *Freedom and Reason* (Oxford University Press, 1962) 152–6; 'Right and Wrong', in John Macquarrie, ed., *Dictionary of Christian Ethics* (London: SCM Press, 1967) 299. See also W. D. Ross, *The Right and the Good* (Oxford: Clarendon Press, 1930).

77 Bruno Schüller, *Die Begründung sittlicher Urteile* (Düsseldorf: Patmos, 1980); 'Neuere Beiträge zum Thema "Begründung sittlicher Normen"', 'Various Types of Grounding Ethical Norms', 'The Debate on the Specific Character of Christian Ethics'.

78 Josef Fuchs, 'Moral Truth – Between Objectivism and Subjectivism', *Christian Ethics in a Secular Arena*, 29–41; 'Moral Truths – Truths of Salvation?', Ibid., 48–68; 'Vatican II: Salvation, Personal Morality, Right Behavior', *Christian Morality: The Word Becomes Flesh*, 19–27; 'Morality: Person and Acts', Ibid., 105–17; 'Good Acts and Good Persons', *Considering Veritatis Splendor*, 21–6.

79 Janssens, 'Ontic Good and Evil'; 'Norms and Priorities in a Love Ethics'.

80 Klaus Demmer, 'Sittlich handeln aus Erfahrung', *Gregorianum* 59 (1978) 678; 'Sittlich handeln als Zeugnis geben', *Gregorianum* 64 (1983) 457–60; *Deuten und handeln* (Freiburg, Switzerland: Universitaetsverlag, 1985).

81 Richard McCormick, 'Bishops as Teachers, Scholars as Listeners', *The Critical Calling* (Washington, DC: Georgetown University Press, 1989) 95–110; *Notes in Moral Theology 1981–1984* (Lanham, MD: University Press of America, 1984) 92, 105–16, 158.

82 Bernard Hoose, *Proportionalism* (Washington, DC: Georgetown University Press, 1987) 41–67.

83 Keenan, *Goodness and Rightness in Thomas Aquinas's Summa Theologiae* (Washington, DC: Georgetown University Press, 1992); 'Die erworbenen Tugenden als richtige (nicht gute) Lebensführung: ein genauerer Ausdruck ethischer Beschreibung', in Franz Furger, ed., *Ethische Theorie Praktisch* (Münster: Aschendorff, 1991) 19–35; 'Distinguishing Charity As Goodness and Prudence As Rightness: A Key to Thomas', *Pars Secunda, The Thomist* 56 (1992) 407–26; 'Can a Wrong Action Be Good? The Development of Theological Opinion on Erroneous Conscience', *Église et Théologie* 24 (1993) 205–19; see Edward Krasevac, '*Goodness and Rightness* Ten Years Later: A Look Back at James Keenan and his Critics', *American Catholic Philosophical Quarterly* 77 (2003) 535–48; Livio Melina, 'The Fullness of Christian Action: Beyond Moralism and Antimoralism', *Logos* 8.3 (2005) 123–40.

84 Josef Fuchs, 'Human Authority – between the Sacral and the Secular', *Christian Ethics in a Secular Arena*, 111–12.

85 Josef Fuchs, 'Vatican II: Salvation, Personal Morality, Right Behavior', *Christian Morality: The Word Becomes Flesh*, 19–27.

86 Frequently held by Klaus Demmer, 'Sittlich handeln aus Erfahrung', 678; 'Sittlich handeln als Zeugnis geben', 457–60; *Deuten und Handeln*, 32, 43, 176.

87 See Karl Rahner, 'The Commandment of Love in Relation to the Other Commandments', *Theological Investigations V* (Baltimore: Helicon Press, 1966) 439–59; 'Reflections on the Unity of the Love of Neighbor and the Love of God', *Theological Investigations VI* (Baltimore: Helicon Press, 1969) 231–59.

88 Besides the citations above referring to Rahner and Gilleman, see George Klubertanz, 'Ethics and Theology', *The Modern Schoolman* 27 (1949) 29–39.

89 On charity as commanding and not eliciting, see *Summa Theologiae* II.II. 23. 4. ad2; *De caritate* 5 ad3.
90 *Summa Theologiae* II.II. 23. 2. ad3.
91 *Summa Theologiae* II.II. 25.
92 *De caritate*, 7.
93 Schüller, *Die Begründung sittlicher Urteile*, 136, 304.
94 '. . . caritas dicitur perfecta quando aliquis secundum totum suum posse diligit', *Summa Theologiae*, II.II. 24. 8c.
95 Keane, 'The Objective Moral Order', 274ff.
96 Schüller, 'Various Types of Grounding Ethical Norms', 191; 'Neuere Beiträge . . .', 157.
97 Fuchs, *Essere del Signore*, 198–9.
98 Demmer, *Deuten und Handeln*, 175ff; 'Erwaegungen zum intrinsece malum', *Gregorianum* 68 (1987) 613–37.
99 Schüller argues that the moral self-determination of a person precedes logically all other acting. For instance, he uses 'Urgewissen' in 'Gewissen und Schuld', in Josef Fuchs, ed., *Das Gewissen* (Düsseldorf: Patmos, 1979) 40; in *Die Begründung sittlicher Urteile*, he uses 'sittliche Uralternative' (137–8), 'sittliche Ureinsicht' (136), and 'Grundhaltung' (300). Motivation appears in 'Various Types of Grounding for Ethical Norms', 191; 'Neuere Beiträge . . .', 129.
100 On sin as failure, see Bretzke, 'Sin and Failure in a Morally Complex World', *A Morally Complex World*, 191–208; Sean Fagan, *Has Sin Changed?* (Dublin: Gill and Macmilllan, 1978); Kenneth R. Himes, 'Human Failings: The Meanings and Metaphors of Sin', *Moral Theology*, 145–61; Keenan, 'The Problem with Thomas Aquinas's Concept of Sin', *Heythrop Journal* 35 (1994) 401–20; ibid., 'Sin', *Moral Wisdom: Lessons and Texts from the Catholic Tradition* (Lanham, MD: Sheed and Ward, 2004) 47–66; Marciano Vidal, *Como hablar del pecado hoy* (Madrid: PPC, 1977); Ronald A. Mercier, 'What Are We to Make of Sin?', *Josephinum* 10.2 (2003) 271–84.
101 John Langan, 'Sins of Malice in the Moral Psychology of Thomas Aquinas', *The Annual of the Society of Christian Ethics* 12 (1987) 179–98.
102 Karl Menninger, *Whatever Became of Sin?* (New York: Bantam Books, 1978) 221, cf. 171ff. Repeatedly, he implies that *acedia* is the heart of sin, cf. 69, 74, 120, 125, 200, 208, 252–4.
103 Darlene Fozard Weaver, 'How Sin Works: A Review Essay', *Journal of Religious Ethics* 29 (2001) 473–501, at 473; Weaver, 'Taking Sin Seriously', *Journal of Religious Ethics* 31 (2003) 45–74.
104 Böckle, *Fundamental Moral Theology*, 87–124; see Herbert Schlögel, *Und virgib uns meine Schuld Wie auch wir . . .* (Stuttgart: Bibelwerk, 2007).
105 Michael Fahey, 'Janssens, Louis, 1908–2001', *TS* 63 (2002) 2.
106 Piet Fransen, 'Pour une Psychologie de la grace divine', *Lumen vitae* 12 (1957) 209–40, in Thomas Kopfensteiner, 'The Theory of Fundamental Option', *Christian Ethics* 123–34, at 124.
107 Bernhard Häring, 'Sin in Post-Vatican II Theology', *Personalist Morals* 87–107, at 93. Ibid., *Free and Faithful in Christ*, I, 164–222. See Richard Gula, 'Freedom and Knowledge', *Reason Informed by Faith*, 75–88.
108 Böckle, *Fundamental Moral Theology*, 55.
109 On Rahner's transcendental freedom, see 'Theology of Freedom', *Theological Investigations VI* (New York: Seabury Press, 1969) 178–96. See Brian Linnane, 'Rahner's Fundamental Option and Virtue Ethics', *Philosophy and Theology* 15

(2003) 229–54.

110 Josef Fuchs, *Essere del Signore* (Rome: Gregorian University Press, 1981) 108ff; 'Basic Freedom and Morality', *Human Values and Christian Morality* (Dublin: Gill and MacMillan, 1970) 92–111; 'Our Image of God and the Morality of Innerworldly Behavior', *Christian Morality: The Word Becomes Flesh*, 28–49.

111 Graham, *Josef Fuchs on Natural Law*, 116–47.

112 Ibid.

113 Jean Porter, 'Moral Language and the Language of Grace: The Fundamental Option and the Virtue of Charity', *Philosophy and Theology* 10 (1997) 171–81.

114 Fuchs, 'Good acts and good persons', *The Tablet* 6 (November 1993) 1444–5.

115 Kopfensteiner, 'The Theory of Fundamental Option', 124. Two other fine presentations: Eugene Cooper, 'The Fundamental Option', *Irish Theological Quarterly* 39 (1972) 383–92; Paul Qureshi, 'Sin, Fundamental Option and Conversion', *Irish Theological Quarterly* 71 (2006) 272–84.

116 Marciano Vidal, *Opción fundamental y actitudes éticas* (Madrid: Fundación Santa María-SM, 1991); Terrence Kennedy, '"Fundamental Option" Can Radically Change as Result of Popular Acts', *L'Osservatore Romano* 5 (1994) 10; Andrzej Szostek, 'Man's Fundamental Option Can Be Radically Altered by Individual Acts', *L'Osservatore Romano* 16 (1994) 14. For critique, Joseph Boyle, 'Freedom, the Human Person, and Human Action', William E. May, ed., *Principles of Catholic Moral Life* (Chicago: Franciscan Herald Press, 1981) 237–66. For defense see Joseph Selling, 'The Context and the Arguments of *Veritatis Splendor*', *The Splendor of Accuracy*, 11–70.

117 Kopfensteiner, 'The Theory of Fundamental Option', 130.

118 *Veritatis Splendor*, 65.

119 Darlene Fozard Weaver, 'Intimacy with God and Self-Relation in the World: The Fundamental Option and Categorical Activity', in William Mattison, ed., *New Wine, New Wineskins* (Lanham: Rowman and Littlefield, 2005) 143–63.

120 Demmer, *Shaping the Moral Life*, 51.

121 Enda McDonagh, 'The Moral Subject', *Irish Theological Quarterly* 39 (1972) 3–22; ibid., 'The Structure and Basis of Moral Experience', *Irish Theological Quarterly* 38 (1971) 3–20.

122 Mark Graham, 'Rethinking Morality's Relationship to Salvation: Josef Fuchs, SJ, on Moral Goodness', *TS* 64.4 (2003) 750–72.

123 Cristina Traina, *Feminism and The Natural Law.*

124 Ibid., 6.

125 Ibid., 158; Cahill, *Sex, Gender, and Christian Ethics* (Cambridge: Cambridge University Press, 1996) 12.

126 Traina, 17.

9

Toward a Global Discourse on Suffering and Solidarity

Margaret Farley has identified love and suffering as the two central experiences that all human beings encounter. Throughout this work we have seen love at the heart of the Christian moral life.[1] But we have not seen an attentiveness to suffering even when we reviewed the manuals used during the Second World War.

For all the innovation of European moralists in the twentieth century, above all in laying claim to the conscience through an autonomous ethics, they explored mostly conceptual and attendant philosophical concerns. They were not adverse to mentioning suffering and poverty, but they approached these topics as general rather than specific issues. Moreover, the ambit of their experiential concern has been mostly limited to the community of academic theologians from which they came. In short, the practicality of life, the needs of the poor, the variety of experiences of suffering, and the call to justice were infrequently addressed by the major fundamental moral theologians whom we have studied.

Exceptions included Marciano Vidal from Spain,[2] Enrico Chiavacci from Italy, Antonio Autiero from Italy and Germany, Kevin Kelly from England, and Enda McDonagh from Ireland who attended to more concrete needs of the marginalized. As McDonagh noted, 'The sense of the margins and the people at the margins of society and church began for me' at the beginning.[3]

For McDonagh and Kelly,[4] their pastoral experiences led them into their own option for their national poor. Not surprisingly, they were two of the first ethicists to write about HIV/AIDS. Chiavacci and Autiero have also made considerable social contributions. Chiavacci wrote on peace and globalization fifteen years ago, developed a comprehensive theological ethics with deep social claims, and later addressed the question of justice and globalization.[5] Autiero has frequently written on bioethical issues,[6] but also on the stranger and the other,[7] and in 1983 was probably the first Catholic ethicist to write on two major issues: HIV/AIDS[8] and the environment.[9]

Unlike their predecessors, today's Europeans like Bernard Hoose, Linda Hogan, Julie Clague, Marie-Jo Thiel, Marianne Heimbach-Steins, Julio Martinez, and Andrea Vicini, to name a few, are much more like McDonagh, Vidal, and Autiero. Still, in order to appreciate a more practical yet foundational moral theology, we should leave Europe and see the work being done by ethicists from other parts of the world, where the call to respond to human suffering shapes contemporary theological ethics.

The Australian ethicist, Robert Gascoigne, proposes suffering as one of the sources of moral reasoning. Suffering 'threatens to render Christian proclamation null and void, to overwhelm our attempts to envision a life of goodness and hope and to understand the complex threads of human experience as held together by a God-given dignity. Yet, although it is suffering that most confounds our search for ethical intelligibility, it is likewise suffering that is the most profound source of insight and conversion.'[10]

Still, suffering prompts us to face the fact that we are often the cause of others' suffering. For this reason, theological ethics turns to a conversion that responds to suffering through compassion.

Today, theological ethicists around the world issue a call for a humane answer to the cry of suffering. From Tanzania, Laurenti Magesa discusses the horrendous suffering in Africa:

> A significant part of the history of Africa and its peoples is slavery and colonialism. There has never been a tragedy in human history to rival these experiences in cruelty and destructiveness of human dignity and identity. In a very fundamental way, they have formed the concrete perception of the African peoples all over the continent in their own and other people's eyes as really 'non-people', whose life and civilization are not of much significance, if indeed any at all, for humanity . . . If there is hunger, mismanagement of human and material resources, civil strife and war in Africa today, the source of it can be traced back directly or indirectly to these experiences. On the material economic scene, the poverty of Africa, a continent incredibly rich in material resources, is a direct result of the exploitation of imperialism and colonialism, both of which continue to devastate the continent and its peoples under the name of globalization.[11]

From Brazil, Ronaldo Zacharias writes about miserable suffering and an outright insensitivity throughout Brazil to the plight of suffering among the world's poor:

> Poverty, in all of its dehumanizing forms, has become a scourge that is manifested in many different ways: the lack of food, housing, work, health care, and basic respect for the human dignity of every person. The country stands by watching as extreme forms of poverty give rise to a

> series of explosive social upheavals. The globalization of misery places before us a challenge of incalculable proportions: how do we begin to respond to the needs of the excluded, the marginalized and those who have lost everything?[12]

From Sri Lanka, Vimal Tirimanna writes about the overwhelming inequity in distribution of goods:

> The pathetic part of this story is that if something serious is not done in the concrete level to check this injustice, the 'winners' are going to continue to gain more and more, while the 'losers' are going to continue to lose more and more. The scandalizing gap of inequality is ever-widening, in each passing year, as the HDRs (Human Development Reports) since 1990 have revealed so convincingly . . . The distance between the incomes of the richest and poorest country was about 3 to 1 in 1820, 35 to 1 in 1950, 44 to 1 in 1973, and 71 to 1 in 1992.

Tirimanna adds: 'In the midst of a globalized world, 10.7 million children every year do not live to see their fifth birthday, and more than 1 billion people survive in abject poverty on less than $1 a day.'[13]

These powerful citations show that, though the irruption of suffering into Catholic theological ethics is fairly universal, it appears locally in the theology of indigenous ethicists on each continent. The emergence of local theological ethicists establishing a local agenda appropriate for their own continents has meant that Catholic ethics is no longer singularly European. To appreciate how ethics has been shaped by local cultural experience and theology, we turn now to each of the continents and their own agendas for moral theology today.

Latin America

From Latin America, liberation theology brought with it a deep concern for oppressive suffering and promoted in its responses the formation of base communities and the option for the poor. Gustavo Gutiérrez above all awakened the world to the experiences and voices of those long ignored. He announced that the bursting in of the poor is a new historical event: they were previously absent from theology.

In *A Theology of Liberation: History, Politics, Salvation* (1971), he summoned readers to make an option for the poor, by politically and religiously standing in solidarity with those marginalized by power and economic forces.[14] The option for the poor became a hermeneutical principle for interpreting the legitimacy and purpose of theology.[15] Through it, he endorsed a critical reflection on praxis and made us realize that the end of ethics is action. Our action was to respond to the world of suffering, inhabited by the poor.

In the world of suffering are interlocking patterns of oppression and domination, established by unexamined yet causal discriminating structures of economic and social power. These structures became the subject of analysis and in time were called 'structures of sin', and people in positions of authority were seen as morally responsible for them. Later, social sin was attributed not only to those in designated power, but to the societies themselves whereby ordinary members' implicit tolerance and complacent ignorance of these structures allowed them to be beneficiaries of the very structures that continued to alienate and oppress the poor.

There had been no theological agenda like this. Relying on the developments of theology particularly as an outgrowth of *Gaudium et Spes*, Gutiérrez brought poverty and politics into theological context and discourse. Later he turned to other resources from the tradition, both biblical and historical, to assert that the call to attend to human suffering has been an enduring one. In *On Job: God Talk and the Suffering of the Innocent*,[16] he proposed the two languages of prophecy and contemplation. The first is mindful of God's call for a new earth, a new sense of justice and equity. The prophetic call to respond to God's poor exists 'not because they are necessarily better than others, morally or religiously, but simply because they are poor and living in an inhuman situation that is contrary to God's will'.[17] The second language is not a treatment of monastic silence but rather a sustained consideration of Job's complaint and lament, a hopeful plea to God to answer his condition.

In *Las Casas: In Search of the Poor of Jesus Christ*,[18] Gutiérrez turned to the liberating figure of Bartolomé de las Casas, OP (1484–1566), whose *Defense of the Indians*[19] is a compelling and electrifying argument to consider the wickedness of oppression, slavery, and torture.[20] In *Las Casas* he gave us an example of a life of critical reflection on praxis, highlighting that the option for the poor coupled with solidarity with another's experience can prompt us to understand why the kingdom of God is such a relevant object of human hope.

Other major figures followed Gutiérrez, above all the Brazilians Leonardo and Clodovis Boff[21] and the Argentine-born, Mexican philosopher Enrique Dussel.[22] More recently, from El Salvador, Jon Sobrino calls for theology as an *Intellectus Amoris* and insists that theology is always in relationship to actual concrete realities, locating itself in the profound suffering of the world. Determining the place of theology is, then, an option since the world of suffering is the privileged place for doing theology.[23]

Sobrino's theology depends on the historicity of Jesus.[24] He sees the failure of Christologies to capture the historical death of Jesus on the cross as the fundamental oversight that leads us to ignore the call of the kingdom and the need to respond to the option of the poor. We are saved singularly by the historical passion, death, and resurrection of Jesus; that moment is the intervention in history of God.[25]

Sobrino sees the historicity of Jesus as key for understanding the promise of the kingdom.[26] 'The Kingdom of God', he writes, 'in no way distances us from the God of the Kingdom. It can make him closer and even more "human".

This is what was made present by Jesus' course through this world.'[27] Thus, just as God in Jesus Christ did not abandon the historical world to its wretchedness, neither can we.[28] That *imitatio Christi* is, then, the embodiment of the spirituality that we need to follow Christ in administering to those who suffer.[29]

Sobrino is indebted to Ignacio Ellacuría for his understanding of history: 'Christian eternity is inexorably linked to temporality ever since the Word became history.'[30] Ellacuría, who was later among the Jesuits assassinated in El Salvador, proposed a great and necessary dialectic, between prophecy and the kingdom. We are called to actualize the prophetic, to make the kingdom concrete in the here and now. But each prophetic moment leads to a new understanding of the kingdom, and each new understanding insists on a prophetic moment.[31]

In Latin America, moral theology has a deep resonance with the proposals of liberation theology: a critical reflection on praxis, a call to respond to human suffering, the option for the poor, and the naming of social sin and the structures of sin. While solidarity helps it to become more social and more communal, still liberation theology depends on and develops the autonomous conscience.[32]

In Latin American theological ethics, Peru's Francisco Moreno Rejon offers a moral theology that brings together the perspective of the poor, with recourse to the social sciences and a scripture-based kingdom of God ethics.[33] The Brazilians Antonio Moser and Bernardino Leers propose a Christological ethics to form the conscience through a conscientization of the forces impeding the kingdom through the idolatries of power, money, technology, pleasure, and superiority.[34] Another Brazilian, Rogue Junges, considers moral conduct in the light of the Christ-event. Launching his investigation from the ethical meaning of the kingdom of God revealed in Jesus of Nazareth, Junges re-examines the fundamental categories of the theological ethics: fundamental option, moral conscience, moral values and norms, the sentiment of guilt and sin, theological and moral conversion, moral maturity, and virtues.[35]

From Chile, Tony Mifsud publishes a multi-volume study on critical issues of our day in fundamental, social, sexual, and bioethics. More recently he has developed a comprehensive handbook for ordinary discernment on contemporary issues.[36] In the area of bioethics, the Mexican Eduard Bonnín develops an ethics of life out of a liberation theology,[37] but Brazil's Márcio Fabri dos Anjos reflects on how a liberation theology allows us to reflect on issues of power and vulnerability that so dominate the field of bioethics.[38]

A significant recent development in liberation theology is the irruption of women into liberation theology. From Brazil, Ivone Gebara defines the option for the poor as an option for poor women, analyses women's experience of salvation and evil, develops a distinctive spirituality for women, and writes on the environment from an eco-feminist perspective.[39] With another Brazilian, Maria Clara Bingemer, she proposes a theology of Mary as the Mother of God and mother of the poor.[40] Bingemer is also a prolific theologian, having published manuscripts on the power and vulnerability of love in Simone Weil, woman's body and the experience of God, the Trinity, Christology, inter-religious dialogue, gender, and the family.[41]

Women in Latin America,[42] like Uruguayan Ana María Bidegain[43] and Costa Rican Elsa Tamez, bring together women's voices and contributions across the Latin American terrain. In the United States, the Mexican-born María Pilar Aquino argues that women have a different epistemological horizon than men. Pilar Aquino uses feminist methods to reinterpret the saving historical value of reality in light of new theological criteria; to unmask and dismantle theological formulations that perpetuate the interpretation of humanity in patriarchal terms; to recognize and describe women's history; and to reflect on women's use of the Bible in their quest to understand and speak about God. Throughout, she calls for a hermeneutics of suspicion and daring.[44]

The Cuban, Ada Maria Isasi-Diaz, proposes *Mujerista* strategies for women, particularly a strong political agenda in which salvation and liberation are seen as two aspects of one process. She writes, 'As Latinas become increasingly aware of the injustices we suffer, we reject any concept of salvation that does not affect our present and future reality.'[45] She advances liberty, both psychologically and socially, without buying into the myth of individual achievement, and justice as both a disposition and a way of acting.

The cause of liberation theology in Latin America did not develop with ease. In 1968 the Latin American Episcopal Conference (CELAM) met in Medellín, Colombia and endorsed liberation theology, with its attention to the base communities and the option for the poor. In 1972, the conservative Bishop Alfonso López Trujillo became the General Secretary of CELAM and used his influence until his resignation in 1984 to curtail the conference's support of liberation theology. Still, in 1979 at the CELAM meeting in Puebla, despite his efforts, Trujillo's agenda was opposed by supporters of liberation theology.[46]

Advocates of liberation theology found themselves at risk on two main fronts. First, a terrible string of assassinations occurred. The killings in El Salvador alone were extraordinary. On 12 March 1977, Fr Rutillo Grande was murdered. Three years later, after five other priests were assassinated in El Salvador, Grande's friend Oscar Romero, the Archbishop of San Salvador, was gunned down on 24 March 1980. Nine months later, on 2 December, three American sisters and a lay woman were murdered by a military death squad. On 16 November 1989, the El Salvadoran army attacked the Jesuit compound at the University of Central America and assassinated six Jesuits (among them Ignacio Ellacuría, Segundo Montes, and Ignacio Martin-Baró) and their housekeeper and her daughter. The only Jesuit to escape, Jon Sobrino, was lecturing in Asia at the time, but since then he has been the compelling witness to their martyrdom.[47]

Second, the Vatican maintained a constant public questioning of the traditional orthodoxy of liberation theology. In 1984, Cardinal Joseph Ratzinger issued his critical *Instruction on Certain Aspects of 'Theology of Liberation'*;[48] in 1986, the cardinal issued a less critical and more moderate analysis of liberation theology, *Instruction on Christian Freedom and Liberation.*[49] At the same time, the Congregation for the Doctrine of the Faith investigated liberation theology's leading advocates. In 1985, they issued a critical notification on Leonardo Boff's book on the Church;[50] in 1993, the congregation sent complaints to the Peruvian bishops regarding Gustavo Gutiérrez; in 1995, the congregation silenced Ivone Gebara for two years; and in 2006, it published its *Notification* on the books of Jon Sobrino.[51]

Despite these setbacks, concepts like option for the poor, structures of sin, critical reflection on praxis, liberation, and the overall call of theology to respond to the irruption of suffering into theology, are now constitutively foundational to theology in general and moral theology in particular. We cannot do theology today without attending to the defining concerns of Guttiérez, Boff, Gebara, Sobrino, and others.

Africa

The irruption of the suffering poor did not enter African theology as a delayed afterthought. If there is one part of the world that most people think of when they consider human suffering as a social reality, it is Africa. The world has become more familiar with Africa, through globalized communications that narrate frequently the advance of HIV/AIDS, the enduring tragedy of malaria and tuberculosis, and the internecine struggles that pit poor aggressor against poor aggressor. Often, however, the questions of how this has happened are rarely presented.

African theology has been attentive not only to the challenges facing Africa, but also the gifts animating it. If liberation theology is the offering from Latin America, then an inculturation that is critically approached through liberation theology is Africa's contribution to the Church and the world. Africa yearns for its identity and finds that by understanding its past it can establish the future.

From the Ivory Coast, Mawuto Roger Afan describes the fundamental challenges facing Africa today: an identity crisis, the post-colonial moves to democracy, and the reconstruction of Africa itself. With African nations experiencing greater instability, the ethicist is urgently called to retrieve from the African traditions a rootedness that could stabilize social upheaval.[52]

The personal identity of the African is probably even more critical than the issue of social stability. Years ago the Cameroonian Englebert Mveng considered the suffering nature of this identity so extreme as to describe it as the 'structural sin' of 'anthropological poverty'.[53] Magesa incorporates this phenomenon into his own reflections: 'African self-doubt is perhaps the most embracing factor in African "anthropological poverty", the kind of poverty which is not merely material but affects the personality itself. It has enormous ethical consequences, one of which is the psychological situation which instinctively obstructs initiative in many areas of personal and social development.'[54]

Writing about African suffering and identity is not without risk. On 22 April 1995, Mveng was assassinated. He had been the leader of a variety of movements, all related to forming intellectual, theological, and artistic communities for the building up of a more just Africa. He encouraged, founded and led greater associations among these constituencies to help retrieve and shape African identity.[55] A vocal critic of political and ecclesial life, Mveng's colleague, Jean-Marc Ela, went into voluntary exile immediately after Mveng's assassination. Ela was the father of African liberation theology. Aside from a year as the Joseph Professor at Boston College, he spent his exile in French Canada. Ela died on 26 December 2008, in exile.[56] With Uganda's John Mary Waliggo's death eight months earlier, on 19 April 2008, Africa lost some of its premier theologians.

Many Catholic ethicists teach outside of their country and often outside their continent. From the Democratic Republic of Congo, Bénézet Bujo teaches in Fribourg in Switzerland, and the Congolese Juvenal Ilunga Muya teaches in Rome at the Urbanianum. In the United States, the Ugandan, Emanuel Katongole, teaches at Emory; the Kenyan, Teresia Hinga, teaches at Santa Clara; and the Nigerian, Paulinus Odozor, teaches in Notre Dame.

Still Africa is developing faculties of theological ethics. In Nairobi there are two major faculties of theological ethics. Emmanuel Barbara, Paul Chummar, Richard Rwiza, and Juvenalis Baitu are at the Catholic University of East Africa; and Aquiline Tarimo, Paulin Manwelo, Laurenti Magesa, Anne Nasimiyu-Wasike, and A. E. Orobator are at the neighboring Jesuit School of Theology at Hekima; At Kinshasa we find M. Théotime Kibanga, Ferdinand Banga, Sébastien Muyengo, and Pierre Bwalwel.

As African theological ethics takes shape, some ethicists are reminding others of their forebears. Bénézet Bujo and Juvenal Ilunga Muya edited a homage to nine French-speaking African theologians who paved the way for contemporary African theology.[57] Premier among them was Bishop Tharcisse Tshibangu, the only African expert at Vatican II and among the first members of the International Theological Commission. He developed in 1960 a specifically African theology, proposing that certain African epistemological insights and local practices were different from European ones.[58] The Belgian Alfred Vanneste, dean of the faculty of theology in Kinshasa, responded affirming the universality of theology and denying the specificity of an African theology.[59] Forty years later, Bujo notes that Tshibangu implicitly contested the presupposition that 'the African tradition has been precisely the weak point of the Africans in the face of Western civilization'. Moreover, while many want to reduce the 'whole question of African theology to social and economic problems', Tshibangu's proposal offered 'an inculturation worthy of the name (that) necessarily ends up in an integral human liberation and development'.[60]

Later Bujo and Ilunga Muya published a second volume, wherein Charles Nyamiti was considered 'the vibrant pioneer of African inculturated theology'.[61] Nyamiti was well known for his contributions in Christology and ecclesiology and his ability to look at them in the context of African ancestor worship.[62] Tschibangu and Nyamiti were trailblazers in leading others to the African need for inculturation.[63] Since then, Bénézet Bujo has become the most eloquent promoter of African inculturation in moral theology.[64]

Proposing a 'palaver' (meaning 'word') ethics, Bujo sees it as effective: through discourse the community comes to resolve crisis, heal the sick, and determine itself for the future. Palaver is how the community comes to fuller realization. As Muya writes:

> In the logic of the palaver, everyone has the right to speak. In this sense the palaver guarantees equality and everyone's access to speak in view of building up the community. The final decision arrived at its end is not the result of compromise or of voting according to the majority, but of a solid consensus among all members. The fundamental experience at the basis of the word is that of communion. Communion is not true unless it promises and guarantees the originality of each member, and unless each member is conscious of not being free except in relation with the community . . . Individual freedom is not therefore a value absolute in itself, but in relation to the community, in the same sense that the community is not an absolute value but one linked to the individuals.[65]

Muya makes it clear that the Communion-oriented stance of a palaver ethics does not deny autonomy, an important interest of Bujo and others.[66] Relationality does not compromise autonomy, nor does autonomy compromise relationality.[67] Still, while focusing on community, Muya points out that the palaver is tri-dimensional as it engages the ancestors, the living and the not-yet-born. By nature, then, there is always a plurality of perspectives, both among the living individuals within the community and by contact with those from the past and expected from the future. This plurality extends, then, beyond the confines of the community.[68]

Bujo develops the dynamics of his ethics as it pertains to leadership:

> . . . [t]he chief must pay attention to everything that happens in the community. Above all he is obliged to receive everything by patient listening and then to try to digest it well. Being a good listener and digesting the word are linked in general to Black Africa. He is the last to speak, after having carefully examined all the aspects of a problem and digested the word well. But first he must propose his own word for debate, at least in the palaver of the elders. In other words, the word must be made available for rumination.[69]

To make the discourse effective, the chief and all the participants in the palaver must have large, broad ears and they must distinguish themselves as listeners before they speak.[70] When they speak, they must be willing to share the word with other members of the palaver, since it is too large and wide for the mouth of one individual.

One critical area in which inculturation plays a major role is HIV/AIDS. In Africa there is overriding insistence that the HIV infection cannot be understood, inhibited or treated by a simple clinical study of the disease. Only by understanding the African context in which this infection has inculturated can we respond to those at risk, infected, or suffering from full-blown AIDS. Toward this end, Laurenti Magesa looks at practices of the African religion upholding a pan-African life ethic; he uses that life ethic as the standard for more effective teaching on HIV/AIDS.[71] The Ugandan Emmanuel Katongole becomes suspicious of 'miracle Western medicines' and asks what are appropriate medical approaches for Africa.[72] Bujo works with Michael Czerny in developing the theological reflections specific to AIDS in Africa,[73] while Uganda's Peter Kanyandago reflects on the nature of God in a time of AIDS.[74] Still, inculturation does not guarantee unanimity in addressing the challenges of AIDS: the debate over whether condoms are an appropriate part of HIV prevention strategies is a case in point.[75]

Other ethicists write on HIV/AIDS in more local contexts. James Good looks at HIV/AIDS among desert nomads in Kenya,[76]while James Olaitan Ajayi studies challenges regarding women's empowerment in Nigeria.[77] His co-citizen Paulinus Odozor gives us local cases to examine the standards of moral reasoning when facing HIV/AIDS.[78]

Many see the local church as key for successful support of peoples with or at risk of HIV/AIDS.[79] Two theologians examine the Church's mission in Nairobi to see how effective it is in the face of such challenges.[80] Stuart Bate in South Africa inquires about clergy formation for ministry to people at risk.[81] Therese Tinkasiimire looks at how the Ugandan church witnesses to cultural practices that both help and harm those most affected by the disease.[82]

Nigeria's Agbonkhianmeghe Orobator asks what happens when AIDS comes to church.[83] Elsewhere he demonstrates how the sociological category of crisis correlates with the theological conception of *kairos* and contends that the identity of the African church is measured by its response to the HIV crisis.[84] Finally, he pressed for new paradigms of a discourse on sexual ethics from an African perspective, describing the experience of women as instructive, not only because they are the predominant victims, but because they are on the front line for the care of people living with HIV/AIDS. Their non-risk-averse combating of AIDS should prompt church leaders to risk sacrificing some of their own 'disincarnate moral fixations' for a more context-based approach to sexual integrity.[85]

Finally, through the African Jesuit AIDS network and its director Michael Czerny,[86] we find another set of distinctive contributions. Paterne Mombe looks for signs of hope in the management of HIV,[87] Ghislain Tshikendwa Matadi applies the wisdom of Job to the experience of those afflicted with AIDS,[88] and Peter Knox looks at local beliefs, particularly regarding ancestors, as a resource to minister to the sick and suffering in Africa today.[89]

As important as inculturation is in Africa, Jean-Marc Ela was actually somewhat suspicious of it. If the African Church becomes more truly African, will it become better? If African society heeds its ancient cultures, will it actually move forward? In short, is the retrieval of African culture coupled with any critical reflection?

Ela preferred a liberation theology approach: the African church, its leaders and members need to heed the liberating gospel which confronts local cultures with the kingdom of God as expressed in Jesus Christ and in the love, justice, equity, and option for the poor that characterizes the gospel message. Ela offered a ringing corrective to African contextual theology. As a noted sociologist and theologian, he demanded a concrete and not a conceptual liberation: we must know the Africa that we are talking about, not to accept it, but to liberate it.[90]

Ela challenged the communities of faith to 'make an effort to redefine themselves in terms of service to persons stripped of their rights'. Indeed: 'Our primordial sacrament should be the poor and the oppressed, those disturbing witnesses of God in the warp and woof of our history. African reality imposes on the church a kind *of pedagogy of the discovery of situations of sin and oppression* – situations that rear their heads in contradiction with the project of the salvation and liberation in Jesus Christ.'[91]

The influence of liberation theology is palpable. Tanzanian Aquiline Tarimo looks for resources from Ignacio Ellacuría and develops a constructive human rights agenda.[92] Feminists like Teresia Hinga,[93] Mercy Amba Oduyoye,[94] and Anne Nasimyu-Wasike[95] bring a definitively feminist liberation approach to their theology by reflecting on women's experience, patriarchal dominance, the practices of local culture, and the fundamental call of scripture to hear the cry of the poor.

If Ela brought liberation theology into African theological discourse, Laurenti Magesa considered it as a companion and not a replacement for inculturation.[96] While identified with liberation theology,[97] Magesa equally promotes a theology of inculturation, especially in his landmark work on the pan-African culture of life that imbued African religion.[98] He studies the challenges of Africa today: those resulting from gender inequities, elitism, political and economic corruption, and the longstanding compromise of the environment. He turns to the two movements of inculturation theology and liberation theology, which include feminist contributions. He admonishes theologians to recognize that these are complementary theologies and that no true African theological ethicist can afford to overlook either of these significant theological claims. He urges theologians to locate themselves more immediately with 'the wretched of the earth' and to find more constructive ways of encouraging Africa's hierarchy to promote, rather than inhibit, the type of theological discourse Africa needs, one that is relevant and action-oriented for God's people.[99]

John Mary Waliggo was also deeply concerned about the effectiveness of theology in responding to suffering and empowering the poor. Waliggo attended less to theological reflection and more to activism in response to the situation of suffering. If he resonated with any particular theological premises, it would be the emerging African feminist ethics which links liberation to the very specific context of economics and power.[100]

Like Magesa, Waliggo wrote on inculturation too.[101] But the specificity of the context Waliggo addressed was always a globalized world that compromises a good deal of equitable justice for the present and future of Africa.[102] Still, Waliggo always exuded hope, as in his tribute to the AIDS activist Noerine Kaleeba[103] and in his comment on the African Synod of 1994.[104]

Lastly, Orobator has written on the Church as a practical institution with a historical tradition rooted in hope while facing ethical challenges. He reflects on the Church as family, a very African line of thought, the specific image of the Church used at the synod.[105] In another book, through the use of African narratives,[106] Orobator explores central issues of contemporary faith: from the (non) naming of God to the Trinity, from Christology to mercy and grace; and from the kingdom to the communion of saints. This master-storyteller draws his material from the traditional stories of his fellow Nigerian Chinua Achebe's *Things Fall Apart*.[107]

Orobator also co-authored with Elias Opongo a manual on the social justice tradition for local communities. Using simple, sample cases, for example, the right to land and housing, standing up against corruption, and encountering ethnic discrimination, the authors lead communities to understand how they can analyse contemporary challenges and act to resolve them. The manual promotes the social, moral formation of parishes.[108] Like their work, Tanzania's Richard N. Rwiza offers a book on the connection of conscience with virtue ethics and argues that the acting person is called to self-development as both critic and member of her/his culture.[109] In all this, we can see a liberating inculturation theology entering its second generation.

Asia

Until recently, theological ethics in India was taught using a moral manual written by the German Karl Peschke.[110] Later, Soosai Arokiasamy emerged as a pioneer for an indigenous, contemporary Indian theological ethics. His interests embraced ordinary people, liberation theology, cultural context, the need for dialogue, and the critical reconstruction of the tradition.[111] Bishop Gali Bali provided a description of Arokiasamy's contributions.

> The thrust of theological thinking of Fr. Arokiasamy is in the line of people's theology and inculturation in the liberative sense. Arokiasamy

> further affirms that in the new method of people's theology, Scripture will be appropriated through a re-reading of it by the people, and tradition will be discerningly re-interpreted by, and integrated into, the people's dynamic and context-related praxis of faith.[112]

In addressing the great caste distinctions in India, Arokiasamy and others have argued that until the option for the poor embraces the most marginalized, the *dalits*, its theological ethics will not realize its call to be liberating.[113] Like them, John Chathanatt, who wrote on Gandhi and Gutiérrez as two liberation paradigms,[114] argues that an Indian liberative inculturation must turn to concrete economic questions and structural issues of marginalization.[115] For this more inclusive agenda, Indian ethicists often turn to the language of human rights.[116]

Clement Campos portrays India as rife with cultural complexity and social inequality and examines a host of the major issues his nation faces: globalization, environment, access to health care (in a land with great health-care resources), discrimination based on gender, caste, and religion, violence, and the failure to recognize human rights. In each instance, he highlights the work of contemporary Indian theological ethicists responding to these needs, but he concludes with outstanding challenges facing today's ethicists: to move both beyond the confines of a seminary setting so as to become more involved in political debate on issues of urgent social concern; to go beyond the search for pastoral solutions so as to offer ethical solutions to the dilemmas that confront individuals; to dialogue with other religions and cultures and the poor so as to participate in humanity's search for the truth by which we all live; and finally to develop a moral theology that is contextualized, truly Indian, authentically human, and socially liberative.[117]

To illustrate his point, Campos describes a major ecological crisis brewing in India. The approach of the Indian theologians is 'to draw from the wisdom of the indigenous peoples who through their myths and rituals, their respect for mother earth, and their simple lifestyle have fostered conservation and a symbiotic relationship with nature'.[118] From the ancient religions and their scriptures, which reveal a mystical perception of the earth as the home in which one experiences the life-giving power of the Divine, Indian theologians develop their arguments. In these sources they find complements for biblically based insights of creation and care for the earth.

Campos adds: 'What Indian eco-ethics also stresses is the need to repair the rape of nature by rendering justice to the victims of such exploitation.'[119] The poor, the first victims always, have a claim to the earth's resources for the fulfillment of basic needs of decent human living.

A young theologian, Pushpa Joseph, notes that poor women are especially affected by the ecological crisis, and yet their own approach to the land provides a needed resource for a new ethics.[120] Elsewhere, she turns to the spirituality of tribal Indian women to articulate a response to the Indian AIDS crisis.[121]

From Sri Lanka, Vimal Tirimanna writes on suffering and economic disparities in a globalized world, an argument that he developed earlier.[122] More recently he has faced issues of religion, violence, and civil strife in a collection of essays.[123]

In facing the challenges of globalization from the Philippines, Agnes Brazal highlights the multitudinous resources with which creative Filipino ethicists engage.[124] The Catholic social tradition and the scriptures are a central source of ethical norms and 'images' necessary for what Fausto Gomez calls 'good globalization/localization'.[125] Elsewhere he invokes a theology of the Eucharist to develop an ethic of global justice.[126] Finally, using the teachings of Thomas Aquinas on justice, property, and the poor, Gomez argues that '"superfluous goods" belong in justice to the poor'.[127]

Like Gomez, Monica Jalandoni also turns to Aquinas, but to understand the fortitude of Filipino women.[128] Aloysius Cartagenas proposes the common good tradition as a way of helping Filipinos to understand citizenship as an expression of discipleship and a path to holiness. Basic ecclesial communities, he argues, should function as 'democratic communities that search for and envision the common good' and must serve as forums where the voices of the marginalized can be heard.[129] Ronaldo Tuazon sees that the narratives from the margins further the Filipino grasp of justice and the common good.[130] Christina Astorga looks to Filipino history, particularly the experience of the people power revolution, as providing a resource to strengthen national resolve to respond to globalization.[131] On issues of sexuality, Brazal turns to the self-understanding and experiences of women across Asia,[132] while Astorga reflects on the feminization of poverty, especially among migrant workers in and from the Philippines.[133]

Beyond these theological and ethical sources, Brazal and others insist on the resourcefulness of interdisciplinarity.[134] She gives evidence of both the need and the failure to utilize interdisciplinary resources in her discussion about sex education and HIV/AIDS in the Philippines.[135] Similarly, Cartagenas criticizes recent, local Catholic social teaching for not depending more on these interdisciplinary sources.[136]

Since poverty in Asia interweaves with cultural and religious identities, any attempt to respond must take seriously Asia's religiousness. For this reason, Carlos Ronquillo proposes an 'option for the poor other'. The 'other' includes the 'oppressed, the "non-person", the "non-christian", the "uncultured", the women and children'. This option for the poor 'other', Ronquillo emphasizes, involves a triple dialogue with the poor, the living cultures and religions of Asia.[137]

As we can see, these Asian writers are not hesitant to use a variety of sources incorporated into local contexts. For instance, Osama Takeuchi brings the writings of Josef Fuchs on conscience into a Japanese context.[138] Haruko K. Okano invokes a feminist understanding of moral responsibility to critique her own culture.[139] Among the specific problems in Japan, she names 'the potentially dangerous side of homogeneity or nationalistic togetherness, that is, the crass distinction between "us and others"' and the principle of harmony that 'not just ignores those who are different or strange' but actively excludes them. While acknowledging the good of fundamental national principles, she brings to them an ethical critique in their encounter with the other.[140]

Finally, as witnesses to the future of theological ethics, from Hong Kong, Lúcás Chan Yiu Sing uses the virtues for cross-cultural dialogue: to better understand scriptural ethics, Confucian ethics, and the possibility of discourse between the two.[141] From Vietnam, Y-Lan Tran, a physician and the first Catholic woman ethicist from her country, calls for dignity, justice, and care in response to HIV/AIDS in her home land.[142]

North America, particularly the United States

Because of its geographical proximity, and more importantly its deep historical (and often oppressive) involvement in Latin America, moral theology in the United States was deeply affected by the irruption of liberation theology onto the theological scene.[143]

In 1970 Philip Scharper with Miguel D'Escoto co-founded Orbis Press and published Gutiérrez's *Theology of Liberation* in English. From then on, through Scharper's initiatives, Orbis became a publishing powerhouse of liberation theology.

Later, a variety of American writers promoted the new theology from the south: Penny Lernoux,[144] Arthur McGovern,[145] Thomas Schubeck,[146] Alfred Hennelly,[147] Roger Haight,[148] and, more recently, Dean Brackley[149] and Kevin Burke.[150] Though many of these authors were describing the theological arguments from Latin America for Latin America, central premises from liberation theology began to be incorporated by North American theologians into Catholic social teaching and the overall theological foundations of Catholic theological ethics:[151] 'structures of sin',[152] social sin,[153] and the option for the poor.[154]

The clearest connection between liberation theology in Latin America and theological movements in the United States is black theology. One year after publishing *Black Theology and Black Power*,[155] James Cone published *A Black Theology of Liberation*.[156] Later, in response to reviews that criticized Cone's dependence on European theologians, he offered a theology of black traditions and experience in *The God of the Oppressed*.[157]

M. Shawn Copeland, a womanist who reflects on the experience of women of color, particularly African-American women, is arguably the most prolific Catholic theological writer in black theology. She has written about liberation theology for women,[158] the nature, method and traditions of black theology,[159] racism,[160] and the experience and narratives of suffering of black women who live a theology of resistance, coupled with some sass.[161] More recently, she has developed from those narratives a theology of freedom.[162]

Bryan Massingale is black Catholic theology's leading theological ethicist. In his dissertation he studied the social dimensions of sin and reconciliation in the works of James Cone and Gustavo Gutiérrez.[163] In the 1990s he wrote about racism and Catholic social teaching,[164] and critiqued US academic theology's failure to reflect on racism and the civil rights movement.[165] Responding to Massingale's essay, Michael Fahey, editor of *Theological Studies*, dedicated an issue 'to make amends for its shameful avoidance of the evil of racism in the United States'.[166] The collection celebrated the thirtieth anniversary of *A Black Theology of Liberation*.[167] There, Massingale returned to Cone to compare his work with recent Catholic Episcopal teaching on racism.[168] Like Copeland, Massingale presses his readers to see the racism they perpetuate and the profound relationship it has with poverty.[169]

On the topic of HIV/AIDS, we find several black ethicists. Massingale considers the resources of resurrection faith and the spirituals to develop a response to the disease.[170] Diana Hayes criticizes the American black Catholic response to intravenous drug users,[171] and Shawnee Marie Daniels-Sykes writes on the treatment of HIV-infected older African-Americans.[172]

Recently, Massingale has advocated for a more radical change in Catholic theological ethics. Arguing that revisionism is over, he contends that moral theologians must offer the Church a faithful or radical reconstruction of the tradition. He explains: '"Reconstruction" emphasizes the need for a more fundamental or "radical" (in the sense of radix or "root") rethinking and rearticulation of the demands of faith than that conveyed by the term "revision".'[173]

Concrete social change that promotes justice, I think, signifies the purpose of a great deal of theological ethics in the United States. On 3 May 1983, the United States Conference of Catholic Bishops issued their long-awaited, transparently drafted, landmark statement, *The Challenge of Peace: God's Promise and Our Response*.[174] This prophetic and ethically well-argued statement gave the Church in the United States a sense that working for justice was its mission. Later, the architect of the pastoral, Joseph Bernardin, developed a broadly inclusive consistent ethics of life through a series of 35 lectures.[175] Three years later, on 13 November 1986, the bishops addressed the ethical issues related to the economy, in *Economic Justice for All*.[176] These events empowered Christians around the country to reflect on the relationship of justice, the Church, and the world.

A leader in this reflection has been the social ethicist David Hollenbach. Hollenbach has addressed a wide array of issues: mediating claims in conflict, promoting a new perspective for an equitable justice, developing the respect of human rights, analysing issues of war and peace in a nuclear age, and deepening the notion of common good to reflect better the world in which we live.[177] More recently he has addressed the issues of refugees and forced migration.[178] In all his writings, he instructs his fellow ethicist to be vigilant about the miscarriages of justice and to be effective in the pursuit of a more equitable world.[179]

In moral theology itself, the move toward just responses to suffering in the world has been made by women scholars like Lisa Sowle Cahill, Margaret Farley, Cristina Traina, Anne Patrick, Christine Firer Hinze, Christine Gudorf, Barbara Andolsen, Susan Ross, Patricia Beattie Jung, Maura Ryan, Mary Jo Iozzio, Maria Cimperman, and Marilyn Martone. Their investigations, like their proposals, are specific and concrete; for instance, Martone writes about the unjust and irrational challenges that parents, especially mothers, encounter in health care as they care for a child who has sustained significant brain injuries.[180] Patrick addresses the shift in theological ethics from the patriarchal moral manuals to the liberating call to autonomy, but insists that that call must be in conscience, promoting egalitarianism, and heeding the voices of the marginalized.[181] Cimperman asks why the world is slow to respond to the international HIV/AIDS crisis and proposes a more comprehensive embodied, relational anthropology.[182] Iozzio, acknowledging that women bear the disproportionate burden of HIV, assembles an international group of 25 women theologians to tackle regional challenges emerging from the virus.[183]

Women have extended the boundaries of theological ethics by incorporating into it the work of the Catholic social tradition and its engagement of the common good, solidarity, social justice, and the option for the poor. In their contributions, theological ethics is not solely a personalist ethics, even one constitutively relational. Theological ethics is about the formation of communities of justice and love through practices that forge a unity of concern and an expressive solidarity.

These women (and also many men)[184] theologians approach their arguments with distinctly feminist perspectives, which, as Copeland and Elisabeth Schüssler Fiorenza explain, is a critical theology of liberation.[185] Margaret Farley argues that feminist ethics is opposed to discrimination and patterns of domination, and is necessarily pro-women. It is suspicious of traditional interpretations of women (and men), any form of inequity, and any deductive logic that guides moral decisions. Systemically it manifests itself in very diverse ways.[186] While agreeing that the contemporary diversity of feminism is significant, Susan Ross underlines fairly constant points of agreement: the priority of experience, attention to difference, appreciation for embodiment, opposition to patriarchal control, and care for the environment. While inclined to context and social location, it has recently led to greater cross-cultural discourse and justice-based transcultural standards.[187]

While systematic theologians gave feminism its fundamental theological foundations,[188] feminist ethicists have definitively extended their claims into the concrete world of sexual,[189] social,[190] and bioethics.[191] Among these, Lisa Sowle Cahill has been the pioneer of the inclusive agenda of connecting feminism to the Catholic social tradition and bringing that connection to the major areas of applied ethics.

In 1985, Cahill wrote on an ethics of sexuality and explored the sources of the Christian ethics: scripture, tradition, human nature, and experience. These categories were seen not as distinct, but rather as inter-related and mutually defining. In this context, she developed certain concepts that became foundational for her own positions: feminism, the common good, and moral practices.[192]

Always working within the tradition, but seeking to reinterpret it, Cahill advances a sexual ethics that is deeply relational, promoting gender equity, depending on the scriptures (in particular the narratives of practices that formed communities of faith and justice),[193] and contending that sexuality should fortify not privacy but rather integral relationships within the common good.

In 1992 she further defined her ideas on sexuality ('sex is fundamentally and above all a relational capacity'), looking at the experience of women, and mindful of ethics' need to use the resources of other disciplines.[194] In 1996, in *Sex, Gender and Christian Ethics*, she proposed that human sexual differentiation and sexual reproduction 'stand as experiences which begin in humanity's primal bodily existence, and which all cultures institutionalize (differently) as gender, marriage and family. Human flourishing, as sexually embodied, depends on the realization of the *equality of the sexes*, male and female; and in their sexual union, on the further values of *reproduction*, *pleasure* and *intimacy*.' She added two other integral components: that social institutions ought to be ethically responsible to these values and that though local cultures develop their own social institutions, that hardly guarantees that all institutions are ethically the same.[195] On this last point, we saw in her debate with Jean Porter, that Cahill, while recognizing the evolution of norms from local cultures, believes in the consensual establishment of universal norms as not only a possibility but a necessity.[196]

Throughout her writings, Cahill upholds sexuality, family,[197] and marriage,[198] and seeks to eradicate domination and inequities. She recognizes a disconnect between church teachings and the actual practices that often promote oppressive expressions of marital and familial relationships, but rather than advocating the dismantlement of these institutions, she seeks to radically reform them. She is, then, a self-described Catholic feminist[199] who scrutinizes ecclesial and social practices that undermine the very values promoted by the narrative of its own tradition.[200]

Later, she developed her ideas on the just-war argument as an instructive guide for containing violence.[201] More recently, she has turned to bioethics. In 2003, she gave a major lecture on bioethics.[202] Here she turned to the common good, solidarity, structural injustice, and sin, and the option for the poor, and brought the Catholic social tradition, once practically hermetically sealed unto itself, into bioethics.[203] The result has been an extraordinarily practical and relevant bioethics. In it, she insists on justice, examines the economic realities that drive so much research while at the same time disenfranchising those most in need, chides the glorification and fascination with a technology that is more market- than person-driven, and remains in solidarity with women throughout the world, particularly those most alienated from medical advances today.

Like Waliggo, Ela, Massingale and others, Cahill's purpose in writing is to bring about actions, practices, and policies that achieve a greater solidarity and equity throughout the world.[204] As she said in her presentation in Padova at the international conference of Catholic Theological Ethics, moral truth 'corresponds to the reality of human interdependence and to the possibility of our being in solidarity with one another to relieve human suffering'.[205]

She added:

> Modern terms such as 'human dignity', 'full humanity', 'democracy', 'human rights', 'equality', 'solidarity', and 'equal opportunity' are ways of challenging inequitable access patterns. Such language represents a social, political and legal ethos in which participation in the common good and access to basic goods of society is universally shared, even though on many possible cultural models. This is the modern definition of social justice, and social justice is an indispensable constituent of contemporary moral theology.[206]

In sum, Cahill brings the resources of the Catholic social tradition in its advocacy for justice into the framework of sexuality and bioethics. She insists that, as we do theology, we examine narrative claims, social practices, and institutional structures. She advocates an action-oriented ethics that seeks to extend the parameters of discourse and participation and is mindful of the biases of classicism, sexism, and racism.

As we leave the United States, we should note a new generation of theological ethicists very intent on constructing a positive, relational, confessional, contemporary ethics. David Matzko McCarthy claims that, earlier in the United States, Catholics were members of identifiable communities in which they were enclosed, but in the postmodern world, without such subcultures, the Catholic question in the United States is not how do we get to the table, but rather what do we bring to it?[207]

These scholars have published a collection of essays entitled *New Wine, New Wineskins*.[208] Much work concerns the identity of the theological ethicist as a person of faith within a community and an institution. For instance, Margaret Pfeil calls moral theologians to exercise discipleship.[209] Echoing a claim by Vincent Twomey that 'Holiness is the ultimate object of morality',[210] Christopher Steck writes, 'Christian moral theology . . . requires that its practioner have a well-formed heart that is attuned to the Gospel and the values at its core.'[211]

Christopher Vogt writes that the 'work of a lay theologian is not a typical lay vocation' and proposes that local bishops should invite lay theologians to preach.[212] Elsewhere, Vogt in an inspiriting essay proposes why we can and should embrace the intravenous drug user as our neighbor.[213]

Among these new scholars, six of them have written or edited introductory textbooks, an astonishing achievement that follows the lead of others from earlier generations. In part because theology is still a requisite for undergraduates at many (predominantly Catholic) universities and because graduate and professional ministerial programs continue to expand, the need for textbooks in moral theology is more evident in the United States than elsewhere. In the 1970s there was Timothy O'Connell's ground-breaking *Principles for a Catholic Morality*.[214] In 1989 two complementary texts were published by Paulist Press: Richard Gula's *Reason Informed by Faith* and Ronald Hamel and Kenneth Himes (eds) *Introduction to Christian Ethics*. Two years later William May published *An Introduction to Moral Theology* (1991).[215] More recently we have seen Bernard Hoose's edition of *Christian Ethics* (1998), and Russell Connors and Patrick McCormick's *Character, Choices and Community* (1998) and later their 'workbook', *Facing Ethical Issues* (2002).[216] Other books include Curran's *The Catholic Moral Tradition Today* (1999); Romanus Cessario's *Introduction to Moral Theology*,[217] Paulinus Odozor's *Moral Theology in an Age of Renewal* (2003), Servais Pinckaers' *Morality: The Catholic View* (2003),[218] James Bretzke's *A Morally Complex World: Engaging Contemporary Moral Theology* (2004), and my own *Moral Wisdom* (2004). The texts by new scholars are: David Matzko McCarthy and M. Therese Lysaught (eds) *Gathered for the Journey* (2007);[219] Jozef Zalot and Benedict Guevin, *Catholic Ethics in Today's World* (2008);[220] David Cloutier, *Love Reason, and God's Story* (2008)[221] and William Mattison, *Introducing Moral Theology* (2008).[222]

Cross-cultural discourse, ethics in the Church, and globalization

At the end of the century, Catholic theological ethics became inclined to cross-cultural discourse. Above all, the development of regional indigenous faculties of theology across the world made the need for cross-cultural discourse all the more apparent.

This was a long time coming. Since 1965, the journal *Concilium* in its six linguistic editions has more than any other journal promoted international discourse. In 1965, Richard McCormick took the reins of the 'Moral Notes' at *Theological Studies* and mediated an international conversation that continues today after more than 40 years. More recently, Christine Gudorf and Regina Wolfe edited *Ethics and World Religions: Cross-Cultural Case Studies*.[223] And, in *Catholic Ethicists on HIV/AIDS Prevention*, 34 ethicists from more than 25 countries worked together for the first international project on a globalized threat.

When 400 moral theologians gathered in July 2006 in Padova, Italy, for the first international conference on Catholic Theological Ethics, cross-cultural discourse in moral theology hit a new plateau. The meeting itself was successful and the conference papers have been published in English, Spanish, Italian, Portuguese, Filipino, and Indian editions.[224] Since then there has been much more cross-cultural collaboration: the project of 25 women ethicists writing on

HIV/AIDS in *Calling for Justice*, a meeting in Manila in August 2008 of East Asian moralists,[225] and plans for the second international conference, to be held in Trento, Italy, 24–27 July 2010.[226]

One interesting development has been the appeal of virtue ethics to mediate this discourse. Virtue ethics is rooted in the priority of being over action and argues that the cultivation of normative dispositions and attendant practices is the stuff of ethics. In 1990, Jean Porter initiated discussion on a Catholic moral theology founded in the virtues.[227] Since then, Protestants, Orthodox, and Catholics have written on the topic.[228]

We have seen throughout this work an emerging affinity for the virtues as a retrieved foundation for Catholic ethics. Lottin, Tillmann, Gilleman, and Häring strongly advocated for virtue. More recently, Spohn, Harrington and I wrote that virtue ethics is the most appropriate mode for developing a scripture-based ethics; throughout the Bible, we see how the Lord asks us to become a certain kind of people. At the same time, Christopher Vogt provides a ground-breaking essay on common good and virtue ethics, using the virtues of solidarity, compassion, and hospitality as foundational sources.[229]

Virtue ethics is suitable for cross-cultural dialogue. Jean Porter notes that 'the language of virtue builds in a kind of flexibility, even ambiguity, that is not so evident in the languages of law and duty'.[230] In my own work, I have argued that every culture promotes for each of its members a threefold summons to be virtuous: in treating all people impartially and fairly, in maintaining faithful bonds with those whom we are in specific relationships, and in caring for ourselves as a unique responsibility. These virtues (justice, fidelity, and self-care) are more or less analogously found in every society and it is the virtue of practical wisdom or prudence that arbitrates their claims.[231]

Cross-cultural dialog results in part because through virtue, ethicists have a common conceptual framework. The more ethicists use the virtues, the more they work beyond local contexts.[232] More than anyone, James Bretzke has used the virtues to introduce East Asian religious ethics to English-speaking Christian moralists.[233] Years earlier, Lee Yearly used a similar approach by comparing the views of Mencius and Aquinas on the virtue of courage.[234] More recently, Aaron Stalnaker studied Xunzi and Augustine, whose use of the virtues allowed them to develop sophisticated accounts of transformative spiritual exercises.[235] In the future, virtue ought to help further discourse between Christian and other religious ethics, like Judaism, Islam, Hinduism, and Buddhism.

Some use the virtues to build up the community of faith: Günther Virt writes about the virtues of humility, *epikeia*, and truthfulness to secure the specifically Christian formation of conscience.[236] Vincent LeClercq proposes virtues for the formation of clergy[237] and Christopher Vogt and William McDonough each offer the virtues for a new Christian *Ars Moriendi*.[238]

Others use virtue in the field of church ethics. Ten years ago, the Mennonite Joseph Kotva and I invited 25 Protestants and Catholics to reflect on virtue and power in the lives of ministers and their communities.[239] Recently Gerard Mannion offered a virtue ecclesiology, which, he writes, 'might enable Christians to explore in a comparative fashion what sort of communities their churches are in reality and what they aspire to be in accordance with the gospel and the rich traditions of Christianity'.[240]

Studying the Church as a universal sacrament of holiness, Herbert Schlögel urges ethicists to take seriously the task of reflecting on the Church not only in its teachings but in its practices.[241] The Church is the community that remembers and narrates the person of Jesus Christ and a community of solidarity that continually tests its convictions and probes its tradition.[242]

The pedophile scandal provided an enormous catalyst for launching the field of church ethics.[243] This cannot be emphasized enough: it is nearly impossible to find essays before 1990 by theological ethicists writing critically of the Church's leadership, practices, and institutional structures. Before 1990, ethicists admonished, advised, and instructed lay persons and civil society. With the scandal coupled with the shift in theological ethics from a clerical to a lay-led field of theological inquiry, at least 100 theologians and ethicists have written about the need for greater moral and ecclesial accountability in church governance.

In 1994, and again in 2005, *Theological Studies* provided two bibliographically rich reflections on the topic.[244] From *Concilium*, three women edited an international collection of essays on the institutional dimensions of the crisis,[245] while Stephen Pope offered a collection of essays that looked at lay leadership and responsibility in the Church.[246] Two other collections looked to multidisciplinary sources so as to address issues of moral leadership and accountability.[247]

Ethicists report that the fundamental problem facing the Church is the gulf between the teachings of the leadership and the needs and faith that the people of God hold. Two major European ethicists, France's Paul Valadier and Italy's Giuseppe Angelini, debated this topic at Padova under the heading of *sensus fidelium*. Though Angelini pleaded for a deeper, non-reductive understanding of *sensus*, Valadier argued that the magisterium must urgently understand better the conscientious claims of the people of God. Leadership ought to gather people together to reflect with realism on their faith and on their location in the world and in history.[248]

From Tanzania, Magesa argues that African church leaders must rethink their ecclesial structures and re-examine the apostolic conception of the Church as the People of God.[249] Magesa wants the Church to remember its past, to act as a social and political conscience, to restore health, to defend the oppressed, and in particular to liberate women. In another work, he explores the actual attempts by the Church to inculturate in Kenya, Tanzania, and Uganda.[250]

In a collection from *Concilium*, Jon Sobrino and Felix Wilfred raised questions about how church leaders understand themselves and the needs of the Church. For them, the identity crisis concerns Christianity itself, and especially its leadership which fails to realize that there is a crisis in the first place.[251] From

Uganda, Peter Kanyandago writes: 'The churches seem to be living as if there is no crisis.' He adds: 'The biggest challenge facing the African churches seems to be the failure to create an interface between what people are living and experiencing, and the Christian message as conveyed mainly through the western historical and cultural influence that has strongly marked African Christianity. This separation between reality and what Christianity stands for is a form of schizophrenia.'[252]

From Japan, Adolfo Nicolas comments, 'In Asia we are in crisis because our message is not made visible in our life.' Thus, 'in this kind of crisis, we are transformed from judging others to being judged ourselves'.[253] From Italy, Antonio Autiero recently called for space in the Church so as to see whether we can address these living challenges. He contended that the problem 'is above all the knowledge that normative and strictly deductive superstructures expressed in authoritarian control suffocate the space of authentic liberty in the existence of adult subjects who are mature enough to make autonomous and responsible moral choices. Now it is time to ask whether and how far the Church presents itself to postmoderns as an inhabitable home from this point of view also.'

He then reflected on 'the most recent developments', and stated:

> One cannot deny that there is a movement away from the Church, quite explicitly or sometimes even simply pragmatically, precisely on account of the Church's insistence on moral themes public or private, marked by normative solutions that make little sense to the critical consciousness of contemporary men and women.[254]

As ethicists look at the structures of the Church, they also examine structures in the world, above all, with regard to globalization. Throughout this chapter we have seen how ethicists from Latin America, Africa, and Asia decry not only the inequity of globalization, but also its ability to alienate more and more from policy-making decisions. Waliggo called this alienation 'the first and most hideous injustice of globalization': 'people in the developing world are thus mere *recipients* of the already laid down agenda of current globalization. The recipients are told over and over again that they have no alternative but to accept it or gradually become isolated and die out!'[255]

Theologians from Latin America and the United States have proposed a strategy of international, cosmopolitan solidarity. From Argentina, Humberto Miguel Yáñez offers a theological anthropology of hope and solidarity from the theology of Juan Alfaro. Solidarity aims to incorporate the marginalized, to humanize economic and social structures, and to temper competitiveness and individualism.[256] From Chile, Tony Mifsud sees solidarity as integral to ethical discernment.[257] From Argentina, Aldo Marcelo Cáceres argues that religious traditions bring to globalization an essential awareness of our humanity that promotes a solidarity across national frontiers.[258]

From the United States, Daniel Groody writes:

> The central questions about globalization ultimately are not about efficiency or profitability but about human life and human freedom. Christian theology's principal task in the modern world is not to reject globalization but to humanize it . . . By necessity, the realization of our interconnectedness as human beings challenges us to work for what John Paul II referred to as a 'globalization without marginalization' or 'a globalization of solidarity', which arguably ought to be the ultimate *telos* of globalization.[259]

Kenneth Himes reminds us that John Paul II's encyclical *Sollicitudo Rei Socialis* provides the most commonly cited reflection on solidarity in Catholic social tradition. There the Pope discusses interdependence as 'a *system determining* relationships in the contemporary world' and solidarity as the 'correlative response as a moral and social attitude, as a "virtue".'[260]

Hollenbach argues that, since globalization structuralizes inequality and marginalization, we need to establish normative standards of solidarity that are as sophisticated and as interlocking as the network of globalization itself.[261]

A review of the works of theological ethics across the globe shows great diversity, but also foundational agreement. After considering proportionalism as an alternative to neo-manualism, many theologians realized that they needed a theological framework to contextualize their work: the Europeans developed an autonomous ethics, the Latin Americans liberation theology, the Africans a liberative inculturation approach, the Asians a liberative inculturation with inter-religious dialogue, and the North Americans the Catholic social tradition in any number of contexts. These defining foundational contexts were constructed in large part for six reasons. Indigenous theologians began to respond to the global irruption of suffering by taking a local and at times effective stance of responsive solidarity. They coupled their solidarity with a theological argument that was identifiable with the specific philosophical needs of their local cultures. Third, their local educational institutions developed into more sophisticated centers of higher learning and gave these theologians teaching positions, graduate students, academic journals, and publishing houses through which they could promote their theological arguments. Fourth, in those instances where local or international hierarchy investigated and/or censured theologians, the theologians often transfered to other teaching positions, and continued their work. Fifth, while the tussle between Episcopal concern for orthodoxy and the theologians' need for space in their theological investigations became a way of life, local theological arguments became more identifiable with the local culture. Parish priests, lay leaders, and Episcopal authority eventually appropriated the theologians' modified claims. Sixth, globalization prompted theologians to act locally but to discuss and collaborate cross-culturally. Journals, visiting professorships, email, and international conferencing permitted a greater sharing of distinctive theological claims across cultural contexts.

What about tomorrow? While in the 1970s and 1980s many theologians were European trained, especially those who became the founders of their local theologies, the advancement of local university theology departments over the last fifteen years has created the opportunity for local students to study on their own continents. As we move through the early years of the twenty-first century, we ought to expect the next generation to reflect even more specifically on the concrete ethical and theological needs of their local contexts while forging trans-cultural consensus on matters of faith, conscience, justice, and solidarity.

A contemporary work: Margaret Farley, *Just Love: A Framework for Christian Sexual Ethics*

Margaret Farley's long-awaited work offers a comprehensive Catholic feminist treatment of sexuality, love, and relationships. As such, it is emblematic of the developments of theological ethics over the last century and highlights well its accomplishments. First, a work by a woman theologian, it provides a comprehensive theological anthropology that resonates with people's experiences both across the globe as well as throughout history. Second, that anthropological vision is relational and embodied, and, while hope-filled, it is also very realistic, appreciating the limitations, vulnerabilities, and frailties of humanity. Third, while sensitive to local claims, Farley is interested in forging consensus on minimal but universal standards of sexual conduct. In both the regard for the local and the global, her work is very catholic. Fourth, Farley aims for an effective work that actually affects the way people live. Like most contemporary theological ethicists, she wants to enter into people's lives, their ways of relating, and their normal standards of conduct. Fifth, as a Catholic feminist, she insists that sexuality is not a private issue but rather a public one. The Church's long interest in sexuality is coupled with a feminist suspicion of embodied ways of seeking and expressing intimacy. Sixth, while the work emerges from the best of Catholic theological ethics, it is not restrictively Catholic. Rather Farley engages other religious traditions as well, believing that the development of universal ethical standards depends in part on the way faith communities envision the human. Finally, she upholds the conscience of the person, and rather than imitating the manuals by presenting a list of prohibitive norms aimed to compel the reader, Farley offers guidelines to bring the reader to greater conscientiousness, maturity, and responsibility.

She begins her work by surveying the traditions of the Greeks and Romans, Judaism, and Christianity to see how they valued sexuality and reflected normatively on it. From Christianity, for instance, we inherit an ethic that '(1) values marriage and procreation on the one hand and singleness and celibacy on the other; (2) gives as much or more importance to internal attitudes and thoughts as to external actions; and (3) affirms a sexual symbolic meaning for sexual intercourse, yet both subordinates it as a value to other human values and finds in it a possibility for evil.'[262]

Farley then turns globally and studies a variety of contemporary cultures and their traditions, from Samoa to Nairobi, from Mecca to Bombay. In these cross-cultural studies, she finds, 'The closer we come to each of these contexts, the most important factor that emerges may not be either difference or similarity. It may be the very plasticity of human sexuality, its susceptibility to different meanings and expressive forms.'[263]

While respecting that plasticity especially as it manifests itself in the complexity of gender, she notes three minimalist claims about our gender: it should not divide us, or be based on complementarity or on the differentiation of roles.[264] Inevitably Farley turns to experience: 'My attention is focused on experience (though I know there is no such thing as "raw" or "pure" experience). I want to ask all over again how it is that humans are complex beings who experience themselves as bodies but not only as bodies, as spirits but not only as spirits.'[265] Here her work is unmistakably feminist, seeking 'to remedy the deficiencies of the past, particularly theories that have had bad consequences for women'.[266]

Based on these investigations, she offers us a normative ethic of sexuality based on a love that is just. 'Love is true and just, right and good, insofar as it is a true response to the reality of the beloved, a genuine union between the one who loves and the one loved, and an accurate and adequate affirmation of the beloved.'[267] The framework, then, is not justice and love, but justice in loving. From this framework she articulates a set of norms that are 'not merely ideals; they are bottom-line requirements', which each admit of degrees. They concern: no unjust harm, free consent, mutuality, equality, commitment, fruitfulness, and social justice. These are tools more for thinking than resolving questions about sexual ethics.

She concludes by summarizing her position: 'It is not easy to introduce conversations of justice into every sexual relation and the evaluation of every sexual activity. But if sexuality is to be creative and not destructive, then there is no substitute for discerning ever more carefully whether our expressions of it are just.'[268]

Farley's universally oriented guidance for sexual conduct strikes me, as by extension, equally applicable to all dimensions of human life. As we conclude our study of the incredible twentieth century, we can now, in our own time and place, most likely in our communities of faith, recognize God's call to discipleship. As we listen to the summons, we should be able to hear the will of God in the sanctuary of our consciences calling us to just love.

Notes

1 Edward Vacek, *Love, Human and Divine: The Heart of Christian Ethics* (Washington, DC: Georgetown University Press, 1994); Timothy Jackson, *The Priority of Love: Christian Charity and Social Justice* (Princeton: Princeton University Press, 2003); David Matzko McCarthy, 'Love in Fundamental Moral Theology', *Moral Theology*, 181–206; Keenan, 'Love', *Moral Wisdom*, 9–26.

2 Marciano Vidal, 'La preferencia por el pobre, criterio de moral', *Studia Moralia* 20 (1982) 277–304; *Feminismo y ética. Cómo 'feminizar' la moral* (Madrid: PPC, 2000).

3 Enda McDonagh, *Immersed in Mystery: Enroute to Theology* (Dublin: Veritas, 2007) 43; see also *Gift and Call: Towards a Christian Theology of Morality* (Dublin: Gill and Macmillan, 1975); *Doing the Truth* (1979); *Vulnerable to the Holy: in Faith, Morality and Art* (Dublin: St Columba's, 2004); 'The Good News in Moral Theology, of Hospitality, Healing, and Hope', *Moral Theology for the Twenty-First Century* 80–6; 'The Reign of God: Signposts for Catholic Theology', *CEHP*, 317–23.

4 Kevin Kelly, *New Directions in Moral Theology* (London: Geoffrey Chapman, 1992); *New Directions in Sexual Morality: Moral Theology and the Challenge of AIDS* (London: Geoffrey Chapman, 1998); *From A Parish Base* (London: Darton, Longman and Todd, 1999); 'A Moral Theologian Faces the New Millennium in a Time of AIDS', *CEHP*, 324–32.

5 Enrico Chiavacci, *Dal dominio alla pace. Scritti sulla globalizzazione* (Molfetta: La Meridiana, 1993); 'Globalization and Justice: New Horizons for Moral Theology', *CTEWC*, 239–44. Also his comprehensive, *Teologia Morale Fondamentale*.

6 See Autiero's thoughts on bioethics, Stephan Goertz and Katharina Klöcker, *Theologie trifft Bioethik* (Ostfildern: Grünewald, 2008); on his work on rights in bioethics, 'L'etica della salute. Tra diritti negati e dovere di solidarietá', *Global Bioethics*' 3 (1993) 157–63.

7 Autiero, *Das Fremde, das Andere und das Selbst: Provokationen an die theologische Ethik* (Münster: Antrittsvorlesung, 1993).

8 Autiero, 'L'etica di fronte alla malattia. Il paradigma della AIDS', in Marian Nalepa and Terrence Kennedy, eds, *La Coscienza Morale Oggi* (Rome: Edacalf, 1987) 599–615; 'Anthropologische und ethische Überlegungen zum Thema AIDS', in H. R. Zielinski, ed., *Prüfsteine medizinischer Ethik* (Grevenbroich: AMEG, 1988) 51–85; 'Quale etica per una sessualitá al positivo?', in A. Cargnel, ed., *AIDS e assistenza domiciliare. Esperienze a confronto* (Rome: Sedac, 1995) 291–7; 'AIDS. Quale sfida per l'etica?', *Rivista di teologia morale* 80 (1988) 13–19.

9 Autiero, 'Essere nel mondo. Ecologia dei bisogni', in Tullo Goffi and G. Piana, eds, *Corso di morale*, Vol. II (Brescia: Queriniana, 1983) 97–125; 'Ambiti e prospettive dell'etica medica', *Studia moralia* 2 (1983) 405–15; 'Le sfide etiche del III millennio: il paradigma dell'ecologia', *Problemi di Bioetica* 7 (1990) 39–49; 'Esiste un'etica ambientale?', in V. Domenicelli, ed., *Diritto pubblico dell'ambiente* (Padova: CEDAM, 1996), 7–27; 'Veröffentlicht etiche per la sostenibilità', in Simone Morandini, ed., *Per la sostenibilitá: Etica ambientale e antropologia* (Padova: Gregoriana, 2007) 111–19. Morandini is the leading European Catholic ethicist on the environment, *La creazione in dono: Giovanni Paolo II e l'ambiente* (Bologna: EMI, 2005); *Teologia ed ecologia* (Brescia: Morcelliana, 2005); *Creazione* (Bologna: EMI, 2005); *Termometro terra: Scienza, etica e politica di fronteal mutamento climatico* (Bologna: EMI, 2004); *Nel tempo dell'ecologia. Etica teologica e questione ambientale* (Bologna: EDB, 1999); 'Reflections on the Relationship between Ecology and Theological Ethics', in Linda Hogan, ed., *Applied Ethics in a World Church: The*

Padua Conference (Maryknoll: Orbis, 2008) 73–82.

10 Robert Gascoigne, 'Suffering and Theological Ethics: Intimidation and Hope', *CTEWC*, 163–6, at 163.

11 See Peter Kanyandago, ed., *Marginalized Africa: An International Perspective* (Nairobi: Paulines Publications Africa, 2002).

12 Ronaldo Zacharias, 'Dreaming of a New Moral Theology for Brazil', *CTEWC*, 116–23, at 117.

13 Vimal Tirimanna, 'Globalization Needs to Count Human Persons', *CTEWC*, 245–52, at 246.

14 Gustavo Gutiérrez, *A Theology of Liberation: History, Politics, Salvation* (Maryknoll: Orbis, 1971).

15 Gustavo Gutiérrez, 'Option for the Poor', in Ignacio Ellacuria and Jon Sobrino, eds, *Mysterium Liberationis: Fundamental Concepts of Liberation Theology* (Maryknoll: Orbis, 1993) 235–50; James Nickoloff, ed., *Gustavo Gutiérrez: Essential Writings* (Maryknoll: Orbis Books, 1996).

16 Gutiérrez, *On Job: God Talk and the Suffering of the Innocent* (Maryknoll: Orbis, 1987).

17 Ibid., 94.

18 Gutiérrez, *Las Casas: In Search of the Poor of Jesus Christ* (Maryknoll: Orbis, 1993); Helen Rand Parish, María Concepta Maciel, and Gustavo Gutiérrez, *Bartolomé de las Casas: Liberation of the Oppressed* (Berkeley: University of California, 1984).

19 Bartolomé de Las Casas, *Defense of the Indians* (North Illinois University Press, 1992); see also Bartolomé de las Casas, Helen Rand Parish, ed., *The Only Way* (New York, NY: Paulist Press, 1992); Francis P. Sulivan, ed., *Indian Freedom: The Cause of Bartolomé de las Casas: A Reader* (Kansas City: Sheed and Ward, 1995).

20 Roger Ruston, 'Part III: Mexico and Peru: Bartolomé de las Casas', *Human Rights and the Image of God* (London: SCM Press, 2004) 119–90; Thomas O'Meara, 'The Dominican School of Salamanca and the Spanish Conquest of America: Some Bibliographical Notes', *The Thomist* 56.4 (1992) 555–82.

21 Leonardo Boff and Clodovis Boff, *Introducing Liberation Theology* (Maryknoll: Orbis, 1987); Leonardo Boff, *Jesus Christ Liberator: A Critical Christology for Our Times* (Maryknoll: Orbis Books, 1978); *Liberating Grace* (Maryknoll: Orbis Books, 1979); Clodovis Boff, 'Epistemology and Method of the Theology of Liberation', *Mysterium Liberationis*, 57–84.

22 Enrique Dussel, *Ethics and the Theology of Liberation* (Maryknoll: Orbis, 1978); *The History of the Church in Latin America: Colonialism to Liberation (1492–1979)* (Grand Rapids: Eerdmans, 1981); *Etica de la liberacion en la edad de la globalizacion y la exclusion* (Madrid: Trotta, 1998); Roberto Goizueta, *Liberation Method and Dialogue: Enrique Dussel and North American Theological Discourse* (Atlanta: Scholar's Press, 1987).

23 Jon Sobrino, 'Theology in a Suffering World', *The Principle of Mercy* (Maryknoll: Orbis, 1994) 27–46; Dean Brackley, 'Theology and Solidarity: Learning from Sobrino's Method', in Stephen Pope, ed., *Hope and Solidarity: Jon Sobrino's Challenge to Christian Theology* (Maryknoll: Orbis, 2008) 3–15 (hereafter *Hope and Solidarity*).

24 Jon Sobrino, *Christology at the Crossroads* (Maryknoll: Orbis, 1976); *Jesus the Liberator: A Historical-theological Reading of Jesus of Nazareth* (New York: Orbis Books, 1993); Daniel Harrington, 'What God Jesus Killed?: Sobrino's Historical Theological Reading of Scripture', *Hope and Solidarity*, 79–89.

25 Roberto Goizueta, 'The Christology of Jon Sobrino', *Hope and Solidarity*, 90–103.

26 Jon Sobrino, 'The Central Position of the Reign of God in Liberation Theology', *Mysterium Liberationis*, 350–487; 'Systematic Christology: Jesus Christ, the Absolute Mediator of the Reign of God', 440–61; Sobrino, *No Salvation Outside the Poor: Prophetic-Utopian Essays* (Maryknoll: Orbis, 2008); Lisa Sowle Cahill, 'Christ and Kingdom', *Hope and Solidarity*, 242–53.
27 Jon Sobrino, 'The Coming Kingdom or God's Present Reign', Andrés Torres Queiruga et al., eds, *Jesus as Christ: What Is at Stake in Christology?* (London: SCM, 2008) 44–54, at 53.
28 Stephen Pope, 'On Not Abandoning the Historical World to its Wretchedness', *Hope and Solidarity*, 44–62.
29 Jon Sobrino, 'Spirituality and the Following of Jesus', *Mysterium Liberationis*, 677–701.
30 Ignacio Ellacuría, 'Utopia and Prophecy in Latin America', *Mysterium Liberationis*, 289–328, at 289; 'The Historicity of Christian Salvation', ibid., 251–88; 'The Church of the Poor, Historical Sacrament of Liberatino', Ibid., 543–63.
31 Ignacio Ellacuría, *Escritos teologicos* (San Salvador: UCA Press, 2000).
32 Marciano Vidal, 'Is Morality based on Autonomy Compatible with the Ethics of Liberation?', in Dietmar Mieth and Jacques Pohier, eds, *Ethics of Liberation or the Liberation of Ethics* (London: T&T Clark, 1984) 80–6; Dietmar Mieth, 'Autonomy or Liberation – Two Paradigms of Christian Ethics?', ibid., 87–93.
33 Francisco Moreno Rejon, *Salvar la Vida de los Pobres: Aportes a la Teología Moral* (Lima: CEPA, 1986); *Moral Theology from the Poor: Moral Challenges of the Theology of Liberation* (Quezon City: Claretian Press, 1988); 'Fundamental Moral Theology in the Theology of Liberation', *Mysterium Liberationis*, ibid., 210–21; 'Seeking the Kingdom and its Justice: the Development of the Ethic of Liberation', *Ethics of Liberation*, 35–41.
34 Antonio Moser and Bernardino Leers, *Moral Theology: Dead Ends and Alternatives* (Maryknoll: Orbis, 1990); Antonio Moser, 'The Representation of God in the Ethic of Liberation', *The Ethics of Liberation*, 42–7.
35 Rogue Junges, *Evento Cristo e Ação Humana. Temas fundamentais da Ética teológica* (São Leopoldo: Unisinos, 2001).
36 Tony Mifsud, *Moral de Discernimento* (Santiago de Chile: San Pablo, 1987); *Ethos Cotidiano: Un Proceso de discernimento* (Santiago de Chile: Universidad Alberto Hurtado, 2006); 'The Development of a Liberation Ethic in the Documents of the Church since Vatican II', *Ethics of Liberation*, 48–53.
37 E. Bonnín, *Moral De La Vida: Manual De Bioética Teológica* (Dabar, 2005).
38 Márcio Fabri dos Anjos, 'Teología de la Liberación', in Juan Carlos Tealdi, ed., *Diccionario Latinoamericano de Bioética* (Bogota: UNESCO, 2008) 12–14; 'Challenges of Pluralism to Moral Theology', *CTEWC*, 228–36; 'Power and Vulnerability: A Contribution of Developing Countries to the Ethical Debate on Genetics', in Lisa Sowle Cahill, ed., *Genetics, Theology and Ethics: An Interdisciplinary Conversation* (New York: The Crossroad Publishing Company, 2005) 137–57; 'Bioética em perspectiva de libertação', in Volnei Garrafa and Leo Pessini, eds, *Bioética: poder e justiça* (São Paulo: SBB & Loyola & S. Camilo, 2003) 455–65; 'Power, Ethics and the Poor in Human Genetic Research', in Lisa Sowle Cahill and Maureen Junker Kenny, eds, *The Ethics of Genetic Engineering* (New York: Orbis Books, 1998) 73–82; 'Medical Ethics in the Developing World: A Liberation Theology Perspective', *Journal of Medicine and Philosophy* 21 (1996) 629–37.
39 Ivone Gebara, 'Option for the Poor as an Option for Poor Women', in Elisabeth Schüssler Fiorenza, ed., *Women, Work, and Poverty* (New York: Orbis, 1987) 110–

17; 'Women Doing Theology in Latin America', in Elsa Tamez, ed., *Through Her Eyes: Women's Theology from Latin America* (Maryknoll, NY: Orbis Books, 1989) 37–48; 'Women and Spirituality: A Latin American Perspective', *The Way* 38 (1998) 240–51; *As incômodas filhas de Eva na Igreja da América Latina*, 2nd edn (São Paulo: Paulinas, 1990); *Longing for Running Water: Ecofeminism and Liberation* (Minneapolis: Fortress, 1999); *Out of the Depths: Women's Experience of Evil and Salvation* (Minneapolis: Augsburg-Fortress, 2002). *Teologia Ecofeminista. Ensaio para repensar o conhecimento e a religião* (São Paulo: Olho d'Água, 1997); *As águas do meu poço. Reflexões sobre experiências de liberdade* (São Paulo: Paulinas, 2005);

40 Ivone Gebara and Maria Clara Bingemer, *A mulher faz Teologia* (Petrópolis: Vozes, 1986); 'Mary', *Mysterium Liberationis*, 482–96; *Mary: Mother of God, Mother of the Poor* (London: Wipf & Stock Publishers, 2004).

41 Maria Clara Bingemer, 'Family and Religion in Brazil: Tensions and Perspectives', *INTAMS Review* 10.2 (2004) 177–84; *Cuerpo de mujer y experiência de Dios. Sentir y experimentar a Dios de un modo femenino* (Buenos Aires: San Benito, 2007); *Simone Weil: la fuerza y la debilidad del amor* (Pamplona: Verbo Divino, 2009); 'Reflections on the Trinity', *Through Her Eyes*, 56–80; 'A mulher na Igreja hoje. A partir e além do Concílio Vaticano II', *Revista Eclesiástica Brasileira* 63, no. 249 (2003) 23–46; 'Saborear a fé em meio à pluralidade. Os caminhos da teologia em meio ao diálogo inter-religioso', *Perspectiva Teológica* 36, no. 99 (2004) 221–39; 'Masculinity, Feminity, and the Christ', *Jesus as Christ*, 73–83.

42 Ana María Trepedino and Margarida L. Ribeiro Brandao, 'Women and the Theology of Liberation', *Mysterium Liberationis*, 221–31.

43 Ana María Bidegain, 'Women and the Theology of Liberation', *Through Her Eyes*, 15–36.

44 María Pilar Aquino, *Our Cry For Life: Feminist Theology from Latin America* (Maryknoll, NY: Orbis Books, 1993); 'Women's Contribution to Theology in Latin America', in Charles Curran, Margaret Farley, and Richard McCormick, eds, *Feminist Ethic and the Catholic Moral Tradition* (Mahwah: Paulist Press, 1996) 90–119 (hereafter *Feminist Ethics*); with Elsa Tamez, *Teología Feminista Latinoamericana* (Quito: Ediciones Abya-Yala, 1998); with Roberto Goizueta, eds, *Theology: Expanding the Borders* (Mystic, CT: Twenty-Third Publications, 1998); with Daisy L. Machado and Jeanette Rodríguez, eds, *A Reader in Latina Feminist Theology. Religion and Justice* (Austin: University of Texas Press, 2002) .

45 Ada Maria Isasi-Diaz, 'Defining our *Proyecto Historico: Mujerista* Strategies for Liberation', *Feminist Ethics*, 120–35, at 121; *En la Lucha – In the Struggle: A Hispanic Women's Liberation Theology* (Minneapolis: Augsburg Fortress Publishers, 1993, 2003); *La Lucha Continues* (Maryknoll: Orbis, 2004).

46 Two very different works, with the same title cover the events from Medellín to Puebla: Alfonso López Trujillo, *De Medellín a Puebla* (Madrid: Editorial Católica, 1980); Enrique Dussel, *De Medellín a Puebla: Una decada de sangre y esperanza, 1968–1979* (Madrid: Edicol, 1979); see also Paul Sigmund, 'The Birth of Liberation Theology: Medellin and Beyond', 'The Battle of Puebla', *Liberation Theology at the Crossroads* (New York: Oxford University Press, 1990) 28–39, 93–107.

47 See Sobrino, *The Principle of Mercy: Taking the Crucified People from the Cross* (Maryknoll: Orbis Books, 1994); *Witnesses to the Kingdom: The Martyrs of El Salvador and the Crucified Peoples* (Maryknoll: Orbis Press, 2003).

48 Cardinal Joseph Ratzinger, *Instruction on Certain Aspects of the 'Theology of Liberation*, 6 August 1984: http://www.vatican.va/roman_curia/congregations/cfaith/documents/rc_con_cfaith_doc_19840806_theology-liberation_en.html.

49 Cardinal Joseph Ratzinger, *Instruction on Christian Freedom and Liberation*, 22 March 1986: http://www.vatican.va/roman_curia/congregations/cfaith/documents/rc_con_cfaith_doc_19860322_freedom-liberation_en.html.

50 Congregation for the Doctrine of the Faith, *Notification on the Book «Church: Charism and Power. Essay on militant Ecclesiology» by Father Leonardo Boff, O.F.M., 11 March 1985, AAS* 77 (1985) 756–62.

51 Congregation for the Doctrine of the Faith, *Notification on the Works of Father Jon Sobrino SJ*, 26 November 2006: http://www.vatican.va/roman_curia/congregations/cfaith/documents/rc_con_cfaith_doc_20061126_notification-sobrino_en.html.

52 Mawuto R. Afan, 'The Main "Building Sites" of Ethics in West Africa', *CTEWC*, 39–48.

53 Engelbert Mveng, 'Impoverishment and Liberation: A Theological Approach for Africa and the Third World', in Rosino Gibellni, ed., *Paths of African Theology* (Maryknoll: Orbis, 1994) 154–63; *Theologie, Liberation Et Cultures Africaines: Dialogue Sur L'anthropologie Negro-Africaine* (Yaoundé: Présence Africaine, 1996); 'La théologie africaine de la libération', *Theologies of the Third World: Convergences and Differences* 219 (1988) 31–51.

54 Laurenti Magesa, 'Locating the Church among the Wretched of the Earth', *CTEWC* , 49–56, at 50.

55 Meinrad Hebga, 'Engelbert Mveng: a Pioneer of African Theology', in Bénézet Bujo and Juvénqal Ilunga Muya, eds, *African Theology in the 21st Century: The Contribution of the Pioneers* (Nairobi: Paulines Publications, 2003) 39–46 (hereafter *African Theology 1*); Yvon Elenga, *Père Engelbert Mveng SJ: un pionnier. Recueil d'hommages à l'occasion du dixième anniversaire de sa mort* (Kinshasa: Editions Loyola-Canisius, 2005).

56 Y. Assogba, *Jean-Marc Ela: Le sociologue et théologien africain en boubou* (Paris: L'Harmattan, 1999).

57 See above, *African Theology 1*.

58 Emmanuel Ntakarutimana, 'Msgr. Tharcisse Tshibangu: Champion of an "African-coloured" Theology', *African Theology 1*, 47–63.

59 The debate appeared in 'Débat sur la "Theologie Africaine"', *Revue du Clergé Africain* 15 (1960) 333–52; reprinted in *African Theology 1*, 183–99.

60 Bujo, 'Introduction to the Tshibangu and Vanneste Debate', *African Theology 1*, 179–82.

61 Patrick Watchege, 'Charles Nyamiti: The Vibrant Pioneer of African Inculturated Theology', *African Theology: The Contribution of the Pioneers* 2 (Nairobi: Paulines edition, 2006) 149–62 (hereafter *African Theology 2*); Mike Vahakangas, *In Search of Foundations for African Catholicism: Charles Nyamiti's Theological Methodology* (Leiden: Brill, 1999).

62 Charles Nyamiti, 'African Christologies Today', in Robert Schretiter, ed., *Faces of Jesus in Africa* (Maryknoll: Orbis, 1991) 3–23; *Some Contemporary Models of African Ecclesiology: A Critical Assessment in the Light of Biblical and Church Teaching* (Nairobi: CUEA Publications, 2007); *Jesus Christ, the Ancestor of Humankind: An Essay on African Christology* (Nairobi: CUEA Publications, 2006).

63 Peter Schineller, *A Handbook on Inculturation* (New York: Paulist, 1990); Aylward Shorter, *Toward a Theology of Inculturation* (Maryknoll, NY: Orbis, 1995).

64 Bénézet Bujo, *African Christian Morality at the Age of Inculturation* (Nairobi: St Paul, 1990); *African Theology in its Social Context* (Maryknoll: Orbis, 1992); Michael Kirwen, ed., *African Cultural Knowledge: Themes and Embedded Beliefs* (Nairobi:

MIAS Books, 2005).

65 Juvénal Ilunga Muya, 'Bénézet Bujo: The Awakening of a Systematic and Authentically African Thought', *African Theology 1*, 107–49, at 130–1.

66 Bénézet Bujo, *Moralautonomie und Normenfindung bei Thomas von Aquin* (Vienna: Schöningh, 1979).

67 Bénézet Bujo, *The Ethical Dimension of Community: The African Model and the Dialogue between North and South* (Nairobi: St Paul, 1997) 15–89; Elochukwu E. Uzukwu, *A Listening Church: Autonomy and Communion in African Churches* (Maryknoll, NY: Orbis, 1996); William O'Neill, 'African Moral Theology', *TS* 62 (2001) 122–39, at 128. I am indebted to O'Neill for his remarkably helpful essay.

68 See Margaret Pfeil, 'The Interpretive Task of Moral Theology: Cultural and Epistemological Considerations', *Josephinum Journal of Theology* 10 (2003) 261–70 who makes a similar point, using Bujo as well.

69 Bénézet Bujo, *Foundations of an African Ethic: Beyond the Universal Claims of Western Morality* (New York: Crossroad, 2001) 185–6.

70 Paulinus Ikechukwu Odozor raises critical questions about Bujo's approach to inculturation, 'An African Moral Theology of Inculturation', *TS* 69 (2008) 583–609.

71 Laurenti Magesa, 'Recognizing the Reality of African Religion in Tanzania', *CEHP*, 76–84.

72 Emmanuel Katongole, 'AIDS, Africa, and the "Age of Miraculous Medicine"', *Applied Ethics* 137–46; *A Future for Africa: Critical Essays in Christian Social Imagination* (Scranton: University of Scranton Press, 2005).

73 Bénézet Bujo and Michael Czerny, *AIDS in Africa: Theological Reflections* (Nairobi: Paulines, 2007).

74 Peter Kanyandago, 'Is God African? Theological Reflections on the AIDS Scourge', in N. W. Ndung'u and P. N. Mwaura, eds, *Challenges and Prospects of the Church in Africa* (Nairobi: Paulines Publications Africa, 2005) 145–59; Peter Kanyandago, ed., *The Cries of the Poor: Questions and Responses for African Christianity* (Kisubi: Marianum Press Ltd, 2002).

75 Paul Chummar, 'HIV/AIDS in Africa: A Task for an Inculturated Theological Ethics', *Applied Ethics*, 155–62; Agbonkhianmeghe Orobator, 'Ethics of HIV/AIDS Prevention: Paradigms of a New Discourse from an African Perspective', ibid., 147–54.

76 James Good, 'HIV/AIDS among Desert Nomads in Kenya', *CEHP*, 91–5.

77 James Olaitan Ajayi, *The HIV/AIDS Epidemic in Nigeria: Some Ethical Considerations* (Rome: Gregorian University Press, 2003).

78 Paulinus Ikechukwu Odozor, 'Casuistry and AIDS', *CEHP*, 294–302.

79 Catholic Bishops of Africa and Madagascar, *Speak Out on HIV & AIDS: Our Prayer is Always Full of Hope* (Nairobi: Paulines Publications Africa, 2004).

80 Aylward Shorter and Edwin Onyancha, *The Church and AIDS in Africa: A Case Study: Nairobi City* (Nairobi, Kenya: St Paul Publications/Daughters of St Paul, 1998).

81 Stuart Bate, 'Differences in Confessional Advice in South Africa', *CEHP*, 212–20.

82 Therese Tinkasiimire, 'Responses to HIV/AIDS in Hoima Diocese, Uganda', in Mary Jo Iozzio, ed., *Calling for Justice throughout the World: Catholic Women Theologians on the HIV/AIDS Pandemic* (New York: Continuum, 2008) 183–91.

83 Agbonkhianmeghe E. Orobator, 'When AIDS Comes to Church', *AIDS in Africa*, 120–8.

84 Orobator, *From Crisis to Kairos: The Mission of the Church in the Time of HIV/AIDS,*

Refugees and Poverty (Nairobi: Paulines, 2005).

85 Orobator, 'Ethics of HIV/AIDS Prevention'. For the work of such women, see Margaret Farley, 'Partnership in Hope: Gender, Faith, and Responses to HIV/AIDS in Africa', *Journal of Feminist Studies in Religion* 20.1 (2004) 133–48.

86 Michael Czerny, ed., *AIDS and the Church in Africa* (Nairobi: Paulines Publications, 2005): http://www.jesuitaids.net/.

87 Paterne-Auxence Mombe, *Rays of Hope: Managing HIV and AIDS in Africa* (Nairobi: Paulines, 2003, 2008).

88 Ghislain Tshikendwa Matadi, *Suffering, Belief, Hope: The Wisdom of Job for an AIDS-Stricken Africa* (Nairobi: Paulines, 2008).

89 Peter Knox, *AIDS, Ancestors and Salvation: Local Beliefs in Christian Ministry to the Sick* (Nairobi: Paulines, 2008).

90 Jean-Marc Ela, *Le Cri de l'homme africain* (Pans: Harmattan, 1980); 'La Foi des pauvres en acte', *Telema* 35 (July–September 1983) 45–72; *Ma foi d'africain* (Pans: Karthala, 1985), *Afrique, L'irruption des Pauvres* (Paris: Harmattan, 2000); *African Cry* (London: Wipf & Stock Publishers, 2005); Bénézet Bujo, 'Jean-Marc Ela: Champion of a Theology Under the Trees', *African Theology 2*, 182–214.

91 Ela, 'Christianity and Liberation in Africa', *Paths of African Theology*, 143–4.

92 Aquiline Tarimo and William O'Neill, 'What San Salvador Says to Nairobi: The Liberation Ethics of Ignacio Ellacuría', *Love that Produces Hope*, 237–49. See also Tarimo, *Human Rights, Cultural Differences, and the Church in Africa* (Morogoro, Tanzania: Salvatorian Institute of Philosophy and Theology, 2004); *Applied Ethics and Africa's Social Reconstruction* (Nairobi: Acton Publishers, 2005); 'Globalization and African Economic Reforms', *Applied Ethics*, 32–8.

93 Teresia Hinga, 'Between Colonialism and Inculturation, Feminist Theologies in Africa', *The Power of Naming: A Concilium Reader in Feminist Liberation Theology* (New York: Orbis, 1996) 36–45; 'Jesus Christ and the Liberation of Women in Africa', in Mercy Amba Oduyoye and Musimbi R. A. Kanyoro, eds, *The Will to Arise Women, Tradition, and the Church in Africa* (Maryknoll, NY: Orbis Books, 2001) 183–95; 'Becoming Better Samaritans: Gender, Catholic Social Teaching and the Quest for Alternative Models of Doing Social Justice in Africa', *Applied Ethics*, 85–97.

94 Mercy Amba Oduyoye, *Daughters of Anowa African Women and Patriarchy* (Maryknoll: Orbis, 1995); Oduyoye, 'Feminist Theology in an African Perspective', *Paths of African Theology*, 166–81; *Introducing African Women's Theology* (Cleveland: Pilgrim Press, 2001).

95 Anne Nasimiyu-Wasike, 'Christianity and the African Rituals of Birth and Naming' and 'Polygamy: A Feminist Critique', *The Will to Arise*, 40–53, 101–18; Nasimiyu-Wasike, 'Christology and an African Woman's Experience', *Faces of Jesus in Africa*, 70–84; see Ursula King, ed., *Feminist Theology from the Third World* (Maryknoll, NY: Orbis, 1994).

96 For the relationship between the two, see Emmanuel Martey, *African Theology: Inculturation and Liberation* (Maryknoll, NY: Orbis, 1994).

97 Laurenti Magesa, 'Christ the Liberator and Africa Today', *Faces of Jesus*, 151–63; Richard Rwiza, 'Laurenti Magesa: An African Liberation Theologian', *African Theology 2*, 231–58.

98 Laurenti Magesa, *African Religion: The Moral Traditions of Abundant Life* (Maryknoll, NY: Orbis, 1997).

99 Magesa, 'Locating the Church among the Wretched of the Earth'.

100 Waliggo, 'African Christology in a Situation of Suffering', *Faces of Jesus*, 164–80.

101 Waliggo, ed., *Inculturation: Its Meaning and Urgency* (Kampala: St Paul Publications, 1986), in particular, his essay 'Making a Church that is truly African', 11–31.

102 Waliggo, 'Inculturation in the Age of Globalization', in Patrick Ryan, ed., *Challenges to Theology in Africa Today* (Nairobi: CUEA Publications, 2002) 95–113; Peter Kanyadago, 'John Mary Waliggo: The Theology of John Mary Waliggo', *African Theology 2*, 215–30.

103 Waliggo, 'A Woman Confronts Social Stigma in Uganda', *CEHP*, 56–58.

104 Waliggo, '"The Synod of Hope" at a Time of Crisis in Africa', in Maura Browne, ed., *The African Synod: Documents, Reflections, Perspectives* (Maryknoll, NY: Orbis, 1996) 199–210; see a bibliography from the Synod: http://www.afrikaworld.net/synod/bibliography.htm; also, Sébastien Muyengo Mulombe, 'Authenticity and Credibility: Moral Challenges after the African Synod', *CTEWC*, 57–62; Aylward Shorter, *Christianity and the African Imagination After the Synod Resources for Inculturation* (Nairobi: Paulines, 1998).

105 Agbonkhianmeghe E. Orobator, *The Church as Family: African Ecclesiology in Its Social Context* (Nairobi: Paulines, 2000).

106 Joseph Healey and Donald Sybertz, *Towards an African Narrative Theology* (Nairobi: Paulines Publications Africa, 1996).

107 Orobator, *Theology Brewed in an African Pot* (Maryknoll, NY: Orbis, 2008).

108 Elias Opongo and Agbonkhianmeghe Orobator, *Faith Doing Justice: A Manual for Social Analysis, Catholic Social Teachings and Social Justice* (Nairobi: Paulines Africa Publications, 2007). From England, see Philomena Cullen, Bernard Hoose, and Gerard Mannion, eds, *Catholic Social Justice: Theological and Practical Explorations* (London: Continuum, 2007).

109 Richard N. Rwiza, *Formation of Christian Conscience in Modern Africa* (Nairobi: Paulines Edition, 2001); Anozie Onyema, *The Moral Significance of African Traditional Religion for Christian Conscience* (Port Harcourt: Lynno Nigeria Coy, 2004).

110 Karl H. Peschke, *Christian Ethics: Moral Theology in the Light of Vatican II*, Vol. 1: *General Moral Theology* (Bangalore: Theological Publications in India, 1991); *Christian Ethics: Moral Theology in the Light of Vatican II*, Vol. 2: *Special Moral Theology* (Bangalore: Theological Publications in India, 1992).

111 Soosai Arokiasamy, *Social Sin: Its Challenges to Christian Life* (Bangalore: Claretian Publications, 1991).

112 Gali Bali, 'Rev. Fr. Soosai Arokiasamy, SJ: Man of the Church', *Vidyajyoti Journal of Theological Reflection* 66 (2002) 567–73, at 570–1. See Arokiasamy, 'Traditional Theology and People's Theology: Tasks and Prospects', *Jeevadhara* 136 (1993) 309–18.

113 Arokiasamy, 'Sarvodaya through Antodaya: The Liberation of the Poor in the Contextualization of Morals', *Vidyajyoti Journal of Theological Reflection* 51, no. 11 (November 1987) 545–64; Xavier Ilango, 'Morality from a Dalit Perspective', *Jeevadhara* 28, no. 168 (November 1998) 426–40.

114 John Chathanatt, *Gandhi and Gutiérrez: Two Paradigms of Liberative Transformation* (New Delhi: Decent Publishers, 2004).

115 Chathanatt, 'Reclaiming our Vintage Values: This Hour of the Economic History of India', *Jeevadhara* 26, no. 156 (November 1996) 435–56; 'An Ethical Analysis of Globalization from an Indian Perspective', *Applied Ethics*, 21–31.

116 Arokiasamy, 'Human Rights: Collective, Societal and Liberational Perspectives', *Jeevadhara* 21 (January 1991) 53–62; Chathanatt, 'Human Rights: A Historical Overview', *Vidyajyoti Journal of Theological Reflection* 31 (February 2001) 11–122; George V. Lobo, *Human Rights in the Indian Context* (New Delhi: The Commis-

sion for Justice Peace and Development, Catholic Bishops' Conference of India, 1991); Aloysius Pieris, 'Human Rights Language and Liberation Theology', *Vidyajyoti Journal of Theological Reflection* 51, no. 11 (November 1988) 522–36.

117 Clement Campos, 'Doing Christian Ethics in India's World of Cultural Complexity and Social Inequality', *CTEWC*, 82–90; 'A Catholic Hospital in India is Asked to Cooperate with an HIV Prevention Program', *CEHP*, 199–210.

118 Campos, 'Doing Christian Ethics', 84. See two issues of *Jeevadhara* dedicated to ecological issues – 18.103 (January 1988) and 21.126 (November 1991) and the statement of the Indian Theological Association, 'Ecological Crisis: An Indian Christian Response', in Jacob Parapally, ed., *Theologizing in Context: Statements of the Indian Theological Association* (Bangalore: Dharmaram Publications, 2002) 252–64.

119 Campos, 84; Arokiasamy, 'Liberation Ethics of Ecology', *Jeevadhara*, 18.103, 32–9.

120 Pushpa Joseph, 'Women's Perspectives in Bioethics: A Case Study from Tribal India', *Applied Ethics*, 98–108.

121 Pushpa Joseph, 'Retrieving Spirituality as a Resource for Coping with HIV/AIDS: Perspectives from South India', *Calling for Justice*, 192–202; Metti Amirtham, 'Women Confronting Stigma in Tamil Nadu', ibid., 174–82. On a related topic, see Joseph Fonseca, *Marriage in India* (Bangalore: Redemptorist Publications, 1989).

122 Vimal Tirimanna, 'Moral Theological Implications of Globalization from a Third World Perspective', *Vidyajyoti Journal of Theological Reflection* 65.4 (April 2001) 296–8.

123 Tirimanna, *Catholic Teaching on Violence, War and Peace in Our Contemporary World* (Bangalore: Asia Trading Corporation, 2006).

124 Agnes Brazal, 'Globalization and Catholic Theological Ethics: A Southeast Asian Perspective', *CTEWC*, 74–82.

125 Fausto Gomez, 'Globalization: Ethical and Christian Perspective', *Religious Life Asia* 3.2 (April–June, 2001) 45–63; see Dominador Bombongan, Jr, 'From Dependency to Globalization: A Changed Context for Liberation Theology', *Hapág* 1, no. 2 (2004) 33–63.

126 Fausto Gomez, 'The Holy Eucharist and Commitment to Justice and Solidarity', *Philippiniana Sacra* 22, no. 66 (September–December 1987) 403–20.

127 Fausto Gomez, 'St Thomas Aquinas: Justice, Property and the Poor', *Philippiniana Sacra* 30.89 (May–August 1995) 251–76.

128 Monica Jalandoni, 'The Fortitude of Filipino Women', in Agnes Brazal, Aloysius Cartagenas, Eric Genilo, and James Keenan, eds, *Transformative Theological Ethics: East Asian Contexts* (Quezon City: Ateoneo de Manila University Press, forthcoming).

129 Aloysius Cartagenas, 'The State of the Nation and its Implications to the Church's Social Praxis', *Talad* (2001) 123.

130 Ronaldo Tuazon, 'Narrating Christian Ethics from the Margins', *Hapág* 4 (2007) 27–60.

131 Astorga, 'Culture, Religion, and Moral Vision: A Theological Discourse on the Filipino People Power Revolution of 1986', *TS* 67 (2006) 567–601.

132 Agnes Brazal and Andrea Lizares Si, eds, *Body and Sexuality* (Quezon City: Ateneo de Manila, 2007).

133 Ma. Christina Astorga, 'The Feminization of AIDS in the Philippines', *Calling for Justice*, 157–66.

134 Brazal and Daniel Pilario, 'Disciplines, Interdisciplinarity, and Theology', *Hapág* 4

(2007) 5–25.

135 Brazal, 'Information, Sex Education, and Church Intervention in Public Policy in the Philippines', *Calling for Justice*, 61–7.

136 Cartagenas, 'The Challenge of Interdisciplinarity to Catholic Social Teaching', *Hapág* 4 (2007) 103–31.

137 Carlos Ronquillo, 'Moral Responsibility in Asia: A Proposed Approach', *Maryhill School of Theology Review* 3.2 (2000) 217–35.

138 Takeuchi, *Conscience and Personality*.

139 Haruko K. Okano, *Die Stellung Der Frau Im Shinto* (Wiesbaden: Otto Harrassowitz, 1976).

140 Okano, 'Moral Responsibility in the Japanese Context', *Für die Freiheit*, 162–9, at 167, 168 respectively.

141 Lucas Chan yiu Sing, 'As West Meets East: Reading Xunzi's A Discussion of Rites Through the Lens of Contemporary Western Ritual Theories', in Martin Stuflesser and Stephan Winter, eds, *'Ahme nach, was du vollziehst' Positionsbestimmungen zum Verhältnis von Liturgie und Ethik* (Regensburg: Friedrich Pustet, 2009) 101–20; 'Boaz as a Model of Hospitality for Community Rebuilding in the Postexilic Period and the Modern World', *Budhi* (2006/7); Lucas Chan and James Keenan, 'Bridging Christian Ethics and Confucianism through Virtue Ethics', *Chinese Cross Currents* 5, no. 3 (2007) 74–85.

142 Y-Lan Tran, 'HIV/AIDS in Vietnam: Calling for Dignity, Justice and Care', *Calling for Justice*, 31–7.

143 Juan José Tamayo, 'Reception of the Theology of Liberation', *Mysterium Liberationis*, 33–56.

144 Penny Lernoux, *Cry of the People* (Garden City: Doubleday, 1980).

145 Arthur McGovern, *Liberation Theology and Its Critics: Toward an Assessment* (Maryknoll, NY: Orbis, 1989).

146 Thomas Schubeck, *Liberation Ethics* (Minneapolis: Augsburg, 1993); 'Ethics and Liberation Theology', *TS* 56 (1995) 107–58.

147 Alfred Hennelly, *Theology for a Liberating Church: The New Praxis of Freedom* (Washington, DC: Georgetown University Press, 1988); *Liberation Theology: A Documentary History* (Maryknoll, NY: Orbis 1990); *Liberation Theologies: The Global Pursuit of Justice* (New London: Twenty-Third Publications, 1995).

148 Roger Haight, *An Alternative Vision: An Introduction to Liberation Theology* (New York: Paulist Press, 1989).

149 Dean Brackley, *Divine Revolution: Salvation and Liberation in Catholic Thought* (London: Wipf and Stock, 2004). Brackley co-authored with Schubeck, 'Moral Theology in Latin America', *TS* 63 (2002) 123–38.

150 Kevin Burke, *The Ground Beneath the Cross: The Theology of Ignacio Ellacuría* (Washington, DC: Georgetown University Press, 2004); Burke and Robert Lassalle Klein, *The Love that Produces Hope: The Thought of Ignacio Ellacuría* (Collegeville: Liturgical Press, 2006); Michael Lee, *Bearing the Weight of Salvation: The Soteriology of Ignacio Ellacuría* (New York: Crossroad, 2009).

151 Kenneth Himes, 'Liberation Theology and Catholic Social Teaching', *Hope and Solidarity*, 228–41.

152 Gregory Baum, 'Structures of Sin', in Gregory Baum and Robert Ellsberg, eds, *The Logic of Solidarity: Commentaries on Pope John Paul II's Encyclical 'On Social Concern'* (Maryknoll, NY: Orbis, 1989) 110–17.

153 Peter Henriot, 'The Concept of Social Sin', *Catholic Mind* (1973) 38–53; Kenneth Himes, 'Social Sin and the Role of the Individual', *Annual of the Society of Christian*

Ethics (1986) 183–213; Mark O'Keefe, *What Are they Saying about Social Sin?* (New York: Paulist Press, 1990); Margaret Pfeil, 'Doctrinal Implications of Magisterial Use of the Language of Social Sin', *Louvain Studies* 27 (2002) 132–52, at 152.

154 Donal Dorr, *Option for the Poor: A Hundred Years of Vatican Social Teaching* (Maryknoll, NY: Orbis, 1983); Joseph Curran, 'Mercy and Justice in the Face of Suffering: The Preferential Option for the Poor', *Hope and Solidarity* 201–14; Margaret Pfeil, 'Power and the Preferential Option for the Poor', ibid., 215–27.

155 James Cone, *Black Theology and Black Power* (Maryknoll, NY: Orbis, 1969, 1987).

156 Cone, *A Black Theology of Liberation* (Maryknoll, NY: Orbis, 1970).

157 Cone, *The God of the Oppressed* (Maryknoll, NY: Orbis, 1987).

158 M. Shawn Copeland, 'Critical Theologics for the Liberation of Women', *The Power of Naming*, 141–51.

159 Copeland, 'Black Political Theologies', in Peter Scott and William Cavanaugh, eds, *The Blackwell Companion to Political Theology* (Oxford: Blackwell Publishers, 2003) 271–87; 'Doing Black Catholic Theology: Rhythm, Structure, and Aesthetics', *Chicago Studies* 42.2 (Summer 2003) 127–41; 'Tradition and the Traditions of African American Catholicism', *TS* 61 (2000) 632–71; 'Method in Emerging Black Catholic Theology', in Diana Hayes and Cyprian Davis, eds, *Taking Down Our Harps* (Maryknoll, NY: Orbis, 1998) 120–44. See also Jamie Phelps, 'Inculturating Jesus', *Taking Down Our Harps*, 67–101; ibid., 'Communion Ecclesiology and Black Liberation Theology', 61 *TS* (2000) 672–99.

160 Copeland, 'The Interaction of Racism, Sexism and Classism in Women's Exploitation', in Elisabeth Schüssler Fiorenza, ed., *Women, Work, and Poverty* (New York: Orbis, 1987) 19–27; 'Race', Gareth Jones, ed., *The Blackwell Companion to Modern Theology* (Oxford: Blackwell Publishers, 2003) 499–511.

161 Copeland, 'The Church Is Marked by Suffering', in William Madges and Michael J. Daley, eds, *The Many Marks of the Church* (New London, CT: Twenty-Third Publications, 2006) 212–16; Copeland, '"Wading Through Many Sorrows": Toward a Theology of Suffering in a Womanist Perspective', in Charles Curran, Margaret Farley and Richard McCormick, eds, *Feminist Ethics and the Catholic Moral Tradition* (Mahwah: Paulist Press, 1996) 136–63.

162 Copeland, *Enfleshing Freedom: Body, Race, and Being* (Minneapolis: Fortress, 2008).

163 Bryan Massingale, *The Social Dimensions of Sin and Reconciliation in the Theologies of James Cone and Gustavo Gutiérrez* (Rome: Academina Alphonsiana, 1991).

164 Massingale, 'Ethical Reflection Upon Environmental Racism in the Light of Catholic Social Teaching', in Todd David Whitmore and Maura Ryan, eds, *The Challenge of Global Stewardship: Roman Catholic Response* (Notre Dame: University of Notre Dame Press, 1997).

165 Massingale, 'The African American Experience and US Roman Catholic Ethics'.

166 Michael Fahey, 'From the Editor's Desk', 61 *TS* (2000) 603.

167 Cone, 'Black Liberation Theology and Black Catholics: A Critical Conversation', *TS* 61 (2000) 731–47.

168 Massingale, 'James Cone and Recent Catholic Episcopal Teaching on Racism', *TS* 61 (2000) 700–30.

169 Massingale, *Poverty and Racism: Overlapping Threats to the Common Good* (Washington, DC: Catholic Charities USA, 2008); 'The Scandal of Poverty: "Cultural Indifference" and the Option for the Poor Post-Katrina', *Journal of Religion and Society*, Supplement Series 4 (2008) 55–72; 'Racial Reconciliation in Christian Ethics: Toward Starting a Conversation', *Journal of the Black Catholic Theological Symposium* 2 (2008) 31–57.

170 Massingale, 'HIV/AIDS and the Bodies of Black Peoples: The Spirituals and Resurrection Faith', in M. Shawn Copeland, ed., *Uncommon Faithfulness: The Black Catholic Experience* (Maryknoll, NY: Orbis, 2009).

171 Diana Hayes, 'Come Ye Disconsolate: American Black Catholics, Their Church, HIV/AIDS', *CEHP*, 96–106.

172 Shawnee Marie Daniels-Sykes, 'Hidden in Plain View: Older African Americans', *Calling for Justice*, 147–56.

173 Massingale, 'Beyond Revision: A Younger Moralist looks at Charles E. Curran', *A Call to Fidelity*, 253–72, at 267–8.

174 United States Conference of Catholic Bishops, *The Challenge of Peace: God's Promise and Our Response*, 3 May 1983: www.usccb.org/sdwp/international/TheChallengeofPeace.pdf.

175 Thomas Nairn, ed., *The Seamless Garment: Writings on the Consistent Ethic of Life* (Maryknoll, NY: Orbis, 2008); Nairn, ed., *The Consistent Ethic of Life*.

176 United States Conference of Catholic Bishops, *Economic Justice for All*, 13 November 1986: www.usccb.org/sdwp/international/EconomicJusticeforAll.pdf.

177 David Hollenbach, *Claims in Conflict: Retrieving and Renewing the Catholic Human Rights Tradition* (Mahwah: Paulist Press 1979); *Nuclear Ethics: A Christian Moral Argument* (Mahwah: Paulist Press, 1983); *The Common Good and Christian Ethics* (New York: Cambridge University Press, 2002); *Justice, Peace, and Human Rights: American Catholic Social Ethics in a Pluralistic World* (New York: Crossroad, 1988); *The Global Face of Public Faith: Politics, Human Rights, and Christian Faith* (Washington, DC: Georgetown University Press, 2003).

178 Hollenbach, ed., *Refugee Rights: Ethics, Advocacy, and Africa* (Washington, DC: Georgetown University Press, 2008).

179 Hollenbach, 'Catholic Ethics in a World Church: A US View', *CTEWC*, 140–6.

180 Marilyn Martone, 'Another Voice', *Hastings Center Report* (March/April 2006); 'Ethical Issues in Rehabilitation in the Home-Care Setting', *Journal of Clinical Ethics* (Winter 2004) 292–9; 'Making Health Care Decisions Without a Prognosis: Life in a Brain Trauma Unit', *Annual of the Society of Christian Ethics* 20 (2000) 309–27.

181 Anne E. Patrick, *Liberating Conscience: Feminist Explorations in Catholic Moral Theology* (New York: Continuum, 1996).

182 Maria Cimperman, *When God's People Have HIV/AIDS: An Approach to Ethics* (Maryknoll, NY: Orbis, 2005).

183 Iozzio, *Calling for Justice*.

184 For instance, Edward Vacek, 'Feminism and the Vatican', *TS* 66 (2005) 159–77.

185 Elisabeth Schüssler Fiorenza, 'Feminist Theology as a Critical Theology of Liberation', *TS* 36 (1975) 605–26; 'Discipleship and Patriarchy', *Feminist Ethics*, 33–651 *In Memory of Her: A Feminist Theological Reconstruction of Christian Origins* (New York: Crossroad, 1992).

186 Margaret Farley, 'Feminist Ethics', *Feminist Ethics*, 5–10; 'A Feminist Respect of Persons', ibid., 164–83.

187 Susan Ross, 'Feminist Theology: A Review of Literature', *Feminist Ethics*, 11–31; Lisa Sowle Cahill, 'Feminist Ethics, Differences, and Common Ground', ibid., 184–205; Barbara Andolsen, 'Whose Sexuality? Whose Tradition? Women, Experience, and Roman Catholic Sexual Ethics', ibid., 207–39.

188 See Rosemary Radford Ruether, *Sexism and God Talk* (Boston: Beacon, 1983); Anne Carr, *Transforming Grace: Christian Tradition and Women's Experience* (San Francisco: Harper and Row, 1988); Sandra Schneiders, *Beyond Patching: Faith and*

Feminism in the Catholic Church (Mahwah: Paulist, 1991); Elisabeth Johnson, *She Who Is: The Mystery of God in Feminist Discourse* (New York: Crossroad, 1992).

189 Christine Gudorf, *The Body, Sex and Pleasure* (Cleveland: Pilgrim Press, 1994); Patricia Beattie Jung, ed., *Sexual Diversity and Catholicism: Toward the Development of Moral Theology* (Collegeville: Liturgical, 2001); Aline Kalbian, *Sexing the Church: Gender, Power, and Ethics in Contemporary Catholicism* (Bloomington: Indiana University Press, 2005).

190 Anne Patrick, 'Toward Renewing "The Life and Culture of Fallen Man", *Gaudium et Spes* as Catalyst for Catholic Feminist Theology', *Feminist Ethics*, 483–510; Christine Firer Hinze, 'Social and Economic Ethics', *TS* 70 (2009) 159–77; ibid., 'Bridge Discourse on Wage Justice: Roman Catholic and Feminist Perspectives on the Family Living Wage', *Feminist Ethics*' 511–40; Mary Elsbernd, 'Social Ethics', *TS* 66 (2005) 137–58; Elsbernd and Reimund Bieringer, *When Love is Not Enough: A Theo-Ethic of Justice* (Collegeville: Liturgical Press, 2002).

191 Maura Ryan, 'Health and Human Rights', *TS* (2008) 144–63; 'Beyond a Western Ethics', *TS* 65 (2004) 158–78; 'The Argument for Unlimited Procreative Liberty: A Feminist Critique', *Feminist Ethics*, 383–401.

192 Cahill, *Between the Sexes: Toward a Christian Ethics of Sexuality* (Fortress and Paulist Presses, 1985).

193 Cahill, 'Sexual Ethics: A Feminist Biblical Perspective', *Interpretation* 49 (January 1995) 5–16.

194 Cahill, *Women and Sexuality* (Mahwah: Paulist, 1992) 78.

195 Cahill, *Sex, Gender and Christian Ethics* (New York: Cambridge University Press, 1996) 110.

196 See also, Cahill, 'Community and Universals: A Misplaced Debate in Christian Ethics', *Annual of the Society of Christian Ethics* 18 (1998) 3–12.

197 Cahill, *Family: A Christian Social Perspective* (Minneapolis: Fortress, 2000); 'Feminist Theology, Catholicism, and the Family', in Magdala Thompson, ed., *Full of Hope: Critical Social Perspectives on Theology* (Mahwah: Paulist Press, 2003).

198 Cahill, 'Marriage: Developments in Catholic Theology and Ethics', *TS* 64 (2003) 78–105; 'Equality in Marriage; The Biblical Challenge', in Todd A. Salzman, Thomas M. Kelly, and John J. O'Keefe, eds, *Marriage in the Catholic Tradition: Scripture, Tradition, and Experience* (New York: Crossroad, 2004) 66–75.

199 Cahill, 'On Being a Catholic Feminist' (Bannan Center for Jesuit Education: Santa Clara University, 2003).

200 Cahill, 'Catholic Sexual Ethics and the Dignity of the Person: A Double Message', *TS* 50 (March 1989) 120–50; 'Feminist ethics', *TS* 51 (March 1990) 49–64.

201 Cahill, '"Love Your Enemies": Discipleship, Pacifism and Just War Theory' (Minneapolis: Fortress, 1994); 'Just Peacemaking: Theory, Practice, and Prospects', *The Journal of the Society of Christian Ethics* 22 (2003).

202 Cahill, *Bioethics and the Common Good* (Marquette University Press, 2003).

203 Cahill, ed., *Genetics, Theology, Ethics*; 'Bioethics', *TS* 67 (2006) 120–42; 'Bioethics, Relationships, and Participation in the Common Good', in Carol Taylor and Roberto Dell'Oro, eds, *Health and Human Flourishing: Religion, Medicine and Moral Anthropology* (Washington, DC: Georgetown University Press, 2006); 'AIDS, Justice and the Common Good', *CEHP*, 282–93; 'Realigning Catholic Priorities: Bioethics and the Common Good', *America* (13 September 2004) 11–13; 'Women's Health and Human Flourishing', in Elio Sgreccia, ed., *Women's Health Issues* (Rome: Societa Editrice Universo, 2003) 93–103; 'Bioethics, Theology, and Social Change', *Journal of Religious Ethics* 31/3 (2003) 363–98; 'Biotech and

Justice: Catching Up with the Real World Order', *Hastings Center Report* 34/4 (2003) 33–44.

204 Cahill, *Theological Bioethics: Participation, Justice and Change* (Washington, DC: Georgetown University Press, 2005).

205 Cahill, 'Moral Theology: From Evolutionary to Revolutionary Change', *CTEWC*, 221–7, at 223.

206 Ibid., 225.

207 David McCarthy, 'Shifting Settings From Subculture to Pluralism: Catholic Moral Theology in an Evangelical Key', *Communio* 31 (2004) 85–110.

208 William Mattison III, ed., *New Wine, New Wineskins: A Next Generation Reflects on Key Issues in Catholic Moral Theology* (Lanham, MD: Rowman and Littlefield, 2005).

209 Margaret Pfeil, 'Transparent Mediation: The Vocation of the Theologian as Disciple', Ibid., 67–76, at 73.

210 D. Vincent Twomey, 'Moral Renewal through Renewed Moral Reasoning', *Josephinum* 10.2 (2003) 210–29, at 228.

211 Christopher Steck, 'Saintly Voyeurism: A Methodological Necessity for the Christian Ethicist?', *New Wine*, 25–44, at 40. Also, Richard Gula, *The Call to Holiness: Embracing a Fully Christian Life* (Mahwah: Paulist Press, 2003).

212 Christopher Vogt, 'Finding a Place at the Heart of the Church', *New Wine*, 45–65, at 52.

213 Vogt, 'Recognizing the Addict as Neighbor: Christian Hospitality and the Establishment of Safe Injection Facilities in Canada', *Theoforum* 35 (2004) 317–42.

214 Timothy O'Connell, *Principles for a Catholic Morality* (Minneapolis: Winston Oak Press, 1976).

215 William May, *An Introduction to Moral Theology* (Huntington, IN: Our Sunday's Visitor, 1991).

216 Russell Connors and Patrick McCormick, *Character, Choices and Community* (Mahwah: Paulist Press, 1998); Connors and McCormick, *Facing Ethical Issues* (Mahwah: Paulist Press, 2002).

217 Romanus Cessario, *Introduction to Moral Theology* (Washington, DC: CUA Press, 2001).

218 Servais Pinckaers, *Morality: The Catholic View* (St Augustine's Press, 2003).

219 David Matzko MCarthy and M. Therese Lysaught, eds, *Gathered for the Journey* (Grand Rapids: Eerdmans, 2007).

220 Jozef Zalot and Benedict Guevin, *Catholic Ethics in Today's World* (Winoma: St. Mary's Press, 2008).

221 David Cloutier, *Love Reason, and God's Story* (Winoma: St. Mary's Press, 2008).

222 William Mattison, *Introducing Moral Theology* (Grand Rapids: Brazos Press, 2008).

223 Christine Gudorf and Regina Wolfe, eds, *Ethics and World Religions: Cross-Cultural Case Studies* (Maryknoll: Orbis, 1999).

224 James Keenan, 'Introduction', *CTEWC*, 1–6; Linda Hogan, 'Cross Cultural Conversations', *Applied Ethics*, 1–11.

225 See *Transformative Theological Ethics*, above.

226 See www.catholicethics.com.

227 Jean Porter, *The Recovery of Virtue: The Relevance of Aquinas for Christian Ethics* (Louisville, Kentucky: Westminster Press, 1990). The philosophical summons came from Alasdair MacIntyre, *After Virtue: A Study in Moral Theory* (Notre Dame: UND Press, 1981).

228 Gilbert Meilaender, *The Theory and Practice of Virtue* (Notre Dame: UND Press,

1984); William Spohn, 'The Return of the Virtues', *TS* 53 (1992) 60–75; Joseph Kotva, Jr, *The Christian Case for Virtue Ethics* (Washington, DC: Georgetown University Press, 1996); Diana Fritz Cates, *Choosing to Feel: Virtue, Friendship and Compassion for Friends* (Notre Dame: Notre Dame University Press, 1997); Joseph Woodill, *The Fellowship of Life: Virtue Ethics and Orthodox Christianity* (Washington, DC: Georgetown University Press, 1998). Recently, M. Cathleen Kaveny integrates the virtues into human rights in 'Imagination, Virtue, and Human Rights: Lessons from Australian and US Law', *Theological Studies* 78 (2009) 109–39.

229 Christopher Vogt, 'Fostering a Catholic Commitment to the Common Good: An Approach Rooted in Virtue Ethics', *TS* 68.2 (2007) 394–417.

230 Jean Porter, 'Virtue', *Oxford Handbook*, 205–19, at 219 and 206 respectively.

231 Keenan, 'Virtue Ethics: Making a Case as It Comes of Age', *Thought* 67 (1992) 115–27; 'Proposing Cardinal Virtues', *TS* 56.4 (1995) 709–29; *Virtues for Ordinary Christians* (Kansas City: Sheed and Ward, 1996); 'Virtue and Identity', in Hermann Häring, Maureen Junker-Kenny, and Dietmar Mieth, eds, *Creating Identity: Biographical, Moral, Religious* (London: SCM Press, 2000) 69–77; 'Engaging Virtue Ethics in the Philippines', *Landas*, 15.1 (2001) 101–16; 'Virtue Ethics,'*Christian Ethics*, 84–94; 'Virtue Ethics and Sexual Ethics', *Louvain Studies* 30:3 (2005) 183–203; 'What Does Virtue Ethics Bring to Genetics?', Lisa Sowle Cahill, ed., *Genetics, Theology, Ethics: An Interdisciplinary Conversation* (New York: Herder, 2005) 97–113.

232 Dietmar Mieth, *Die neuen Tugenden* (Düsseldorf: Patmos, 1984); Herbert Schlögel, 'Tugend, Kasuistik, Biographie', *Catholica* 51 (1997) 187–200; Keenan, 'L'Etica delle Virtù: Per una sua Promozione fra I Teologi moralisti italiani', *Rassegna di Teologia* 44 (2003) 569–90; Keenan, 'Riscoprire la via delle virtù: giustizia, fedeltà, cura di se stessi, prudenza, misericordia', *Teologia in America Del Nord* (Padova: Messaggero di S. Antonio, 2008) 119–34.

233 James Bretzke 'The Tao of Confucian Virtue Ethics', *International Philosophical Quarterly* 35 (1995) 25–41, 137; 'The Common Good in a Cross-Cultural Perspective: Insights from the Confucian Moral Community', *Annual Publication of the College Theology Society* 41 (1996) 83–105; 'Moral Theology Out of East Asia', *TS* 61 (2000) 106–21; *Bibliography on East Asian Religion and Philosophy* (Philadelphia: Mellen Press, 2001); 'Human Rights or Human Rites?: A Confucian Cross-Cultural Perspective', *East Asian Pastoral Review* 41/1 (2003) 44–67; 'A New Pentecost for Moral Theology: The Challenge of Inculturation of Ethics', *Josephinum* 10:2 (2003) 250–60.

234 Lee Yearly, *Mencius and Aquinas: Theories of Virtue and Conceptions of Courage* (Albany: SUNY Press, 1990); Edward Slingerland, 'Virtue Ethics, the *Analects*, and the Problem of Commensurability', *Journal of Religious Ethics* 29.1 (Summer 2001) 97–125.

235 Aaron Stalnaker, *Overcoming Our Evil: Human Nature and Spiritual Exercises in Xunzi and Augustine* (Washington, DC: Georgetown University Press, 2006).

236 Günther Virt, *Damit Menschsein Zukunft hat: Theologische Ethik im Einsatz für eine humane Gesellschaft* (Würzburg: Echter Verlag, 2007).

237 Vincent LeClercq, 'La morale des vertus dans la formation des futures pretres', *Seminarium* 46.4 (2006) 895–921.

238 Christopher Vogt, *Patience, Compassion, Hope, and the Christian Art of Dying Well* (Lanham, MD: Rowman & Littlefield, 2004); William McDonough, 'Etty Hillesum's Learning to Live and Preparing to Die: *Complacentia Boni* as the Beginning of Acquired and Infused Virtue', *Journal of the Society of Christian Ethics* 25.2 (2005)

179–202; See, Daniel Daly, 'Prudence and the Debate on Dying', *Health Progress* 88.5 (2007) 49–55.

239 James Keenan and Joseph Kotva, eds, *Practice What You Preach: Virtues, Ethics and Power in the Lives of Pastoral Ministers and Their Congregations* (Franklin, WI: Sheed and Ward, 1999).

240 Gerard Mannion, *Ecclesiology and Postmodernity: Questions for the Church in Our Time* (Collegeville: Liturgical Press, 2007) 227.

241 Herbert Schlögel, 'Kirche und Theologische Ethik'.

242 Herbert Schlögel, 'Kirchenbilder in der Moraltheologie', *Stimmen der Zeit* 210 (1992) 109–14; idem, 'In Medio Ecclesiae. Ekklesiologische Aspectke in der Moraltheologie', in Klaus Demmer and Karl-Heinz Ducke, eds, *Moraltheologie im Dienst der Kirche* (Leipzig: Benino, 1992) 57–67; *Kirche, Moral, Spiritualität* (Münster: Lit verlag, 2001).

243 Barry McMillan, 'Scapegoating in a Time of Crisis', *The Furrow* 53 (2002) 276–81.

244 Norbert Rigali, 'Church Responses to Pedophilia', *TS* 55 (1994) 124–39; Keenan, 'Ethics and the Crisis in the Church', *TS* 66.1 (2005) 117–36.

245 Regina Ammicht-Quinn, Hille Haker, and Maureen Junker-Kenny, *The Structural Betrayal of Trust*, *Concilium* 2004/3 (London: SCM, 2004).

246 Stephen J. Pope, ed., *Common Calling: The Laity and Governance of the Church* (Washington: Georgetown University, 2004) 165–80; 'Accountability and Sexual Abuse in the United States: Lessons for the Universal Church', *Irish Theological Quarterly* 69 (2004) 73–88.

247 Francis Oakley and Bruce Russett, eds, *Governance, Accountability, and the Future of the Catholic Church* (New York: Continuum, 2004); Jean Bartunek, Mary Ann Hinsdale, and James Keenan, eds, *Church Ethics and its Organizational Context* (Lanham, MD: Sheed and Ward, 2005).

248 Paul Valadier, 'Has the Concept of *Sensus Fidelium* Fallen into Desuetude?', *CTEWC*, 187–92; Giuseppe Angelini, 'The *Sensus Fidelium* and Moral Discernment', *CTEWC*, 202–9.

249 Laurenti Magesa, *Le Catholicisme Africain en Mutation: Des Modèles d'Église pour un Siècle nouveau* (Yaounde, Cameroun: Edition Clé, 2001).

250 Laurenti Magesa, *Anatomy of Inculturation: Transforming the Church in Africa* (Maryknoll, NY: Orbis, 2004).

251 Jon Sobrino and Felix Wilfred, eds, *Christianity in Crisis?* (London: SCM Press, 2005) 7.

252 Peter Kanyandago, 'African Churches and the Crisis of Christianity', ibid., 71–5, at 71–2.

253 Adolfo Nicolas, 'Christianity in Crisis: Asia. Which Asia? Which Christianity? Which Crisis?', ibid., 64–70, at 66–7.

254 Antonio Autiero, 'The Human Being between Polis and Ekklesia', *Studia Liturgica* 30 (2008) 17–30.

255 Waliggo, 'A Call for Prophetic Action', *CTEWC*, 253–62, at 254.

256 Humberto Miguel Yáñez, *Esperanza y Solidaridad* (Madrid: Comillas, 1999).

257 Mifsud, *Ethos Cotidiano* (Santiago: Universidad Alberto Hurtado, 2006). See also Alain Thomasset, 'Les pratiques sociales chrétiennes et leur force de conviction dans une société pluraliste', in Philippe Bordeyne and Alain Thomasset, eds, *Les communautés chrétiennes et la formation morale des sujets* (Paris: Cerf, 2008) 259–88.

258 Aldo Marcelo Cáceres, *Una ética para la globalización* (Buenos Aires: San Augustin, 2005).

259 Daniel Groody, 'Globalizing Solidarity: Christian Anthropology and the Chal-

lenge of Human Liberation', *TS* 69 ((2008) 250–69, at 267. Groody refers us to John Paul II, *Ecclesia in America*, no. 55 (Washington: United States Catholic Conference, 1999). See Groody, *Globalization, Spirituality, and Justice: Navigating the Path to Peace* (Maryknoll, NY: Orbis, 2007).

260 Kenneth Himes, 'Globalization with a Human Face: Catholic Social Teaching', *TS* 69 (2008) 269–89, at 276. John Paul II, *Sollicitudo rei socialis*, no. 38 (30 December 1987): http://www.vatican.va/holy_father/john_paul_ii/encyclicals/documents/hf_jp-ii_enc_30121987_sollicitudo-rei-socialis_en.html. See Charles Curran, Kenneth Himes, and Thomas Shannon, 'Commentary on *Sollicitudo rei socialis*', *in* Himes, et al., *Modern Catholic Social Teaching* (Washington: Georgetown University, 2005) 415–35, esp. 426–30.

261 Hollenbach, *Common Good*, 220.

262 Margaret Farley, *Just Love: A Framework for Christian Sexual Ethics* (New York: Continuum Press, 2006) at 38.

263 Ibid., 104.

264 Ibid., 156–7.

265 Ibid, 116. See Jennifer Beste, 'Limits of the Appeal to Women's Experiences Reconsidered', *Horizons* 33.1 (2006) 54–77.

266 Farley, 114.

267 Ibid., 198.

268 Farley, 311. See Maura A. Ryan and Brian F. Linnane, *A Just and True Love: Feminism at the Frontiers of Theological Ethics: Essays in Honor of Margaret A. Farley* (Notre Dame: University of Notre Dame Press, 2007).

Afterword: The Encyclicals of Pope Benedict XVI

This book was going to press just as Pope Benedict XVI promulgated his long-awaited encyclical, *Caritas in Veritate* (*Charity in Truth*). Signed on 29 June 2009, the letter was published on 7 July on the eve of the G8 summit and his meeting with American President Barack Obama.

At the beginning of his pontificate the Pope published in Christmas 2005 *Deus Caritas Est.* The first encyclical is a scholarly work: he cites the scriptures (Deuteronomy, Leviticus, John, Paul), Augustine and Ambrose, and refers to Plato and Descartes, as well as Pope John Paul II and the *Code of Canon Law*. At a time when critics of religion see faith lives as leading to bigotry and violence, the Pope counteracts the charges by naming charity as the heart of Christianity.

In the first paragraph he writes: 'In a world where the name of God is sometimes associated with vengeance or even a duty of hatred and violence, this message is both timely and significant. For this reason, I wish in my first Encyclical to speak of the love which God lavishes upon us and which we in turn must share with others.'

He adds that the encyclical has two parts; the first 'is more speculative, since I wanted here – at the beginning of my Pontificate – to clarify some essential facts concerning the love which God mysteriously and gratuitously offers to man, together with the intrinsic link between that Love and the reality of human love. The second part is more concrete, since it treats the ecclesial exercise of the commandment of love of neighbor.'

Unlike Pope John Paul's *Veritatis Splendor*, there's no hint of a divide between some theologians and the papacy. Rather this is a very positive beginning to the papacy's tenure, highlighting the world's need for God and the Church, and recognizing as we have always believed, the centrality of charity as God's gift of love to us. Similarly, the Pope commented on neighbor love as a response to God's love and saw the works of mercy as expressions of that love.

If there were any critical theological questions raised regarding the encyclical, it was about how constitutive justice was of charity, with some wondering why there was not much attention to issues of structural injustices. This concern noted, for the most part, the encyclical offered to the Church and the world great signs of hope.

Not surprisingly, then, his next encyclical addressed hope. Turning to Romans 8.24, the encyclical *Spe Salvi* (*In Hope We Are Saved*) appeared on 30 November 2007. In it the Pope develops a contemporary read on a faith-based hope, offering hope as a new sign of light in the world, a hope that is communal, expresses itself in prayer, and is at the heart of all upright and serious human conduct.

Thus, after writing on charity and a faith-based hope, he returned recently to the topic of charity, particularly how it affects the issues of structural injustice and the environment. Urging formidable links between solidarity and subsidiarity, the Pope sees charity as animating the possibility of a much-needed change in the world's structural distribution of resources. Against the backdrop of Pope Paul VI's *Progressio Populorum* (26 March 1967), the Pope remarks frequently that globalization has changed not only the way economic structures exist, but worse, it has made the possibility of humanizing those structures even more challenging to attain. By the wealthier nations' construction of a distribution of labor that serves the former's needs for low-cost products, the wealthy tier harnesses the poor in a world where equity recedes more and more. In the globalized world, the Pope also addresses the need for a social response to the challenges of the environment.

But the Pope is not simply offering a socio-economic plan. This encyclical is rooted in the scriptures, sees charity at the heart of the Church's social doctrine, and is as concerned about a culture affected by faithlessness as it is by greed.

Foundational insights from the scriptures and the Church's tradition direct the reader to consider concrete practical responses to the challenges facing the world today, while at the same time providing the resources for animating and guiding that response.

The encyclical marks, then, not just the development of church social teaching itself, but demonstrates the mutual and interactive need to integrate theological ethics with that social teaching: each field needs the other. In many ways, the encyclical exemplifies the developments of theological ethics over the last 70 years.

Index